Grassroots
with Readings

The Writer's Workbook

Ninth Edition

Grassroots
with Readings

The Writer's Workbook

Ninth Edition

Susan Fawcett

HEINLE
CENGAGE Learning™

Australia • Brazil • Japan • Korea • Mexico • Singapore • Spain • United Kingdom • United States

HEINLE
CENGAGE Learning™

Grassroots with Readings: The Writer's Workbook, Ninth Edition
Susan Fawcett

Executive Publisher: Pat Coryell

Editor-in-Chief: Carrie Brandon

Sponsoring Editor: Joann Kozyrev

Senior Marketing Manager: Tom Ziolkowski

Senior Development Editor: Martha Bustin

Senior Project Editor: Nancy Blodget

Art and Design Manager: Jill Haber

Cover Design Director: Tony Saizon

Senior Photo Editor: Jennifer Meyer Dare

Senior Composition Buyer: Chuck Dutton

New Title Project Manager: James Lonergan

Editorial Assistant: Daisuke Yasutake

Marketing Assistant: Bettina Chiu

Editorial Assistant: Jill Clark

Cover Image: © Fabio Cardoso/CORBIS

Acknowledgement appear on page 450

For product information and technology assistance, contact us at **Cengage Learning Customer & Sales Support, 1-800-354-9706**

For permission to use material from this text or product, submit all requests online at **www.cengage.com/permissions**. Further permissions questions can be e-mailed to **permissionrequest@cengage.com**.

Library of Congress Control Number: 2007934925

Instructor's Annotated Edition:

ISBN-13: 978-0-618-95544-2

ISBN-10: 0-618-95544-5

Student Edition:

ISBN-13: 978-0-618-95521-3

ISBN-10: 0-618-95521-6

Heinle
20 Channel Center Street
Boston, MA 02210
USA

Cengage Learning is a leading provider of customized learning solutions with office locations around the globe, including Singapore, the United Kingdom, Australia, Mexico, Brazil, and Japan. Locate your local office at **international.cengage.com/region**

Cengage Learning products are represented in Canada by Nelson Education, Ltd.

To learn more about Heinle, visit **www.cengage.com/heinle**

Purchase any of our products at your local college store or at our preferred online store **www.ichapters.com**

Printed in the United States of America
4 5 6 7 11 10 09

Brief Contents

Contents

UNIT 4 Joining Ideas Together

UNIT 5 Choosing the Right Noun, Pronoun, Adjective, Adverb, or Preposition   224

UNIT 6 Revising for Consistency and Parallelism   280

UNIT 9 Reading Selections and Quotation Bank

Quotation Bank 434

THE NINTH EDITION OF

Grassroots with Readings:
The Writer's Workbook

Inspire Success with Grassroots!

MOTIVATE

"*Grassroots* has energy, it includes great visuals, it is thought provoking, and it is geared towards mature students, who like to know they are well thought of."

— Sarah Lahm, *Normandale Community College*

ENGAGE

"The clarity of the explanations and the way the students respond to the book have been our deciding factors."

— Margaret E. Welsh, *Plaza College*

SUCCEED

"*Grassroots* pushes the lower-level students, and they are better prepared for subsequent courses as a result."

— Adrienne Mews, *Lane Community College*

"*Grassroots*, 9th edition, marks a fresh approach to an already cutting-edge book. It is THE book to use."

— Lisa Moslow, *Erie Community College*

Grassroots with Readings

A Clear Approach That Works with Students

MOTIVATE

High-Interest Content

A hallmark of the *Grassroots* approach is the continuous discourse practice or model passage on an engaging, informative, and timely topic. Examples include:

- **Critical thinking about media**
  Students learning about sentence structure read about the appeal of horror movies.

- **Life skills**
  While studying comma splices, students learn why many job recruiters are now checking applicants' Facebook™ sites.

- **Role models**
  Students focusing on verb tense and fragments read about community activist Majora Carter, leader Nelson Mandela, and car designer Ralph Gilles.

These high-interest practices promote cultural literacy, model good writing, contain helpful life-skill tips, engage students' interest, and, most of all, improve learning outcomes.

Movie poster, 1958. Horror movies allow people to face their fears and dark wishes in a safe way, claim psychologists.
The Everett Collection.

in safe settings. (8) Many teenagers, in particular, need to test their tolerance for threatening situations. (9) In addition, parents often declare horror movies inappropriate. (10) Therefore, adolescents want to see this forbidden entertainment

PRACTICE 8

Proofread the paragraph for fragments. Circle the number of every fragment, and then write your corrections above the lines.

(1) Ralph Gilles is famous as the designer of the Chrysler 300C. (2) Which won many design awards. (3) Raised in Canada by Haitian parents, Gilles was in awe of his mother. (4) Because she gave her all to various thankless jobs and still told her children success stories. (5) When he was a boy, (6) Gilles loved to draw futuristic cars in his notebooks. (7) An aunt noticed his design gifts and urged him to write to Lee Iacocca. (8) Who was then chairman of the Chrysler Corporation. (9) Amazingly, after the embarrassed fourteen-year-old sent a letter and some

Designer Ralph Gilles poses with the car that made him famous.
Getty Images News.

> "I really like the exercises, and how many of the grammar sections include paragraphs and actual chunks of writing material so that the skill is simulated in a more realistic way."
>
> — Amy Carratini, *Housatonic Community College*

funeral pyre grows a white flower now known as the narcissus. (11) The story of this arrogant young man also gave modern psychology the term *narcissist*, a person so admiring of himself that he cannot love others.

Narcissus, 1597–1599, as imagined by the painter Caravaggio. Oil on canvas, 110 × 92 cm. What would a twenty-first-century Narcissus look like?

Photo credit: Scala/Art Resource, NY.

6. People pay to get into the festival _____ they then enter a volunteer and gift economy.

7. Commercial vendors are not allowed _____ can participants buy or sell anything using money.

8. People focus instead on giving something to the group _____ the festival encourages "radical self-expression."

Two Burning Man participants frame the wooden statue of Burning Man, lit at the festival's end.

© Peter Menzel/ www.menzelphoto.com.

MOTIVATE

Nearly Doubled Visual Image Program

Forty compelling visual images have been carefully chosen to:

● Engage students

● Prompt them to pause and think more deeply

● Connect what they know already from their lives with what they are learning

● Increase comprehension

These images and their captions provide opportunities for critical thinking and set up thought-provoking writing or discussion prompts.

"*Grassroots* has it right regarding visuals. They are not distracting, and they reinforce the text and support the teaching. The quality of the visuals is excellent, and for our highly visual students, this is a great way to add an extra dimension of understanding."

—- Ann Fellinger, *Pulaski Technical College*

ENGAGE
New Readings

Five new readings (below) and a new array of accompanying photos add to the diversity, humor, insight, and inspiration of this collection.

- ● *Daring to Dream Big* by Diane Sawyer, on the importance of goals

- ● *Don't Share Your Life with Me* by Ellen Goodman, on cell phone manners

- ● *Beauty Is Not Just Smaller Than Life* by Leonard Pitts Jr., on the obsession with thinness

- ● *Quitting Hip-Hop* by Michaela angela Davis, on reexamining a popular form

- ● *Stuff* by Richard Rodriguez, on Americans' overaccumulation of things

The twenty readings in *Grassroots* can be flexibly clustered to explore a variety of topics and themes—for example, Work, Overcoming Obstacles, Education, Gender Roles, and Identity.

Fashion week in São Paolo, Brazil, where two anorexic models died in 2006. Whereas the average American woman wears a size 13, the average model wears a 2.

AP Images.

Approximately 5 million to 10 million women and girls (and 1 million boys and men) suffer from eating disorders—primarily anorexia and bulimia—which are sometimes fatal. That same *Psychology Today* recounted the results of a body image survey of 4,000 women and men. Almost 90 percent of the women wanted to lose weight. 9

Score one for pop culture. I mean, one of its primary functions is to make us dissatisfied with what we are, make us want what it is selling. Right now, it's selling the canard[6] that the average supermodel's body is achievable or even desirable for the average girl. And girls are getting sick, even dying, as a result. 10

There are those feminists who would argue that the solution is for men to stop objectifying[7] women, but their reasoning flies in the face of human nature. If somebody hadn't objectified somebody else, none of us would be here to argue about it. And anyone who doesn't think women fantasize about a masculine ideal has never seen a soap opera or romance novel. 11

I'm not out to stop—as if I could!—the endless mating dance of male and female. I'd just like to see something done to protect our girls and women from its more insidious[8] effects. Just like to see the gatekeepers of media become more conscientious about depicting the beauty of women and girls in all its dimensions. 12

Not just breasts, but brains, heart, humor, compassion, love. 13

It is a pipe dream, yes. So I guess those of us who care about such things will have to be satisfied with concentrating on those girls closest to us—our daughters, our nieces, our sisters and friends—and exhorting[9] them to value themselves for *all* the things they are. 14

Writing Assignments

1. Describe a time when you immersed yourself in and truly savored a specific sensual experience—a moonlit swim, a delicious meal, a slow stroll down your favorite street, or the like. Describe this experience, including details about what you saw, smelled, tasted, touched, and heard.

2. Which of your possessions are crucial to your happiness? What things do you own now that you could live without? What possessions do you lack that you believe will make you happier?

3. In 1993, photographer Peter Menzel asked "statistically average" families in different countries to pose in front of their houses with every possession they owned. In a group with four of five classmates, carefully observe and discuss two of these families and their "stuff." From each family's home, location, and possessions, can you make any guesses about its values, daily life, or priorities? Is each family like or different from families you know?

A family from Bhutan and all its possessions.

© Peter Menzel/
www.menzelphoto.com.

"The readings are excellent choices. They engage the students, and we base our writing on subjects related to them."

— Lupe Wilson, *Del Mar College*

CHAPTER 27 Commas

ENGAGE
Paced Inductive Lessons

The proven inductive *Grassroots* teaching method works for both instructors and students. It is based on the Fawcett MAP: illustrative *model* and brief *analysis*, followed by lots of *practice*. Grammatical and writing topics are:

- Broken down into manageable segments

- Presented with minimal verbiage through a boxed example, bulleted thinking questions, and an easy-to-read rule

- Reinforced with numerous, paced practices

- Clarified with diagrams for the visual learner

- Applied in Chapter 30, "Putting Your Proofreading Skills to Work," where students tackle passages with a real-world mix of errors; in Chapter and Unit Review activities; and in engaging writing assignments.

PRACTICE 4

Proofread this paragraph, correcting any errors above the lines. (You should find twenty individual errors.) To review, see these chapters:

Chapter 7   sentence fragments

Chapter 8   subject/verb agreement errors

Chapter 27   comma errors

Chapter 28   apostrophe errors

(1) Every spring and summer, storm chaser's spreads out across the Midwestern part of the United States known as Tornado Alley. (2) Armed with video cameras maps and radios. (3) These lovers of violent weather follows huge weather systems called supercells, which sometimes produces tornadoes. (4) On a good day, a storm chaser may find a supercell. (5) And get close enough to film the brief, destructive life of a tornado. (6) Some joins the storm-chasing tours offered every summer by universities or private companies. (7) Others learn what they can from Internet websites and sets off on their own to hunt tornadoes. (8) Storm chasing can be very dangerous. (9) A large tornado spins winds between 125 and 175 mph, tearing roofs off houses ripping limbs from trees, and overturning cars. (10) The greatest danger comes from airborne branches boards shingles and glass hurtling through the air like deadly weapons. (11) Even if a supercell don't spawn tornadoes. (12) It often

Storm chasers confront a deadly twister in Tornado Alley.

©Carsten Peter/National Geographic Image Collection.

"*Grassroots* gives students editing tools and techniques they can use both inside and outside the class. Also, the emphasis on sentence structure is an asset."

—— Sandia Tuttle, *Grossmont College*

SUCCEED

Focus on Writing

Varied writing opportunities are consistently interspersed with grammatical instruction so students can incorporate what they are learning into their own writing.

- Step-by-step paragraph and essay instruction in Unit 1

- New, expanded coverage of writing topic sentences

- Chapter and unit writing assignments that build on grammatical practices

- "Spotlight on Writing" and "Writing Ideas" to launch each unit

- Writers' Workshops with student writing to conclude each unit

- New photo captions that pose thinking and writing questions

- More Exploring Online web links with writing ideas

UNIT 3

WRITERS' WORKSHOP

Tell a Family Story

A **narrative** tells a story. It presents the most important events in the story, usually in time order. Here, a student tells of her mother-in-law's inspiring journey to self-realization.

In your group or class, read this narrative essay aloud, if possible. As you read, underline any words or details that strike you as vivid or powerful.

Somebody Named Seeta

(1) Someone I deeply admire is my mother-in-law, Seeta, who struggled for years to become her best self. She was born in poverty on the sunny island of Trinidad. Seeta's father drank and beat his wife, and sadly, her mother accepted this lifestyle. Her parents did not believe in sending girls to school, so Seeta's daily chores began at 4:00 a.m. when she milked the cows. Then she fed the hens, scrubbed the house, cooked, and tended babies (as the third child in a family of ten children). During stolen moments, she taught herself to read. At age sixteen, this skinny girl with long black hair ran away from home.

(2) Seeta had nowhere to go, so her friend's family took her in. They believed in education, yet Seeta struggled for years to catch up and finish school. Even so, she calls this time her "foot in the door." She married my father-in-law and had four children, longing inside to become "somebody"

Spotlight on Writing

Notice the way this writer uses strong, simple sentences to capture a moment with her grandfather, her *abuelo*. If possible, read the paragraph aloud.

My grandfather has misplaced his words again. He is trying to find my name in the kaleidoscope of images that his mind has become. His face brightens like a child's who has just remembered his lesson. He points to me and says my mother's name. I smile back and kiss him on the cheek. It doesn't matter what names he remembers anymore. Every day he is more confused, his memory slipping back a little further in time. Today he has no grandchildren yet. Tomorrow he will be a young man courting my grandmother again, quoting bits of poetry to her. In months to come, he will begin calling her Mama.

Judith Ortiz Cofer, "The Witch's Husband"

- How does the writer feel about her grandfather? Which sentences tell you this?

- Why do you think the writer arranges the last three sentences in the order that she does?

 *Writing Ideas*

- *A visit with a loved (or feared) relative*
- *Your relationship with someone who has a disability*

"Written on a student's level in a way a student could understand and be interested in. . . . The clear transition from prewriting into paragraph structure backed up with editing is a major draw."

— Mark Schneberger, *Oklahoma City Community College*

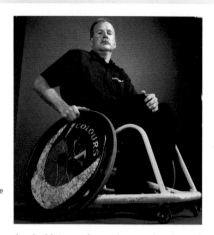

John Box, wheelchair athlete and founder of Colours Wheelchair.

Michael Grecco/Getty Exclusive.

the wheelchair manufacturer, however, the salespeople ignored him as if his disability made him invisible.

(7) Back home, furious and feeling frustration, John and his brother Mike decided to design one's own sports wheelchair. (8) The result inspired them to start a company and name her Colours. (9) Colours Wheelchair sells high-performance chairs with edgy names like Hammer, Avenger, Swoosh, and one is called Boing. (10) John Box, the company's president, hires other "wheelers," and he or she often contribute new product ideas. (11) The company also sponsors seventy-five wheelchair athletes. (12) In fact, fourteen-year-old Aaron Fotheringham, a wheelchair skateboarder, recently became the first human to perform a somersault flip in a wheelchair.

(13) Today John Box and his brother not only want to expand his or her successful company but also in educating the public about disability. (14) "A person doesn't lose their personality by becoming disabled," declares John. (15) The disabled, he says, can be funny, brilliance, pregnant, competing, sexy, or none of the above, just like everyone else.

 EXPLORING ONLINE

Visit the Colours Wheelchair website and examine the photos, video, and presentation of disabled people. What is the message this website is sending? Do these images of the disabled differ from other images you have seen?

PEER FEEDBACK SHEET

To _____ From _____ Date _____

1. What I like about this piece of writing is _____
   _____
   _____

2. Your main point seems to be _____
   _____
   _____

3. These particular words or lines struck me as powerful.
   Words or lines: I like them because

SUCCEED

More on Critical Thinking

To better foster college-level thinking skills, *Grassroots* contains:

- **Many opportunities for collaborative problem-solving and peer feedback**

- **Many print and online exercises on the revision process**

- **Thought-provoking readings and practice exercises**

- **Contextualized visuals to discuss and analyze**

- **Writers' Workshops fostering peer critique**

- **More Exploring Online tasks and writing assigments**

These recurring critical thinking features help students develop habits of questioning assumptions, presenting evidence, considering alternative views, and drawing reasonable conclusions.

"I like the pertinent topics that are used for the various exercises. I also like the Critical Thinking sections at the end of some exercises."

— Anna Maheshwari, *Schoolcraft College*

Comprehensive Support for Instructors and Students

Newly minted and seasoned professionals alike will find that the *Grassroots* program is a complete teaching and learning package that they can use to motivate, engage, and inspire their students.

Online Study Center™ Student Website for *Grassroots*

Online Study Center™ Student Website for *Grassroots*, Cengage Learning's online writing program, benefits Developmental English students at all skill levels and saves time for instructors. Online resources for students include:

- Self-study ACE tests with immediate feedback for students
- A list of Live Links from the text
- Career and Job Resource Center
- ESL Resources
- Supplemental material on Writing Better Paragraphs and Essays

With a passkey, students can access this additional premium material:

- Interactive tutorials
- CL Interactives powered by the Associated Press—multimedia activities for critical thinking and viewing
- CL News Now powered by the Associated Press
- Total Practice Zone
- Online handbook
- GEAR, *Grassroots* Exercises and Review

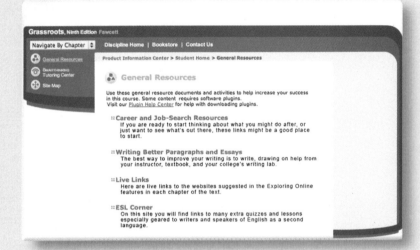

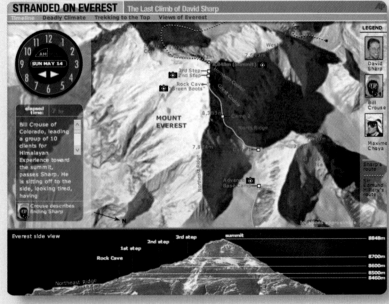

(From CL Interactives powered by the Associated Press.)

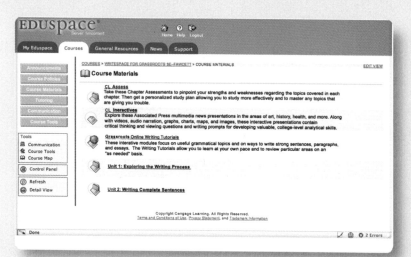

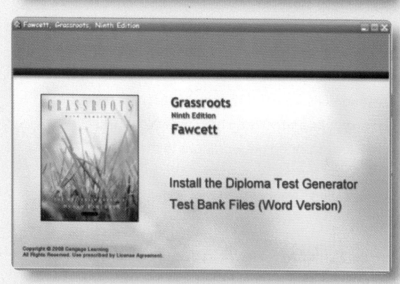

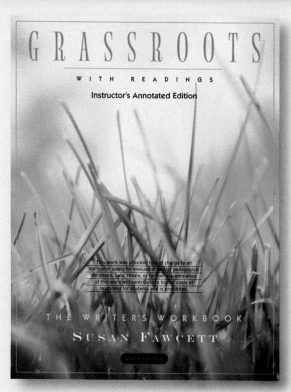

Online Study Center™ with Eduspace®
Online Writing Program

Online Study Center™ with Eduspace® provides an online course management system with tools such as:

- A powerful gradebook, with *Grassroots* Practices and Chapter Tests

- CL Assess, a diagnostic testing program that creates individualized study plans

- Safe Assignment, for plagiarism prevention

- Discussion board

Online Study Center™ Instructor Website

The passkey-protected instructor website provides:

- New Instructor's Resource Manual with suggestions for teaching writing, notes on how best to teach each unit and reading, and icons for new multimedia activities keyed to the text

- Expanded Test Bank with diagnostic, mastery, unit, and chapter tests

- 123 PowerPoint slides keyed to *Grassroots*

- Student Answer Key

Diploma Testing CD: *Grassroots* Test Bank

The expanded and improved test bank provides diagnostic, mastery, unit, and chapter tests. It is also available on the instructor website.

Instructor's Annotated Edition

Now with more and better ESL Tips by ESL expert Linda Fellag, this instructor's annotated edition also contains additional Teaching Tips from Susan Fawcett and answers to practices.

ABOUT THE AUTHOR

SUSAN FAWCETT is the author of the market-leading textbook series *Grassroots* and *Evergreen*, as well as *Business English: Skills for Success*. The inductive, step-by-step lessons and activities in these textbooks come from her successful teaching career as a professor of English and director of the writing lab at Bronx Community College, CUNY. In 2000, *Evergreen* won the McGuffey Prize for sustained excellence in a language and literature text, awarded by the Text and Academic Authors Association.

Professor Fawcett's formal education took place at Ohio University, the University of London, and Columbia University, with the support of Fulbright and Woodrow Wilson fellowships. However, her writing skills were truly honed by teaching college writers, writing textbooks, and revising her own articles and poems for submission. Through presentations in the United States and South Africa, she has worked to improve college writing instruction and to promote textbook authorship by minority faculty.

In her spare time, she loves to kayak, sing, and travel with friends and family.

Preface

Grassroots with Readings grew out of my classroom teaching experience at Bronx Community College of the City University of New York. It is designed for a range of students—native and nonnative, diverse in age, ethnicity, and background—who have not yet mastered the basic writing skills so necessary for success in college and most careers. Through its clear, paced lessons, inspiring student and professional models, and variety of high-interest practices and writing assignments, *Grassroots* has helped nearly two million students become better writers.

I am excited about this sparkling, new Ninth Edition. I have kept the carefully honed flow of grammar and writing lessons that have prompted so many instructors and students to tell me that *Grassroots* keeps fulfilling its promise to help students improve their writing. However, I have thoroughly updated the text in light of the college and workplace challenges our students face in the twenty-first century, integrating features and emphases that better address contemporary realities. To sharpen *Grassroots'* effectiveness, I have added forty-five new high-interest models and exercises on a range of lively topics. These topics engage students and help them to practice their writing skills in a meaningful context. And *Grassroots'* much-praised reading selections have been enriched with five dynamic new readings, plus fresh photos and prompts for thinking and writing.

Increasingly, students today must become not only competent writers but critical thinkers and viewers as well. The integrated four-color visual image program in the last edition was so enthusiastically received that I have nearly doubled the number of images in this edition, adding new photographs, paintings, and cartoons that always reinforce the subject matter. Many captions now contain critical thinking questions to help students view the images more analytically. Because critical thinking skills are so vital for students at every level, I have embedded more thinking activities throughout the text, always related to the lesson at hand.

More nonnative students are entering basic writing classes than ever before—and yet most instructors are not trained in ESL but learn, as I did, flying by the seats of their pants. Therefore, many new Teaching Tips and ESL Tips appear in the margins of the Instructor's Annotated Edition. These tips suggest classroom approaches, alert teachers to trouble spots, and point out ESL coverage integrated throughout the text.

Computer and web resources are opening new avenues for students to learn more effectively and for faculty to improve their teaching and lighten the grading load. Thus, additional Exploring Online web links or searches now appear throughout this edition, guiding students to online practice or exploration and tying to *Grassroots'* extensive new technology package. Other improvements include more coverage of writing topic sentences, more continuous, high-interest—as opposed to single-sentence—practices, and more examples of student writing.

Special Features of *Grassroots with Readings*, Ninth Edition

Many New High-Interest Models and Practices. Forty-five new high-interest practices and models enrich *Grassroots*, Ninth Edition, each on an informative and timely topic. New subjects include the young founders of Yahoo!, Google, and YouTube; traits of high achievers; *Ugly Betty* as social critique; the trend among job recruiters to check applicants' Facebook and MySpace pages; opportunities for majors in paralegal studies; ingredients of a successful apology; good credit card habits; and profiles of community activist Majora Carter, car designer Ralph Gilles, and wheelchair entrepreneur John Box.

xxvii

These high-interest practices promote cultural literacy, model good writing, contain helpful life-skill tips, engage students' interest, and most of all, improve learning outcomes.

25 Percent New Reading Selections.   *Grassroots'* readings have been widely praised for their ability to spark discussion, critical thinking, and strong written responses. Five fresh readings, each selected with the help of detailed feedback from instructors and students, increase the overall strength of this collection. In "Daring to Dream Big," the new model essay with annotations, Diane Sawyer discusses the importance of aspiration. Ellen Goodman writes in "Don't Share Your Life with Me" about annoying cell phone manners or, rather, lack of manners, as an invasion of privacy. Leonard Pitts Jr. explores the obsession with thinness in his column "Beauty Is Not Just Smaller Than Life." In "Quitting Hip-Hop," music writer Michaela angela Davis explains her painful divorce from a form she still loves. Finally, Richard Rodriguez takes on Americans' overaccumulation of material possessions in his essay "Stuff."

In all, the twenty readings in *Grassroots* can be flexibly clustered to explore a variety of topics and themes—for example, Work, Overcoming Obstacles, Education, Gender Roles, and Identity.

Expanded Visual Image Program.   *Grassroots* now contains nearly double the previous number of full-color visuals, all carefully placed for maximum pedagogical effectiveness. Each photo, painting, and cartoon has been chosen to capture students' interest, encourage critical viewing, and prompt viewers to connect with what they are learning. For example, new images show America Ferrera as "Ugly Betty," a character whose inner qualities illumine the shallowness around her; a student of garbology, an environmental field of increasing importance; Jane Goodall communicating with a chimpanzee; Caravaggio's painting of Narcissus, with a caption asking students what a twenty-first-century Narcissus might look like; and Robert Polidori's photograph of a once-ordinary living room ravaged by Hurricane Katrina.

Strong images such as these, with their accompanying captions and prompts, provide rich opportunities for students' discussion, critical thinking, and writing.

Expanded Coverage of Topic Sentences.   In response to instructor feedback, the Ninth Edition has been revised to include expanded material on writing topic sentences. Specifically, Chapter 3, Developing Effective Paragraphs, now covers topic sentences and controlling ideas in greater depth and offers many more practices. These new practices are built on a range of thought-provoking subjects, such as the innovative uses of iPods; the dynamic president of the Congressional Hispanic Caucus, Esther Aguilera; a student writer's inspirational lessons from a hardworking father; and the advantages of bilingualism. A unique new practice asking students to place nouns in a sequence from concrete to most abstract launches the section.

Overall, the expanded coverage of topic sentences and the new practices provide instructors with better tools to help their students write effectively.

More Critical Thinking and Viewing.   The Ninth Edition of *Grassroots* fosters college-level thinking skills through a multifaceted approach.

● Many new collaborative exercises provide opportunities for problem solving, discussion, and peer feedback.

● More "Exploring Online" features invite students to visit a relevant website, answer questions about it, and write.

- Fifteen new paragraph-length writing assignments give students many more chances to practice and develop their thinking and writing skills.

- The twenty thought-provoking Readings in Unit 9 and the book's many contextualized visuals offer many occasions for analysis or debate.

- More photo captions and Teaching Tips in this edition contain open-ended thinking questions.

- Finally, two special features at the end of each unit—Writers' Workshops showcasing student work and Writing Assignments—reinforce the message that good writing and critical thinking are inseparable.

Complementing the book's strong core of grammar and writing lessons, these features help students develop habits like considering alternative views, inferring, questioning assumptions, and drawing reasonable conclusions.

Comprehensive Support

Grassroots is a complete learning and teaching program for any instructor. Both full-time and part-time instructors will appreciate the time-saving resources provided in *Grassroots'* complete package of technology and print materials.

- **Online Study Center™ Student Website for *Grassroots*.** Online Study Center™ Student Website for *Grassroots*, Cengage Learning's online writing program, benefits Developmental English students at all skill levels and saves time for instructors.

    This helpful site offers many new computer-scored ACE self-tests that provide students with immediate feedback; a list of Live Links from the text; Career and Job Resource Center; ESL Resources; and supplemental material on Writing Better Paragraphs and Essays.

    With a passkey, students can access additional premium material. They receive all material on the student website, plus tutorials; CL Interactives powered by Associated Press; CL News Now powered by Associated Press; Total Practice Zone; an online handbook created for developmental students; and GEAR, *Grassroots* Exercises and Review.

- **Online Study Center™ with Eduspace® Online Writing Program.** For instructors who would like an online course management system, Online Study Center™ with Eduspace® makes available additional assets such as a powerful gradebook; CL Assess, a diagnostic testing program that creates individualized study plans; Safe Assignment for plagiarism prevention; and a discussion board.

- **Online Study Center™ Instructor Website.** The passkey-protected instructor website provides useful instructor resources such as the Instructor's Resource Manual with the author's suggestions for teaching writing as well as her notes on how to best teach each unit and reading; the Test Bank with diagnostic, mastery, unit, and chapter tests; 123 PowerPoint slides keyed to *Grassroots*; and the Student Answer Key.

- **Diploma Testing CD: *Grassroots* Test Bank.** Now expanded and improved, this test bank provides diagnostic, mastery, unit, and chapter tests that can be customized, edited, and printed. This test bank is also available on the instructor website.

- **Instructor's Annotated Edition.** Now with more and better ESL Tips by ESL expert Linda Fellag of the Community College of Philadelphia, this instructor's annotated edition likewise contains additional Teaching Tips from Susan Fawcett and answers to practices.

Flexible Organization of the Text

The range of material and flexible format of *Grassroots with Readings* make this worktext and its much-expanded technology package adaptable to almost any teaching and learning situation: classroom, laboratory, or self-teaching. Each chapter is a self-contained lesson, so instructors may teach the chapters in any sequence that fits their course design. *Grassroots* is versatile enough to support many different approaches to basic writing instruction.

Acknowledgments

The author wishes to thank these reviewers and colleagues. Their thoughtful comments and suggestions helped strengthen this Ninth Edition.

Carolyn Barr, *Broward Community College*

Elaine Bassett, *Troy University*

Frieda Campbell-Peltier, *Portland Community College*

Amy Carattini, *Housatonic Community College*

Barbara Craig, *Del Mar College*

Ann Fellinger, *Pulaski Technical College*

Tom Ghering, *Ivy Tech Community College of Indiana*

Susan Graf, *Penn State University Mont Alto Campus*

Todd Helmer, *Brown College*

Deanna Highe, *Central Piedmont Community College*

Teresa Jenkins, *Denmark Technical College*

Doug Joyce, *McCook Community College*

John Kordalewski, *Bunker Hill Community College*

Sarah Lahm, *Normandale Community College*

Anna Maheshwari, *Schoolcraft College*

Linda McLintock, *Germanna Community College*

Adrienne Mews, *Lane Community College*

Kerry Moley, *Palm Beach Community College*

Lisa Moslow, *Erie Community College South Campus*

Caryn Newburger, *Austin Community College*

Bakkah Rasheed-Shabazz, *Wayne County Community College District*

Richard Sabree, *Community College of Philadelphia*

Mark Schneberger, *Oklahoma City Community College*

Shusmita Sen, *Spokane Community College*

Sandia Tuttle, *Grossmont College*

Margaret Welsh, *Plaza College*

Kenneth Wilson, *Cuyahoga Community College*

Lupe Wilson, *Del Mar College*

I am indebted to my editors at Cengage Learning who worked hard to make this simply the best revision of *Grassroots* yet. My deep thanks to Joann Kozyrev, Sponsoring Editor, for her unfailing support, humor, and belief in my textbooks; Martha Bustin, Senior Development Editor, whose love of *Grassroots* and attention to detail have enriched this book; Henry Rachlin, the best textbook designer anywhere; Nancy Blodget, Senior Project Editor, for converting my giant manuscript into this lovely volume, bringing kindness and grace to the process; Marcy Kagan, photo researcher and artist, whose eye taught me and whose friendship touched me; Jill Clark, Editorial Assistant, whose careful scrutiny of untold numbers of proofs earned her the unofficial "Eagle Eye" award as well as my deepest gratitude; and Daisuke Yasutake, Editorial Assistant, whose many capabilities keep us all moving forward. I am grateful to Tom Ziolkowski, Marketing Manager, for his vision and enthusiasm for my textbooks and their mission.

The talented Ann Marie Radaskiewicz has played a vital role, researching and drafting a number of Practices and creating many new electronic tests and exercises for *Grassroots'* online resources. Her professionalism and can-do cheer make working with her a delight. Professor Linda Fellag of the Community College of Philadelphia also enriched this edition, writing useful new ESL Tips that will help many instructors better serve their nonnative and bilingual students.

Love and gratitude to the friends and family who supported me during the long days and nights of this revision, brought me flowers and goodies, and basically loved me anyway—especially Maggie Smith, Colleen Huff, Trisha Nelson, Pamela Tudor, Sondra Zeidenstein, David Fawcett, and Ed Brown. My husband, Richard Donovan, patiently listened to drafts, clipped articles for me on juicy topics, and suggested sports figures and issues that might appeal to *Grassroots'* readers—those students and faculty in whose dreams we both believe.

I dedicate this Ninth Edition to my mother, Harriet Fawcett, whose passionate fight back from a massive stroke to life and art inspires all who know her.

S.F.

Writing Forceful Paragraphs

The goal of *Grassroots* is to make you a better writer, and Unit 1 is key to your success. In this unit, you will

- Learn the importance of subject, audience, and purpose

- Learn the parts of a good paragraph

- Practice the paragraph-writing process

- Learn how to revise and improve your paragraphs

- Apply these skills to exam questions and short essays

Spotlight on Writing

Here, writer Alice Walker recalls her mother's extraordinary talent. If possible, read the paragraph aloud.

My mother adorned with flowers whatever shabby house we were forced to live in, and not just your typical straggly country stand of zinnias, either. She planted ambitious gardens—and still does—with over fifty different varieties of plants that bloom profusely from early March until late November. Before she left home for the fields, she watered her flowers, chopped up the grass, and laid out new beds. When she returned from the fields, she might divide clumps of bulbs, dig a cold pit, uproot and replant roses, or prune branches from her taller bushes or trees—until night came and it was too dark to see.

Alice Walker, "In Search of Our Mothers' Gardens"

- Ms. Walker's words bring to life her mother's passion for flowers. Are any details especially vivid? Why do you think Walker's mother worked so hard on her gardening?

- Words are powerful: they can make us remember, see, feel, or think in certain ways. Unit 1 will introduce you to the power of writing well.

 Writing Ideas

- *An activity that your parent or guardian passionately enjoyed*

- *Someone who inspired you with her or his ambition or creativity*

CHAPTER 1

Exploring the Writing Process

PART A The Writing Process

PART B Subject, Audience, and Purpose

PART C Guidelines for Submitting Written Work

Did you know that the most successful students and employees are people who write well? In fact, many good jobs today require excellent writing and communication skills in fields as varied as computer technology, health sciences, education, and social services.

The goal of this book is to help you become a better and more confident writer. You will realize that the ability to write well is not a magical talent that some people possess and others don't but rather a life skill that can be learned. I invite you now to make a decision to excel in this course. It will be one of the best investments you could ever make in yourself, your education, and your future. Let *Grassroots* be your guide, and enjoy the journey.

PART A The Writing Process

This chapter will give you an overview of the writing process, as well as some tips on how to approach your writing assignments in college. Many people have the mistaken idea that good writers just sit down and write a perfect paper or assignment from start to finish. In fact, experienced writers go through a **process** consisting of steps like these:

1 Prewriting
- Thinking about possible subjects
- Freely jotting down ideas on paper or computer
- Narrowing the subject and writing it as one sentence
- Deciding which ideas to include
- Arranging ideas in a plan or outline

2 Writing
- Writing a first draft

3 Rewriting
- Rethinking, rearranging, and revising as necessary
- Writing one or more new drafts
- Proofreading for grammar and spelling errors

Writing is a personal and sometimes messy process. Writers don't all perform these steps in the same order, and they may have to go through some steps more than once. However, most writers **prewrite, write, rewrite**—and **proofread.** The rest of this unit and much of the book will show you how.

PRACTICE 1

Self-Assessment

Choose something that you wrote recently for a class or for work and think about the *process* you followed in writing it. With a group of three or four classmates, or in your notebook, answer these questions:

1. Did I do any planning or prewriting—or did I just start writing the assignment?

2. How much time did I spend improving and revising my work?

3. Was I able to spot and correct my own grammar and spelling errors?

4. What one change in my writing process would most improve my writing? Taking more time for prewriting? Spending more time revising? Improving my grammar or spelling skills?

PRACTICE 2

Bring in several newspaper help-wanted sections. In a group with four or five classmates, study the ads in career fields that interest you. Next, count the number of ads that stress writing and communication skills. Alternately, if you have Internet access, you could visit a job-search website like **<http://www.monster.com>** and perform the same exercise. Be prepared to present your findings to the class.

PART B   Subject, Audience, and Purpose

As you begin a writing assignment, give some thought to your **subject, audience,** and **purpose.**

When your instructor assigns a broad **subject,** try to focus on one aspect that interests you. For example, suppose the broad subject is *music,* and you play the conga drums. You might focus on why you play them rather than some other instrument or on what drumming means to you. Whenever possible, choose subjects you know and care about: observing your neighborhood come to life in the morning, riding a dirt bike, helping a child become more confident, learning more about your computer. Your answers to such questions, like those listed below, will suggest promising writing ideas. Keep a list of the best ones.

To find or focus your subject, ask

- What special experience or knowledge do I have?

- What angers, saddens, or inspires me?

- What campus, job, or community problem do I have ideas about solving?

- What story in the news affected me recently?

How you approach your subject will depend on your **audience,** your readers. Are you writing for classmates, a professor, people who know about your subject, or people who do not? For instance, if you are writing about weight training, and your readers have never been inside a gym, you will approach your subject in a simple and basic way, perhaps stressing the benefits of weightlifting. An audience of bodybuilders, however, already knows these things; for bodybuilders, you would write in more depth, perhaps focusing on how to develop one muscle group.

> To focus on your audience, ask
>
> - For whom am I writing? Who will read this?
>
> - Are they beginners or experts? How much do they know about the subject?
>
> - Do I think they will agree or disagree with my ideas?

Finally, keeping your **purpose** in mind helps you know what to write. Do you want to explain something to your readers, convince them that a certain point of view is correct, entertain them, or just tell a good story? If your purpose is to persuade parents to support having school uniforms, you can explain that uniforms lower clothing costs and may reduce student crime. However, if your purpose is to convince students that uniforms are a good idea, you might approach the subject differently, emphasizing how stylish the uniforms look or why students from other schools feel that uniforms improve their school atmosphere.

PRACTICE 3

List five subjects you might like to write about. Consider your audience and purpose. For whom are you writing? What do you want them to know about your subject? For ideas, reread the boxed questions.

	Subject	**Audience**	**Purpose**
EXAMPLE: 1.	how to make a Greek salad	inexperienced cooks	to show how easy it is to make a great Greek salad
2.	_____	_____	_____
3.	_____	_____	_____
4.	_____	_____	_____
5.	_____	_____	_____

PRACTICE 4

With a group of three or four classmates, or on your own, jot down ideas for the following two writing tasks. Notice how your points and details differ depending on your audience and purpose. (If you are not employed, write about a job with which you are familiar.)

1. For a new coworker, you plan to write a description of a typical day on your job. Your purpose is to help train this person, who will perform the same duties you do. Your supervisor will need to approve what you write.

2. For one of your closest friends, you plan to write a description of a typical day on your job. Your purpose is to make your friend laugh because he or she has been feeling down recently.

PRACTICE 5

Study the advertisement shown below and then answer these questions: What *subject* is the ad addressing? Who do you think is the target *audience*? What is the ad's intended *purpose*? In your view, how successful is the ad in achieving its purpose? Why or why not?

©2004 People for the Ethical Treatment of Animals.

PRACTICE 6

In a group with three or four classmates, read the following classified ads from real city newspapers around the country. The *subject* of each ad is a product or service that is for sale, the *audience* is the potential customer, and the *purpose* is to convince that customer to buy the product or service. How does each ad writer undercut his or her purpose? How would you revise each ad so that it better achieves its apparent purpose?

1. Do you need a dramatic new look? Visit our plastered surgeons.

2. We do not tear your clothing with machinery. We do it carefully by hand.

3. Now is your chance to have your ears pierced and get an extra pair to take home free.

4. Tired of cleaning yourself? Let me do it.

5. Auto repair service. Try us once, and you'll never go anywhere again.

PART C   Guidelines for Submitting Written Work

Learn your instructor's requirements for submitting written work, as these may vary from class to class. Here are some general guidelines. Write in any special instructions.

1. Choose sturdy, white, 8½-by-11-inch paper, lined if you write by hand, plain if you use a computer.

2. Clearly write your name, the date, and any other required information, using the format requested by your instructor.

3. If you write by hand, do so neatly in black or dark blue ink.

4. Write on only one side of the paper.

5. Double-space if you write on a computer. Some instructors also want handwriting double-spaced.

6. Leave margins of at least one inch on all sides.

7. Number each page of your assignment, starting with page 2. Place the numbers at the top of each page, either centered or in the top right corner.

Other guidelines: _____

_____

_____

CHAPTER HIGHLIGHTS

Tips for Succeeding in This Course

● **Remember that writing is a process: prewriting, writing, and rewriting.**

● **Before you write, always be clear about your subject, audience, and purpose.**

● **Follow your instructor's guidelines for submitting written work.**

● **Practice.**

EXPLORING ONLINE

Throughout this text, the Exploring Online feature will suggest ways that you can use the Internet to improve your writing and grammar skills. You will find that if you need extra writing help, online writing centers (called OWLs) can be a great resource. Many provide extra review or practice in areas in which you might need assistance. You will want to do some searching to find the best sites for your needs, but here are two excellent OWL sites to explore:

<http://owl.english.purdue.edu/> Purdue University.

<http://grammar.ccc.commnet.edu/grammar/> Capital Community College.

<http://college.cengage.com/devenglish> For more exercises, quizzes, and live links to all websites in this chapter, visit this link, click Developmental Writing, and find the home page for *Grassroots*, 9/e. Bookmark the *Grassroots* student website for future visits as you work through this book.

Prewriting to Generate Ideas

PART A Freewriting

PART B Brainstorming

PART C Clustering

PART D Keeping a Journal

The author of this book used to teach ice skating. On the first day of class, her students practiced falling. Once they knew how to fall without fear, they were free to learn to skate.

Writing is much like ice skating: the more you practice, the better you get. If you are free to make mistakes, you'll want to practice, and you'll look forward to new writing challenges.

The problem is that many people avoid writing. Faced with an English composition or a report at work, they put it off and then scribble something at the last minute. Other people sit staring at the blank page or computer screen—writing a sentence, crossing it out, unable to get started. In this chapter, you will learn four useful prewriting techniques that will help you jump-start your writing process and generate lots of ideas: freewriting, brainstorming, clustering, and keeping a journal.

PART A Freewriting

Freewriting is a method many writers use to warm up and get ideas. Here are the guidelines: For five or ten full minutes, write without stopping. Don't worry about grammar or about writing complete sentences; just set a timer and go. If you get stuck, repeat or rhyme the last word you wrote, but keep writing nonstop until the timer sounds. Afterward, read what you have written, and underline any parts you like.

Freewriting is a wonderful way to let your ideas pour out without getting stuck by worrying too soon about correctness or "good writing." Sometimes freewriting produces nonsense, but often it provides interesting ideas for further thinking and writing. **Focused freewriting** can help you find subjects to write about.

Focused Freewriting

In *focused freewriting*, you try to focus your thoughts on one subject as you freewrite. The subject can be one assigned by your instructor, one you choose, or one you discover in unfocused freewriting.

Here is one student's focused freewriting on the topic *someone who strongly influenced me.*

Thin, thinner, weak, weaker. You stopped cooking for yourself—forced yourself to choke down cans of nutrition. Your chest caved in; your bones stuck out. You never asked, Why me? With a weak laugh you asked, Why not me? I had a wonderful life, a great job, a good marriage while it lasted. Have beautiful kids. Your wife divorced you—couldn't stand to watch you die, couldn't stand to have her life fall apart the way your body was falling apart. I watched you stumble, trip over your own feet, sink, fall down. I held you up. Now I wonder which one of us was holding the other one up. I saw you shiver in your summer jacket because you didn't have the strength to put on your heavy coat. Bought you a feather-light winter jacket, saw your eyes fill with tears of pleasure and gratitude. You said they would find you at the bottom of the stairs. When they called to tell me we'd lost you, the news wasn't unexpected, but the pain came in huge waves. Heart gave out, they said. Your daughter found you crumpled at the foot of the stairs. How did you know? What else did you guess?

Daniel Corteau, student

● This student later used his freewriting as the basis for an excellent paragraph.

● Underline any words or lines that you find especially striking or powerful. Be prepared to discuss your choices.

● How was the writer influenced by the man he describes?

PRACTICE 1

1. Set a timer for ten minutes, or have someone time you. Freewrite without stopping for the full ten minutes. Repeat or rhyme words if you get stuck, but keep writing! Don't let your pen or pencil leave the page or your fingers leave the keyboard.

2. When you finish, write down one or two words that describe how you feel while freewriting. _____

3. Now read your freewriting. Underline any words or lines you like—anything that strikes you as powerful, moving, funny, or important. If nothing strikes you, that's okay.

PRACTICE 2

Now choose one word or idea from your freewriting or from the following list. Focus your thoughts on it, and do a ten-minute focused freewriting. Try to stick to the topic, but don't worry too much about it. Just keep writing! When you finish, read and underline any striking lines or ideas.

1. home
2. a good student
3. the biggest lie
4. a dream
5. someone who influenced you
6. your experiences with writing
7. the smell of _____
8. strength

PRACTICE 3

Try two more focused freewritings at home, each one ten minutes long. Do them at different times of the day when you have a few quiet moments. If possible, use a timer: set it for ten minutes, and then write fast until it rings. Later, read your freewritings, and underline any ideas or passages you might like to write more about.

PART B   Brainstorming

Brainstorming means freely jotting down ideas about a topic on paper or on a computer. As in freewriting, the purpose of brainstorming is to get as many ideas down as possible so that you will have something to work with later. Just write down everything that comes to mind about a topic—words and phrases, ideas, details, examples, little stories. Once you have brainstormed, read over your list, underlining any ideas you might want to develop further.

Here is one student's brainstorming list on *an interesting job:*

> midtown messenger
>
> frustrating but free
>
> I know the city backward and forward
>
> good bike needed
>
> fast, ever-changing, dangerous
>
> drivers hate messengers—we dart in and out of traffic
>
> old clothes don't get respect
>
> I wear the best Descent racing gear, a Giro helmet
>
> people respect you more
>
> I got tipped $100 for carrying a crystal vase from the showroom to Wall Street in 15 minutes
>
> other times I get stiffed
>
> lessons I've learned—controlling my temper
>
> having dignity
>
> staying calm no matter what—insane drivers, deadlines, rudeness
>
> weirdly, I like my job

As he brainstormed, this writer produced many interesting facts and details about his job as a bicycle messenger, all in just a few minutes. He might want to underline the ideas that most interest him—perhaps the time he was tipped $100—and then brainstorm again for more details.

PRACTICE 4

Choose one of the following topics that interests you, and write it at the top of your page. Then brainstorm! Write anything that comes into your head about the topic. Let your ideas flow.

1. a singer or a musician
2. the future
3. an intriguing job
4. a story in the news
5. the best/worst class I've ever had
6. making a difference
7. a place to which I never want to return
8. a community problem

After you fill a page with your list, read it over, underlining the most interesting ideas. Draw arrows to connect related ideas. Do you find one idea that might be the subject of a paper?

PART C   Clustering

Some writers find **clustering** or **mapping** an effective way to get ideas onto paper. To begin clustering, write one idea or topic—usually one word—in the center of your paper. Then let your mind make associations, and write those ideas down, branching out from the center. When one idea suggests other ideas, details, or examples, jot down those around it in a cluster, like this:

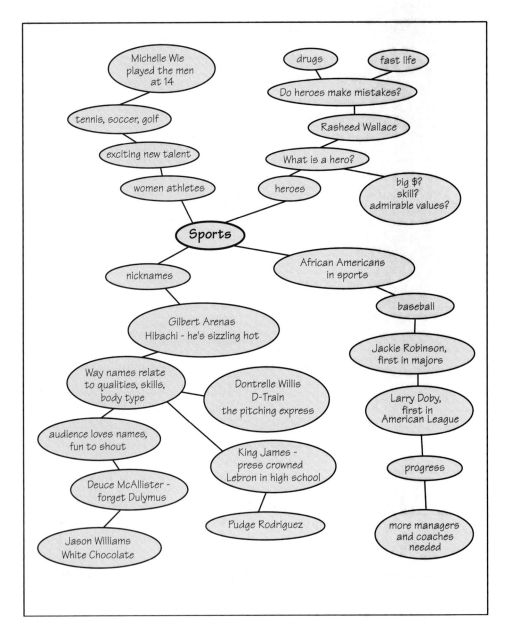

Once this student filled a page with clustered ideas about the word *sports*, his next step was choosing the cluster that most interested him and writing further. He might even have wanted to freewrite for more ideas.

PRACTICE 5

Read over the clustering map on page 12. If you were giving advice to the writer, which cluster or branch do you think would make the most interesting paper? Why?

PRACTICE 6

Choose one of these topics or another topic that interests you. Write it in the center of a piece of paper and then try clustering. Keep writing down associations until you have filled the page.

1. movies	5. my hometown
2. a pet	6. self-esteem
3. a lesson	7. a relative
4. sports	8. someone I don't understand

PART D Keeping a Journal

Keeping a **journal** is an excellent way to practice your writing skills and to discover ideas for future writing. Most of all, your journal is a place to record your private thoughts and important experiences. Open a journal file on your computer, or get yourself a special book with 8½-by-11-inch lined paper. Every night, or several times a week, write for at least ten minutes in your journal.

What you write about will be limited only by your imagination. Here are some ideas:

● Write in detail about things that matter to you—family relationships, falling in (or out of) love, an experience at school or work, something important you just learned, something you did well.

● List your personal goals, and brainstorm possible steps toward achieving them.

● Write about problems you are having, and "think on paper" about ways to solve them.

● Comment on classroom instruction or assignments, and evaluate your learning progress. What needs work? What questions do you need to ask? Write out a study plan for yourself and refer to it regularly.

● Write down your responses to your reading—class assignments, newspaper items, magazine articles, websites that impress or anger you.

● Read through the quotations at the end of this book until you find one that strikes you. Then copy it into your journal, think about it, and write. For example, Agnes Repplier says, "It is not easy to find happiness in ourselves, and it is not possible to find it elsewhere." Do you agree with her?

● Be alert to interesting writing topics all around you. If possible, carry a notebook during the day for "fast sketches." Jot down moving or funny moments, people or things that catch your attention—an overworked waitress in a restaurant, a scene at the day-care center where you leave your child, a man trying to persuade an officer not to give him a parking ticket.

You will soon find that ideas for writing will occur to you all day long. Before they slip away, capture them in words. Writing is like ice skating. You have to practice.

PRACTICE 7

Write in your journal for at least ten minutes three times a week.

At the end of each week, read what you have written. Underline striking passages, and mark interesting topics and ideas that you would like to explore further.

As you complete the exercises in this book and work on the writing assignments, try all four techniques—freewriting, brainstorming, clustering, and keeping a journal—and see which ones work best for you.

PRACTICE 8

From your journal, choose one or two passages that you might want to rewrite and allow others to read. Put a check beside each of those passages so that you can find them easily later. Underline the parts you like best. Can you already see ways you might rewrite and improve the writing?

CHAPTER HIGHLIGHTS

To get started and to discover your ideas, try these techniques.

- **Focused freewriting: freewriting for five or ten minutes about one topic**

- **Brainstorming: freely jotting down many ideas about a topic**

- **Clustering: making word associations on paper**

- **Keeping a journal: writing regularly about things that interest and move you**

EXPLORING ONLINE

<http://owl.english.purdue.edu/owl/resources/673/01> If you still feel stuck when you start to write, try these techniques from Purdue University's famous OWL (Online Writing Lab).

<http://depts.gallaudet.edu/englishworks/writing/prewriting.html> Review or print this handy chart of prewriting strategies.

<http://college.cengage.com/devenglish> For more exercises, quizzes, and live links to all websites in this chapter, visit this link, click Developmental Writing, and find the home page for *Grassroots*, 9/e. Bookmark the *Grassroots* student website for future visits as you work through this book.

Developing Effective Paragraphs

The **paragraph** is the basic unit of writing. This chapter will guide you through the process of writing paragraphs.

CHAPTER 3

PART A Defining the Paragraph and the Topic Sentence

A *paragraph* is a group of related sentences that develop one main idea. Although a paragraph has no definite length, it is often four to twelve sentences long. A paragraph usually appears with other paragraphs in a longer piece of writing—an essay, a letter, or an article, for example.

A paragraph looks like this on the page:

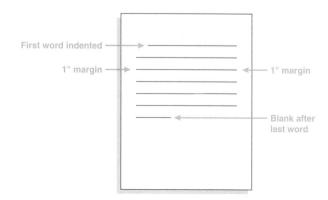

First word indented

1" margin   1" margin

Blank after last word

- Clearly **indent** the first word of every paragraph about 1 inch (one tab on the computer).

- Extend every line of a paragraph as close to the right-hand margin as possible.

- If the last word of the paragraph comes before the end of the line, however, leave the rest of the line blank.

Topic Sentence and Body

Most paragraphs contain one main idea to which all the sentences relate. The **topic sentence** states this main idea. The **body** of the paragraph supports this main idea with specific details, facts, and examples.

> When I was growing up, my older brother Joe was the greatest person in my world. If anyone teased me about my braces or buckteeth, he fiercely defended me. When one boy insisted on calling me "Fang," Joe threatened to knock his teeth out. It worked—no more teasing. My brother always chose me to play on his baseball teams though I was a terrible hitter. Even after he got his driver's license, he didn't abandon me. Instead, every Sunday, the two of us went for a drive. We might stop for cheeseburgers, go to a computer showroom, drive past some girl's house, or just laugh and talk. It was one of childhood's mysteries that such a wonderful brother loved me.
>
> *Jeremiah Woolrich, student*

- The first sentence of this paragraph is the *topic sentence*. It states in a general way the main idea of the paragraph: that *Joe was the greatest person in my world*. Although the topic sentence can appear anywhere in the paragraph, it is often the first sentence.

- The rest of the paragraph, the *body*, fully explains this statement with details about braces and buckteeth, baseball teams, Sunday drives, cheeseburgers, and so forth.

- Note that the final sentence provides a brief conclusion so that the paragraph *feels* finished.

PRACTICE 1

Each group of sentences below can be arranged and written as a paragraph. Circle the letter of the sentence that would be the best topic sentence. REMEMBER: The topic sentence states the main idea of the entire paragraph and includes all the other ideas.

EXAMPLE: a. Speed-walking three times a week is part of my routine.

b. Staying healthy and fit is important to me.

c. Every night, I get at least seven hours of sleep.

d. I eat as many fresh fruits and vegetables as possible.

(Sentence b is more general than the other sentences; it would be the best topic sentence.)

1. a. Some colleges are experimenting with using iPods to deliver instructional material, complete with musical clips, news, and even video.

   b. Runners, hikers, and bicyclists sometimes use their iPods as personal trainers that plan a route and then provide maps, distances, and time goals.

   c. Although most people still think of the iPod as a digital music player, others are using these gadgets in creative and innovative ways.

   d. Video iPod owners can search for their soul mates using PodDater software to download short video clips and profiles of available singles.

2. a. Trained bomb-sniffing dogs have a nearly perfect record of separating real explosives from false alarms.

   b. Most air travelers love these dogs, prompting one police officer to say that people react to his Labrador retriever, Chili, as if she were Julia Roberts.

   c. Bomb-sniffing dogs have become an important and often-beloved security safeguard at airports.

   d. Because dogs are mobile—unlike machines—they can easily lead their handlers to the source of a problem.

3. a. When his family moved to Los Angeles in 1974, ten-year-old Lenny won a place in the California Boys Choir and taught himself to play many instruments.

   b. As a teen, he studied music at the Berkeley Hills School and created the dramatic look for which he is now famous.

   c. Before he was ten, he had convinced his parents to take him to concerts by James Brown, Duke Ellington, and the Jackson 5.

   d. Lenny and his father produced his first album, *Let Love Rule*, which won him a Virgin Records contract and huge numbers of fans.

   e. A childhood love of performing music launched rocker and songwriter Lenny Kravitz on the path to stardom.

   f. As a toddler in Brooklyn, New York, Lenny made his own drum set out of pots and pans.

4. a. Physical courage allows soldiers or athletes to endure bodily pain or danger.

   b. Those with social courage dare to expose their deep feelings in order to build close relationships.

   c. Those rare people who stand up for their beliefs despite public pressure possess moral courage.

   d. Inventors and artists show creative courage when they break out of old ways of seeing and doing things.

   e. Psychologist Rollo May claimed that there are four different types of courage.

5. a. She watched her mother and father, who had only an elementary school education, struggle to feed and clothe the family.

   b. Today, Aguilera is president of the Congressional Hispanic Caucus Institute (CHCI), which supports Hispanic students with scholarships and internships.

   c. For Esther Aguilera, education is the key that unlocks the American dream.

   d. Esther became an excellent student, earned her bachelor's degree in public policy, and decided to help other Hispanics aim high and succeed in college.

   e. Born in Mexico, five-year-old Esther arrived in California with her parents and five siblings.

6. a. Many old toys and household objects are now collectors' items.

   b. A Barbie or Madame Alexander doll from the 1950s can bring more than $1,000.

   c. Old baseball cards are worth money to collectors.

   d. Fiesta china, made in the 1930s, has become popular again.

7. a. You should read the ingredients on every package of food you buy.

   b. Children should not eat mandelona, which is made from peanuts soaked in almond flavoring.

   c. Avoid buying food from bins that do not list ingredients.

   d. If your child is allergic to peanuts, you need to be constantly on the alert.

   e. In a restaurant, tongs may have been used to pick up items containing peanuts.

8. a. In our increasingly global economy, employees who can communicate with non-English-speaking customers and overseas colleagues are in demand at many American companies.

   b. People who can speak and write two languages fluently possess a valuable professional, social, and mental asset.

   c. Studies confirm that bilingualism boosts brain power because adults who grew up speaking two language stay sharper and quicker later in life.

   d. Bilingualism brings personal rewards, such as the ability to bridge cultural boundaries and broaden one's social network to include people of other nationalities and ethnic groups.

PART B Narrowing the Topic and Writing the Topic Sentence

The rest of this chapter will guide you through the process of writing paragraphs of your own. Here are the steps we will discuss:

1. Narrowing the topic and writing the topic sentence

2. Generating ideas for the body

3. Selecting and dropping ideas

4. Grouping ideas in a plan

5. Writing and revising the paragraph

6. Writing the final draft

Narrowing the Topic

Often your first step as a writer will be **narrowing** a broad topic—one assigned by your instructor, one you have thought of yourself, or one suggested by a particular writing task, like a letter. That is, you must cut the topic down to size and choose one aspect that interests you.

Assume, for example, that you are asked to write a paragraph describing a person you know. The trick is to choose someone you would *like* to write about, someone who interests you and would probably also interest your audience of readers.

At this point, many writers find it helpful to think on paper by *brainstorming, freewriting,* or *clustering.** As you jot down or freely write ideas, ask yourself questions.

---

*Brainstorming is discussed further in Part C. Also see Chapter 2 for more information about prewriting.

Whom do I love, hate, or admire? Who is the funniest or most unusual person I know? Is there a family member or friend about whom others might like to read?

Suppose you choose to write about your friend Beverly. *Beverly* is too broad a topic for one paragraph. Therefore, you should limit your topic further, choosing just one of her qualities or acts. What is unusual about her? What might interest others? Perhaps what stands out in your mind is that Beverly is a determined person who doesn't let difficulties defeat her. You have now *narrowed* your broad topic to *Beverly's determination*.

PRACTICE 2

Good writers need a clear understanding of general and specific—that is, which ideas are general and which are specific. Number the items in each group below, with 1 being the most specific and limited, 2 being the second most specific, and the highest number being the most general.

1. ___ chairs

   ___ furniture

   ___ Grandma's mahogany rocking chair

   ___ household contents

2. ___ CDs of Malian singer Habib Koité

   ___ music

   ___ African music

   ___ music of Mali, West Africa

   ___ sound

3. ___ rose

   ___ flowering plants

   ___ living things

   ___ plants

   ___ the Betty Boop rose

4. ___ *Union-Tribune* sports writer Jim Jackson

   ___ California

   ___ North America

   ___ *San Diego Union-Tribune* office building

   ___ Earth

5. ___ athletes

   ___ Brodeur's agility

   ___ hockey players

   ___ goalies

   ___ New Jersey Devils goalie Martin Brodeur

Writing the Topic Sentence

The next step is to write your **topic sentence,** which clearly states, in sentence form, your narrowed topic and a point about that topic. This step helps you further focus your topic by forcing you to make a statement about it. That statement sets forth one main idea that the rest of your paragraph will support and explain. A topic sentence can be very simple *(Beverly is very determined)*, or, better yet, it can state your attitude or point of view about the topic *(Beverly's determination inspires admiration)*.

Think of the topic sentence as having two parts: a **topic** and a **controlling idea.** The controlling idea states the writer's attitude, angle, or point of view about the topic.

> topic   controlling idea
>
> **Topic sentence:**   Beverly's determination inspires admiration.

All topics can have many possible topic sentences, depending on the writer's interests and point of view. The controlling idea helps you focus on just one aspect. Here are three possible topic sentences about the topic *attending college:*

> (1) Attending college has revolutionized my career plans.
>
> (2) Attending college has put me in debt.
>
> (3) Attending college is exhausting but rewarding.

- These topic sentences all explore the same topic—attending college—but each controlling idea is different. The controlling idea in topic sentence (1) is *has revolutionized my career plans.*

- What is the controlling idea in topic sentence (2)?

  _____

- What is the controlling idea in topic sentence (3)?

  _____

- Notice the way each controlling idea lets the reader know what that paragraph will be about. By choosing different key words, a writer can angle any topic in different directions. If you were assigned the topic *attending college*, what would your topic sentence be?

  _____

  _____

PRACTICE 3

Read each topic sentence below. Circle the topic and underline the controlling idea.

EXAMPLE: (Computer games) improved my study skills.

1. Hybrid cars offer monetary advantages over gasoline vehicles.

2. White-water rafting increased my self-confidence.

3. Ed Bradley achieved many firsts as a television journalist.

4. Immigrants frequently are stereotyped by native-born Americans.

5. A course in financial planning should be required of all college freshmen.

Writing Limited and Complete Topic Sentences

Check to make sure your topic sentence is *limited* and *complete*. Your topic sentence should be **limited.** It should make a point that is neither too broad nor too narrow to be supported in a paragraph. As a rule, the more specific and well defined the topic sentence, the better the paragraph. Which of these topic sentences do you think will produce the best paragraph?

(1) My recent trip to Colorado was really bad.

(2) My recent trip to Colorado was disappointing because the weather ruined my camping plans.

● Topic sentence (1) is so broad that the paragraph could include almost anything.

● Topic sentence (2), on the other hand, is *limited* enough to provide the main idea for a good paragraph: how terrible weather ruined the writer's camping plans.

(3) The Each-One-Reach-One tutoring program encourages academic excellence at Chester Elementary School.

(4) Tutoring programs can be found all over the country.

● Topic sentence (3) is limited enough to provide the main idea for a good paragraph. Reading this topic sentence, what do you expect the paragraph to include?

_____

_____

● Topic sentence (4) lacks a limited point. Reading this sentence, someone cannot guess what the paragraph will be about.

In addition, the topic sentence must be a **complete sentence;** it must contain a subject and a verb and express a complete thought.* Do not confuse a topic with a topic sentence. For example, *the heroism of Christopher Reeve* cannot be a topic sentence because it is not a complete sentence. Here is one possible topic sentence: *Christopher Reeve's work with other spinal-cord injury patients made him a true hero.*

For now, it is best to place your topic sentence at the beginning of the paragraph. After you have mastered this pattern, you can try variations. Placed first, the topic sentence clearly establishes the focus of your paragraph and helps grab

_____

*For more work on writing complete sentences, see Chapters 6 and 7.

the reader's attention. Wherever the topic sentence appears, all other sentences must relate to it and support it with specific details, facts, examples, arguments, and explanations. If necessary, you can revise the topic sentence later to make it more accurately match the paragraph you have written.

Caution: Do not begin a topic sentence with *This paragraph will be about . . .* or *I am going to write about . . .* These extra words contribute nothing. Instead, make your point directly. Make every word in the topic sentence count.

PRACTICE 4

Put a check beside each topic sentence that is limited enough to be the topic sentence of a good paragraph. If you think a topic sentence is too broad, limit the topic according to your own interests; then write a new, specific topic sentence.

EXAMPLES:

✔   E-mail has changed my life in three ways.

  Rewrite: _____

  I am going to write about cell phones.

  Rewrite: *Talking on a cell phone can distract drivers to the point of causing accidents.*

1. Working in the complaint department taught me tolerance.

  Rewrite: _____

  _____

2. A subject I want to write about is money.

  Rewrite: _____

  _____

3. This paragraph will discuss food.

  Rewrite: _____

  _____

4. Some things about college have been great.

  Rewrite: _____

  _____

5. Living in a one-room apartment forces a person to be organized.

  Rewrite: _____

  _____

PRACTICE 5

Here is a list of topics. Choose one that interests you from this list or from your own list in Chapter 1 on page 6. Narrow the topic, and write a topic sentence limited enough to provide the main idea for a good paragraph. Make sure that your topic sentence is a complete sentence.

A talented musician	An act of courage
Why get an education?	Advertising con jobs
AIDS	Clothing styles on campus

Narrowed topic: _____

Topic sentence: _____

_____

PART C   Generating Ideas for the Body of the Paragraph

Rich supporting detail is one key to effective writing. A good way to generate ideas for the body of a paragraph is by *brainstorming*, freely jotting down ideas. This important step may take just a few minutes, but it gets your ideas on paper and may pull ideas out of you that you didn't even know you had.

Freely jot down anything that might relate to your topic—details, examples, little stories. Don't worry at this point if some ideas don't seem to belong. For now, just keep jotting them down.

Here is a possible brainstorming list for the topic sentence *Beverly inspires admiration because she is so determined.*

1. saved enough money for college
2. worked days, went to school nights
3. has beautiful brown eyes
4. nervous about learning to drive but didn't give up
5. failed road test twice—passed eventually
6. her favorite color—wine red
7. received degree in accounting
8. she is really admirable
9. with lots of will power, quit smoking
10. used to be a heavy smoker
11. married to Virgil
12. I like Virgil too
13. now a good driver
14. never got a ticket
15. hasn't touched another cigarette

As you saw in Part B, some writers brainstorm or use other prewriting techniques *before* they write the topic sentence. Do what works best for you.

PRACTICE 6

Now choose the topic from Practice 4 or Practice 5 that most interests you. Write your limited topic sentence here.

Topic sentence: _____

_____

Next, brainstorm, freewrite, or cluster for specific ideas to develop a paragraph. On paper or on a computer, write anything that comes to you about your topic sentence. Just let ideas pour out—details, memories, facts. Try to fill at least one page.

PRACTICE 7

Many writers adjust the topic sentence *after* they have finished drafting the paragraph. In a group of three or four classmates, study the body of each of the following paragraphs. Then, working together, write the most exact and interesting topic sentence you can.

1. Topic sentence: _____

   _____

The first advantage is the wide choice of movies. Most multiplexes have eight, twelve, or even twenty screens playing at once, so the moviegoer has a good chance of finding a movie that she or he actually wants to see. A second advantage of the multiplex is comfortable seating. Most multiplexes have large stadium seats that lean back like lounge chairs. Finally, the multiplex is a lively and pleasant place to be on Friday or Saturday night. In a college town, for example, the moviegoer is likely to run into friends and classmates, a definite plus—unless she or he hates crowds or wants to spend the evening hiding in the dark with a jumbo tub of popcorn. Some might long for the small movie houses of the past, but nostalgia can't outweigh the advantages of the multiplex.

2. Topic sentence: _____

   _____

Despite his pressured schedule, he always found time to play with my sisters and me, tell us stories, and make us feel loved. From his example, I learned that men can be loving and show affection. In addition, he often sat with me and discussed the responsibilities of being a man. He instilled in me principles and morals that I would not have learned from the guys on the corner. My hero felt that a man should be the provider for his family. He demonstrated this by working two jobs, seven days a week. After many years, my father saved enough money to make a down payment on a three-bedroom house next to a park. He accomplished all this with only a sixth-grade education. The values on which I now base my life were given to me by my hero, an unknown man who deserves to be famous.

Robert Fields, student

3. Topic sentence: _____

   _____

Frigid air would hit us in the eyes when we stepped out the door to catch the school bus. Even though our faces were wrapped in scarves and our heads covered with wool caps, the cold snatched our breath away. A thin layer of snow crunched loudly under our boots as we ran gasping out to the road. I knew that the famous Minnesota wind chill was pulling temperatures well below zero, but I tried not to think about that. Instead, I liked to see how everything in the yard was frozen motionless, even the blades of grass that shone like little glass knives.

Ari Henson, student

PART D Selecting and Dropping Ideas

This may be the easiest step in paragraph writing because all you have to do is select those ideas that best support your topic sentence and drop those that do not. Also drop ideas that just repeat the topic sentence and add nothing new to the paragraph.

Here is the brainstorming list for the topic sentence *Beverly inspires admiration because she is so determined.* Which ideas would you drop? Why?

1. saved enough money for college
2. worked days, went to school nights
3. has beautiful brown eyes
4. nervous about learning to drive but didn't give up
5. failed road test twice—passed eventually
6. her favorite color—wine red
7. received degree in accounting
8. she is really admirable
9. with lots of will power, quit smoking
10. used to be a heavy smoker
11. married to Virgil
12. I like Virgil too
13. now a good driver
14. never got a ticket
15. hasn't touched another cigarette

You probably dropped ideas 3, 6, 11, and 12 because they do not relate to the topic. You also should have dropped idea 8 because it merely repeats the topic sentence.

PRACTICE 8

Read through your own brainstorming list in Practice 6. Select the ideas that best support your topic sentence, and cross out those that do not. In addition, drop ideas that merely repeat the topic sentence. You should be able to give good reasons for keeping or dropping each idea in the list.

PART E Arranging Ideas in a Plan or an Outline

Next, choose an **order** in which to arrange your ideas. First, group together ideas that have something in common, that are related or alike in some way. Then decide which ideas should come first, which second, and so on. Many writers do this by numbering the ideas on their list.

Here is a plan for a paragraph about Beverly's determination.

Topic sentence: Beverly inspires admiration because she is so determined.

> worked days, went to school nights
>
> saved enough money for college
>
> received degree in accounting

> nervous about learning to drive but didn't give up
>
> failed road test twice—passed eventually
>
> now a good driver
>
> never got a ticket

> used to be a heavy smoker
>
> with lots of will power, quit smoking
>
> hasn't touched another cigarette

● How are the ideas in each group related? _____

_____

● Does it make sense to discuss college first, driving second, and smoking last?

Why? _____

_____

Keep in mind that there is more than one way to arrange ideas. As you group your own brainstorming list, think of what you want to say; then arrange your ideas accordingly.*

PRACTICE 9

On paper or on a computer, make a plan or outline from your brainstormed list of ideas. First, group together related ideas. Then decide which ideas will come first, which second, and so on.

PART F Writing and Revising the Paragraph

Writing the First Draft

By now, you should have a clear plan or outline from which to write the first draft of your paragraph. The **first draft** should contain all the ideas you have decided

_____
*For more work on choosing an order, see Chapter 4, Part B.

to use, in the order in which you have chosen to present them. Writing on every other line will leave room for later changes.

Explain your ideas fully, including details that will interest or amuse the reader. If you are unsure about something, put a check in the margin and come back to it later, but avoid getting stuck on any one word, sentence, or idea. If possible, set the paper aside for several hours or several days; this step will help you read it later with a fresh eye.

PRACTICE 10

On paper or on a computer, write a first draft of the paragraph you have been working on.

Revising

Whether you are a beginning writer or a professional, you must **revise**—that is, rewrite what you have written in order to improve it. You might cross out and rewrite words or entire sentences. You might add, drop, or rearrange details.

As you revise, keep the reader in mind. Ask yourself these questions:

● Is my topic sentence clear?

● Can the reader easily follow my ideas?

● Is the order of ideas logical?

● Will this paragraph keep the reader interested?

In addition, revise your paragraph for *support* and for *unity*.

Revising for Support

Make sure your paragraph contains excellent **support**—that is, specific details, facts, and examples that fully explain your topic sentence.

Avoid simply repeating the same idea in different words, especially the idea in the topic sentence. Repeated ideas are just padding, a sign that you need to brainstorm or freewrite again for new ideas. Which of the following two paragraphs contains the best and most interesting support?

A.   Every Saturday morning, Fourteenth Street is alive with activity. From one end of the street to the other, people are out doing everything imaginable. Vendors sell many different items on the street, and storekeepers will do just about anything to get customers into their stores. They will use signs, and they will use music. There is a tremendous amount of activity on Fourteenth Street, and just watching it is enjoyable.

B.   Every Saturday morning, Fourteenth Street is alive with activity. Vendors line the sidewalks, selling everything from DVD players to wigs. Trying to lure customers inside, the shops blast pop music into the street or hang brightly colored banners announcing "Grand Opening Sale" or "Everything Must Go." Shoppers jam the sidewalks, both serious bargain hunters and families just out for a stroll, munching chilidogs as they survey the merchandise. Here and there, a panhandler hustles for handouts, taking advantage of the Saturday crowd.

● The body of *paragraph A* contains vague and general statements, so the reader gets no clear picture of the activity on Fourteenth Street.

- The body of *paragraph B*, however, includes many specific *details* that clearly explain the topic sentence: *vendors selling everything from DVD players to wigs, shops blasting pop music, brightly colored banners.*

- What other details in *paragraph B* help you see just how Fourteenth Street is alive with activity?

_____

_____

_____

_____

PRACTICE 11

Check the following paragraphs for strong, specific support. Mark places that need more details or explanation, and cross out any weak or repeated words. Then revise and rewrite each paragraph *as if you had written it*, inventing and adding support when you need to.

Paragraph A: Aunt Alethia was one of the most important people in my life. She had a strong influence on me. No matter how busy she was, she always had time for me. She paid attention to small things about me that no one else seemed to notice. When I was successful, she praised me. When I was feeling down, she gave me pep talks. She was truly wise and shared her wisdom with me. My aunt was a great person who had a major influence on my life.

Paragraph B: Just getting to school safely can be a challenge for many young people. Young as he is, my son has been robbed once and bullied on several occasions. The robbery was very frightening, for it involved a weapon. What was taken was a small thing, but it meant a lot to my son. It angers me that just getting to school is so dangerous. Something needs to be done.

Revising for Unity

While writing, you may sometimes drift away from your topic and include information that does not belong in the paragraph. It is important, therefore, to revise your paragraph for **unity**—that is, to drop any ideas or sentences that do not relate to the topic sentence.

This paragraph lacks unity:

(1) Franklin Mars, a Minnesota candy maker, created many popular candy snacks. (2) Milky Way, his first bar, was an instant hit. (3) Snickers, which he introduced in 1930, also sold very well. (4) Milton Hershey developed the very first candy bar in 1894. (5) M&Ms were a later Mars creation, supposedly designed so that soldiers could enjoy a sugar boost without getting sticky trigger fingers.

- What is the topic sentence in this paragraph? _____

- Which sentence does *not* relate to the topic sentence? _____

- Sentence (4) has nothing to do with the main idea, that *Franklin Mars created many popular candy snacks.* Therefore, sentence (4) should be dropped.

PRACTICE 12

Check the following paragraphs for unity. If a paragraph is unified, write U in the blank. If it is not, write the number of the sentence that does not belong in the paragraph.

1. ___   (1) Families who nourish their children with words as well as food at dinnertime produce better future readers. (2) Researchers at Harvard University studied the dinner conversations of sixty-eight families. (3) What they found was that parents who use a few new words in conversation with their three- and four-year-olds each night quickly build the children's vocabularies and their later reading skills. (4) The researchers point out that children can learn from eight to twenty-eight new words a day, so they need to be "fed" new words. (5) Excellent "big words" for preschoolers include *parachute, emerald, instrument,* and *education,* the researchers say.

2. ___   (1) Personalized license plates have become very popular. (2) These "vanity plates" allow car owners to express their sense of humor, marital status, pet peeves, or ethnic pride. (3) Of course, every car must display a plate on the rear bumper or in the back window. (4) Drivers have created messages such as ROCK ON, NT GUILTY, and (on a tow truck) ITZ GONE. (5) In some states, as many as one in seven autos has a personalized plate. (6) Recently, *Parade* magazine chose the nation's top ten vanity plates, including XQQSME on a Massachusetts plate, ULIV1S on an Arkansas plate, and on an SUV in Missouri, a message to be read in the rear-view mirror— TI-3VOM.

3. ___   (1) Swimming is excellent exercise. (2) Swimming vigorously for just twelve minutes provides aerobic benefits to the heart. (3) Unlike jogging and many other aerobic sports, however, swimming does not jolt the bones and muscles with sudden pressure. (4) Furthermore, the motions of swimming, such as reaching out in the crawl, stretch the muscles in a healthy, natural way. (5) Some swimmers wear goggles to keep chlorine or salt out of their eyes whereas others do not.

Peer Feedback for Revising

You may wish to show your first draft or read it aloud to a respected friend or classmate. Ask this person to give an honest reader response, not to rewrite your work. To elicit useful responses, ask specific questions of your own, or use the Peer Feedback Sheet on the following page. You may want to photocopy the sheet rather than write on it so that you can reuse it.

PRACTICE 13

Now read the first draft of your paragraph with a critical eye. Revise and rewrite it, checking especially for a clear topic sentence, strong support, and unity.

PRACTICE 14

Exchange *revised* paragraphs with a classmate. Ask specific questions or use the Peer Feedback Sheet.

When you *give* feedback, try to be as honest and specific as possible; saying a paper is "good," "nice," or "bad" doesn't really help the writer. When you *receive* feedback, think over your classmate's responses. Do they ring true?

Now revise a second time, with the aim of writing a fine paragraph.

PEER FEEDBACK SHEET

To _____   From _____   Date _____

1. What I like about this piece of writing is _____

    _____

    _____

2. Your main point seems to be _____

    _____

    _____

3. These particular words or lines struck me as powerful.

    Words or lines: I like them because

    _____   _____

    _____   _____

    _____   _____

    _____   _____

4. Some things aren't clear to me. These lines or parts could be improved (meaning not clear; supporting points missing; order mixed up; writing not lively):

    Lines or parts: Need improving because

    _____   _____

    _____   _____

    _____   _____

    _____   _____

5. The one change you could make that would most improve this piece of writing is

    _____

    _____

    _____

PART G   Writing the Final Draft

When you are satisfied with your revisions, recopy your paper. Be sure to include all your corrections, and write neatly and legibly—a carelessly scribbled paper seems to say that you don't care about your work.

The first draft of the paragraph about Beverly, with the writer's changes, and the revised final draft follow. Compare them.

First Draft with Revisions

(1) Beverly inspires admiration because she is so determined. (2) Although she
doing what?   *Is*
could not afford to attend college right after high school, she worked to save
How long?! Better support needed—show her hard work!
money. (3) It took a long time, but she got her degree. (4) She is now a good driver.

(5) At first, she was very nervous about getting behind the wheel and even failed
The third time,
the road test twice, but she didn't quit. (6) She passed eventually. (7) Her husband,
Drop Virgil—he doesn't belong   ^
Virgil, loves to drive; he races cars on the weekend. (8) Anyway, Beverly has never
how long??
gotten a ticket. (9) A year ago, Beverly quit smoking. (10) For a while, she had a
too general—add details here
rough time, but she hasn't touched a cigarette. (11) Now she says that the urge to
better conclusion needed
smoke has faded away. (12) She doesn't let difficulties defeat her.

Guide the reader better from point to point! Choppy—

Final Draft

(1) Beverly inspires admiration because she is so determined. (2) Although she could not afford to attend college right after high school, she worked as a cashier to save money for tuition. (3) It took her five years working days and going to school nights, but she recently received a BS in accounting. (4) Thanks to this same determination, Beverly is now a good driver. (5) At first, she was very nervous about getting behind the wheel and even failed the road test twice, but she didn't give up. (6) The third time, she passed, and she has never gotten a ticket. (7) A year ago, Beverly quit smoking. (8) For a month or more, she chewed her nails and endless packs of gum, but she hasn't touched a cigarette. (9) Now she says that the urge to smoke has faded away. (10) When Beverly sets a goal for herself, she doesn't let difficulties defeat her.

● This paragraph provides good support for the topic sentence. The writer has made sentences (2) and (3) more specific by adding *as a cashier, for tuition, five years working days and going to school nights,* and *recently received a BS in accounting.*

● What other revisions did the writer make? How do these revisions improve the paragraph? _____

_____

_____

_____

● *Transitional expressions* are words and phrases that guide the reader smoothly from point to point. In sentence (5) of the final draft, *at first* is a transitional expression showing time. What other transitional expressions of time are used?

_____

_____

● What phrase provides a transition from sentence (3) to (4)?

_____

● Note that the last sentence now provides a brief *conclusion* so that the paragraph *feels* finished.

Proofreading

Finally, carefully **proofread** your paper for grammatical and spelling errors, consulting your dictionary and this book as necessary. Errors in your writing will lower your grades in almost all college courses. Writing errors may also affect your job opportunities. Units 2 through 8 of this textbook will help you improve your grammar, punctuation, and spelling skills.

Some students find it useful to point to each word and say it softly. This method helps them catch errors as well as any words they may have left out as they wrote, especially little words like *and, at, of,* and *on*.

In which of these sentences have words been omitted?

> (1) Despite its faulty landing gear, the 777 managed land safely.
>
> (2) Plans for the new gym were on display the library.
>
> (3) Mr. Sampson winked at his reflection in the bathroom mirror.

● Words are missing in sentences (1) and (2).
● Sentence (1) requires *to* before *land*.
● What word is omitted in sentence (2)? _____
● Where should this word be placed? _____

PRACTICE 15

Proofread these sentences for omitted words. Add the necessary words above the lines. Some sentences may already be correct.

EXAMPLE: People were not always able ^to^ tell time accurately.

1. People used to guess the time day by watching the sun move across the sky.

2. Sunrise and sunset were easy recognize.

3. Recognizing noon easy, too.

4. However, telling time by the position of sun was very difficult at other times.

5. People noticed that shadows lengthened during the day.

6. They found it easier to tell time by looking at the shadows than by looking the sun.

7. People stuck poles into the ground to time by the length of the shadows.

8. Those the first shadow clocks, or sundials.

9. In 300 BC, Chaldean astronomer invented a more accurate, bowl-shaped sundial.

10. Today, most sundials decorative, but they can still be used to tell time.

PRACTICE 16

Proofread the final draft of your paragraph, checking for grammar or spelling errors and omitted words.

PRACTICE 17

Writing and Revising Paragraphs

The assignments that follow will give you practice in writing and revising basic paragraphs. In each assignment, aim for (1) a clear topic sentence and (2) sentences that fully support and explain the topic sentence. As you write, refer to the checklist in the Chapter Highlights on page 34.

Paragraph 1: Describe a public place. Reread paragraph B on page 27. Then choose a place in your neighborhood that is "alive with activity"—a park, street, restaurant, or club. In your topic sentence, name the place and say when it is most active; for example, "Every Saturday night, the Blue Dog Café is alive with activity." Begin by freewriting or by jotting down as many details about the scene as possible. Then describe the scene. Arrange your observations in a logical order. Revise for support, making sure that your details are so lively and interesting that your readers will see the place as clearly as you do.

Paragraph 2: Describe a portrait. Study this photograph of actor Johnny Depp. Notice his pose and expression, eyes, glasses, mouth, beard, and his hand on the

Actor Johnny Depp.

© Fred Prouser/Reuters/CORBIS.

brim of his hat. Now write a paragraph in which you describe this portrait for someone who has not seen it. In your topic sentence, state one overall impression or feeling that this portrait conveys. Support this impression with specific details. If you prefer, use Google Images or another search engine, find an expressive portrait, and describe that instead. Conclude your paragraph; don't just stop.

Paragraph 3: Evaluate your strengths as a writer. In writing as in life, it helps to know your true strengths as well as your weaknesses. You may not realize it, but you probably already possess several skills and personality traits that can nourish good writing. These include being observant and paying attention to details, imagining, feeling deep emotions, wanting to learn the truth, knowing how and where to find the answers to questions, thinking creatively, being well organized, and being persistent. Which of these abilities do you already possess? Do you possess other skills or traits that might help your writing? Describe *three* of your strengths as a writer. As you revise, make sure your ideas follow a logical order. Proofread carefully.

Paragraph 4: Choose your time of day. Many people have a favorite time of day—the freshness of early morning, 5 p.m. when work ends, late at night when the children are asleep. In your topic sentence, name your favorite time of day. Then develop the paragraph by explaining why you look forward to this time and exactly how you spend it. Check your work for any omitted words.

CHAPTER HIGHLIGHTS

Checklist for Writing an Effective Paragraph

- **Narrow the topic:** Cut the topic down to one aspect that interests you and will probably interest your readers.

- **Write the topic sentence. (You may wish to brainstorm or freewrite first.)**

- **Brainstorm, freewrite, or cluster ideas for the body:** Write down anything and everything that might relate to your topic.

- **Select and drop ideas:** Select those ideas that relate to your topic, and drop those that do not.

- **Group together ideas that have something in common; then arrange the ideas in a plan.**

- **Write your first draft.**

- **Read what you have written, making any necessary corrections and additions. Revise for support and unity.**

- **Write the final draft of your paragraph neatly and legibly, making sure to indent the first word.**

- **Proofread for grammar, punctuation, spelling, and omitted words. Make neat corrections in ink.**

EXPLORING ONLINE

<http://grammar.ccc.commnet.edu/grammar/paragraphs.htm> Review paragraph unity and topic sentences.

<http://college.cengage.com/devenglish> For more exercises, quizzes, and live links to all websites in this chapter, visit this link, click Developmental Writing, and find the home page for *Grassroots*, 9/e. Bookmark the *Grassroots* student website for future visits as you work through this book.

CHAPTER 4

Improving Your Paragraphs

PART A More Work on Support: Examples

PART B More Work on Arranging Ideas: Coherence

PART C More Work on Revising: Exact and Concise Language

PART D Turning Assignments into Paragraphs

In Chapter 3, you practiced the steps of the paragraph-writing process. This chapter builds on that work. It explains several skills that can greatly improve your writing: using examples; achieving coherence; choosing exact, concise language; and turning assignments into paragraphs.

PART A   More Work on Support: Examples

One effective way to make your writing specific is by using **examples.** Someone might write, "Divers in Monterey Bay can observe many beautiful fish. For instance, tiger-striped treefish are common." The first sentence makes a general statement about the beautiful fish in Monterey Bay. The second sentence gives a specific example of such fish: *tiger-striped treefish.*

Use one, two, or three well-chosen examples to develop a paragraph.

> Many of the computer industry's best innovators were young when they first achieved success. For example, David Filo and Jerry Yang were graduate students at Stanford when they realized that their hobby of listing the best pages on the World Wide Web might become a business. They created Yahoo!, a Web index now logging 500 million visits a month. Two more youthful examples are Google founders Larry Page and Sergey Brin. They were students in their twenties when they got the idea for one of the Internet's most popular search engines. In 2004, just six years after launching their new company, Page and Brin became multibillionaires by selling Google shares to the public. A third pair of young computer geniuses created the video-sharing website YouTube .com. Chad Hurley and Steven Chen worked in Hurley's garage to solve a personal problem: they wanted to figure out an easier way to share video clips with each other via the Internet. The popularity of their site exploded, and just one year later, Hurley and Chen sold YouTube to Google for $1.65 million.

● The writer begins this paragraph with a topic sentence about the youth of many computer innovators.

● What three examples does the writer provide as support?

Example 1: _____

Example 2: _____

Example 3: _____

● Note that the topic sentence and the examples make a rough plan for the paragraph.

The simplest way to tell a reader that an example will follow is to say so, using a transitional expression: *For example, David Filo . . .*

> ### Transitional Expressions to Introduce Examples
>
> | for example | for instance |
> |---|---|
> | to illustrate | another example |

PRACTICE 1

Each example in a paragraph must clearly relate to and explain the topic sentence. Each of the following topic sentences is followed by several examples. Circle the letter of any example that does *not* clearly illustrate the topic sentence. Be prepared to explain your choices.

EXAMPLE: Some animals and insects camouflage themselves in interesting ways.

    a. Snowshoe rabbits turn from brown to white in winter, thus blending into the snow.

    b. The cheetah's spotted coat makes it hard to see in the dry African bush.

    (c.) The bull alligator smashes its tail against the water and roars during mating season.

    d. The walking stick is brown and irregular, much like the twigs among which this insect hides.

1. State troopers report that many people do dangerous and outrageous things while driving.

    a. One woman applied mascara, pressing her face close to the rear-view mirror as she drove 65 miles an hour.

    b. A woman shopped in a Detroit supermarket while wearing a Queen Elizabeth mask and a crown.

    c. Another man glanced up and down as he changed lanes, writing in a spiral notebook propped against the steering wheel.

    d. A man ate scrambled eggs with a fork—from a plate on his dashboard.

2. Several players from Japanese baseball leagues have achieved success in the United States's major leagues.

    a. Since 1995, Hideo Nomo has pitched for the Los Angeles Dodgers, Boston Red Sox, and Baltimore Orioles.

    b. Left-fielder Hideki Matsui joined the New York Yankees in 2003, becoming a vital team member and the highest-paid Japanese player in baseball.

    c. After the Seattle Mariners signed outfielder Ichiro Suzuki of Japan's Pacific League in 2001, the all-star shattered a number of major league records.

    d. Baseball has been played and loved for many years in Japan.

3. Mrs. Makarem is well loved in this community for her generous heart.
   a. Her door is always open to neighborhood children, who stop by for lemonade or advice.
   b. When the Padilla family had a fire, Mrs. Makarem collected clothes and blankets for them.
   c. "Hello, dear," she says with a smile to everyone she passes on the street.
   d. Born in Caracas, Venezuela, she has lived on Bay Road for thirty-two years.

4. A number of unusual, specialized scholarships are offered by colleges across the United States.
   a. The Icy Frost Bridge Scholarship at Indiana's DePauw University is awarded to female music students who sing or play the national anthem "with sincerity."
   b. Brighton College, a secondary school for boys and girls in England, pays the full tuition of a student with the last name of *Peyton*.
   c. Left-handed, financially needy students can get special scholarships at Juniata College in Pennsylvania.
   d. Wisconsin's Ripon College offers $1,500 to students with a 3.0 average who once were Badger Girls or Badger Boys.

5. English borrows words from many other languages.
   a. The Spanish *la reata* gives us *lariat*, "a rope."
   b. The expression *gung ho* comes from the Chinese *keng ho*, which literally means "more fire."
   c. *Diss* is a term meaning "disrespect."
   d. *Kimono* is the Japanese word for "thing for wearing."

PRACTICE 2

The secret of good illustration lies in well-chosen and well-written examples. Think of one example that illustrates each of the following general statements. Write out the example in sentence form—one to three sentences—as clearly and exactly as possible.

1. Many films today have amazing special effects.

   Example: _____

   _____

2. Television programs have reached new lows in the past few years.

   Example: _____

   _____

3. Dan is always buying strange gadgets.

   Example: _____

   _____

4. Even when she is very busy, Grace finds ways to exercise.

   Example: _____

   _____

5. Children often say surprising things.

   Example: _____

   _____

PRACTICE 3

Writing Assignment

Write a paragraph developed by examples. Make sure your topic sentence can be supported by examples. Prewrite and pick the best one to three examples to explain your topic sentence. Here are some ideas for topics:

offensive "reality" television shows   ads that appeal to _____

great places to study on campus   disastrous wedding stories

PART B   More Work on Arranging Ideas: Coherence

Every paragraph should have **coherence**. A paragraph *coheres*—holds together—when its ideas are arranged in a clear and logical order.

Sometimes the order of ideas flows logically from your topic. However, three basic ways to organize ideas are **time order, space order,** and **order of importance.**

Time Order

Time order means arranging ideas chronologically, from present to past or from past to present. Careful use of time order helps avoid such confusing writing as *Oops, I forgot to mention before that . . .*

Most instructions, histories, processes, and stories follow the logical order of time.

> The talent and drive of surfer Lisa Andersen quickly propelled her to the top of her sport. In 1983, thirteen-year-old Andersen paddled a friend's surfboard into the ocean off the coast of Florida's Ormond Beach, caught a breaking wave, and easily rode it to shore. Thrilled to discover this natural talent, she realized that she might have the potential to become a serious female surfer. Soon, in hopes of gaining a competitive edge, she began practicing with only her most skilled male counterparts. In 1987, this strategy paid off when she won the U.S. amateur women's surfing contest. Later that same year, Lisa turned professional; by 1992, she was winning major competitions and training for the world championship. Almost immediately, however, news that she was pregnant put any plans to win the 1993 championship on hold. Andersen says that although it cost her one year's title, the birth of her daughter Erica motivated her to go all the way to the top. In 1994, Lisa was crowned world surfing champion, a title she won again in 1995, 1996, and 1997. Today, the four-time winner is credited with inspiring a generation of young women to enter the once male-dominated world of surfing.

● The paragraph moves in time from Lisa Andersen's first surfing experience as a teenager to her world championship victories.

● Note how some transitional expressions—*in 1983, soon, later that same year, almost immediately,* and *today*—show time and connect the events in the paragraph.

> ## Transitional Expressions to Show Time
>
> first, second, third
>
> then, next, finally
>
> before, during, after
>
> soon, the following month, the next year

PRACTICE 4

Arrange each set of sentences in time order, numbering them 1, 2, 3, and so on. Be prepared to explain your choices.

1. In eighty years, the T-shirt rose from simple underwear to fashion statement.

   ___ During World War II, women factory workers started wearing T-shirts on the job.

   ___ Hippies in the 1960s tie-dyed their T-shirts and wore them printed with messages.

   ___ Now, five billion T-shirts are sold worldwide each year.

   ___ The first American T-shirts were cotton underwear, worn home by soldiers returning from France after World War I.

2. The short life of Sadako Sasaki has inspired millions to value peace.

   ___ Sadako was just two years old in 1945 when the atom bomb destroyed her city, Hiroshima.

   ___ From her sickbed, Sadako set out to make 1,000 paper cranes, birds that, in Japan, symbolize long life and hope.

   ___ Although she died before making 1,000, classmates finished her project and published a book of her letters.

   ___ At age eleven, already a talented runner, she was crushed to learn that she had leukemia, caused by radiation from the bomb.

   ___ Now, every year, the Folded Crane Club places 1,000 cranes at the foot of a statue of Sadako, honoring her wish that all children might enjoy peace and a long life.

3. Scientists who study the body's daily rhythms can suggest the ideal time of day for different activities.

   ___ Taking vitamins with breakfast helps the body absorb them.

   ___ Allergy medication should be taken just before bedtime to combat early-morning hay fever—usually the worst of the day.

   ___ The best time to work out is 3 p.m. to 5 p.m., when strength, flexibility, and body temperature are greatest.

   ___ Ideal naptime is 1 p.m. to 3 p.m., when body temperature falls, making sleep easier.

PRACTICE 5

Writing Assignment

Have you ever been through something that lasted only a few moments but was unforgettable—for example, a sports victory, an accident, or a kiss? Write a paragraph telling about such an event. As you prewrite, pick the highlights of the experience and arrange them in time order. As you write, try to capture the drama of what happened. Use transitional expressions of time to make the story flow smoothly.

Space Order

Space order means describing a person, a place, or a thing from top to bottom, from left to right, from foreground to background, and so on.

Space order is most often used in descriptions because it moves from detail to detail, like a camera's eye.

> When the city presses in on me, I return in my mind to my hometown in St. Mary, Jamaica. I am alone, high in the mango tree on our property on the hilltop. The wind is blowing hard as usual, making a scared noise as it passes through the lush vegetation. I look down at the coconut growth with its green flooring of banana plants. Beyond that is a wide valley and then the round hills. Farther out lies the sea, and I count the ships as they pass to and from the harbor while I relax on my special branch and eat mangoes.
>
> *Daniel Dawes, student*

● The writer describes this scene from his vantage point high in a tree. His description follows space order, moving from the plants below him, farther out to the valley and the hills, and then even farther, to the sea.

● Notice how *transitional expressions* indicating space—*beyond that, then,* and *farther out*—help the reader follow and "see" the details.

Transitional Expressions to Show Space Order

to the left, in the center, to the right

behind, beside, in front of

next, beyond that, farther out

PRACTICE 6

Arrange each set of details according to space order, numbering them 1, 2, 3, and so on. Be prepared to explain your choices.

1. After the party, the living room was a mess.

   _____ greasy pizza boxes on the coffee table

   _____ empty soda cans on the floor

   _____ deflated balloons on the ceiling light

   _____ pictures hanging at odd angles on the wall

2. The nurse quietly strode into my aunt's hospital room.

_____ black and silver stethoscope draped around his neck

_____ crisp, white cotton pants and short-sleeved tunic

_____ reassuring smile

_____ blue paper covers on his shoes

_____ kind, dark brown eyes

3. The taxicab crawled through rush-hour traffic in the rain-drenched city.

_____ fare meter on the dashboard ticking relentlessly

_____ headlights barely piercing the stormy, gray dusk

_____ windshield wipers losing their battle with the latest cloudburst

_____ backseat passengers frantically checking their watches

_____ driver wishing hopelessly that he could be home watching the news

PRACTICE 7

Writing Assignment

Study this portrait of Dr. Mae Jemison, the first woman of color ever to soar into space. Notice her facial expression, posture, clothing, equipment, and other details. Then describe the photograph to someone who has never seen it. In your topic sentence, state one feeling, impression, or message this picture conveys and then choose details that support this idea. Arrange these details in space order—from left to right, top to bottom, and so on. As you revise, make sure that your sentences flow clearly and smoothly.

To learn more about the life of this remarkable astronaut, search Google or use your favorite search engine.

Astronaut Mae Jemison.

JSC Digital Image Collection/NASA.

Gehry's Disney Concert Hall
in Los Angeles.

Richard Cummins/CORBIS.

Order of Importance

Order of importance means arranging your ideas from most to least important—or vice versa.

> Frank Gehry is one of the greatest living architects. There are at least three reasons for his worldwide influence. Most important, Gehry has created new shapes for buildings, literally moving outside the boxes in which we often live and work. He has found ways to build walls that look like mountains, sails, and wings. In addition, Gehry uses new materials—or old materials in new ways. Going beyond plaster and wood, Gehry's buildings have rounded metal walls, curves made of glass, and stone in strange places. Third, because of its striking looks, a Gehry building can bring tourist dollars and international attention to a town or city. This happened when Gehry designed the now-famous Guggenheim Museum building in the little town of Bilbao, Spain. And like the latest blockbuster movie, the Disney Concert Hall in Los Angeles recently opened to rave reviews.

● The three reasons in this paragraph are discussed from the most important reason to the least important.

● Note that the words *most important, in addition,* and *third* help the reader move from one reason to another.

Sometimes you may wish to begin with the least important idea and build toward a climax at the end of the paragraph. Paragraphs arranged from the least important idea to the most important idea can have dramatic power.

> Although my fourteen-year-old daughter learned a great deal from living with a Pennsylvania Amish family last summer, adjusting to their strict lifestyle was difficult for her. Kay admitted that the fresh food served on the farm was great, but she missed her diet colas. More difficult was the fact that

she had to wear long dresses—no more jeans and baby tees. Still worse in her view were the hours. A suburban girl and self-confessed night person, my daughter had to get up at 5 a.m. to milk cows! By far the most difficult adjustment concerned boys. If an Amish woman is not married, she cannot spend time with males, and this rule now applied to Kay. Yes, she suffered and complained, but by summer's end, she was a different girl—more open-minded and proud of the fact that all these deprivations put her more in touch with herself.

Lucy Auletta, student

● The adjustment difficulties this writer's daughter had are arranged from least

to most important. How many difficulties are discussed? _____

● Note how the words *more difficult, still worse,* and *by far the most difficult adjust-ment* help the reader move from one idea to the next.

Transitional Expressions to Show Importance

first, next, finally

more, most

less, least

PRACTICE 8

Arrange the ideas that develop each topic sentence in order of importance, numbering them 1, 2, and 3. Begin with the most important idea, or reverse the order if you think that a paragraph would be more effective if it began with the least important idea. Be prepared to explain your choices. Then, on a separate sheet of paper, write the ideas in a paragraph.

1. For three reasons, joining a serious study group is an excellent idea.

   _____ A study group exposes you to new points of view and effective study habits.

   _____ Joining a study group is a good way to make new friends.

   _____ Statistics show that students who regularly attend a study group get better grades and are less likely to drop out of college.

2. A hidden epidemic of steroid use among young women—for weight control or enhanced athletic performance—is causing serious consequences.

   _____ Steroid use, which has been linked to heart attacks, strokes, and some cancers, can be fatal.

   _____ Many female steroid users not only lose hair on their heads but also grow extra body hair.

   _____ Steroids prematurely stop bones from lengthening, so developing girls who take the drug may permanently stunt their growth.

3. At 2 a.m., arriving on the scene of a rollover accident with injuries, the fire rescue team had to act quickly.

_____ One team member lit flares and placed them on the road to warn other drivers to slow down.

_____ On the ambulance radio, a team member called for "sanders" to drop sand on local roads, which were becoming slippery in the falling snow.

_____ A lone woman, conscious with head injuries, was carefully moved from the driver's seat into the ambulance.

_____ Someone held the woman's dog, who was shivering but seemed unhurt.

PRACTICE 9

Writing Assignment

Write a paragraph to persuade a certain group of people to do something they don't do now. For example, you could write to convince couch potatoes to begin exercising, senior citizens to take a free class at your college, or nonvoters to register and cast a ballot. Discuss the three most important reasons why your readers should follow your advice, and arrange these reasons in order of importance—least to most important or most to least important, whichever you think would make a better paragraph. Don't forget to use transitional expressions. If you wish, use humor to win over your audience.

PART C More Work on Revising: Exact and Concise Language

Good writers do not settle for the first words that spill onto their paper or computer screen. Instead, they revise what they have written, replacing vague words with exact language and repetitious words with concise language.

Exact Language

As a rule, the more specific, detailed, and exact the language is, the better the writing. Which sentence in each of the following pairs contains the more vivid and exact language?

(1) The office was noisy.
(2) In the office, phones jangled, faxes whined, and copy machines hummed.

(3) What my tutor said made me feel good.
(4) When my tutor whispered, "Fine job," I felt like singing.

● Sentence (2) is more exact than sentence (1) because _phones jangled, faxes whined, and copy machines hummed_ provide more vivid information than the general word _noisy_.

● What exact words does sentence (4) use to replace the general words _said_ and

made me feel good? _____

You do not need a large vocabulary to write exactly and well, but you do need to work at finding the right words to fit each sentence.

PRACTICE 10

These sentences contain vague language. Revise each one, using vivid and exact language wherever possible.

EXAMPLE: A man went through the crowd.

Revise: _A man in a blue leather jacket pushed through the crowd._

_____

1. An automobile went down the street.

   Revise: _____

   _____

2. This apartment has problems.

   Revise: _____

   _____

3. When Allison comes home, her pet greets her.

   Revise: _____

   _____

4. This magazine is interesting.

   Revise: _____

   _____

5. The expression on his face made me feel comfortable.

   Revise: _____

   _____

6. My job is fun.

   Revise: _____

   _____

7. There was a big storm here last week.

   Revise: _____

   _____

8. The emergency room has a lot of people in it.

   Revise: _____

   _____

Concise Language

Concise writing never uses five or six words when two or three will do. It avoids repetitious and unnecessary words that add nothing to the meaning of a sentence. As you revise your writing, cross out unnecessary words and phrases.

Which sentence in each of the following pairs is more concise?

> (1) Because of the fact that Larissa owns an antiques shop, she is always poking around in dusty attics.
> (2) Because Larissa owns an antiques shop, she is always poking around in dusty attics.
>
> (3) Mr. Tibbs entered a large, dark blue room.
> (4) Mr. Tibbs entered a room that was large in size and dark blue in color.

● Sentences (2) and (3) are concise; sentences (1) and (4) are wordy.

● In sentence (1), *because of the fact that* is a wordy way of saying *because*.

● In sentence (4), *in size* and *in color* just repeat which ideas?

_____

Of course, conciseness does not mean writing short, choppy sentences. It does mean dropping unnecessary words and phrases.

PRACTICE 11

The following sentences are wordy. In a group with two or three others, make each sentence more concise by deleting unnecessary words, rewording slightly as necessary. Write your revised sentences on the lines provided.

EXAMPLE: Venice, an Italian city in Italy, is trying to reduce its huge number of visitors who go to see it.

Revise: Venice, a city in Italy, is trying to reduce its huge number of visitors.

_____

1. For a great many hundreds of years, this beautiful city of such loveliness has been a major tourist attraction.

   Revise: _____

   _____

2. The reasons why people go to Venice are because they want to see its priceless art and palaces, famous bridges, and canals that serve as streets.

   Revise: _____

   _____

3. At this time now, however, Venice is being destroyed by floods, by polluted air and water that are dirty, and by tourists who visit it.

   Revise: _____

   _____

4. Twelve million annual visitors invade Venice every year, and most of them are day-trippers who come only for the day and then go home.

   Revise: _____

   _____

5. The day-trippers, who often bring their own drinks and sandwiches with them to eat, spend little money in town, thus contributing very little to the city's economy of money.

   Revise: _____

   _____

6. However, they contribute enormously and in large amounts to the city of Venice's congestion, transportation, and sanitation nightmares.

   Revise: _____

   _____

7. Recently, the city tried to scare off day-trippers with a negative publicity campaign that gave bad publicity about the city.

   Revise: _____

   _____

8. Posters showed tourists being devoured and eaten by Venice's well-known and famous pigeons.

   Revise: _____

   _____

9. An immense giant toilet plunger became the symbol of a city that some say is the city that is the most romantic city in the world.

   Revise: _____

   _____

10. Unfortunately, the bad publicity did not work or stop tourists from pouring into Venice, so city officials are trying a new plan—asking visitors to make reservations to visit the city on a particular day.

    Revise: _____

    _____

PRACTICE 12

Review

Following are statements from real accident reports collected by an insurance company. As you will see, these writers need help with more than their fenders!

In a group with four or five classmates, read each statement and try to understand what each writer *meant* to say. Then revise each statement so that it says exactly and concisely what the writer intended.

1. "The guy was all over the place. I had to swerve a number of times before I hit him."

2. "The telephone pole was approaching fast. I was attempting to swerve out of its path when it struck my front end."

3. "Coming home, I drove into the wrong house and collided with a tree I don't have."

4. "I was on my way to the doctor's with rear-end trouble when my universal joint gave way, causing me to have an accident."

5. "I was driving my car out of the driveway in the usual manner when it was struck by the other car in the same place it had been struck several times before."

PRACTICE 13

Review

Choose a paragraph or paper you wrote recently. Read it with a fresh eye, checking for exact and concise language. Then rewrite it, eliminating all vague or wordy language.

PART D   Turning Assignments into Paragraphs

In Chapter 3, Part B, you learned how to narrow a broad topic and write a specific topic sentence. Sometimes, however, your assignment may take the form of a specific question, and your job may be to answer the question in one paragraph.

For example, this question asks you to take a stand for or against a particular issue.

Are professional athletes overpaid?

You can often turn this kind of question into a topic sentence:

(1) Professional athletes are overpaid.

(2) Professional athletes are not overpaid.

(3) Professional athletes are sometimes overpaid.

● These three topic sentences take different points of view.

● The words *are*, *are not*, and *sometimes* make each writer's opinion clear.

Sometimes you will be asked to agree or disagree with a statement:

(4) Salary is the most important factor in job satisfaction. Agree or disagree.

● This is really a question in disguise: *Is salary the most important factor in job satisfaction?*

In the topic sentence, make your opinion clear and repeat key words.

(5) Salary is the most important factor in job satisfaction.

(6) Salary is not the most important factor in job satisfaction.

(7) Salary is only one among several important factors in job satisfaction.

● The words *is*, *is not*, and *is only one among several* make each writer's opinion clear.

● Note how the topic sentences repeat the key words from the statement—*salary*, *important factor*, *job satisfaction*.

Once you have written the topic sentence, follow the steps described in Chapter 2—freewriting, brainstorming, or clustering; selecting; grouping—and then write your paragraph. Be sure that all ideas in the paragraph support the opinion you have stated in the topic sentence.

PRACTICE 14

Here are four exam questions. Write one topic sentence to answer each of them. REMEMBER: Make your opinion clear in the topic sentence and repeat key words from the question.

1. Should computer education be required in every public high school?

   Topic sentence: _____

   _____

2. Would you advise your best friend to buy a new car or a used car?

   Topic sentence: _____

   _____

3. Is there too much bad news on television news programs?

   Topic sentence: _____

   _____

4. How have your interests changed in the past five years?

   Topic sentence: _____

   _____

PRACTICE 15

Imagine that your instructor has just written the exam questions from Practice 14 on the board. Choose the question that most interests you and write a paragraph answering that question. Prewrite, select, and arrange ideas before you compose your paragraph. Then read your work, making neat corrections in ink.

PRACTICE 16

Here are four statements. Agree or disagree, and write a topic sentence for each.

1. All higher education should be free. Agree or disagree.

   Topic sentence: _____

   _____

2. Expecting one's spouse to be perfect is the most important reason for the high divorce rate in the United States. Agree or disagree.

   Topic sentence: _____

   _____

3. Parents should give children money when they need it rather than give them an allowance. Agree or disagree.

   Topic sentence: _____

   _____

4. Silence is golden. Agree or disagree.

   Topic sentence: _____

   _____

PRACTICE 17

Choose the statement in Practice 16 that most interests you. Then write a paragraph in which you agree or disagree.

CHAPTER HIGHLIGHTS

To improve your writing, try these techniques:

- Use well-chosen examples to develop a paragraph.
- Organize your ideas by time order.
- Organize your ideas by space order.
- Organize your ideas by order of importance, either from the most important to the least or from the least important to the most.
- Use language that is exact and concise.
- Turn assignment questions into topic sentences.

EXPLORING ONLINE

<http://writesite.cuny.edu/projects/keywords/example/hand2.html> Online process: Develop your idea with examples.

<http://owl.english.purdue.edu/handouts/general/gl_cohere.html> Review ways to add coherence to your writing.

<http://college.cengage.com/devenglish> For more exercises, quizzes, and live links to all websites in this chapter, visit this link, click Developmental Writing, and find the home page for *Grassroots*, 9/e. Bookmark the *Grassroots* student website for future visits as you work through this book.

CHAPTER 5
Moving from Paragraph to Essay

PART A Defining the Essay and the Thesis Statement

PART B The Process of Writing an Essay

So far, you have written single paragraphs, but to succeed in college and at work, you will need to handle longer writing assignments as well. This chapter will help you apply your paragraph-writing skills to planning and writing short essays.

PART A Defining the Essay and the Thesis Statement

An **essay** is a group of paragraphs about one subject. In many ways, an essay is like a paragraph in longer, fuller form. Both have an introduction, a body, and a conclusion. Both explain one main idea with details, facts, and examples.

An essay is not just a padded paragraph, however. An essay is longer because it contains more ideas.

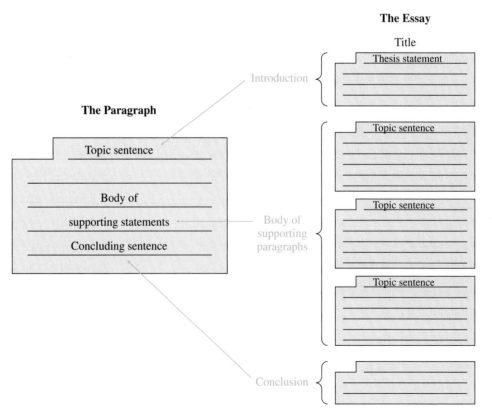

The paragraphs in an essay are part of a larger whole, so each one has a special purpose.

- The **introductory paragraph** opens the essay and tries to catch the reader's interest. It usually contains a **thesis statement,** one sentence that states the main idea of the entire essay.

- The **body** of an essay contains one, two, three, or more paragraphs, each one making a different point about the main idea.

- The **conclusion** brings the essay to a close. It might be a sentence or a paragraph long.

Here is a student essay:

Tae Kwon Do

WINETH WILLIAMS

(1) Tae kwon do is a Korean martial art. It is a way of fighting and self-defense based on an understanding of both body and mind. As a college student, I discovered tae kwon do. Even though I was physically fit and planned to become a police officer, I thought that women needed special skills to protect themselves. Tae kwon do teaches these skills and much more. The person who practices tae kwon do gains discipline, maturity, and a changed self-concept.

(2) First, the discipline of tae kwon do helps the student outfight and outsmart her opponent. For a while, I didn't appreciate the discipline. We had to move in certain ways, and we had to yell. Yelling made me laugh. Our teacher told us to shout with great force, "Keeah!" Yelling keeps the mind from focusing on being tired and helps the fighter call out the life force, or "chi," from inside her. Once we started sparring, I also had to get past not wanting to hurt anyone. Later I understood that if I punched or kicked my opponent, it meant that he or she should have been blocking and was not using good skills.

(3) Second, with practice, tae kwon do increases maturity. I have a hot temper. Before tae kwon do, I would walk dark streets and take chances, almost daring trouble. I reacted to every look or challenge. Practicing this martial art, I started to see the world more realistically. I developed more respect for the true danger in the streets. I spoke and behaved in ways to avoid trouble. My reactions became less emotional and more rational.

(4) Finally, after a year or so, tae kwon do can change the student's self-concept. This happened to me. On one hand, I became confident that I had the skills to take care of business if necessary. On the other hand, the better I got, the more I acted like a pussycat instead of a lion. That may sound strange, but inside myself, I knew that I had nothing to prove to anybody.

(5) As I discovered firsthand, the practice of tae kwon do can bring personal benefits that go far beyond self-defense.

- The last sentence in the introduction (underlined) is the *thesis statement*. The thesis statement must be general enough to include the topic sentence of every paragraph in the body of the essay.

- Underline the topic sentences of paragraphs (2), (3), and (4). Note that the thesis statement and the topic sentences make a rough plan of the entire essay.

- **Transitional expressions** are words and phrases that guide the reader from point to point and from paragraph to paragraph. What transition does this student use between paragraphs (1) and (2)? Between (2) and (3)? Between (3) and (4)?

_____

- The last paragraph provides a brief *conclusion.**

PRACTICE 1

To help you understand the structure of an essay, complete this plan for "Tae Kwon Do." Under each topic sentence, jot down the writer's two or three main supporting points as if you were making a plan for the essay. (In fact, the writer probably made such a plan before she wrote her first draft.)

Paragraph 1. **INTRODUCTION**

Thesis statement: The person who practices tae kwon do gains discipline, maturity, and a changed self-concept.

Paragraph 2. **Topic sentence:** First, the discipline of tae kwon do helps the student outfight and outsmart her opponent.

Point 1: _____

Point 2: _____

Point 3: _____

Paragraph 3. **Topic sentence:** Second, with practice, tae kwon do increases maturity.

Point 1: _____

Point 2: _____

Paragraph 4. **Topic sentence:** Finally, after a year or so, tae kwon do can change the student's self-concept.

Point 1: _____

Point 2: _____

Point 3: _____

Paragraph 5. **CONCLUSION**

_____

*To read essays by other students, see the Writers' Workshops in Units 3, 6, 7, and 8.

PRACTICE 2

Discuss with several classmates or write your answers to these questions.

1. Did Wineth Williams' introduction (paragraph 1) catch and hold your interest? Would this essay be just as good or better if it had no introduction but started right in with the thesis statement? Why or why not?

2. In paragraph (4), the writer says she now can "take care of business." Is this language appropriate for a college essay? Will readers know what this means?

3. Is the conclusion effective, or is it too short?

4. Williams' audience was her English class. Her purpose (though not directly stated in the essay) was to let people know some of the benefits that come from practicing tae kwon do. Did she achieve her purpose?

5. What did you like best about the essay? What, if anything, would you change?

PART B   The Process of Writing an Essay

Whether you are writing a paragraph or an essay, the writing process is the same. Of course, writing an essay will probably take longer. In this section, you will practice these steps of the essay-writing process:

- Narrowing the subject and writing the thesis statement
- Generating ideas for the body of the essay
- Selecting and arranging ideas in a plan
- Writing and revising your essay

Narrowing the Subject and Writing the Thesis Statement

While an essay subject should be broader than a paragraph topic, a good essay subject also must be narrow enough to write about in detail. For example, the topic *jobs* is broad enough to fill a book. But the far narrower topic *driving a bulldozer at the town dump* could make a good essay. Remember to select or narrow your subject in light of your intended audience and purpose. Who are your readers, and what do you want your essay to achieve?

Writing the *thesis statement* forces you to narrow the topic further: *Driving a bulldozer for the Department of Highways was the best job I ever had.* That could be an intriguing thesis statement, but the writer could focus it even more: *For three reasons, driving a bulldozer for the Department of Highways was the best job I ever had.* The writer might discuss one reason in each of three paragraphs.

Here are two more examples of the narrowing process:

(1) Subject:	music
Narrowed subject:	Cuban singer Lucretia
Thesis statement:	In talent and style, Cuban singer Lucretia might be the next Celia Cruz.
(2) Subject:	pets
Narrowed subject:	pains and pleasures of owning a parrot
Thesis statement:	Owning a parrot will enrich your life with noise, occasional chaos, and lots of laughs.

● On the basis of each thesis statement, what do you expect the essays to discuss?

_____

_____

Although the thesis statement must include all the ideas in the body of the essay, it should also be **clear** and **specific.** Which of these thesis statements is specific enough for a good essay?

> (1) Three foolproof techniques will help you avoid disastrous first dates.
>
> (2) NBA basketball is the most exciting sport in the world.
>
> (3) Dr. Villarosa is a competent and caring physician.

● Thesis statements (1) and (3) are both specific. From (1), a reader might expect to learn about the "three foolproof techniques," each one perhaps explained in a paragraph.

● On the basis of thesis statement (3), what supporting points might the essay

discuss? _____

_____

● Thesis statement (2), however, is too broad for an essay—or even a book. It gives the reader (and writer) no direction.

PRACTICE 3

Choose one of these topics for your own essay. Then narrow the topic and write a clear and specific thesis statement.

The benefits of a sport or practice

The most fascinating/boring/important job I ever had

Qualities of an excellent husband/wife/partner

Narrowed subject: _____

_____

Thesis statement: _____

_____

Generating Ideas for the Body of the Essay

Writers generate support for an essay just as they do for a paragraph—by prewriting to get as many interesting ideas as possible. Once you know your main point and have written a thesis statement, use your favorite prewriting method—freewriting, for example. If you feel stuck, change to brainstorming or clustering. Just keep writing.

PRACTICE 4

Generate as many good ideas as possible to support your thesis statement. Fill at least one or two pages with ideas. As you work, try to imagine how many paragraphs your essay will contain and what each will include.

Selecting and Arranging Ideas in a Plan

Next, underline or mark the most interesting ideas that support your thesis statement. Cross out the rest.

Make a rough **plan** or **outline** that includes an introductory paragraph, two or three paragraphs for the body of the essay, and a brief conclusion. Choose a logical order for presenting your ideas. Which idea will come first, second, third?

For example, the bulldozer operator might explain why that job was "the best" with three reasons, arranged in this order: 1. *On the job, I learned to operate heavy equipment.* 2. *Working alone at the controls gave me time to think.* 3. *One bonus was occasionally finding interesting items beside the road.* This arrangement moves logically from physical skills to mental benefits to a surprising bonus.

PRACTICE 5

Read over your prewriting pages, selecting your best ideas and a logical order in which to present them. Make an outline or a plan that includes an introduction and a thesis statement; two or three supporting paragraphs, each with a clear topic sentence; and a brief conclusion.

Writing and Revising Your Essay

Drafting   Now write your first draft. Try to express your ideas clearly and fully. If a section seems weak or badly written, put a check in the margin and go on; you can come back to that section later, prewriting again if necessary for fresh ideas. Set aside your draft for an hour or a day.

Revising and Proofreading   Revising may be the most important step in the writing process. Reread your essay as if you were reading someone else's work, marking it up as you answer questions like these:

- Are my main idea and my thesis statement clear?

- Have I supported my thesis in a rich and convincing way?

- Does each paragraph in the body clearly explain the main idea?

- Does my essay have a logical order and good transitions?

- Are there any parts that don't belong or don't make sense?

- What one change would most improve my essay?*

You also might wish to ask a respected friend to read or listen to your essay, giving peer feedback before you revise.**

PRACTICE 6

Now read your first draft to see how you can improve it. Trust your instincts about what is alive and interesting and what is dull. Take your time. As you revise, try to make this the best paper you have ever written.

Finally, write a new draft of your essay, using the format preferred by your instructor. Proofread carefully, correcting any grammar or spelling errors.

---

* See Chapter 3, Part F, for more revising ideas.
** See Chapter 3, page 30, for a sample Peer Feedback Sheet.

PRACTICE 7

Exchange essays with a classmate. Write a one-paragraph evaluation of each other's work, saying as specifically as possible what you like about the essay and what might be improved. If you wish, use the Peer Feedback Sheet (page 30).

Possible Topics for Essays

1. The best/worst class I ever had
2. Two sure-fire ways to relax
3. Modern dating
4. A major decision
5. Tips for the new parent (college student, NBA draft pick, cell-phone user, and so forth)
6. A valuable/worthless television show
7. A good friend
8. Can anger be used constructively?
9. How I fell in love with books (German shepherds, rock climbing, video games, and so forth)
10. What childhood taught me about boys/girls in society

CHAPTER HIGHLIGHTS

Checklist for Writing an Effective Essay

- **Narrow the topic in light of your audience and purpose. Be sure you can discuss the topic fully in a short essay.**
- **Write a clear thesis statement. If you have trouble, freewrite or brainstorm first; then narrow the topic and write the thesis statement.**
- **Freewrite, brainstorm, or cluster to generate facts, details, and examples to support your thesis statement.**
- **Plan or outline your essay, choosing two to three main ideas to support the thesis statement.**
- **Write a topic sentence that expresses each main idea.**
- **Decide on a logical order in which to present the paragraphs.**
- **Plan the body of each paragraph, using all you have learned about support and paragraph development.**
- **Write the first draft of your essay.**
- **Revise as necessary, checking your essay for support, unity, and coherence.**
- **Proofread carefully for grammar, punctuation, and spelling.**

EXPLORING ONLINE

<http://www.powa.org/> Review the essay-writing process.

<http://college.cengage.com/devenglish> For more exercises, quizzes, and live links to all websites in this chapter, visit this link, click Developmental Writing, and find the home page for *Grassroots*, 9/e. Bookmark the *Grassroots* student website for future visits as you work through this book.

WRITING ASSIGNMENTS

As you complete each writing assignment, remember to perform these steps:

● Write a clear, complete topic (or thesis) sentence.

● Use freewriting, brainstorming, or clustering to generate ideas for the body of your paragraph or essay.

● Arrange your best ideas in a plan.

● Revise for support, unity, coherence, and exact language.

● Proofread for grammar, punctuation, and spelling errors.

Writing Assignment 1 *Discuss one requirement for a happy family life.* Complete this topic sentence: "A basic requirement for a happy family life is _____." What do you believe a family should have? Is it something material, like a house or a certain amount of money? Is it related to the number or types of people in the family? Does it have to do with nonmaterial things, like communication or support? Begin by jotting down all the reasons why you would require this particular thing. Then choose the three most important reasons and arrange them in order of importance—either from the least to the most important or the reverse. Explain each reason, making clear to the reader why you feel as strongly as you do.

Writing Assignment 2 *Present yourself online.* To meet people and make new friends, many computer users are creating personal Web pages on social networking sites like MySpace and Friendster. Write a description of yourself that you could post in the "About Me" section of your own page on one of these sites. To communicate who you are in just one brief paragraph, think of a one- or two-word phrase that describes you (for example, "proud mom," "daredevil," "computer geek," or "good friend"). Include that phrase in your topic sentence. Then choose specific details and examples to support this description.

Writing Assignment 3 *Interview a classmate about an achievement.* Write about a time your classmate achieved something important, like winning a sales prize at work, losing thirty pounds, or helping a friend through a bad time. To gather interesting facts and details, ask your classmate questions like these and take notes: *Is there one accomplishment of which you are very proud? Why was this achievement so important? Did it change the way you feel about yourself?* Keep asking questions until you feel you have enough information to give your reader a vivid sense of your classmate's triumph.

In your first sentence, state the person's achievement—for instance, *Getting her first A in English was a turning point in Jessica's life.* Then explain specifically why the achievement was so meaningful.

Writing Assignment 4 *Develop a paragraph with examples.* Below are topic sentences for possible paragraphs. Pick the topic sentence that most interests you and write a paragraph, using one to three examples to explain the topic sentence. If you prefer, choose a quotation from the Quotation Bank at the end of this book and explain it with one or more examples.

    a. A sense of humor can make difficult times easier to bear.

    b. Mistakes can be great teachers.

    c. Television commercials often insult my intelligence.

REVIEW

Choosing a Topic Sentence

Each group of sentences could be unscrambled and written as a paragraph. Circle the letter of the sentence that would be the best topic sentence.

1. a. Rooftops and towers made eye-catching shapes against the winter sky.
   b. Far below, the faint sounds of slush and traffic were soothing.
   c. From the apartment-house roof, the urban scene was oddly relaxing.
   d. Stoplights changing color up and down the avenues created a rhythmic pattern invisible from the street.

2. a. Actor Andy Garcia and *CSI Miami* star Adam Rodriguez own homes in Miami.
   b. Mexican actress and singer Lucia Mendez resides there, as does Venezuelan soap opera star Jose Luis Rodriguez.
   c. Singers Ricky Martin and Enrique Iglesias call Miami home.
   d. In recent years, Miami has become the Hollywood of southern America.

Selecting Ideas

Here is a topic sentence and a brainstormed list of possible ideas for a paragraph. Check "Keep" for ideas that best support the topic sentence and "Drop" for ideas that do not.

Topic sentence: Oprah Winfrey is a force for tremendous good in the United States.

Keep   Drop

___   ___   1. on her TV show, often has experts who help people with relationships or finances

___   ___   2. through her book club, inspired millions to start reading and periodically introduces a vast audience to new and old authors

___   ___   3. proves that women don't need to be thin to be beautiful, popular, famous, and greatly loved

___   ___   4. was born in 1954 on a farm in Mississippi

___   ___   5. at age six was sent to Milwaukee; kept cockroaches in a jar as substitute for farm animals

___   ___   6. is a well-known example of someone who overcame many obstacles, including childhood abuse and racial prejudice

___   ___   7. another example of someone who has overcome abuse and prejudice is actress Halle Berry

___   ___   8. physical abuse by a former boyfriend caused Berry to lose 80 percent of her hearing in one ear

___   ___   9. Winfrey gives millions to such causes as helping South African children orphaned by AIDS

___   ___   10. her website and magazine encourage women to develop their spirituality and pursue personal goals

Examining a Paragraph

Read this paragraph and answer the questions.

(1) Students at some American colleges are learning a lot from trash by studying "garbology." (2) Wearing rubber gloves, they might sift through the local dump, counting and collecting treasures that they examine back at the laboratory. (3) First, they learn to look closely and to interpret what they see, thus reading the stories that trash tells. (4) More important, they learn the truth about what Americans buy, what they eat, and how they live. (5) Students at the University of Arizona, for instance, were surprised to find that low-income families in certain areas buy more educational toys for their children than nearby middle-income families do. (6) Most important, students say that garbology courses can motivate them to be better citizens of planet Earth. (7) One young woman, for example, after seeing from hard evidence in her town's landfill how many people really recycled their glass, cans, and newspapers and how many cheated, organized an annual recycling awareness day.

1. Write the number of the topic sentence in the paragraph. _____

2. What kind of order does this writer use? _____

3. Students learn three things in garbology courses. (a) Write the numbers of the sentences stating these. (b) Which two ideas are supported by examples?

   (a) _____   (b) _____

Like his former garbology professor at the University of Arizona, this graduate student at the University of Mexico believes that the only way to know people is by what they throw away.

Louie Psihoyos/Science Faction/Getty Images.

WRITERS' WORKSHOP

Discuss Your Name

Good writers are masters of exact language and thoughtful observation. Read this student's paragraph about her name. Underline any words or details that strike you as well written, interesting, or powerful.

In this paragraph I will write about my name. My name YuMing is made up of two Chinese characters that mean "the universe" and "the crow of a bird." This may seem like a strange name to an American, but in fact it has a special meaning for me. In ancient Chinese literature, there is a story about a bird that was owned by God. This bird was rumored to have the most beautiful voice in the universe. A greedy king wanted this bird, so he had it captured and placed in a big cage. He sat next to this cage day after day waiting for the bird to sing, but the bird stayed silent. After three years, the impatient king threw open the cage door and set the bird free. As the bird flew up toward the heavens, it made its first crow in three years. The sound shocked everyone in the kingdom because they realized the legend was true—they had never heard such a beautiful voice before! My parents told me that they gave me this name because they want me to be like the bird in the story. Though I may stay silent for a while as I establish myself in society, they hope that I will "crow" one day when it is the right time for me, and crow loudly so everyone in the universe can hear.

YuMing Lai, student

1. How effective is YuMing Lai's paragraph about the meaning of her name?

   _____ Good topic sentence?   _____ Rich supporting details?

   _____ Logical organization?   _____ Effective conclusion?

2. Underline the words, details, or sentences you like best. Put a check beside anything that needs improvement.

3. Now discuss your underlinings with your group or class. Try to explain as exactly as you can why you like something. For example, in the last sentence, the way that the writer ties her parents' wish for her to the meaning of the story is moving and surprising.

4. Is YuMing's topic sentence as good as the rest of her paragraph? If not, how might she change it?

5. Did YuMing's thoughts about her name make you think about your own name? Do you like your name? Why or why not? Do you know why your parents chose it?

6. What order does this paragraph employ?

Writing and Revising Ideas

1. Write about the meaning of your name or the name of someone close to you.

2. Visit the government's website below, which lists the most popular baby names in the United States, year by year. Do you see any patterns? How popular is your name? Your parents' names?
   <http://www.ssa.gov/OACT/babynames/>

For help with writing your paragraph, see Chapter 3 and Chapter 4, Parts B and C. As you revise, pay special attention to writing a clear, catchy topic sentence supported by interesting details.

Writing Complete Sentences

The sentence is the basic unit of all writing, so good writers must know how to write clear and correct sentences. In this unit, you will

- Learn to spot subjects and verbs

- Practice writing complete sentences

- Learn to avoid or correct any sentence fragments

Spotlight on Writing

Notice the way this writer uses strong, simple sentences to capture a moment with her grandfather, her *abuelo*. If possible, read the paragraph aloud.

My grandfather has misplaced his words again. He is trying to find my name in the kaleidoscope of images that his mind has become. His face brightens like a child's who has just remembered his lesson. He points to me and says my mother's name. I smile back and kiss him on the cheek. It doesn't matter what names he remembers anymore. Every day he is more confused, his memory slipping back a little further in time. Today he has no grandchildren yet. Tomorrow he will be a young man courting my grandmother again, quoting bits of poetry to her. In months to come, he will begin calling her Mama.

Judith Ortiz Cofer, "The Witch's Husband"

- How does the writer feel about her grandfather? Which sentences tell you this?

- Why do you think the writer arranges the last three sentences in the order that she does?

 Writing Ideas

- *A visit with a loved (or feared) relative*
- *Your relationship with someone who has a disability*

CHAPTER 6

Subjects and Verbs

PART A Defining and Spotting Subjects

The sentence is the basic unit of all writing. To write well, you need to know how to write correct and effective sentences. A **sentence** is a group of words that expresses a complete thought about something or someone. It contains a **subject** and a **verb.**

> (1) _____ jumped over the black Buick, scaled the building, and finally reached the roof.
>
> (2) _____ needs a new coat of paint.

These sentences might be interesting, but they are incomplete.

● In sentence (1), *who* jumped, scaled, and reached? Spider-Man, Alicia Keys, the English teacher?

● Depending on *who* performed the action—jumping, scaling, or reaching—the sentence can be exciting, surprising, or strange.

● What is missing is the *who* word—the *subject*.

● In sentence (2), *what* needs a new coat of paint? The house, the car, the old rocking chair?

● What is missing is the *what* word—the *subject*.

For a sentence to be complete, it must contain a *who* **or** *what* **word—a** *subject.* **The subject tells you** *who* **or** *what* **does something or exists in a certain way.**

The subject is often a *noun,* a word that names a person, place, or thing (such as *Alicia Keys, English teacher,* or *house*). However, a *pronoun (I, you, he, she, it, we,* or *they*) also can be the subject.*

---

*For more work on pronoun subjects, see Chapter 20, Part F.

PRACTICE 1

In each of these sentences, the subject (the *who* or *what* word) is missing. Fill in your own subject to make the sentence complete.

EXAMPLE: A(n) _____ *fox* _____ dashed across the road.

1. The _____ skidded across the ice.

2. The _____ was eager to begin the semester.

3. Because of the crowd, the _____ slipped out unnoticed.

4. For years, _____ piled up in the back of the closet.

5. The cheerful yellow _____ brightened Sheila's mood.

6. _____ and _____ were scattered all over the doctor's desk.

7. The _____ believed that his _____ would return someday.

8. The _____ was in bad shape. The _____ was falling in, and the _____ were all broken.

As you may have noticed, the subject can be a noun only, but it can also include *words that describe the noun* (such as *the, cheerful,* or *yellow*).

The noun or pronoun alone is called the *simple subject;* the noun or pronoun plus the words that describe it are called the *complete subject.*

(3) Three yellow roses grew near the path.

(4) A large box was delivered this morning.

● The simple subject of sentence (3) is the noun *roses.*
● The complete subject is *three yellow roses.*
● What is the simple subject of (4)? _____
● What is the complete subject of (4)? _____

PRACTICE 2

Circle the *simple* subject in each sentence. (A person's complete name—though more than one word—is considered a simple subject.)

EXAMPLE: Many (people) love scary films.

(1) Dr. Leon Rappoport studies the fear factor in movies. (2) Humans have always liked to explore their feelings of fear and anxiety, according to Rappoport. (3) Frightening movies allow them to master those emotions and work through them. (4) Other psychologists agree. (5) People like to be scared in the absence of any real danger. (6) Horror films and stories provide opportunities for such experiences. (7) Also, some moviegoers like to explore their uncivilized, antisocial nature

Movie poster, 1958. Horror movies allow people to face their fears and dark wishes in a safe way, claim psychologists.

The Everett Collection.

in safe settings. (8) Many teenagers, in particular, need to test their tolerance for threatening situations. (9) In addition, parents often declare horror movies inappropriate. (10) Therefore, adolescents want to see this forbidden entertainment more than ever.

PRACTICE 3

In these sentences, the complete subject has been omitted. You must decide where it belongs and fill in a complete subject (a *who* or *what* word along with any words that describe it). Write in any complete subject that makes sense.

EXAMPLE: Raced down the street.

  My worried friend raced down the street.

1. Trained day and night for the big event.

    _____

2. Has a dynamic singing voice.

    _____

3. Landed in the cornfield.

    _____

4. After the show, applauded and screamed for fifteen minutes.

    _____

5. Got out of the large gray van.

    _____

PART B   Spotting Singular and Plural Subjects

Besides being able to spot subjects in sentences, you need to know whether a subject is singular or plural.

> (1) The man jogged around the park.

- The subject of this sentence is *the man*.
- Because *the man* is one person, the subject is *singular*.

Singular means only one of something.

> (2) The man and his friend jogged around the park.

- The subject of sentence (2) is *the man and his friend*.
- Because *the man and his friend* refers to more than one person, the subject is *plural*.

Plural means more than one of something.

PRACTICE 4

Here is a list of possible subjects of sentences. If the subject is singular, put a check in the Singular column; if the subject is plural, put a check in the Plural column.

Possible Subjects	Singular (one)	Plural (more than one)
EXAMPLES: an elephant	✔	
children		✔
1. our cousins	____	____
2. a song and a dance	____	____
3. Kansas	____	____
4. their trophy	____	____
5. women	____	____
6. a rock star and her band	____	____
7. his three pickup trucks	____	____
8. salad dressing	____	____

PRACTICE 5

Circle the complete subjects in these sentences. Then, in the space at the right, write *S* if the subject is singular or *P* if the subject is plural.

EXAMPLE: (This young cartoonist) is getting national attention.   *S*

1. Aaron McGruder was a student at the University of Maryland.   ____
2. Comic books and hip-hop music intrigued him.   ____
3. To Aaron, existing comics did not capture racial diversity in a real way.   ____
4. McGruder decided to create a comic strip called *Boondocks*.   ____

5. The characters were African-American city kids in suburbia.   _____

6. The strip appeared in the college's student paper, *The Diamondback*, in 1997.   _____

7. Rave reviews and a few angry letters poured in.   _____

8. A major music magazine soon began publishing *Boondocks* every day.   _____

9. Aaron's goal is to expand racial dialogue by using humor.   _____

10. The daily strip, a book, and TV projects now keep him very busy.   _____

PART C   Spotting Prepositional Phrases

One group of words that may confuse you as you look for subjects is the prepositional phrase. A **prepositional phrase** contains a *preposition* (a word like *at, from, in,* or *of*) and its *object* (a *noun* or *pronoun*). Here are some prepositional phrases:*

Prepositional Phrase = Preposition + Object		
at work	at	work
behind her	behind	her
of the students	of	the students
on the blue table	on	the blue table

The object of a preposition *cannot* be the subject of a sentence. Therefore, crossing out prepositional phrases can help you find the real subject.

(1) On summer evenings, girls in white dresses stroll under the trees.

(2) On summer evenings, girls in white dresses stroll under the trees.

(3) From dawn to dusk, we hiked.

(4) The president of the college will speak tonight.

● In sentence (1), you may have trouble spotting the subject. However, once the prepositional phrases are crossed out in (2), the subject, *girls*, is easy to see.

● Cross out the prepositional phrase in sentence (3). What is the subject of the sentence? _____

● Cross out the prepositional phrase in sentence (4). What is the subject of the sentence? _____

Here are some common prepositions you should know:

Common Prepositions		
about	after	among
above	against	around
across	along	at

---

*For more work on prepositions, see Chapter 22.

before	from	through(out)
behind	in	to
beside	into	toward
between	like	under
by	of	until
during	off	up
except	on	with
for	over	without

PRACTICE 6

Cross out the prepositional phrase or phrases in each sentence. Then circle the *simple* subject of the sentence.

EXAMPLE: (Millions) of people walk on the Appalachian Trail each year.

1. That famous trail stretches from Springer Mountain in Georgia to Mount Katahdin in Maine.

2. One quarter of the trail goes through Virginia.

3. The majority of walkers hike for one day.

4. Of the four million trail users, two hundred people complete the entire trail every year.

5. For most hikers, the trip through fourteen states takes four or five months.

6. In the spring, many hardy souls begin their 2,158-mile-long journey.

7. These lovers of the wilderness must reach Mount Katahdin before winter.

8. On the trail, men and women battle heat, humidity, bugs, blisters, muscle sprains, and food and water shortages.

9. After beautiful green scenery, the path becomes rocky and mountainous.

10. Hikers in the White Mountains of New Hampshire struggle against high winds.

11. A pebble from Georgia is sometimes added to the pile of stones at the top of Mount Katahdin.

12. At the bottom of the mountain, the conquerors of the Appalachian Trail add their names to the list of successful hikers.

PART D Defining and Spotting Action Verbs

(1) The pears _____ on the trees.

(2) Robert _____ his customer's hand and _____ her dog on the head.

These sentences tell you what or who the subject is—*the pears* and *Robert*—but not what each subject does.

● In sentence (1), what do the pears do? Do they *grow, ripen, rot, stink,* or *glow*?

- All these *action verbs* fit into the blank space in sentence (1), but the meaning of the sentence changes depending on which action verb you use.

- In sentence (2), what actions did Robert perform? He might have *shaken, ignored, kissed, patted,* or *scratched.*

- Depending on which verb you use, the meaning of the sentence changes.

- Some sentences, like sentence (2), contain two or more action verbs.

For a sentence to be complete, it must have a *verb.* **An** *action verb* **tells what action the subject is performing.**

PRACTICE 7

Fill in each blank with an action verb.

1. LeBron James _____ through the air for a slam dunk.

2. An artist _____ the scene at the waterfront.

3. When the rooster _____, the dogs _____.

4. A fierce wind _____ and _____.

5. The audience _____ while the conductor _____.

6. This new kitchen gadget _____ and _____ any vegetable you can imagine.

7. When the dentist _____ his drill, Charlene _____.

8. Will Smith _____ and _____ across the stage.

PRACTICE 8

Circle the action verbs in these sentences. Some sentences contain more than one action verb.

(1) Sometimes the combination of talent and persistence explodes into well-deserved fame and fortune. (2) For almost a year, J. K. Rowling survived on public assistance in Edinburgh, Scotland. (3) Almost every day that year, she brought her baby to a coffee shop near their damp, unheated apartment. (4) In the warmth of the café, the divorced, unemployed mother sat and wrote. (5) Almost at the end of her endurance, she finally finished her first book. (6) Today, Rowling's Harry Potter books sell hundreds of millions of copies in sixty languages. (7) Each book tells about Harry's adventures, both in the everyday world (the Muggles' world) and at a new grade level at Hogwarts School of Witchcraft and Wizardry. (8) The imaginative and very funny series about the courageous young wizard-in-training attracts and enthralls adults as well as children. (9) In fact, the *New York Times* began a children's bestseller list for the first time—after months of Harry Potter books in slots 1, 2, and 3 on the adult bestseller list!

PART E   Defining and Spotting Linking Verbs

The verbs you have been examining so far show action, but a second kind of verb simply links the subject to words that describe or rename it.

> (1) Aunt Claudia sometimes seems a little strange.

● The subject in this sentence is *Aunt Claudia,* but there is no action verb.

● Instead, *seems* links the subject, *Aunt Claudia,* with the descriptive words *a little strange.*

Aunt Claudia	seems	a little strange.
↓	↓	↓
subject	linking verb	descriptive words

> (2) They are reporters for the newspaper.

● The subject is *they.* The word *reporters* renames the subject.

● What verb links the subject, *they,* with the word *reporters?* _____

For a sentence to be complete, it must contain a *verb.* **A** *linking verb* **links the subject with words that describe or rename that subject.**

Here are some linking verbs you should know:

Common Linking Verbs

be (am, is, are, was, were)	look
act	seem
appear	smell
become	sound
feel	taste
get	

● The most common linking verbs are the forms of *to be,* but verbs of the senses, such as *feel, look,* and *smell,* also may be used as linking verbs.

PRACTICE 9

The subjects and descriptive words in these sentences are boxed. Circle the linking verbs.

1. Jerry sounds sleepy today.
2. Ronda always was the best debater on the team.
3. His brother often appeared relaxed and happy.
4. By evening, Harvey felt confident about the exam.
5. Mara and Maude became talent scouts.

PRACTICE 10

Circle the linking verbs in these sentences. Then underline the subject and the descriptive word or words in each sentence.

1. The sweet potato pie tastes delicious.

2. You usually seem energetic.

3. During the summer, she looks calm.

4. Under heavy snow, the new dome roof appeared sturdy.

5. Raphael is a gifted animal trainer.

6. Lately, I feel very competent at work.

7. Luz became a medical technician.

8. Yvonne acted surprised at her baby shower.

PART F   Spotting Verbs of More Than One Word

All the verbs you have dealt with so far have been single words—*look, walked, saw, are, were,* and so on. However, many verbs consist of more than one word.

> (1) Sarah is walking to work.

- The subject is *Sarah.* What is *Sarah* doing?
- *Sarah is walking.*
- *Walking* is the *main verb. Is* is the *helping verb*; without *is, walking* is not a complete verb.

> (2) Should I have written sooner?

- The subject is *I.*
- *Should have written* is the *complete verb.*
- *Written* is the *main verb. Should* and *have* are the *helping verbs*; without *should have, written* is not a complete verb.

> (3) Do you eat fish?

- What is the subject? _____
- What is the main verb? _____
- What is the helping verb? _____

The *complete verb* in a sentence consists of all the helping verbs and the main verb.

PRACTICE 11

The blanks following each sentence tell you how many words make up the complete verb. Fill in the blanks with the complete verb; then circle the main verb.

EXAMPLE: Language researchers at the University of Arizona have been studying parrots.

_____have_____   _____been_____   _(studying)_

1. Dr. Irene Pepperberg has worked with Alex, an African Gray parrot, for years.

_____ _____

2. Nearly one hundred words can be used by this intelligent bird.

_____ _____ _____

3. Alex is believed to understand the words, not just "parrot" sounds.

_____ _____

4. For example, from a tray of objects, Alex can select all the keys, all the wooden items, or all the blue items.

_____ _____

5. Dr. Pepperberg might show Alex a fuzzy cloth ball.

_____ _____

6. The bird will shout, "Wool!"

_____ _____

7. Alex has been counting to six.

_____ _____ _____

8. Currently, he and the other parrots are learning letters and their sounds.

_____ _____

9. Can these birds really be taught to read?

_____ _____ _____

10. Scientists in animal communication are excited by the possibility.

_____ _____

PRACTICE 12

Box the simple subject, circle the main verb, and underline any helping verbs in each of the following sentences.

EXAMPLE: Most people have wondered about the beginning of the universe.

1. Scientists have developed one theory.
2. According to this theory, the universe began with a huge explosion.
3. The explosion has been named the Big Bang.

4. First, all matter must have been packed into a tiny speck under enormous pressure.

5. Then, about 15 billion years ago, that speck burst with amazing force.

6. Everything in the universe has come from the original explosion.

7. In fact, the universe still is expanding from the Big Bang.

8. All of the planets and stars are moving away from each other at an even speed.

9. Will it expand forever?

10. Experts may be debating that question for a long time.

PRACTICE 13

Writing Assignment

Whether you have just graduated from high school or have worked for several years, the first year of college can be difficult. Imagine that you are writing to an incoming student who needs advice and encouragement. Pick one serious problem you had as a first-year student and explain how you coped with it. State the problem clearly. Use examples from your own experience or the experience of others to make your advice more vivid.

CHAPTER HIGHLIGHTS

- **A sentence contains a subject and a verb, and expresses a complete thought:**

       S   *V*
  Jennifer swims every day.

             S   *V*
  The two students have tutored in the writing lab.

- **An action verb tells what the subject is doing:**
  Toni Morrison *writes* novels.

- **A linking verb links the subject with words that describe or rename it:**
  Her novels *are* bestsellers.

- **Don't mistake the object of a prepositional phrase for a subject:**

       S   *PP*
  The red car [in the showroom] is a Corvette.

    PP   *S*
  [In my dream,] *a sailor and his parrot* were singing.

CHAPTER REVIEW

Circle the simple subjects, crossing out any confusing prepositional phrases. Then underline the complete verbs. If you have difficulty with this review, consider rereading the lesson.

Target Practice: Setting Attainable Goals

(1) Successful people know an important secret about setting and reaching goals. (2) These high achievers break their big goals down into smaller, more manageable steps or targets. (3) Then they hit the targets, one by one. (4) Otherwise, a huge goal might seem impossible.

(5) To turn a major goal into smaller steps, many achievers think backward. (6) Dillon, for example, wanted to lose twenty pounds by graduation. (7) That much weight must be lost gradually. (8) So Dillon decided to set smaller targets for himself. (9) First, Dillon eliminated between-meal snacks. (10) On the new plan, he might eat an occasional apple, but only in emergencies. (11) Second, Dillon gave up second helpings at any meal—no matter what. (12) His third target was a walk after dinner. (13) Every night, this purposeful dieter would check off the day's successes.

(14) Even high achievers do not complete a major goal, like losing a lot of weight, every day. (15) Yet they can feel satisfaction about moving forward one step at a time. (16) The photographer at Dillon's graduation captured his beaming smile. (17) Under that cap and gown, Dillon's weight had dropped by twenty-two pounds.

EXPLORING ONLINE

<http://grammar.ccc.commnet.edu/grammar/quizzes/subjector.htm> Interactive quiz: Identify the subjects.

<http://grammar.ccc.commnet.edu/grammar/quizzes/verbmaster.htm> Interactive quiz: Identify verbs of one or more words.

<http://college.cengage.com/devenglish> For more exercises, quizzes, and live links to all websites in this chapter, visit this link, click Developmental Writing, and find the home page for *Grassroots*, 9/e. Bookmark the *Grassroots* student website for future visits as you work through this book.

CHAPTER 7

Avoiding Sentence Fragments

PART A Writing Sentences with Subjects and Verbs

PART B Writing Sentences with Complete Verbs

PART C Completing the Thought

PART A   Writing Sentences with Subjects and Verbs

Which of these groups of words is a sentence? Be prepared to explain your answers.

> (1) People will bet on almost anything.
> (2) For example, every winter the Nenana River in Alaska.
> (3) Often make bets on the date of the breakup of the ice.
> (4) Must guess the exact day and time of day.
> (5) Recently, the lucky guess won $300,000.

- In (2), you probably wanted to know what the Nenana River *does.* The idea is not complete because there is no *verb.*

- In (3) and (4), you probably wanted to know *who* often makes bets on the date of the breakup of the ice and *who* must guess the exact day and time of day.

    The ideas are not complete. What is missing? _____

- But in sentences (1) and (5), you knew *who did what.* These ideas are complete.

    Why? _____

Below are the same groups of words written as complete sentences:

> (1) People will bet on almost anything.
> (2) For example, every winter the Nenana River in Alaska freezes.
> (3) The townspeople often make bets on the date of the breakup of the ice.
> (4) Someone must guess the exact day and time of day.
> (5) Recently, the lucky guess won $300,000.

Every *sentence* **must have both a subject and a verb—and must express a complete thought.**

A *fragment* lacks either a subject or a complete verb—or does not express a complete thought.

PRACTICE 1

All of the following are *fragments;* they lack a subject, a verb, or both. Add a subject, a verb, or both to make the fragments into sentences.

EXAMPLE:　Raising onions in the backyard.

　　　　　　Rewrite: _Charles is raising onions in the backyard._ _____

1. Melts easily.

   Rewrite: _____

2. That couple on the street corner.

   Rewrite: _____

3. One of the fans.

   Rewrite: _____

4. Manages a Software City store.

   Rewrite: _____

5. The tip of her nose.

   Rewrite: _____

6. DVD players.

   Rewrite: _____

7. Makes me nervous.

   Rewrite: _____

8. A person who likes to take risks.

   Rewrite: _____

PART B　Writing Sentences with Complete Verbs

Do not be fooled by incomplete verbs.

> (1) She leaving for the city.
>
> (2) The students gone to the cafeteria for dessert.

● *Leaving* seems to be the verb in (1).

● *Gone* seems to be the verb in (2).

But . . .

● An *-ing* word like *leaving* is not by itself a verb.

● A word like *gone* is not by itself a verb.

(1) She $\left.\begin{array}{c} is \\ was \end{array}\right\}$ leaving for the city.

(2) The students $\left.\begin{array}{c} have \\ had \end{array}\right\}$ gone to the cafeteria for dessert.

● To be a verb, an *-ing* word (called a *present participle*) must be combined with some form of the verb *to be*.*

Helping Verb		Main Verb
am	were	
is	has been	
are	have been	jogging
was	had been	

● To be a verb, a word like *gone* (called a *past participle*) must be combined with some form of *to have* or *to be*.**

Helping Verb		Main Verb
am	have	
is	had	
are	has been	
was	have been	forgotten
were	had been	
has		

PRACTICE 2

All of the following are fragments; they have only a partial or an incomplete verb. Complete each verb in order to make these fragments into sentences.

EXAMPLE: Both children grown tall this year.
Rewrite: *Both children have grown tall this year.* _____

1. The Australian winning the tennis match.
   Rewrite: _____

2. Her parents gone to the movies.
   Rewrite: _____

3. Steve's letter published in the *Miami Herald*.
   Rewrite: _____

4. My physics professor always forgetting the assignment.
   Rewrite: _____

5. This sari made of scarlet silk.
   Rewrite: _____

———————
*For a detailed explanation of present participles, see Chapter 11.
**For a detailed explanation of past participles, see Chapter 10.

6. For the past two years, Joan working at a computer company.

Rewrite: _____

7. You ever been to Alaska?

Rewrite: _____

8. Yesterday, Ed's wet gloves taken from the radiator.

Rewrite: _____

PRACTICE 3

All of the following are fragments; they lack a subject, and they contain only a partial verb. Make these fragments into sentences by adding a subject and by completing the verb.

EXAMPLE: Written by Ray Bradbury.

Rewrite: This science fiction thriller was written by Ray Bradbury.

1. Forgotten the password.

Rewrite: _____

2. Now running the copy center.

Rewrite: _____

3. Making sculpture from old car parts.

Rewrite: _____

4. Been working at the state capitol building.

Rewrite: _____

5. Creeping along the windowsill.

Rewrite: _____

6. Driven that tractor for years.

Rewrite: _____

7. Slept through the TV program.

Rewrite: _____

8. Been to a wrestling match.

Rewrite: _____

PRACTICE 4

Fragments are most likely to occur in paragraphs or longer pieces of writing. Proofread the paragraph below for fragments; check for missing subjects, missing verbs, or incomplete verbs. Circle the number of every fragment; then write your corrections above the lines.

   (1) On a routine day in 1946, a scientist at the Raytheon Company his hand into his pants pocket for a candy bar. (2) The chocolate, however, a messy, sticky mass of gunk. (3) Dr. Percy Spencer had been testing a magnetron tube. (4) Could the chocolate have melted from radiation leaking from the tube? (5) Spencer sent out

for a bag of popcorn kernels. (6) Put the kernels near the tube. (7) Within minutes, corn popping wildly onto the lab floor. (8) Within a short time, Raytheon working on the development of the microwave oven. (9) Microwave cooking the first new method of preparing food since the discovery of fire more than a million years ago. (10) Was the first cooking technique that did not directly or indirectly apply fire to food.

PART C   Completing the Thought

Can these ideas stand by themselves?

> (1) Because oranges are rich in vitamin C.
>
> (2) Although Sam is sleepy.

- These ideas have a subject and a verb (find them), but they cannot stand alone because you expect something else to follow.
- Because oranges are rich in vitamin C, *then what*? Should you *eat them, sell them,* or *make marmalade*?
- Although Sam is sleepy, *what will he do*? Will he *wash the dishes, walk the dog,* or *go to the gym*?

> (1) Because oranges are rich in vitamin C, *I eat one every day.*
>
> (2) Although Sam is sleepy, *he will work late tonight.*

- These sentences are now complete.
- Words like *because* and *although* make an idea incomplete unless another idea is added to complete the thought.*

PRACTICE 5

Make these fragments into sentences by adding some idea that completes the thought.

EXAMPLE: Because I miss my family, <u>I am going home for the weekend.</u>

1. As May stepped off the elevator, _____

2. If you are driving to Main Street, _____

3. While Kimi studied chemistry, _____

4. Because you believe in yourself, _____

5. Although spiders scare most people, _____

6. Unless the surgery is absolutely necessary, _____

---

*For more work on this type of sentence, see Chapter 14.

7. Whenever I hear Macy Gray sing, _____

8. Although these air conditioners are expensive to run, _____

_____

Can these ideas stand by themselves?

(3) Graciela, who has a one-year-old daughter.

(4) A course that I will always remember.

● In each of these examples, you expect something else to follow. Graciela, who has a one-year-old daughter, *is doing what*? Does she *attend town meetings, knit sweaters,* or *fly planes*?

● A course that I will always remember *is what*? The thought must be completed.

(3) Graciela, who has a one-year-old daughter, *attends Gordon College.*

(4) A course that I will always remember *is documentary filmmaking.*

● These sentences are now complete.*

PRACTICE 6

Make these fragments into sentences by completing the thought.

EXAMPLE: Kent, who is a good friend of mine, _rarely writes to me._

1. The horoscopes that appear in the daily papers _____

2. Couples who never argue _____

3. Robert, who is a superb pole-vaulter, _____

4. Radio programs that ask listeners to call in are _____

5. A person who has coped with a great loss _____

6. My dog, which is the smartest animal alive, _____

7. Libraries that are up to date _____

8. The video that we watched last night _____

9. A person who becomes upset easily _____

10. A country that I have always wanted to visit _____

PRACTICE 7

To each fragment, add a subject, a verb, or whatever is required to complete the thought.

1. Visiting the White House.

   Rewrite: _____

2. That digital clock blinking for hours.

   Rewrite: _____

*For more work on this type of sentence, see Chapter 17, Part A.

3. People who can't say no to their children.

   Rewrite: _____

4. Make tables from driftwood they find on the beach.

   Rewrite: _____

5. Over the roof and into the garden.

   Rewrite: _____

6. Raúl completed a culinary arts program, and now he a well-known chef.

   Rewrite: _____

7. Chess, which is a difficult game to play.

   Rewrite: _____

8. Whenever Dolly starts to yodel.

   Rewrite: _____

PRACTICE 8

Proofread the paragraph for fragments. Circle the number of every fragment, and then write your corrections above the lines.

(1) Ralph Gilles is famous as the designer of the Chrysler 300C. (2) Which won many design awards. (3) Raised in Canada by Haitian parents, Gilles was in awe of his mother. (4) Because she gave her all to various thankless jobs and still told her children success stories. (5) When he was a boy, (6) Gilles loved to draw futuristic cars in his notebooks. (7) An aunt noticed his design gifts and urged him to write to Lee Iacocca. (8) Who was then chairman of the Chrysler Corporation. (9) Amazingly, after the embarrassed fourteen-year-old sent a letter and some

Designer Ralph Gilles poses with the car that made him famous.

Getty Images News.

sketches. (10) An executive responded with encouragement. (11) And a list of colleges from which Chrysler hired designers. (12) Later Gilles took the advice, attended Detroit's College for Creative Studies, and landed his first job at Chrysler. (13) Talent and hard work earned him promotions, the title of director of truck design, and media stardom. (14) While Gilles is designing the next generation of vehicles. (15) He is also inspiring the next generation of young people. (16) He tells the kids who write him or attend his talks, "Dream out loud."

PRACTICE 9

Writing Assignment

Working in a small group, choose one of the sentences below that could begin a short story.

1. As soon as Sean replaced the receiver, he knew he had to take action.

2. Suddenly, the bright blue sky turned dark.

3. No matter where she looked, Elena could not find her diary.

Next, each person in the group should write his or her own short story, starting with that sentence. First decide what type of story yours will be—science fiction, romance, action, comedy, murder mystery, and so on; perhaps each person will choose a different type. It may help you to imagine the story later becoming a TV show. As you write, be careful to avoid fragments, making sure each sentence has a subject and a complete verb—and expresses a complete thought.

Then exchange papers, checking each other's work for fragments. If time permits, read the papers aloud to the group. Are you surprised by the different ways in which that first sentence was developed?

CHAPTER HIGHLIGHTS

A sentence fragment is an error because it lacks

- **a subject:**   Was buying a gold ring. (*incorrect*)
  Diamond Jim was buying a gold ring. (*correct*)

- **a verb:**   The basketball game Friday at noon. (*incorrect*)
  The basketball game *was played* Friday at noon. (*correct*)

- **a complete thought:**   While Teresa was swimming. (*incorrect*)
  While Teresa was swimming, she lost a contact lens. (*correct*)

  The woman who bought your car. (*incorrect*)
  The woman who bought your car is walking down the highway. (*correct*)

CHAPTER REVIEW

Circle the number of each fragment. Correct it in any way that makes sense, changing it into a separate idea or adding it to another sentence.

A.   (1) Many people seem to forget all about good manners. (2) When they use a cell phone. (3) They rudely allow the ringing phone to interrupt conversations, meetings, appointments, performances, and romantic dinner dates. (4) Some even answer calls in church or at funerals. (5) And then proceed to talk loudly. (6) Forcing others to listen or wait for them to finish talking. (7) Public relations consultant Carol Page, known as the "Miss Manners of Cell Phones." (8) She created *cellmanners.com*. (9) Which is a website promoting cell phone courtesy and civility. (10) Page believes that in order to stop cell phone rudeness. (11) We should fix a "cell glare" on any cell phone user who is behaving badly. (12) If that doesn't work. (13) We can interrupt and gently ask if the phone conversation might be postponed. (14) Setting a good example when you use your own cell phone probably the best way to teach good cellular phone manners to others.

DILBERT© Scott Adams/Distributed by United Feature Syndicate, Inc.

B.   (1) As the demand for paralegals, or legal assistants, grows. (2) More students nationwide are majoring in paralegal studies. (3) Because many different types of law firms and businesses hire paralegals. (4) A paralegal's duties vary with the job setting. (5) For instance, because Denise Cunningham is the only paralegal at a small law firm in Louisville, Kentucky. (6) She has many duties. (7) Cunningham relishes being at the center of things. (8) Researching cases, doing client intake interviews, writing, and even managing the office. (9) When she was earning her associate's degree in paralegal studies from the University of Louisville. Cunningham learned about immigration law, real estate law, family law, and criminal law. (10) Drawn to criminal law, she was hired in 1980 by the attorney with whom she still works today. (11) Her professional rewards include a good salary. (12) And the satisfaction of helping people. (13) In 2006, her boss nominated her for Paralegal of the Year.

EXPLORING ONLINE

<http://www.bls.gov/oco/> Visit this helpful career website, which describes the duties and future outlook for hundreds of professions. Choose one career that interests you, research it, take notes, and write a report on the pros and cons of the job for you.

C.   (1) Braille, which is a system of reading and writing now used by blind people all over the world. (2) Was invented by a fifteen-year-old French boy. (3) In 1824, when Louis Braille entered a school for the blind in Paris. (4) He found that the library had only fourteen books for the blind. (5) These books used a system that he and the other blind students found hard to use. (6) Most of them just gave up. (7) Louis Braille devoted himself to finding a better way. (8) Working with the French army method called night-writing. (9) He came up with a new system in 1829. (10) Although his classmates liked and used Braille. (11) It not widely accepted in England and the United States for another hundred years.

D.   (1) Steel drums wonderful and unusual musical instruments. (2) Steel bands use them to perform calypso, jazz, and popular music. (3) And even classical symphonies. (4) Steel drums were invented in Trinidad. (5) Where they were made from the ends of discarded oil drums. (6) That had been left by the British navy. (7) Although the first steel drums produced only rhythm. (8) Now they can be tuned to play up to five octaves. (9) Steel orchestras produce music. (10) That surrounds and delights listeners without the use of amplifiers. (11) The worldwide popularity of steel drums has been increasing steadily. (12) The Trinidad All Steel Percussion Orchestra was a smash hit. (13) When it first performed in England a number of years ago. (14) Recently, the Northern Illinois University Steel Band has been thrilling audiences from the United States to Taiwan.

EXPLORING ONLINE

<http://owl.english.purdue.edu/handouts/grammar/g_fragEX1.html> Graded quiz: Can you find the fragments?

<http://grammar.ccc.commnet.edu/grammar/cgi-shl/quiz.pl/fragments_add2.htm> Interactive quiz: Find the correct sentence in each group.

<http://college.cengage.com/devenglish> For more exercises, quizzes, and live links to all websites in this chapter, visit this link, click Developmental Writing, and find the home page for *Grassroots,* 9/e. Bookmark the *Grassroots* student website for future visits as you work through this book.

WRITING ASSIGNMENTS

As you complete each writing assignment, remember to perform these steps:

● Write a clear, complete topic sentence.

● Use freewriting, brainstorming, or clustering to generate ideas for your paragraph, essay, or memo.

● Arrange your best ideas in a plan.

● Revise for support, unity, coherence, and exact language.

● Proofread for grammar, punctuation, and spelling errors.

Writing Assignment 1: *Plan to achieve a goal.* Did you know that nearly all successful people are good goal-planners? Choose a goal you would truly love to achieve, and write it down. Next, write down three to six smaller steps or targets that will lead you to your goal. Arrange these in time order. Have you left out any crucial steps? To inspire you and help you plan, reread "Target Practice: Setting Attainable Goals" on page 77, or try out the interactive goal-planner from Paradise Valley Community College at **<http://www.pvc.maricopa.edu/advisement/goalplan.html>.**

Writing Assignment 2: *Describe your place in the family.* Your psychology professor has asked you to write a brief description of your place in the family—as an only child, the youngest child, the middle child, or the oldest child. Did your place provide you with special privileges or lay special responsibilities on you? For instance, youngest children may be babied; oldest children may be expected to act like parents. Does your place in the family have an effect on you as an adult? In your topic sentence, state what role your place in the family played in your development: *Being the _____ child in my family has made me _____.* Proofread for fragments.

Writing Assignment 3: *Write about someone who changed jobs.* Did you, someone you know, or someone you know about change jobs because of a new interest or love for something else? Describe the person's first job and feelings of job satisfaction (or lack of them). What happened to make the person want to make a job switch? How long did the switch take? Was it difficult or easy to accomplish? Describe the person's new job and feelings of job satisfaction (or lack of them). Proofread for fragments.

Writing Assignment 4: *Ask for a raise.* Compose a memo to a boss, real or imagined, attempting to persuade him or her to raise your pay. In your first sentence, state that you are asking for an increase. Be specific: note how the quality of your work, your extra hours, or any special projects you have been involved in have made the business run more smoothly or become more profitable. Do not sound vain, but do praise yourself honestly. Use the memo style shown here. Proofread for fragments.

MEMORANDUM

DATE: Today's date

TO: Your boss's name

FROM: Your name

SUBJECT: Salary Increase

REVIEW

Proofreading and Revising

Proofread the following essay to eliminate all sentence fragments. Circle the number of every fragment. (You should find nine.) Then correct the fragments in any way you choose—by connecting them to a sentence before or after, by completing any incomplete verbs, and so on. Make your corrections above the lines.

Living Without Television

(1) What would you do without your television? (2) Every spring, millions of Americans answer this question for themselves. (3) By taking part in TV Turn-Off Week. (4) They find out that they can in fact lead enjoyable lives without watching TV. (5) Begun in 1995, TV Turn-Off Week now has motivated 24 million participants to spend seven full days. (6) Engaging in activities other than TV viewing. (7) Although many Turn-Off Week participants initially fear that they will be bored without their TVs. (8) They often rediscover the joys of reading, talking to family and friends, going for walks, exercising, and learning new skills like playing the guitar.

(9) Statistics help explain the power of TV Turn-Off Week. (10) Americans watch more than four hours of TV a day. (11) That's two full months each year. (12) Simply turning off the box leaves people with lots of time to do other things. (13) Nearly half of the U.S. population watches TV while eating dinner. (14) Instead of using that time to talk to other family members. (15) Because 56 percent of children have a television set in their bedrooms. (16) They tend to watch programs alone instead of doing homework, interacting with their parents and siblings, or exercising.

(17) Interestingly, the consequences of TV Turn-Off Week seem to be lasting. (18) Many past participants say that they have changed their viewing habits. (19) While a few people go so far as to get rid of their televisions. (20) Most report that they now watch fewer shows. (21) And are less likely to leave the TV sputtering as unwatched background noise. (22) Some move their televisions. (23) Taking them out of bedrooms and the family room. (24) Others cancel or reduce their cable or satellite services. (25) One major benefit is that individuals and families prove to themselves that they can find other, more engaging things to do.

(26) Many parents gain confidence about limiting their children's viewing time.

(27) And more important, about teaching their children how and when to watch TV.

 EXPLORING ONLINE

Turn off all the TVs in your house for one week, keeping notes on any reactions or changes. Use these notes to write about the experience.

<http://tvturnoff.org/> Visit the website and read for ideas. See "Facts and Figures." Then use this information in a composition arguing for or against watching less TV.

WRITERS' WORKSHOP
Discuss an Event That Influenced You

Readers of a final draft can easily forget that they are reading the *end result* of someone else's writing process. The following paragraph is one student's response to the assignment *Write about an event in history that influenced you.*

   In your class or group, read it aloud if possible. As you read, underline any words or lines that strike you as especially powerful.

> Though the Vietnam War ended almost before I was born, it changed my life. My earliest memory is of my father. A grizzled Vietnam warrior who came back spat upon, with one less brother. He wore a big smile playing ball with my brother and me, but even then I felt the grin was a coverup. When the postwar reports were on, his face became despondent. What haunted his heart and mind, I could not know, but I tried in my childish way to reason with him. A simple "It'll be all right, Dad" would bring a bleak smirk to his face. When he was happy, I was happy. When he was down, I was down. Soon the fatherly horseplay stopped, and once-full bottles of liquor were empty. He was there in body. Yet not there. Finally, he was physically gone. Either working a sixty-hour week or out in the streets after a furious fight with my mother. Once they divorced, she moved us to another state. I never came to grips with the turmoil inside my father. I see him as an intricate puzzle, missing one piece. That piece is his humanity, tangled up in history and blown up by a C-19.
>
> *Brian Pereira, student*

1. How effective is Brian Pereira's paragraph?

   _____ Good topic sentence?   _____ Rich supporting details?

   _____ Logical organization?   _____ Effective conclusion?

2. Discuss your underlinings with the group or class. Did others underline the same parts? Explain why you feel particular words or details are effective. For instance, the strong words *bleak smirk* say so much about the father's hopeless mood and the distance between him and his young son.

3. The topic sentence says that the writer's life changed, yet the body of the paragraph speaks mostly about his troubled father. Does the body of the paragraph explain the topic sentence?

4. What order, if any, does this writer follow?

5. If you do not know what a "C-19" is in the last sentence, does that make the conclusion less effective for you?

6. Would you suggest any changes or revisions?

7. Proofread for grammar and spelling. Do you notice any error patterns (two or more errors of the same type) that this student should watch out for?

> Brian Pereira's fine paragraph was the end result of a difficult writing process. Pereira describes his process this way:
>
> > The floor in my room looked like a writer's battleground of crumpled papers. Before this topic was assigned, I had not the slightest idea that this influence even existed, much less knew what it was. I thought hard, started a sentence or two, and threw a smashed paper down in disgust, over and over again. After hours, I realized it—the event in history that influenced me was Vietnam, even though I was too young to remember it! That became my topic sentence.

Writing and Revising Ideas

1. Discuss an event that influenced you.

2. Choose your best recent paper and describe your own writing process—what you did well and not so well.

For help with writing your paragraph, see Chapter 3 and Chapter 4, Part B (see "Time Order"). Give yourself plenty of time to revise. Stick with it, trying to write the best possible paper. Pay special attention to fully supporting your topic with interesting facts and details.

UNIT 3

Using Verbs Effectively

Every sentence contains at least one verb. Because verbs often are action words, they add interest and punch to any piece of writing. In this unit, you will

- Learn to use present, past, and other verb tenses correctly
- Learn when to add -*s* or -*ed*
- Recognize and use past participle forms
- Recognize -*ing* verbs, infinitives, and other special forms

Spotlight on Writing

Notice how vividly this writer describes the scene before him. His verbs are underlined.

Russell Thomas <u>places</u> the toe of his right sneaker one inch behind the three-point line. Inspecting the basket with a level gaze, he <u>bends</u> twice at the knees, <u>raises</u> the ball to shoot, then suddenly <u>looks</u> around. What <u>is</u> it? <u>Has</u> he <u>spotted</u> me, watching from the opposite end of the playground? No, something else <u>is</u> up. He <u>is lifting</u> his nose to the wind like a spaniel; he <u>appears</u> to be gauging air currents. Russell <u>waits</u> until the wind <u>settles</u>, bits of trash feathering lightly to the ground. Then he <u>sends</u> a twenty-five-foot jump shot arcing through the soft summer twilight. It <u>drops</u> without a sound through the dead center of the bare iron rim. So <u>does</u> the next one. So <u>does</u> the one after that. Alone in the gathering dusk, Russell <u>begins</u> to work the perimeter against imaginary defenders, unspooling jump shots from all points.

Darcy Frey, *The Last Shot*

- Simple but well-chosen verbs help bring this description to life. Which verbs most effectively help you see and experience the scene?

- Do you think that the writer realistically captures this young athlete at practice? What, if anything, do you learn about Russell Thomas—his abilities, personality, even his loves—from reading this short passage?

 Writing Ideas

- *A person practicing or performing some sport, art, or task*

- *A time when you watched or overheard someone in a public place*

CHAPTER 8

Present Tense (Agreement)

PART A Defining Agreement

A subject and a present tense verb **agree** if you use the correct form of the verb with each subject. The chart below shows which form of the verb to use for each kind of pronoun subject (we discuss other kinds of subjects later).

Verbs in the Present Tense
(*example verb: to write*)

Singular		Plural	
If the subject is	the verb is	If the subject is	the verb is
↓	↓	↓	↓
1st person: I	write	1st person: we	write
2nd person: you	write	2nd person: you	write
3rd person: he, she, it	writes	3rd person: they	write

PRACTICE 1

Fill in the correct present tense form of the verb.

1. You *ask* questions.	1. He _____ questions.
2. They *decide*.	2. She _____ .
3. I *remember*.	3. He _____ .
4. They *wear* glasses.	4. She _____ glasses.
5. We *hope* so.	5. He _____ so.
6. I *laugh* often.	6. She _____ often.
7. We *study* daily.	7. He _____ daily.
8. He *amazes* me.	8. It _____ me.

Add *-s* or *-es* to a verb in the present tense only when the subject is *third person singular (he, she, it)*.

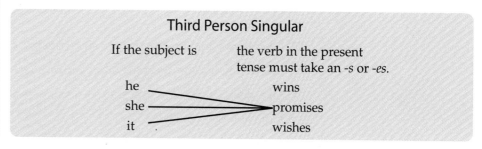

Third Person Singular

If the subject is   the verb in the present
                          tense must take an *-s* or *-es*.

he   wins
she ─────────────────promises
it   wishes

PRACTICE 2

Write the correct form of the verb in the space to the right of the pronoun subject.

EXAMPLE: **to see**   I _____ see _____

                                     they _____ see _____

                                     she _____ sees _____

to find	**to ask**	**to go**
he _____	I _____	it _____
they _____	she _____	you _____
you _____	he _____	we _____

to rest	**to hold**	**to select**
I _____	it _____	she _____
they _____	we _____	he _____
she _____	you _____	I _____

PRACTICE 3

First, underline the subject (always a pronoun) in each sentence below. Then circle the correct verb form. REMEMBER: If the subject of the sentence is *he, she,* or *it* (third person singular), the verb must end in *-s* or *-es* to agree with the subject.

1. According to researcher Deborah Tannen, we sometimes (fail, fails) to under-

    stand how men and women communicate on the job.

2. When working together, they sometimes (differ, differs) in predictable ways.

3. In Tannen's book *Talking from 9 to 5: Women and Men at Work,* she (describe, describes) the following misunderstanding between Amy, a manager, and Donald, her employee.

4. She (read, reads) Donald's report and (find, finds) it unacceptable.

5. She (meet, meets) with him to discuss the necessary revisions.

6. To soften the blow, she (praise, praises) the report's strengths.

7. Then, she (go, goes) on to explain in detail the needed revisions.

8. The next day, he (submit, submits) a second draft with only tiny changes.

9. She (think, thinks) that Donald did not listen to her.

10. He (believe, believes) that Amy first liked his report, then changed her mind.

11. According to the author, they (represent, represents) different communication styles.

12. Like many women supervisors, she (criticize, criticizes) gently, adding positive comments to protect the other person's feelings.

13. Like many male employees, he (expect, expects) more direct—and to him, more honest—criticism.

14. Tannen says that both styles make sense, but they (cause, causes) confusion if not understood.

15. Stereotypes or truth? You (decide, decides) for yourself about the accuracy of Tannen's analysis.

PART B   Troublesome Verb in the Present Tense: TO BE

A few present tense verbs are formed in special ways. The most common of these verbs is *to be.*

Reference Chart: TO BE
(*present tense*)

Singular		Plural	
If the subject is	the verb is	If the subject is	the verb is
↓	↓	↓	↓
1st person: I	am	1st person: we	are
2nd person: you	are	2nd person: you	are
3rd person: he she it	is	3rd person: they	are

This chart can also be read as shown at the top of the next page.

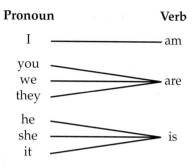

Pronoun	Verb
I	am
you we they	are
he she it	is

PRACTICE 4

Use the charts to fill in the present tense form of *to be* that agrees with the subject.

1. She _____ a member of the Olympic softball team.

2. We _____ both carpenters, but he _____ more skilled than I am.

3. I _____ sorry about your accident; you _____ certainly unlucky with rollerblades.

4. They _____ salmon fishermen.

5. He _____ a gifted website designer.

6. Because she _____ a native of Morocco, she _____ able to speak both Arabic and French.

7. I _____ too nervous to sleep because we _____ having an accounting exam tomorrow.

8. So you _____ the one we have heard so much about!

9. It _____ freezing outside, but he _____ opening all the windows.

10. If it _____ sunny tomorrow, they _____ going hot-air ballooning.

PART C   Troublesome Verb in the Present Tense: TO HAVE

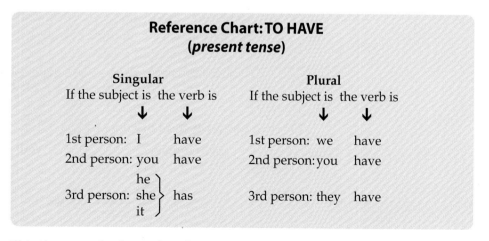

Reference Chart: TO HAVE
(*present tense*)

Singular		**Plural**	
If the subject is	the verb is	If the subject is	the verb is
↓	↓	↓	↓
1st person: I	have	1st person: we	have
2nd person: you	have	2nd person: you	have
3rd person: he she it	has	3rd person: they	have

This chart can also be read as shown at the top of the next page.

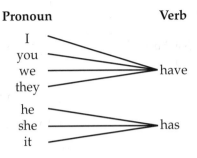

PRACTICE 5

Fill in the present tense form of *to have* that agrees with the subject. Use the charts.

1. He _____ a cabin on Lake Superior.

2. You _____ a wonderful sense of style.

3. ·We _____ to taste these pickled mushrooms.

4. It _____ to be spring because the cherry trees _____ pink blossoms.

5. She _____ the questions, and he _____ the answers.

6. You _____ a suspicious look on your face, and I _____ to know why.

7. They _____ plans to build a fence, but we _____ plans to relax.

8. You _____ one ruby earring, and she _____ the other.

9. It _____ to be repaired, and I _____ just the person to do it for you.

10. If you _____ $50, they _____ an offer you can't refuse.

PART D   Troublesome Verb in the Present Tense: TO DO (+ NOT)

Reference Chart: TO DO
(*present tense*)

Singular		**Plural**	
If the subject is	the verb is	If the subject is	the verb is
↓	↓	↓	↓
1st person: I	do	1st person: we	do
2nd person: you	do	2nd person: you	do
3rd person: he she it	does	3rd person: they	do

The chart can also be read like this:

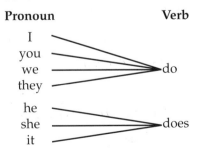

PRACTICE 6

Use the charts to fill in the correct present tense form of *to do*.

1. She always _____ well in math courses.

2. I always _____ badly under pressure.

3. It _____ matter if you forget to vote.

4. They most certainly _____ sell muscle shirts.

5. You _____ the nicest things for people!

6. If you _____ the dishes, I'll _____ the laundry.

7. He _____ seem sorry about forgetting your dog's birthday.

8. You sometimes _____ surprise me.

9. _____ they dance the tarantella?

10. _____ she want to be a welder?

To Do + Not

Once you know how to use *do* and *does,* you are ready for *don't* and *doesn't.*

$$do + not = don't$$
$$does + not = doesn't$$

PRACTICE 7

In the Positive columns, fill in the correct form of *to do* (*do* or *does*) to agree with the pronoun. In the Negative columns, fill in the correct form of *to do* with the negative *not* (*don't* or *doesn't*).

Pronoun	Positive *do/does*	Negative *don't/doesn't*
1. he	does	doesn't
2. we	do	don't
3. I	do	don't
4. they	do	don't
5. she	does	doesn't
6. it	does	doesn't
7. they	do	don't
8. you	do	dont

PRACTICE 8

Fill in either *doesn't* or *don't* in each blank.

1. If they __don't__ turn down that music, I'm going to scream.

2. It just __doesn't__ make sense.

3. You __don't__ have to reply in writing.

4. He __doesn't__ always lock his door at night.

Handwritten margin notes:
TO HAVE
HE / SHE / IT → HAS – DOES
I / WE / THEY / YOU → HAVE – DO

5. We _don't_ mind the rain.

6. If she _doesn't_ stop calling collect, I _don't_ want to talk to her.

7. He _doesn't_ know the whole truth, and they _don't_ want to know.

8. They _don't_ want to miss *Larry King Live* tonight.

9. Although you _don't_ like biking five miles a day to work, it _doesn't_ do your health any harm.

10. When I _don't_ try, I _don't_ succeed.

PRACTICE 9

Review

As you read this paragraph, fill in the correct present tense form of *to be*, *to have*, or *to do* in each blank. Make sure all your verbs agree with their subjects.

(1) He _has_ the expertise of a James Bond or Lara Croft, but he _does_ the real thing, not a movie hero performing fantasy stunts. (2) Right now, he _is_ calm, even though he _is_ ready to leap from the open door of a Navy aircraft. (3) On his back he _has_ an oversized parachute capable of supporting both him and the extra hundred pounds of special equipment packed in his combat vest. (4) When he _does_ hit the water, he _is to be_ ready to face the real challenge: finding and defusing a bomb sixty feet under rough, murky seas. (5) He _has_ a mission and a very tight time frame, and he _does_ not want to let the enemy know he _is to be_ there. (6) Swimming underwater in special scuba gear, he _does_ not release any air bubbles to mark the water's surface. (7) Working in semidarkness, performing dangerous technical tasks, he quickly _does_ the job. (8) However, unlike media heroes, he _does_ n't work alone. (9) He _is to be_ a member of a highly trained team of Navy SEALs. (10) Among the most respected special forces in the world, they _have_ commando divers ready for hazardous duty on sea, air, and land.

PART E   Changing Subjects to Pronouns

So far, you have worked on pronouns as subjects (*I, you, he, she, it, we, they*) and on how to make verbs agree with them. Often, however, the subject of a sentence is not a pronoun but a noun—like *dog, banjo, Ms. Callas, José and Robert, swimming* (as in *Swimming keeps me fit*).

To be sure that your verb agrees with your subject, *mentally* change the subject into a pronoun and then select the correct form of the verb.

Reference Chart: Subject-Verb Agreement

If the subject is	it can be changed to the pronoun
1. the speaker himself or herself ──────────────→	I
2. masculine and singular ──────────────→ (*Bill, one man*)	he
3. feminine and singular ──────────────→ (*Sondra, a woman*)	she
4. neither masculine nor feminine and singular (a thing or an action) ──────────────→ (*this pen, love, running*)	it
5. a group that includes the speaker (I) ──────────────→ (*the family and I*)	we
6. a group of persons or things not including the speaker ──────────────→ (*Jake and Wanda, several pens*)	they
7. the person or persons spoken to ──────────────→	you

PRACTICE 10

Change the subjects into pronouns. REMEMBER: If you add *I* to a group of people, the correct pronoun for the whole group is *we*; if you add *you* to a group, the correct pronoun for the whole group is *you*.

Possible Subject	Pronoun
EXAMPLE: Frank	*he*
1. a huge moose	it
2. a calculator and a checkbook	they
3. Sheila	she
4. my buddies and I	we
5. you and the other actors	you
6. the silk scarf	it
7. Frank and Ted	they
8. her son	he
9. their power drill	it
10. scuba diving	it

PRACTICE 11

Review

Change each subject into a pronoun. Then circle the present tense verb that agrees with that subject. (Use the reference chart on this page if you need to.)

EXAMPLES: Harry = ___*he*___   Harry (whistle, (whistles)).

Sam and I = ___*we*___   Sam and I ((walk), walks).

1. Camilla = ___She___
2. Their concert = ___it___
3. You and Ron = ___you___
4. The men and I = ___we___
5. This blender = ___it___
6. This beach = ___it___
7. Our printer = ___it___
8. Folk dancing = ___it___
9. The museum and garden = ___they___
10. Aunt Lil and I = ___we___

1. Camilla (own, **owns**) a horse farm.
2. Their concert (**is**, are) sold out.
3. You and Ron (**seem**, seems) exhausted.
4. The men and I (**repair**, repairs) potholes.
5. This blender (grate, **grates**) cheese.
6. This beach (**is**, are) deserted.
7. Our printer (jam, **jams**) too often.
8. Folk dancing (**is**, are) our current passion.
9. The museum and garden (is, **are**) open.
10. Aunt Lil and I (**like**, likes) Swedish massages.

PART F Practice in Agreement

PRACTICE 12

Review

Circle the correct verb in each sentence, making sure it agrees with its subject.

More Than Skin-Deep

WOMAN (1)
WOMEN (2)

(1) The television show *Ugly Betty* (**entertains**, entertain) viewers and also (**makes** make) them think. (2) This combination (**does**, do) not often occur in American television. (3) The main character, Betty, (**works**, work) for a snooty high-fashion magazine. (4) Her coworkers (claws, **claw**) their way up the career ladder. (5) Stick-thin women (prances, **prance**) through the offices. (6) In this environment, Betty (**is**, are) the "ugly girl," with blue braces, a normal-size body, and a wacky wardrobe. (7) Viewers (watches, **watch**) as Betty (**works**, work) hard and (**struggles**, struggle) with ethical choices. (8) Her dreams and troubles (reveals, **reveal**) the shallowness of a world where appearances often (matters, **matter**) more than substance.

America Ferrera as *Ugly Betty*. What details of her appearance might contribute to her "fashion outcast" reputation?

The Everett Collection.

(9) The brilliant cast (has, have) a lot to do with this show's success. (10) Actresses with top film credits (includes, include) Salma Hayek, Vanessa Williams, and the star, America Ferrera. (11) Their skills (brings, bring) depth to their characters. (12) In reality a beautiful woman, Ferrera (wears, wear) heavy makeup, dentures, and false eyebrows to become "ugly." (13) Even though viewers (laughs, laugh) at her character's habit of walking into doors and unique fashion selections, Betty's inner beauty always (shines, shine) through. (14) By focusing on ethical issues and making viewers look critically at our culture, *Ugly Betty* (goes, go) deeper than skin-deep.

PRACTICE 13

Review

In each blank, write the *present tense* form of one of the verbs from this list. Your sentences can be funny; just make sure that each verb agrees with each subject.

leap	spin	yip	woof	attend	win	compete
go	love	try	prance	wiggle	fly	encourage

(1) Dogs of every size and shape, their owners, and visitors all _____love_____ the Great American Mutt Show. (2) Sponsored by Tails in Need,

the Mutt Show _encourages_ people to adopt mixed-breed dogs instead of buying pure breeds. (3) Pooches _competes_ in categories like Mostly Terrier, Most Misbehaved, Best Kisser, and Best Lap Dog Over 50 Pounds. (4) In one event, a shepherd mix named Top Gun _flies_ through the air to be crowned Best Jumper while a beagle named Jack _wiggles_ his stumpy tail, energetically claiming the coveted trophy for Best Wag. (5) Four-legged hopefuls _yips_ and _woofes_, trying to snag the award for Best Bark. (6) The proud winner of Best in Show _goes_ home with a trophy designed by Michael Graves—a red fire hydrant topped by a golden bone.

PRACTICE 14

Review

The sentences that follow have singular subjects and verbs. To gain skill in verb agreement, rewrite each sentence, changing the subject from *singular* to *plural*. Then make sure the verb agrees with the new subject. Keep all verbs in the present tense.

EXAMPLE: The train stops at Cold Spring.

Rewrite: The trains stop at Cold Spring.

1. The movie tickets costs too much.

   Rewrite: the movie tickets cost too much

2. The pipeline carries oil from Alaska.

   Rewrite: the pipelines carrie oil from Alaska

3. A white horse grazes by the fence.

   Rewrite: a white horses grazes by the fence

4. My brother knows American Sign Language.

   Rewrite: My brothers know American sign language

5. The family needs good health insurance.

   Rewrite: the families need good health insurance

6. The backup singer wears green contact lenses.

   Rewrite: the backup singers wear green contact

7. My niece wants an iguana.

   Rewrite: My nieces wants an iguana

8. A wave laps softly against the dock.

   Rewrite: waves lap sofltly against the dock.

PRACTICE 15

Review

The sentences that follow have plural subjects and verbs. Rewrite each sentence, changing the subject from *plural* to *singular*. Then make sure the verb agrees with the new subject. Keep all verbs in the present tense.

1. My cousins raise sheep.

   Rewrite: _My cousin raises sheep_

2. The engines roar loudly.

   Rewrite: _the engine roar loudly._

3. The students manage money wisely.

   Rewrite: _the student manages money wisely_

4. The inmates watch *America's Most Wanted*.

   Rewrite: _the inmate watchs American's most Wanted_

5. Overhead, seagulls ride on the wind.

   Rewrite: _Overhead, seagull rides on the Wind_

6. Good card players know when to bluff.

   Rewrite: _Good card player Knows When to bluff_

7. On Saturday, the pharmacists stay late.

   Rewrite: _on Saturday, the pharmacist stays late_

8. The jewels from Bangkok are on display.

   Rewrite: _the Jewel From Bangkok is on display._

PRACTICE 16

Review

Rewrite this paragraph in the present tense by changing the verbs. Write the present tense form of each verb above the lines. (Hint: You should change twenty-two verbs.)

(1) A six-month-old in a highchair watched [watshes] intently as his father whacked [whackes] golf balls into a net in the family garage. (2) When the baby started [startes] to walk, his parents gave [give] him a short putter, which he dragged [drages] around the house. (3) When he was [he is] nine months old, he carefully picked [pickes] up the putter. (4) The child did [does] an exact imitation of his father's hip swivel, swung [swings], and sent [sends] the ball perfectly into the net.

(5) Thunderstruck, the father and mother realized that they had a golf genius on *[realize]* *[they have]* their hands. (6) From the age of eighteen months, the toddler practiced his pitch *[practices]* and putt strokes on a golf course. (7) At age three, on a TV show, the little boy exclaimed that he wanted to beat Jack Nicklaus someday. (8) In fact, he did that at *[exclaimes]* *[wantes]* *[does]* age twenty-one, winning the Masters with the lowest score in tournament history. (9) Suddenly, people all over the world knew the name Tiger Woods. (10) At *[Knows]* twenty-four, Tiger shattered U.S. Open records by a twelve under par and a *[Shatteres]* fifteen-stroke victory and tied Nicklaus's record of the lowest score ever in a U.S. *[Ties]* Open. (11) His influence was enormous. (12) Young people saw golf as exciting, *[is]* *[see]* and the game had thousands of new fans. *[has]*

PART G Special Problems in Agreement

So far, you have learned that if the subject of a sentence is third person singular (*he, she, it*) or a word that can be changed into *he, she,* or *it*, the verb takes *-s* or *-es* in the present tense.

In special cases, however, you will need to know more before you can make your verb agree with your subject.

Focusing on the Subject

(1) A box of chocolates sits on the table.

- *What* sits on the table?
- Don't be confused by the prepositional phrase before the verb—*of chocolates.*
- Just one *box* sits on the table.
- *A box* is the subject. *A box* takes the third person singular verb—*sits.*

A box (of chocolates) sits on the table.
↓ ↓
subject verb
(*singular*) (*singular*)

(2) The children in the park play for hours.

- *Who* play for hours?
- Don't be confused by the prepositional phrase before the verb—*in the park.*
- *The children* play for hours.
- *The children* is the subject. *The children* takes the third person plural verb—*play.*

The children (in the park) play for hours.

↓   ↓

subject   verb
(*plural*)   (*plural*)

(3) The purpose of the exercises is to improve your spelling.

● *What* is to improve your spelling?

● Don't be confused by the prepositional phrase before the verb—*of the exercises*.

● *The purpose* is to improve your spelling.

● *The purpose* is the subject. *The purpose* takes the third person singular verb—*is*.

The purpose (of the exercises) is to improve your spelling.

↓   ↓

subject   verb
(*singular*)   (*singular*)

As you can see from these examples, sometimes what seems to be the subject is really not the subject. Prepositional phrases (groups of words beginning with *of, in, at,* and so on) *cannot* contain the subject of a sentence. One way to find the subject of a sentence that contains a prepositional phrase is to ask yourself *what makes sense as the subject*.

My friends from the old neighborhood often { visits / visit } me.

● Which makes sense as the subject of the sentence: *my friends* or *the old neighborhood*?

(a) My friends . . . visit me.   (b) The old neighborhood . . .
                                             visits me.

● Obviously, sentence (a) makes sense; it clearly expresses the intention of the writer.

PRACTICE 17

In each of these sentences, cross out any confusing prepositional phrases and circle the correct verbs.

1. Greetings around the world (differs, (differ)) from culture to culture.

2. A resident of the United States ((shakes), shake) hands firmly to say hello.

3. Kisses on each check (is, (are)) customary greetings in Latin America and southern Europe.

4. Natives of Hawaii (hugs, (hug)) and (exchanges, (exchange)) breaths in a custom called *alo ha* (sharing of life breath).

5. The Maori people of New Zealand (presses, (press)) noses to greet each other.

6. A person in traditional Japanese circles ((bows), bow) upon meeting someone.

7. A custom among Pakistanis ((is), are) the *salaam,* bowing with the right hand on the forehead.

8. Hindus in India (folds, *fold*) the hands and (tilts, *tilt*) the head forward.

9. The Hindi word for the greeting (*is*, are) *namaste*.

10. This word (*means*, mean) "The divine in me (*salutes*, salute) the divine in you."

Spotting Special Singular Subjects

Either of the students
Neither of the students
Each of the students   } seems happy.
One of the students
Every one of the students

● *Either, neither, each, one,* and *every one* are the real subjects of these sentences.

● *Either, neither, each, one,* and *every one* are special singular subjects. They always take a singular verb.

● REMEMBER: The subject is never part of a prepositional phrase, so *the students* cannot be the subject.

PRACTICE 18

Circle the correct verb.

1. One of the forks (*is*, are) missing.

2. Each of my brothers (wear, *wears*) cinnamon after-shave lotion.

3. Each of us (carry, *carries*) a snakebite kit.

4. Neither of those excuses (sound, *sounds*) believable.

5. One of the taxi drivers (see, *sees*) us.

6. Either of the watches (cost, *costs*) about $30.

7. Neither of those cities (*is*, are) the capital of Brazil.

8. One of the butlers (commit, *commits*) the crime, but which one?

9. One of the desserts in front of you (do, *does*) not contain sugar.

10. Each of the cars (have, *has*) a CD player.

PRACTICE 19

On a separate sheet of paper, write five sentences using the special singular subjects. Make sure your sentences are in the present tense.

Using THERE to Begin a Sentence

(1) *There* is a squirrel in the yard.

(2) *There* are two squirrels in the yard.

● Although sentences sometimes begin with *there, there* cannot be the subject of a sentence.

● Usually, the subject *follows* the verb in sentences that begin with *there.*

To find the real subject (so you will know how to make the verb agree), mentally drop the word *there* and rearrange the sentence to put the subject at the beginning.

(1) There is a squirrel in the yard.
becomes

A squirrel	*is* in the yard.
↓	↓
subject	verb
(*singular*)	(*singular*)

(2) There are two squirrels in the yard.
becomes

Two squirrels	*are* in the yard.
↓	↓
subject	verb
(*plural*)	(*plural*)

BE CAREFUL: Good writers avoid using *there* to begin a sentence. Whenever possible, they write more directly: *Two squirrels are in the yard.*

PRACTICE 20

In each sentence, mentally drop the word *there* and rearrange the sentence to put the subject at the beginning. Then circle the verb that agrees with the subject of the sentence.

1. There (is, are) a daycare center on campus.

2. There (is, are) a scarecrow near the barn.

3. There (is, are) two scarecrows near the barn.

4. There (is, are) one good reason to quit this job—my supervisor.

5. There (is, are) six customers ahead of you.

6. There (is, are) a water fountain in the lounge.

7. There (is, are) a house and a barn in the wheat field.

8. There (is, are) only two shopping days left before my birthday.

9. There (is, are) thousands of plant species in the rain forest.

10. There (is, are) a single blue egg in the nest over the kitchen door.

PRACTICE 21

On paper or on a computer, rewrite each sentence in Practice 20 so that it does not begin with *there is* or *there are*. (You may add or change a word or two if you like.) Sentences (1) and (2) are done for you.

EXAMPLES: 1. *A daycare center is on campus.*

               2. *A scarecrow hangs near the barn.*

Choosing the Correct Verb in Questions

(1) Where is Bob?

(2) Where are Bob and Lee?

(3) Why are they singing?

(4) Have you painted the hall yet?

- In questions, the subject usually *follows* the verb.

- In sentence (1), the subject is *Bob*. *Bob* takes the third person singular verb *is*.

- In sentence (2), the subject is *Bob and Lee*. *Bob and Lee* takes the third person plural verb *are*.

- What is the subject in sentence (3)? _____ What verb does it take?

  _____

- What is the subject in sentence (4)? _____ What verb does it take?

  _____

If you can't find the subject, mentally turn the question around:

(1) Bob is . . .

(2) Bob and Lee are . . .

PRACTICE 22

Circle the correct verb.

1. Where (is, are) my leather bomber jacket?

2. (Have, Has) our waiter gone to lunch?

3. How (is, are) your children enjoying summer camp?

4. Who (is, are) those people on the fire escape?

5. Which (is, are) your day off?

6. Why (do, does) she want to buy another motorcycle?

7. (Have, Has) you considered taking a cruise next year?

8. Where (is, are) Don's income tax forms?

9. (Have, Has) the groundhog raided the zucchini patch today?

10. Well, what (do, does) you know about that?

PRACTICE 23

On paper or on a computer, write five questions of your own. Make sure that your questions are in the present tense and that the verbs agree with the subjects.

Using WHO, WHICH, and THAT as Relative Pronouns

When you use a **relative pronoun**—*who, which,* or *that*—to introduce a dependent idea, make sure you choose the correct verb.*

(1) I know a woman *who* plays expert chess.

● Sentence (1) uses the singular verb *plays* because *who* relates or refers to *a woman* (singular).

(2) Suede coats, *which* stain easily, should not be worn in the rain.

● Sentence (2) uses the plural verb *stain* because *which* relates to the subject *suede coats* (plural).

(3) Computers *that* talk make me nervous.

● Sentence (3) uses the plural verb *talk* because *that* relates to what word?

_____

PRACTICE 24

Write the word that *who, which,* or *that* relates or refers to in the blank at the right; then circle the correct form of the verb.

EXAMPLE: I like people who (is, are) creative.   ____*people*____

1. My office has a robot that (fetch, fetches) the mail.   _____

2. Never buy food in cans that (have, has) dents in them.   _____

3. My husband, who (take, takes) marvelous photographs,

   won the Nikon Prize.   _____

4. He likes women who (is, are) very ambitious.   _____

5. The old house, which (sit, sits) on a cliff above the sea, is

   called Balston Heights.   _____

6. Students who (love, loves) to read usually write well.   _____

_____

*For work on relative pronouns, see Chapter 17.

7. I like a person who (think, thinks) for himself or herself. _____

8. The only airline that (fly, flies) to Charlottesville is
   booked solid. _____

9. People who (live, lives) in glass houses should invest
   in blinds. _____

10. Most students want jobs that (challenge, challenges) them. _____

PRACTICE 25

Review

Proofread the following paragraph for a variety of verb agreement errors. First, underline all present tense verbs. Then correct any errors above the lines.

(1) Many people who love exciting theater admires Anna Deavere Smith. (2) She is well known for her thought-provoking plays. (3) Many of these dramas explores social conflicts in America, bringing important issues to life through the voices of different characters. (4) Smith's newest play, *House Arrest: First Edition*, probe the relationship between the media and the White House. (5) Politicians, journalists, and worried citizens, played by a variety of actors, all speak out. (6) In other shows, Smith brilliantly plays all the roles herself. (7) For example, one show, *Twilight: Los Angeles 1992*, examine the L.A. riots and the beatings of Rodney King and Reginald Denny. (8) Smith, who is African American, movingly expresses the feelings of white people, black people, Korean shopkeepers, angry rioters, and frightened citizens. (9) Once a shy and withdrawn child, Anna Deavere Smith works to open herself to the experiences of others. (10) She believe that both successful acting and successful democracy requires us to grow in tolerance.

PRACTICE 26

Writing Assignment

In a group of three or four classmates, choose an area of the building or campus that contains some interesting action—the hallway, the cafeteria, or a playing field. Go there now and observe what you see, recording details and using verbs in the present tense. Choose as many dynamic action verbs as you can. Keep observing and writing for ten minutes. Then head back to the classroom and write a first draft of a paragraph.

Next, exchange papers within your group. The reader should underline every verb, checking for verb agreement, and tell the writer what he or she liked about the writing and what could be improved.

CHAPTER HIGHLIGHTS

- **A subject and a present tense verb must agree:**

    The light flickers. (*singular subject, singular verb*)

    The lights flicker. (*plural subject, plural verb*)

- **Only third person singular subjects** (*he, she, it*) **take verbs ending in** *-s* **or** *-es.*

- **Three troublesome present tense verbs are** *to be, to have,* **and** *to do.*

- **When a prepositional phrase comes between a subject and a verb, the verb must agree with the subject.**

    The *chairs* on the porch *are* painted white.

- **The subjects** *either, neither, each, one,* **and** *every one* **are always singular.**

    Neither of the mechanics *repairs* transmissions.

- **In a sentence beginning with** *there is* **or** *there are,* **the subject follows the verb.**

    There are three *oysters* on your plate.

- **In questions, the subject usually follows the verb.**

    Where are *Kimi and Fred*?

- **Relative pronouns** (*who, which,* **and** *that*) **refer to the word with which the verb must agree.**

    A *woman who* has children must manage time skillfully.

CHAPTER REVIEW

Proofread this essay carefully for verb agreement. First, underline all present tense verbs. Then correct each verb agreement error.

Advantages and Disadvantages of Online Dating

(1) Every month, about 40 million Americans visits online dating sites like Match.com and Matchmaker.com. (2) In fact, these sites now make more money than any other paid service on the Web. (3) Clearly, many people no longer feels embarrassed about using a dating service. (4) But are websites really good places to find a mate? (5) You decide. (6) There is both advantages and disadvantages to cyberdating.

(7) Some busy people likes the convenience of online dating and the chance to meet people at any time of day or night. (8) The Web makes a better meeting place than bars, they argue. (9) In addition, the sites allow individuals to search for mates with certain qualities or characteristics. (10) According to supporters of cyberdating, this method also encourage people to get to know possible romantic partners better. (11) In cyberspace, they are less likely to be swept away by physical attraction alone.

(12) On the other hand, computer dating also have dangers and drawbacks. (13) Online, many people tends to lie about their physical appearance, age, profession, or personality traits. (14) According to a recent study, about three out of ten people using online sites are married. (15) Others has criminal backgrounds. (16) Therefore, safety remain a constant concern for cyberdaters. (17) Getting to know each other online takes more time. (18) Consequently, the online environment actually slow down the dating process instead of speeding it up.

 ## EXPLORING ONLINE

<http://depts.gallaudet.edu/englishworks/exercises/exgrammar/subver2.htm>
Verb crossword puzzle: Change past tense verbs to present tense.

<http://grammar.ccc.commnet.edu/grammar/quizzes/svagr3.html> Interactive quiz: Choose the correct verbs in this essay about soccer.

<http://college.cengage.com/devenglish> Visit the *Grassroots* 9/e student website for more exercises, quizzes, and live links to all websites mentioned in this chapter.

Past Tense

PART A   Regular Verbs in the Past Tense

Verbs in the past tense express actions that occurred in the past. The italicized words in the following sentences are verbs in the past tense.

> (1) They *noticed* a dent in the fender.
>
> (2) She *played* the guitar very well.
>
> (3) For years I *studied* yoga.

● What ending do all these verbs take? _____

● In general, what ending do you add to put a verb in the past tense? _____

● Verbs that add *-d* or *-ed* to form the past tense are called *regular verbs*.

PRACTICE 1

Some of the verbs in these sentences are in the present tense; others are in the past tense. Circle the verb in each sentence. Write *present* in the column at the right if the verb is in the present tense; write *past* if the verb is in the past tense.

1. Ricardo stroked his beard. _____

2. Light travels 186,000 miles in a second. _____

3. They donate blood every six months. _____

4. Magellan sailed around the world. _____

5. The lake looks as calm as glass. _____

6. Yesterday, Rover buried many bones. _____

7. Mount St. Helens erupted in 1980. _____

8. That chemical plant pollutes our water. _____

9. A robin nested in the mailbox. _____

10. He owns two exercise bikes. _____

PRACTICE 2

Change the verbs in this paragraph to past tense by writing the past tense form above each italicized verb.

(1) Again this year, Carnival *transforms* Rio de Janeiro, Brazil, into one of the most fantastic four-day parties on the planet. (2) On the Friday before Ash Wednesday, thousands of visitors *pour* into the city. (3) They *watch* all-night parades and *admire* the glittering costumes. (4) They *cheer, sweat,* and *dance* the samba. (5) Of course, preparation *starts* long before. (6) For months, members of the samba schools (neighborhood dance clubs) *plan* their floats, *practice* samba steps, and *stay* up for nights making their costumes. (7) Using bright fabrics, sequins, feathers, and chains, both men and women *create* spectacular outfits. (8) Each samba school *constructs* a float that *features* a smoke-breathing dragon or a spouting waterfall. (9) During Carnival, judges *rate* the schools on costumes, dancing, and floats, and then they *award* prizes. (10) Together, Brazilians and their visitors *share* great music, drink, food, fun, and the chance to go a little bit crazy.

As you can see from this exercise, many verbs form the past tense by adding either -*d* or -*ed*.

Furthermore, in the past tense, agreement is not a problem, except for the verb *to be*. This is because verbs in the past tense have only one form, no matter what the subject is.

PRACTICE 3

The verbs have been omitted from this paragraph. Choose verbs from the list below and write a past tense form in each blank space. Do not use any of the verbs twice.

arrive	cry	walk	help
install	climb	pound	learn
grab	hug	smile	work
paint	thank	shout	hurry

(1) Last month, Raoul and I _____ build a Habitat for Humanity house as part of our college's service learning program. (2) On the first day, we _____ at the construction site at dawn. (3) With three other volunteers, we _____ our hammers and _____ onto the roof. (4) We _____ nails for hours while other volunteers _____ the Sheetrock walls. (5) For three weeks, we _____ hard and _____ a lot about plumbing, wiring, and interior finishes. (6) On our last day, the new homeowners _____ with joy and _____ the whole crew.

PRACTICE 4

Fill in the past tense of each verb.

1. Erik Weihenmayer, blinded at age thirteen, _____ (dream) for years of climbing Mount Everest.

2. Mountaineers _____ (laugh) at the idea of a blind man scaling the world's tallest peak—a death trap of rock, wind, and cold.

3. But in 2001, Erik _____ (gather) a climbing team and _____ (start) the trek up Everest.

4. Before the climbers _____ (reach) the first of several camps on the way to the top, Erik _____ (slip) into a crevasse, but he _____ (survive).

5. When he finally _____ (stumble) into the first camp, weak and dehydrated, Erik _____ (wonder) whether he had made a serious mistake.

6. Nevertheless, he and his teammates _____ (vow) to continue the climb.

7. The group _____ (battle) upward through driving snow and icy winds.

8. Erik _____ (manage) to keep up and even _____ (edge) across the long, knife-blade ridge just below the peak, taking tiny steps and using his ice ax as an anchor.

9. Months after he began his journey, the blind mountaineer _____ (step) onto Everest's summit and _____ (stay) for ten minutes to savor his victory.

10. For many people around the world, this achievement _____ (symbolize) the nearly unstoppable human power to reach a goal.

Blind mountaineer Erik Weihenmayer successfully scaled Mount Everest.

Didrick Johnck/CORBIS/Sygma.

PART B   Irregular Verbs in the Past Tense

Instead of adding *-d* or *-ed,* some verbs form the past tense in other ways.

> (1) He *threw* a knuckle ball.
>
> (2) She *gave* him a dollar.
>
> (3) He *rode* from his farm into the town.

- The italicized words in these sentences are also verbs in the past tense.
- Do these verbs form the past tense by adding *-d* or *-ed*? _____
- *Threw, gave,* and *rode* are the past tense of verbs that do not add *-d* or *-ed* to form the past tense.
- Verbs that do not add *-d* or *-ed* to form the past tense are called *irregular verbs.*

A chart listing common irregular verbs follows.

Reference Chart: Irregular Verbs

Simple Form	Past	Simple Form	Past
be	was, were	lose	lost
become	became	make	made
begin	began	mean	meant
blow	blew	meet	met
break	broke	pay	paid
bring	brought	put	put
build	built	quit	quit
burst	burst	read	read
buy	bought	ride	rode
catch	caught	ring	rang
choose	chose	rise	rose
come	came	run	ran
cut	cut	say	said
dive	dove (dived)	see	saw
do	did	seek	sought
draw	drew	sell	sold
drink	drank	send	sent
drive	drove	set	set
eat	ate	shake	shook
fall	fell	shine	shone (shined)
feed	fed	shrink	shrank (shrunk)
feel	felt	sing	sang
fight	fought	sit	sat
find	found	sleep	slept
fly	flew	speak	spoke
forget	forgot	spend	spent
forgive	forgave	spring	sprang
freeze	froze	stand	stood
get	got	steal	stole
give	gave	strike	struck
go	went	swim	swam
grow	grew	swing	swung

Reference Chart: Irregular Verbs (*continued*)

Simple Form	Past	Simple Form	Past
have	had	take	took
hear	heard	teach	taught
hide	hid	tear	tore
hold	held	tell	told
hurt	hurt	think	thought
keep	kept	throw	threw
know	knew	understand	understood
lay	laid	wake	woke
lead	led	wear	wore
leave	left	win	won
let	let	wind	wound
lie	lay	write	wrote

Learn the unfamiliar past tense forms by grouping together verbs that change from present tense to past tense in the same way. For example, some irregular verbs change *ow* in the present to *ew* in the past:

blow	blew	know	knew
grow	grew	throw	threw

Another group changes from *i* in the present to *a* in the past:

begin	began	sing	sang
drink	drank	spring	sprang
ring	rang	swim	swam

As you write, refer to the chart. If you are unsure of the past tense form of a verb that is not in the chart, check a dictionary. For example, if you look up the verb *go* in the dictionary, you will find an entry like this:

go \ went \ gone \ going

The first word listed is used to form the *present* tense of the verb (I *go,* he *goes,* and so on). The second word is the *past* tense (I *went,* he *went,* and so on). The third word is the *past participle* (*gone*), and the last word is the *present participle* (*going*).

Some dictionaries list different forms only for irregular verbs. If no past tense is listed, you know that the verb is regular and that its past tense ends in *-d* or *-ed.*

PRACTICE 5

Use the chart to fill in the correct form of the verb in the past tense.

1. Beryl Markham _____ (grow) up in Kenya, East Africa.

2. As a child, this adventurer _____ (go) hunting with African tribesmen.

3. Once, while a lion attacked her, she _____ (lie) still, thus saving her own life.

4. At age seventeen, she _____ (seek) a license to train horses, becoming the first woman trainer in Kenya.

5. Her friend Tom Black _____ (teach) her how to fly a small plane, the *D. H. Gipsy Moth.*

6. By her late twenties, she _____ (be) a licensed pilot.

7. As Africa's first female bush pilot, Markham regularly _____ (fly) across East Africa, carrying supplies, mail, and passengers.

8. In 1936, she _____ (make) a solo flight across the Atlantic Ocean.

9. Despite poor flying conditions, fatigue, and low fuel, she _____ (keep) her plane in the air for more than twenty hours.

10. Markham _____ (set) a record as the first woman to fly alone non-stop from England to Nova Scotia.

11. In 1942, she _____ (write) *West with the Night,* a book about her thrilling life.

12. This book _____ (become) a classic.

PRACTICE 6

Use the chart to fill in the correct past tense form of each verb.

How to Find a Great Job

(1) Emma _____ (begin) her job search in an organized way. (2) She _____ (think) carefully about her interests and abilities. (3) She _____ (spend) time in the library and _____ (read) books like *What Color Is Your Parachute?* and *Job Hunting on the Internet.* (4) She also _____ (do) online research about interesting professions at sites like Career Infonet (**<http://www.acinet.org/acinet/>**). (5) She _____ (speak) to people with jobs that _____ (have) special appeal for her.

(6) After Emma _____ (understand) her own skills and goals, she _____ (write) a straightforward, one-page, error-free résumé. (7) Her clear objectives statement _____ (tell) prospective employers about her job preferences. (8) After listing her educational experience, she _____ (give) her past employment, with the most recent job first. (9) She _____ (choose) lively action verbs like *calculated, filed, oversaw,* and *inspected* to describe her responsibilities at each job. (10) Her references _____ (be) four people who _____ (know) her work well.

(11) At last, Emma _____ (feel) ready to answer newspaper ads, search for jobs online, and explore every lead she _____ (get). (12) She _____ (put) her résumé on the *monster.com* site so that hundreds of companies would see it. (13) Then, she _____ (take) a friend's good suggestion that they interview each other to practice their skills. (14) A few days later, the phone _____ (ring), and Emma _____ (make) preparations for her first job interview.

PRACTICE 7

Look over the list of irregular verbs on pages 120–121. Pick out the ten verbs that give you the most trouble and list them here.

Simple	Past	Simple	Past
_____	_____	_____	_____
_____	_____	_____	_____
_____	_____	_____	_____
_____	_____	_____	_____
_____	_____	_____	_____

Now, on paper or on a computer, write one paragraph using *all ten* verbs. Your paragraph may be humorous; just make sure your verbs are correct.

PART C   Troublesome Verb in the Past Tense: TO BE

Reference Chart: TO BE
(*past tense*)

	Singular		**Plural**
1st person:	I was ⟶		we were
2nd person:	you were ⟶		you were
3rd person:	he she } was ⟶ it		they were

● Note that the first and third person singular forms are the same—*was.*

PRACTICE 8

In each sentence, circle the correct past tense of the verb *to be*—either *was* or *were*.

1. Our instructor (was, were) a pilot and skydiver.
2. You always (was, were) a good friend.
3. Jorge Luis Borges (was, were) a great twentieth-century writer.
4. Why (was, were) they an hour early for the party?
5. I (was, were) seven when my sister (was, were) born.
6. Carmen (was, were) a Republican, but her cousins (was, were) Democrats.
7. The bride and groom (was, were) present, but where (was, were) the ring?
8. (Was, Were) you seasick on your new houseboat?
9. Either they (was, were) late, or she (was, were) early.
10. At this time last year, Sarni and I (was, were) in Egypt.

To Be + Not

Be careful of verb agreement if you use the past tense of *to be* with *not* as a contraction.

$$was + not = wasn't$$
$$were + not = weren't$$

PRACTICE 9

In each sentence, fill in the blank with either *wasn't* or *weren't*.

1. The printer cartridges _____ on sale.

2. That papaya _____ cheap.

3. He _____ happy about the opening of the nuclear power plant.

4. This fireplace _____ built properly.

5. The parents _____ willing to tolerate drug dealers near the school.

6. That _____ the point!

7. My pet lobster _____ in the aquarium.

8. That history quiz _____ so bad.

9. He and I liked each other, but we _____ able to agree about music.

10. Many young couples _____ able to afford homes.

PART D   Review

PRACTICE 10

Review

Read the following paragraph for meaning. Then write a different past tense verb in every blank.

(1) In 1861, a French naturalist _____ through a dense jungle of Cambodia in Southeast Asia. (2) He _____ to a clearing and _____ across the treetops. (3) He _____ in amazement. (4) Five enormous towers _____ above him. (5) With a pounding heart, he _____ to the most gorgeous temple imaginable. (6) He _____ 250 feet to the top of the highest tower. (7) A huge abandoned city _____ for miles all around him. (8) Carvings of gods and goddesses _____ the palaces and monuments. (9) Unlike the ruins of Greece and Rome, every stone in these buildings _____ in place. (10) Local people _____ this

The lost city of Angkor Wat.

Paul Chesley/National
Geographic/Getty Images.

marvelous lost city Angkor. (11) Five hundred years before, it had been the largest

city in Asia. (12) Then for unknown reasons, its entire population _____.

PRACTICE 11

Review

Rewrite this paragraph, changing the verbs to the past tense.*

(1) Above the office where I work is a karate studio. (2) Every day as I go through my files, make out invoices, and write letters, I hear loud shrieks and crashes from the studio above me. (3) All day long, the walls tremble, the ceiling shakes, and little pieces of plaster fall like snow onto my desk. (4) Sometimes, the noise does not bother me; at other times, I wear earplugs. (5) If I am in a very bad mood, I stand on my desk and pound out reggae rhythms on the ceiling with my shoe. (6) However, I do appreciate one thing. (7) The job teaches me to concentrate, no matter what.

_____

_____

_____

_____

_____

_____

_____

*See also Chapter 23, "Consistent Tense," for more practice.

PRACTICE 12

Writing Assignment

With three or four classmates, invent a group fairy tale. Take five minutes to decide on a subject for your story. On a clean sheet of paper, the first student should write the first sentence—in the past tense, of course. Use vivid action verbs. Each student should write a sentence in turn until the fairy tale is finished.

Have a group member read your story aloud. As you listen, make sure the verbs are correct. Should any verbs be replaced with livelier ones?

CHAPTER HIGHLIGHTS

- **Regular verbs add *-d* or *-ed* to form the past tense:**

    We *decided.*

    The frog *jumped.*

    He *outfoxed* the fox.

- **Irregular verbs in the past tense change in irregular ways:**

    We *took* a marketing course.

    Owen *ran* fast.

    Jan *brought* pineapples.

- ***To be* is the only verb that takes more than one form in the past tense:**

I *was*	we *were*
you *were*	you *were*
he she it *was*	they *were*

CHAPTER REVIEW

Fill in the past tense form of each verb in parentheses. Some verbs are regular; others are irregular.

Homegrown Warrior

(1) Majora Carter _____ (grow) up in a rough neighborhood of New York's South Bronx. (2) When she _____ (leave) for college, she _____ (vow) never to return. (3) Like many inner-city areas, this _____ (be) an industrial wasteland, with decaying building and gray air.

(4) Yet a strange twist of fate _____(bring) Carter home and _____(inspire) her amazing career.

(5) For financial reasons, Majora _____(have) to move back with her parents while she _____(work) on a master's degree in writing. (6) She soon _____(hear) about the city's plan to build yet another solid waste treatment plant in the South Bronx. (7) She and her neighbors _____(discuss) this pattern of dumping unwanted waste in poor areas. (8) They _____(learn) that the toxic effects of sewage plants already in the South Bronx _____(add) to the plague of local health problems, especially asthma. (9) Angry and determined, Carter _____(rally) the residents to fight. (10) Incredibly, they _____(defeat) the city's plan.

(11) Inspired by this success, Carter _____(see) how much more _____(need) to be done. (12) Her group _____(want) clean air, waterfront development, and environmentally friendly jobs. (13) In 2001, she _____(create) Sustainable South Bronx (SSB), an organization dedicated to community restoration. (14) The group _____(assemble) a workforce, _____(build) a park on the site of an old cement plant, and

Green roofs like this one in New York City reduce urban heat and pollution.

Reprinted with permission of Alyson Hurt and www.morethanthis.net.

_____(explore) the idea of a four-mile-long greenway along the water-front. (15) With new respect from local officials and businesses, SSB _____(push) for economic development, too. (16) The slow but sure revival _____(bring) other activists and artists back to the neighborhood.

(17) Carter further _____(study) the connection between environment and health. (18) Her group _____(take) steps to improve residents' fitness, recreation, and nutrition. (19) But the "green roof" _____(become) one of her proudest achievements. (20) Carter _____(demonstrate) how growing plants on city roofs cleans the air, cools buildings, provides healthy food, and reduces water pollution. (21) The idea of green roofs _____(catch) on and _____(get) national attention.

(22) In 2005, at age 38, Majora Carter _____(receive) a MacArthur "Genius" Grant for profoundly improving her community's quality of life. (23) A career she never _____(plan) just _____(keep) blooming.

 ## EXPLORING ONLINE

<http://chompchomp2.com/irregular01/irregular01.htm> Interactive quiz: Choose the correct irregular verbs.

<http://grammar.ccc.commnet.edu/grammar/quizzes/chute.htm> Change present tense verbs to past in this passage from a famous book.

<http://college.cengage.com/devenglish> Visit the *Grassroots* 9/e student website for more exercises, quizzes, and live links to all websites mentioned in this chapter.

The Past Participle in Action

PART A   Defining the Past Participle

Every verb has one form that can be combined with helping verbs like *has* and *have* to make verbs of more than one word. This form is called the **past participle.**

> (1) She has solved the problem.
>
> (2) I have solved the problem.
>
> (3) He had solved the problem already.

● Each of these sentences contains a two-part verb. Circle the first part, or *helping verb,* in each sentence, and write each helping verb in the blanks that follow:

  (1) _____

  (2) _____

  (3) _____

● Underline the second part, or *main verb,* in each sentence. This word, a form of the verb *to solve,* is the same in all three. Write it here: _____

● *Solved* is the past participle of *to solve.*

The past participle never changes, no matter what the subject is and no matter what the helping verb is.

PART B   Past Participles of Regular Verbs

Fill in the past participle in each series below:

Present Tense	Past Tense	Helping Verb + Past Participle
(1) Beth dances.	(1) Beth danced.	(1) Beth has _____ .
(2) They decide.	(2) They decided.	(2) They have _____ .
(3) He jumps.	(3) He jumped.	(3) He has _____ .

● Are the verbs *to dance, to decide,* and *to jump* regular or irregular?

_____ How do you know? _____

● What ending does each verb take in the past tense? _____

● Remember that any verb that forms its past tense by adding *-d* or *-ed* is a *regular*

verb. What past participle ending does each verb take? _____

The past participle forms of regular verbs look exactly like the past tense forms. Both end in *-d* **or** *-ed.*

PRACTICE 1

The first sentence in each of these pairs contains a one-word verb in the past tense. Fill in the past participle of the same verb in the blank in the second sentence.

EXAMPLE: She designed jewelry all her life.

She has ____*designed*____ jewelry all her life.

1. Several students worked in the maternity ward.

   Several students have _____ in the maternity ward.

2. The pot of soup boiled over.

   The pot of soup has _____ over.

3. The chick hatched.

   The chick has _____ .

4. We congratulated Jorgé.

   We have _____ Jorgé.

5. Nelson always studied in the bathtub.

   Nelson has always _____ in the bathtub.

6. Many climbers scaled this mountain.

   Many climbers have _____ this mountain.

7. The landlord asked for a rent increase.

   The landlord has _____ for a rent increase.

8. Sylvia located her long-lost cousin in New Jersey.

   Sylvia has _____ her long-lost cousin in New Jersey.

9. The satellite circled Jupiter.

   The satellite has _____ Jupiter.

10. They signed petitions to save the seals.

    They have _____ petitions to save the seals.

PRACTICE 2

Write the missing two-part verb in each of the following sentences. Use the helping verb *has* or *have* and the past participle of the verb written in parentheses.

EXAMPLE: _____*Have*_____ you ever _____*wished*_____ (to wish) for a new name?

1. Some of us _____ _____ (to want) new names at one time or another.

2. Many famous people _____ _____ (to fulfill) that desire.

3. Some _____ _____ (to use) only their first names.

4. Madonna Louise Ciccone _____ _____ (to drop) everything but Madonna.

5. Beyoncé Knowles _____ _____ (to shorten) her name to Beyoncé.

6. Other celebrities _____ _____ (to retain) their last names and taken new first names.

7. For example, Eldrick Woods _____ _____ (to turn) into Tiger Woods.

8. Comedian Jonathan Leibowitz _____ _____ (to rename) himself Jon Stewart.

9. Replacing both her names, Dana Owens _____ _____ (to transform) herself into Queen Latifah.

10. What new name would you _____ _____ (to pick) for yourself?

PART C   Past Participles of Irregular Verbs

Present Tense	Past Tense	Helping Verb + Past Participle
(1) He sees.	(1) He saw.	(1) He has seen.
(2) I take vitamins.	(2) I took vitamins.	(2) I have taken vitamins.
(3) We sing.	(3) We sang.	(3) We have sung.

● Are the verbs *to see, to take,* and *to sing* regular or irregular? _____

● Like all irregular verbs, *to see, to take,* and *to sing* do not add *-d* or *-ed* to show past tense.

● Most irregular verbs in the past tense are also irregular in the past participle—like *seen, taken,* and *sung.*

● Remember that past participles must be used with helping verbs.*

Because irregular verbs change their spelling in irregular ways, there are no easy rules to explain these changes. Here is a list of some common irregular verbs.

Reference Chart: Irregular Verbs

Simple Form	Past	Past Participle
be	was, were	been
become	became	become
begin	began	begun
blow	blew	blown
break	broke	broken
bring	brought	brought
build	built	built
burst	burst	burst
buy	bought	bought
catch	caught	caught
choose	chose	chosen
come	came	come
cut	cut	cut
dive	dove (dived)	dived
do	did	done
draw	drew	drawn
drink	drank	drunk
drive	drove	driven
eat	ate	eaten
fall	fell	fallen
feed	fed	fed
feel	felt	felt
fight	fought	fought
find	found	found
fly	flew	flown
forget	forgot	forgotten
forgive	forgave	forgiven
freeze	froze	frozen
get	got	gotten (got)
give	gave	given
go	went	gone
grow	grew	grown
have	had	had
hear	heard	heard
hide	hid	hidden
hold	held	held
hurt	hurt	hurt
keep	kept	kept
know	knew	known
lay	laid	laid
lead	led	led
leave	left	left
let	let	let
lie	lay	lain
lose	lost	lost

---

*For work on incomplete verbs, see Chapter 7, Part B.

Reference Chart: Irregular Verbs (*continued*)

Simple Form	Past	Past Participle
make	made	made
mean	meant	meant
meet	met	met
pay	paid	paid
put	put	put
quit	quit	quit
read	read	read
ride	rode	ridden
ring	rang	rung
rise	rose	risen
run	ran	run
say	said	said
see	saw	seen
seek	sought	sought
sell	sold	sold
send	sent	sent
set	set	set
shake	shook	shaken
shine	shone (shined)	shone (shined)
shrink	shrank (shrunk)	shrunk
sing	sang	sung
sit	sat	sat
sleep	slept	slept
speak	spoke	spoken
spend	spent	spent
spring	sprang	sprung
stand	stood	stood
steal	stole	stolen
strike	struck	struck
swim	swam	swum
swing	swung	swung
take	took	taken
teach	taught	taught
tear	tore	torn
tell	told	told
think	thought	thought
throw	threw	thrown
understand	understood	understood
wake	woke (waked)	woken (waked)
wear	wore	worn
win	won	won
wind	wound	wound
write	wrote	written

You already know many of these past participle forms. One way to learn the unfamiliar ones is to group together verbs that change from the present tense to the past tense to the past participle in the same way. For example, some irregular verbs change from *ow* in the present to *ew* in the past to *own* in the past participle.

bl<u>ow</u>	bl<u>ew</u>	bl<u>own</u>
gr<u>ow</u>	gr<u>ew</u>	gr<u>own</u>
kn<u>ow</u>	kn<u>ew</u>	kn<u>own</u>
thr<u>ow</u>	thr<u>ew</u>	thr<u>own</u>

Another group changes from *i* in the present to *a* in the past to *u* in the past participle:

beg<u>i</u>n	beg<u>a</u>n	beg<u>u</u>n
dr<u>i</u>nk	dr<u>a</u>nk	dr<u>u</u>nk
r<u>i</u>ng	r<u>a</u>ng	r<u>u</u>ng
s<u>i</u>ng	s<u>a</u>ng	s<u>u</u>ng
spr<u>i</u>ng	spr<u>a</u>ng	spr<u>u</u>ng
sw<u>i</u>m	sw<u>a</u>m	sw<u>u</u>m

As you write, refer to the chart. If you are unsure of the past participle form of a verb that is not on the chart, check a dictionary. For example, if you look up the verb *see* in the dictionary, you will find an entry like this:

see \ saw \ seen \ seeing

The first word listed is the present tense form of the verb (*I see, she sees,* and so on). The second word listed is the past tense form (*I saw, she saw,* and so on). The third word is the past participle form (*I have seen, she has seen,* and so on), and the last word is the present participle form.

Some dictionaries list different forms only for irregular verbs. If no past tense or past participle form is listed, you know that the verb is regular and that its past participle ends in -*d* or -*ed*.

PRACTICE 3

The first sentence in each pair contains an irregular verb in the past tense. Fill in *has* or *have* plus the past participle of the same verb to complete the second sentence.

EXAMPLE: I ate too much.

I _____have_____ _____eaten_____ too much.

1. The river rose over its banks.

   The river _____ _____ over its banks.

2. She sold her 1956 Buick.

   She _____ _____ her 1956 Buick.

3. For years, we sang in a barbershop quartet.

   For years, we _____ _____ in a barbershop quartet.

4. Crime rates fell recently.

   Crime rates _____ _____ recently.

5. Ralph gave me a red satin bowling jacket.

   Ralph _____ _____ me a red satin bowling jacket.

6. They thought carefully about the problem.

   They _____ _____ carefully about the problem.

7. I kept all your love letters.

   I _____ _____ all your love letters.

8. The Joneses forgot to confirm the reservation.

The Joneses _____ _____ to confirm the reservation.

9. The pond froze solid.

The pond _____ _____ solid.

10. The children knew about those caves for years.

The children _____ _____ about those caves for years.

PRACTICE 4

Now you will be given only the first sentence with its one-word verb in the past tense. Rewrite the entire sentence, changing the verb to a two-word verb—*has* or *have* plus the past participle of the main verb.

EXAMPLE: He took his credit cards with him.

He has taken his credit cards with him. _____

1. They brought their Great Dane to the party.

_____

2. T. J. drove a city bus for two years.

_____

3. She chose a Van Gogh poster for the hallway.

_____

4. I saw a white fox near the barn.

_____

5. A tornado tore through the shopping center.

_____

6. Margo became more self-confident.

_____

7. Councilman Gomez ran a fair campaign.

_____

8. The old barn stood there for years.

_____

9. Sam read about the islands of Fiji.

_____

10. Our conversations were very helpful.

_____

PRACTICE 5

Review

For each verb in the chart that follows, fill in the present tense (third person singular form), the past tense, and the past participle. BE CAREFUL: Some of the verbs are regular, and some are irregular.

Simple	Present Tense (he, she, it)	Past Tense	Past Participle
know	knows	knew	known
catch			
stop			
break			
reach			
bring			
fly			
fall			
feel			
take			
go			

PRACTICE 6

Review

Complete each sentence by filling in the helping verb *has* or *have* and the past participle of the verb in parentheses. Some verbs are regular, and some are irregular.

EXAMPLES: Millions _____have_____ _____heard_____ (hear) them sing.

They _____have_____ _____used_____ (use) words and music to connect with others.

Latinas Break Through

(1) Recently, a new generation of Latina crossover stars _has break._ (break) musical barriers, bringing to American music and films new talent and a Latin flavor. (2) The performer who started it all, Cuban-born Gloria Estefan, now _establish herselfed_ (establish) herself as a hugely successful crossover singer. (3) Her albums, with hits like "Conga" and "Rhythm of the Night," _they have selled_ (sell) millions of copies. (4) In fact, "Conga" was the first song to appear on the pop, soul, Latin, and dance

music charts at the same time. (5) During her long career, Estefan _____

_____ (blaze) many trails. (6) In addition to being the first Latina to win

BMI's Songwriter of the Year award, she _____ _____ (re-

ceive) five Grammies. (7) In 1993, Estefan became the first person ever to sing in

Spanish at the Grammy Awards.

(8) Since then, many young singers _____ _____ (cross)

over to English from a range of Hispanic backgrounds. (9) Selena, for instance, es-

tablished herself as the first female superstar of Tejano music, a Tex-Mex style that

_____ _____ (come) to blend rock, country, conjunto,

norteño, and blues. (10) Selena's 1991 hit "Ven Conmigo" was the first Tejano

record to go gold, and in 1993, she became the first Tejano artist to win a Grammy.

(11) In addition, having five of her Spanish-language albums on the Billboard 200

_____ _____ (earn) her another first. (12) Although her tragic

murder in 1995 cut short her brilliant career, Selena's recordings _____

_____ (encourage) North Americans to appreciate the beauty, exuber-

ance, and variety of Latino music.

(13) Ironically, a film about Selena's life launched the next Latina superstar into

the spotlight. (14) Since her 1997 role as the slain Tejano singer, Puerto Rican Jen-

nifer Lopez _____ _____ (win) acclaim in both her acting and

singing careers. (15) In fact, she was the first U.S. performer to have the number

one album (*Love Don't Cost a Thing*) and the number one movie (*The Wedding Plan-

ner*) during the same week. (16) Today, commanding top fees for her films and cre-

ating her own perfume and clothing lines, J.Lo _____ _____

(become) the highest paid Latina actress in history.

(17) These breakthrough stars _____ _____ (help) blend

Hispanic and Anglo cultures and _____ _____ (open) doors

for a new crop of Latina singers and actresses.

PRACTICE 7

Review

Check your work in the preceding exercises or have it checked. Do you see any
patterns in your errors? Do you tend to miss regular or irregular verbs? To help
yourself learn, copy all four forms of each verb that you missed into your notebook in a chart like the one on the next page. Use the chart to study.

Personal Review Chart

Simple	Present Tense (he, she, it)	Past Tense	Past Participle
go	goes	went	gone

PART D Using the Present Perfect Tense

The **present perfect tense** is composed of the present tense of *to have* (*has* or *have*) plus the past participle.

Present Perfect Tense

Singular

I *have* spoken
you *have* spoken
he
she *has* spoken
it

Plural

we *have* spoken
you *have* spoken

they *have* spoken

Let us see how this tense is used.

(1) They *sang* together last Saturday.

(2) They *have sung* together for three years now.

● In sentence (1), the past tense verb *sang* tells us that they sang together on one occasion, Saturday, but are no longer singing together. The action began and ended in the past.

● In sentence (2), the present perfect verb *have sung* tells us something entirely different: that they have sung together in the past and *are still singing together now*.

(3) Janet *sat* on the beach for three hours.

(4) Valerie *has* just *sat* on the beach for three hours.

● Which woman is probably still sunburned? _____

● In sentence (3), Janet's action began and ended at some time in the past. Perhaps it was ten years ago that she sat on the beach.

● In (4), the present perfect verb *has sat* implies that although the action occurred in the past, it *has just happened*, and Valerie had better put some lotion on her sunburn *now*.

● Notice how the word *just* emphasizes that the action occurred very recently.

Use the *present perfect tense* to show either (1) that an action began in the past and has continued until now or (2) that an action has just happened.

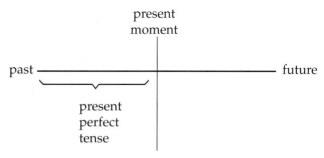

In writing about an action that began in the past and is still continuing, you will often use time words like *for* and *since.*

> (5) We have watched the fireworks *for* three hours.
>
> (6) John has sung in the choir *since* 2002.

In writing about an action that has just happened, you will often use words like *just, recently, already,* and *yet.*

> (7) I have *just* finished the novel.
>
> (8) They have *already* gone to the party.

PRACTICE 8

Paying close attention to meaning, circle the verb that best completes each sentence.

EXAMPLES: Years ago, he (wanted, has wanted) to know how things worked.

Since then, not much (changed, has changed).

1. Even as a young boy in New York City, Dean Kamen (loved, has loved) science and invention.

2. While just a teenager, he (got, has gotten) the job of automating the Times Square ball drop for New Year's Eve.

3. Since that time, Kamen (invented, has invented) many amazing machines, including a stair-climbing wheelchair, a robotic scooter, and a small dialysis machine.

4. For several years now, he (lived and worked, has lived and worked) in a huge, six-sided house in New Hampshire.

5. Inside and out, the house (began, has begun) to look like a fabulous science museum.

6. The collection (expanded, has expanded) to include helicopters, a steam engine, a special Humvee, and a wind turbine.

7. Some years ago, Kamen (decided, has decided) to encourage children to enter science careers.

8. In the 1990s, he (created, has created) FIRST—For Inspiration and Recognition of Science and Technology—to spark kids' interest in science and to sponsor robot-building contests.

9. In a recent speech, Kamen (said, has said), "Teenagers think they will become NBA stars and make millions, but their odds [of doing so] are less than 1 percent."

10. "However, many, many scientists and inventors (made, have made) big money and big contributions as well," he added. "Think about it."

PRACTICE 9

Fill in either the *past* tense or the *present perfect* tense form of each verb in parentheses.

(1) In 1976, the town of Twinsburg, Ohio, _____ (to begin) hosting a gathering of twins from around the world. (2) Every year since then, more and more twins _____ (to attend), wearing matching outfits, crazy hats, and posing for photographers. (3) Last year, 2,064 sets of twins from the United States, Africa, Europe, and South America _____ (to register) for Twins Days. (4) Over the years, fascinated tourists _____ (to double) the fun. (5) More importantly, the annual event _____ (to offer) scientists a rare research opportunity. (6) For example, researchers _____ (to study) identical twins (with identical genes) to see how DNA and environment affect diseases, hair loss, and even personality traits like shyness. (7) By the way, in the 1990s, researchers _____ (to find) that shyness is inherited. (8) Many twins _____ (to assist) scientists by standing in line for hours to answer questions, take tests, and donate their DNA. (9) The twins festival _____ (to afford) them the chance not only to meet other twins but also to contribute to human knowledge.

PART E   Using the Past Perfect Tense

The **past perfect tense** is composed of the past tense of *to have* (*had*) plus the past participle.

Past Perfect Tense

Singular	Plural
I *had* spoken	we *had* spoken
you *had* spoken	you *had* spoken
he she *had* spoken it	they *had* spoken

Let us see how this tense is used.

> (1) Because Bob *had broken* his leg, he *wore* a cast for six months.

● The actions in both parts of this sentence occurred entirely in the past, but one occurred before the other.

● At some time in the past, Bob *wore* (past tense) a cast on the leg that he *had broken* (past perfect tense) at some time before that.

When you are writing in the past tense, use the *past perfect tense* **to show that something happened at an even earlier time.**

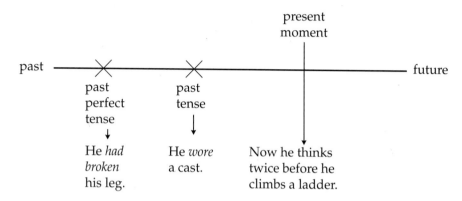

As a general rule, the present perfect tense is used in relation to the present tense, and the past perfect tense is used in relation to the past tense. Read the following pairs of sentences and note the time relation.

> (2) Sid *says* (present) he *has found* (present perfect) a good job.
> (3) Sid *said* (past) he *had found* (past perfect) a good job.
>
> (4) Grace *tells* (present) us she *has won* (present perfect) first prize.
> (5) Grace *told* (past) us she *had won* (past perfect) first prize.

PRACTICE 10

Choose either the present perfect or the past perfect tense of the verb in parentheses to complete each sentence. Match present perfect tense with present tense and past perfect tense with past tense.

1. The newspaper reports that the dictator _has to leave the country_ (to leave) the country.

2. The newspaper reported that the dictator _have to leave the country_ (to leave) the country.

3. I plan to buy a red convertible; I _____ _____ (to want) a convertible for three years now.

4. Last year, I bought a red convertible; I _____ _____ (to want) a convertible for three years before that.

5. Mel _____ _____ (to choose) the steepest trail up the mountain; he was thoroughly worn out.

6. Mel _____ _____ (to choose) the steepest trail up the mountain; he is thoroughly worn out.

7. I am worried about my cat; she _____ _____ (to drink) bubble bath.

8. I was worried about my cat; she _____ _____ (to drink) bubble bath.

9. Sam told us that he _____ _____ (to decide) to major in restaurant management.

10. Sam tells us that he _____ _____ (to decide) to major in restaurant management.

PART F Using the Passive Voice

So far in this chapter, you have combined the past participle with forms of *to have*. But the past participle can also be used with forms of *to be* (*am, is, are, was, were*).

(1) That jam was made by Aunt Clara.

● The subject of the sentence is *that jam*. The verb has two parts: the helping verb *was* and the past participle *made*.

● Note that the subject, *that jam*, does not act but is acted on by the verb. *By Aunt Clara* tells us who performed the action.

That jam *was made* by Aunt Clara.

When the subject is acted on or receives the action, it is passive, and the verb (*to be + past participle*) **is in the** *passive voice.*

Now compare the passive voice with the active voice in these pairs of sentences:

(2) **Passive voice:** Free gifts are given by the bank.
(3) **Active voice:** The bank gives free gifts.

(4) **Passive voice:** We were photographed by a tourist.
(5) **Active voice:** _____

● In sentence (2), the subject, *free gifts,* is passive; it receives the action. In sentence (3), *the bank* is active; it performs the action.

● Note the difference between the passive verb *are given* and the active verb *gives*.

● However, the tense of both sentences is the same. The passive verb *are given* is in the present tense, and so is the active verb *gives*.

● Rewrite sentence (4) in the active voice. Be sure to keep the same verb tense in the new sentence.

Write in the *passive voice* **only when you want to emphasize the receiver of the action rather than the doer. Usually, however, write in the** *active voice* **because sentences in the active voice are livelier and more direct.**

PRACTICE 11

Underline the verb in each sentence. In the blank to the right, write *A* if the verb is written in the active voice and *P* if the verb is in the passive voice.

EXAMPLE: Nelson Mandela <u>is respected</u> worldwide as a leader.   _P_

1. Nelson Mandela was born in South Africa on July 18, 1918, a member of the Xhosa tribe. _____

2. Under the apartheid government, only whites, not the black majority, enjoyed basic rights. _____

3. As a young lawyer, Mandela defended many black clients. _____

4. They were charged with such crimes as "not owning land" or "living in the wrong area." _____

5. Several times, Mandela was arrested for working with the African National Congress, a civil rights group. _____

6. In 1961, he sadly gave up his lifelong belief in nonviolence. _____

7. Training guerrilla fighters, he was imprisoned again, this time with a life sentence. _____

8. Thirty years in jail did not break Mandela. _____

9. Offered freedom to give up his beliefs, he said no. _____

10. Finally released in 1990, this man became a symbol of hope for a new South Africa. _____

11. In 1994, black and white South Africans lined up to vote in the first free elections. _____

12. Gray-haired, iron-willed Nelson Mandela was elected president of his beloved country. _____

PRACTICE 12

In each sentence, underline both parts of the passive verb and circle the complete subject. Then draw an arrow from the verb to the word or words it acts on.

EXAMPLE: (I) <u>was approached</u> by Professor Martin.

1. The skaters were applauded vigorously by the crowd.

2. The corn is picked fresh every morning.

3. These flowered bowls were imported from Mexico.

4. Milos, my cat, was ignored by the mouse.

5. Hasty promises are often broken.

6. An antique train set was sold at the auction.

7. The speech was memorized by both actors.

8. Customers are lured into the store by loud music and bright signs.

9. Dutch is spoken on Curaçao.

10. Our quarrel was quickly forgotten.

PRACTICE 13

Whenever possible, write in the active, not the passive, voice. Rewrite each sentence, changing the verb from the passive to the active voice. Make all necessary verb and subject changes. Be sure to keep each sentence in the original tense.

EXAMPLE: Good medical care is deserved by all human beings.

All human beings deserve good medical care.

1. Doctors Without Borders was created by a small group of French doctors in 1971.

_____

2. Excellent health care was provided by them to people in poor or isolated regions.

_____

3. Soon they were joined by volunteer doctors and nurses from all over the world.

_____

4. Today drugs and medical supplies are brought by the organization to people in need.

_____

Sudanese refugees from Darfur wait in a sandstorm to get medical help at the Doctors Without Borders mobile clinic.

AP Images.

5. Vaccinations are received by children in eighty countries.

_____

6. Crumbling hospitals and clinics are restored by volunteers.

_____

7. Victims of wars also are treated by the DWB staff.

_____

8. Information about humanitarian crises is gotten by the world.

_____

9. Each year, thousands are given the gifts of health and life by these traveling experts.

_____

PART G   Using Past Participles as Adjectives

Sometimes a past participle is not a verb at all but an *adjective*, a word that describes a noun or pronoun.*

> (1) Jay is *married.*
>
> (2) The *broken* window looks terrible.
>
> (3) Two *tired* students slept in the hall.

● In sentence (1), *married* is the past participle of the verb *to marry,* but here it is not a verb. Instead, it describes the subject, *Jay.*

● *Is* links the subject, *Jay,* with the descriptive word, *married.*

● In sentence (2), *broken* is the past participle form of *to break,* but it is used as an adjective to describe the noun *window.*

● In sentence (3), what past participle is an adjective? _____

● Which word does it describe? _____

Past participles like *married, broken,* and *tired* are often used as adjectives.

Some form of the verb *to be* usually links descriptive past participles with the subjects they describe, but here are a few other common linking verbs that you learned in Chapter 6, Part E.

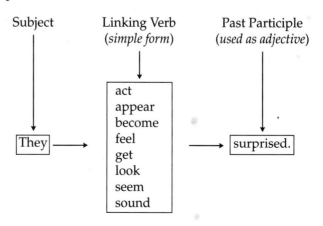

_____
*For more work on adjectives, see Chapter 21.

PRACTICE 14

Underline the linking verb in each sentence. Then circle the descriptive past participle or participles that complete the sentences.

EXAMPLES: The window <u>was</u> (polish, (polished)).

Harry <u>seems</u> very (worry, (worried)) these days.

1. This product is (guarantee, guaranteed) not to explode.

2. Nellie seems (qualify, qualified) for the job.

3. Your aunt appears (delight, delighted) to see you again.

4. After we read the chapter, we were still (confuse, confused).

5. The science laboratory is (air-condition, air-conditioned).

6. David feels (appreciate, appreciated) in his new job.

7. Did you know that one out of two American couples gets (divorce, divorced)?

8. We were (thrill, thrilled) to meet Venus and Serena Williams.

9. During the holidays, Paul feels (depress, depressed).

10. Are the potatoes (fry, fried), (bake, baked), or (boil, boiled)?

PRACTICE 15

Below is a list of verbs. Use the past participles of the verbs as adjectives to describe each noun in the exercise. Then use your adjective-noun combination in a sentence. Use a different past participle for each noun.

bore	freeze	park	train
delight	hide	pollute	wear
dry	lose	tire	worry
embarrass	daze	toast	wrinkle

EXAMPLE: the _____dried_____ fruit

We served the dried fruit for dessert.

1. a( ) _____ man

_____

2. the _____ emeralds

_____

3. these _____ muffins

_____

4. a( ) _____ nurse

_____

5. two _____ passengers

_____

PRACTICE 16

Proofread the following ad copy for past participle errors. First, underline all the past participles. Then make any corrections above the line.

(1) We are please to introduce three automobiles this year, each one created by our experience team of engineers. (2) Our racy new sports model, the Hormone, is guaranteed to provide adventure on the road. (3) It comes equip with a powerful fuel-injected engine, steel-belt tires, and orange flames painted across the hood. (4) Growing families will prefer the Sesame ST. (5) Blue and modest on the outside, the Sesame ST's interior is make for parents and children. (6) Its plastic upholstery is printed with yellow Big Bird designs. (7) Pop-out soda and hamburger holders come preinstall, and the sound system is program for soft rock only, so your kids can't tune in to grunge, hard rock, or rap stations. (8) For the budget-minded car shopper, we offer the Chintz. (9) It comes equip with a two-cylinder engine, steering wheel, and seats. (10) Recently, on *The Tonight Show with Jay Leno,* the Chintz was name "the car that gives you less for less."

PRACTICE 17

Combine each pair of short sentences. First, find and underline the past participle. Then rewrite the two short sentences as one smooth sentence, using the past participle as an adjective.

EXAMPLE: The book is lost. It is worth $1,000.

The lost book is worth $1,000.

1. This rug has been dry-cleaned. It looks new.

   _____

2. His grades have fallen. He can bring them up.

   _____

3. The envelope was sealed. Harriet opened it.

   _____

4. The weather forecast was revised. It calls for sunshine.

   _____

5. These gold chains are overpriced. Do not buy them.

   _____

PRACTICE 18

The sentences in the left column are in the present tense; those in the right column are in the past tense. If the sentence is shown in the present tense on the left, write the sentence in the past tense on the right, and vice versa. REMEMBER: Only the *linking verb*, never the past participle, changes to show tense.

EXAMPLES: Smoking is forbidden.

Smoking was forbidden.

Lunches are served.

Lunches were served.

Present Tense	Past Tense
1. Your car is repaired.	1. _____
2. _____	2. The store looked closed.
3. _____	3. My feelings were hurt.
4. The seats are filled.	4. _____
5. She is relaxed.	5. _____
6. _____	6. You seemed qualified for the job.
7. He is supposed to meet us.*	7. _____
8. They are used to hard work.*	8. _____
9. _____	9. It was written in longhand.
10. You are expected at noon.	10. _____

PRACTICE 19

Writing Assignment

In a group of four or five classmates, write a wacky restaurant menu, using all the past participles that you can think of as adjectives: *steamed* fern roots, *fried* cherries, *caramel-coated* hamburgers, and so forth. Brainstorm. Get creative. Then arrange your menu in an order that makes sense (if that is the correct term for such a menu!).

CHAPTER HIGHLIGHTS

● **Past participles of regular verbs add** *-d* **or** *-ed*, **just like their past tense forms:**

Present	Past	Past Participle
decide	decided	decided
jump	jumped	jumped

---

*For more work on *supposed* and *used*, see Chapter 32, "Look-Alikes/Sound-Alikes."

- **Past participles of irregular verbs change in irregular ways:**

Present	Past	Past Participle
bring	brought	brought
see	saw	seen
take	took	taken

- **Past participles can combine with** *to have:*

  He *has edited* many articles for us. (*present perfect tense*)

  He *had edited* many articles for us. (*past perfect tense*)

- **Past participles can combine with** *to be:*

  The report *was edited* by Mary. (*passive voice*)

- **Past participles can be used as adjectives:**

  The *edited* report arrived today. (*adjective*)

CHAPTER REVIEW

Proofread this student's essay for past participle errors. Correct each error above the line.

Three Ways to Be a Smarter Learner

(1) Once in a great while, a person is born with a photographic memory, allowing him or her to memorize a lot of information with almost no effort. (2) However, most of us have struggle on our own to find the best ways to learn. (3) We have stayed up all night studying. (4) We have mark up our textbooks, highlighting and underlining like skill tattoo artists. (5) Maybe, in frustration, we have even questioned our own intelligence. (6) Although everyone has his or her own learning style, three techniques have make me and others better learners.

(7) The first technique is simple—sit at the front of the class! (8) A student who has choose to sit up front is more likely to stay alert and involve than students at the back and sides. (9) By sitting away from windows or talkative friends, many students discover that they take a greater interest in the classroom subject and take better notes. (10) An extra benefit of sitting up front is that teachers are often impress by students with whom they make eye contact, students whose behavior says, "I care about this class."

(11) Second, make a smart friend. (12) During the first week of class, exchange phone numbers with another front-row student. (13) You are looking for an intelligent, responsible classmate who seems committed to learning—not for a pizza

buddy or a date. (14) Students who have agree in advance to help each other can call if they miss a class. (15) What was discuss that day? (16) Was homework assign or a test announced? (17) Two students who "click" might want to become study partners, meeting regularly to review material and prepare for tests.

(18) Third, ask questions. (19) The student who has sit up front, made a study friend, and pay close attention in class should not be worried about asking the professor questions. (20) Learning a subject is like building a tower. (21) Each new level of understanding must be build solidly on the level below. (22) If an important point or term is unclear, ask for help, in or after class.

(23) Students who use these techniques will be rewarded with increase understanding and better grades—even before they have pull out their pastel highlighters.

Maurice Jabbar, student

 EXPLORING ONLINE

<http://grammar.ccc.commnet.edu/grammar/cgi-shl/par_quiz.pl/final-ed_add2.htm> Quiz with answers: Choose the past or past participle form.

<http://grammar.ccc.commnet.edu/grammar/quizzes/passive_quiz.htm> Interactive quiz: Revise these passive sentences. Make them active.

<http://college.cengage.com/devenglish> Visit the *Grassroots* 9/e student website for more exercises, quizzes, and live links to all websites mentioned in this chapter.

Progressive Tenses
(*TO BE* + *-ING* Verb Form)

PART A   Defining and Writing the Present Progressive Tense

Verbs in the *present progressive tense* have two parts: the present tense form of *to be* (*am, is, are*) plus the *-ing* (or present participle) form of the main verb.

Present Progressive Tense (*example verb: to play*)	
Singular	**Plural**
I am playing	we are playing
you are playing	you are playing
he	
she } is playing	they are playing
it	

Compare the present tense with the present progressive tense below.

(1) Larry works at the bookstore.

(2) Larry is working at the bookstore.

● Sentence (1) is in the present tense. Which word tells you this? __Works__

● Sentence (2) is also in the present tense. Which word tells you this? __is__

● Note that the main verb in sentence (2), *working,* has no tense. Only the helping verb *is* shows tense.

151

PRACTICE 1

Change each one-word present tense verb in the left-hand column to a two-part present progressive verb in the right-hand column. Do this by filling in the missing helping verb (*am*, *is*, or *are*).

EXAMPLES: I fly.   I ____am____ flying.

He wears my sweater.   He ____is____ wearing my sweater.

Present Tense	**Present Progressive Tense**
1. Elsa and I set goals together.	1. Elsa and I _____ setting goals together.
2. They eat quickly.	2. They _____ eating quickly.
3. He plans the wedding.	3. He _____ planning the wedding.
4. Our work begins to pay off.	4. Our work _____ beginning to pay off.
5. We pose for the photographer.	5. We _____ posing for the photographer.
6. Maryann smiles.	6. Maryann _____ smiling.
7. Sal does his Elvis impression.	7. Sal _____ doing his Elvis impression.
8. I speak Portuguese to Manuel.	8. I _____ speaking Portuguese to Manuel.
9. My grandson gets silly.	9. My grandson _____ getting silly.
10. You probably wonder why.	10. You _____ probably wondering why.

REMEMBER: **Every verb in the present progressive tense must have two parts: a helping verb (*am*, *is*, or *are*) and a main verb ending in -*ing*. The helping verb must agree with the subject.**

PRACTICE 2

Below are sentences in the regular present tense. Rewrite each one in the present progressive tense by changing the verb to *am*, *is*, or *are* plus the -*ing* form of the main verb.

EXAMPLE: We play cards.

We are playing cards.

1. The telephone rings.

_____ is ringing

2. Dexter wrestles with his math homework.

_____ is wrestling

3. James and Judy work in the emergency room.

_____ they are working in the emergency room.

4. I keep a journal of thoughts and observations.

   I'm keeping.

5. We polish all our old tools.

   we are polishing

PART B   Defining and Writing the Past Progressive Tense

Verbs in the *past progressive tense* have two parts: the past tense form of *to be* (*was* or *were*) plus the *-ing* form of the main verb.

Past Progressive Tense
(*example verb: to play*)

Singular	**Plural**
I was playing	we were playing
you were playing	you were playing
he	
she ⎱ was playing	they were playing
it	

Compare the past tense with the past progressive tense below.

(1) Larry worked at the bookstore.

(2) Larry was working at the bookstore.

● Sentence (1) is in the past tense. Which word tells you this? ___*worked*___

● Sentence (2) is also in the past tense. Which word tells you this? *he was working*

● Notice that the main verb in sentence (2), *working*, has no tense. Only the helping verb *was* shows tense.

PRACTICE 3

Change each one-word past tense verb in the left-hand column to a two-part past progressive verb in the right-hand column. Do this by filling in the missing helping verb (*was* or *were*).

EXAMPLES:	I flew.	I ___was___ flying.
	He wore my sweater.	He ___was___ wearing my sweater.

Past Tense	**Past Progressive Tense**
1. Elsa and I set goals together.	1. Elsa and I ___are___ setting goals together.
2. They ate quickly.	2. They ___are___ eating quickly.
3. He planned the wedding.	3. He ___is___ planning the wedding.
4. Our work began to pay off.	4. Our work ___are___ beginning to pay off.

5. We posed for the photographer.

6. Maryann smiled.

7. Sal did his Elvis impression.

8. I spoke Portuguese to Manuel.

9. My grandson got silly.

10. You probably wondered why.

5. We _____ posing for the photographer.

6. Maryann _____ smiling.

7. Sal _____ doing his Elvis impression.

8. I _____ speaking Portuguese to Manuel.

9. My grandson _____ getting silly.

10. You _____ probably wondering why.

PRACTICE 4

Below are sentences in the past tense. Rewrite each sentence in the past progressive tense by changing the verb to *was* or *were* plus the *-ing* form of the main verb.

EXAMPLE: You cooked dinner.
You were cooking dinner.

1. The two linebackers growled at each other.
The two linebackers were growling each other.

2. Leroy examined his bank receipt.
he was examining his bank receipt

3. We watched the news.
we were watching the news

4. Marsha read the *Wall Street Journal*.
she was reading the Wall Street jounal.

5. He painted like a professional artist.
he was painting like a professional artist.

PART C   Using the Progressive Tenses

As you read these sentences, do you hear the differences in meaning?

(1) Lenore *plays* the piano.

(2) Dave *is playing* the piano.

● Which person is definitely at the keyboard right now?

● If you said Dave, you are right. He is *now in the process of playing* the piano. Lenore, on the other hand, *does* play the piano; she may also paint, write novels, and play center field, but we do not know from the sentence what she *is doing right now*.

● The present progressive verb *is playing* tells us that the action is *in progress*.

Here is another use of the present progressive tense:

(3) Tony *is coming* here later.

● The present progressive verb *is coming* shows *future* time: Tony is going to come here.

(4) Linda *washed* her hair last night.

(5) Linda *was washing* her hair when we arrived for the party.

● In sentence (4), *washed* implies a completed action.

● The past progressive verb in sentence (5) has a special meaning: that Linda was *in the process* of washing her hair when something else happened (we arrived).

● To say, "Linda *washed* her hair *when* we arrived for the party" means that first we arrived, and then Linda started washing her hair.

Writers in English use the progressive tenses *much less often* than the present tense and past tense. Use the progressive tense only when you want to emphasize that something is or was in the process of happening.

Use the *present progressive tense (am, is, are + -ing)* **to show that an action is in progress now or that it is going to occur in the future.**

Use the *past progressive tense (was, were + -ing)* **to show that an action was in progress at a certain time in the past.**

PRACTICE 5

Read each sentence carefully. Then circle the verb or verbs that best express the meaning of the sentence.

EXAMPLE: Right now, we (write, (are writing)) letters.

1. Thomas Edison (held, (was holding)) 1,093 patents.

2. Where is Ellen? She (drives, is driving) to Omaha.

3. Most mornings we (get, are getting) up at seven.

4. Believe it or not, I (thought, was thinking) about you when you phoned.

5. My dog Gourmand (eats, is eating) anything at all.

6. At this very moment, Gourmand (eats, is eating) the sports page.

7. Max (fried, was frying) onions when the smoke alarm (went, was going) off.

8. Please don't bother me now; I (study, am studying).

9. Newton (sat, was sitting) under a tree when he (discovered, was discovering) gravity.

10. The *Andrea Doria*, a huge pleasure ship, (sank, was sinking) on July 25, 1956.

PART D   Avoiding Incomplete Progressives

Now that you can write both present and past progressive verbs, avoid mistakes like this one:

> We having fun. (*incomplete*)

- Can you see what is missing?

- All by itself, the -*ing* form *having* is not a verb. It has to have a helping verb.

- Because the helping verb is missing, *we having fun* has no time. It could mean *we are having fun* or *we were having fun*.

- *We having fun* is not a sentence. It is a fragment of a sentence.*

PRACTICE 6

Each group of words below is an incomplete sentence. Put an X over the exact spot where a word is missing. Then, in the Present Progressive column, write the word that would complete the sentence in the *present progressive tense*. In the Past Progressive column, write the word that would complete the sentence in the *past progressive tense*.

	Present Progressive	Past Progressive
EXAMPLE: He ˣhaving fun.	is	was
	(He is having fun.)	(He was having fun.)
1. Fran and I watching the sunrise.	are	were
2. You taking a computer course.	are	were
3. A big log floating down the river.		
4. Her study skills improving.		
5. I trying to give up caffeine.		
6. Fights about money getting me down.		
7. Thick fog blanketing the city.		
8. That child reading already.		
9. Your pizza getting cold.		
10. They discussing the terms of the new contract.		they

PRACTICE 7

Writing Assignment

Write a brief account that begins, "We are watching an amazing scene on TV. A man/woman/child/couple/group/animal is trying to_____." Fill in the blank, and then write four or five more sentences describing the unfolding action in the *present progressive* tense—as if the action is taking place right now. Read over what you have written, checking the verbs.

Now rewrite the whole account in the *past progressive* tense. The new version will begin, "We were watching an amazing scene on TV. A man/woman/child/couple/group/animal was trying to_____."

_____
*For more on this type of fragment, see Chapter 7, Part B.

CHAPTER HIGHLIGHTS

- **The progressive tenses combine** *to be* **with the** *-ing* **verb form:**
  present progressive tense: I *am reading.* He *is reading.*
  past progressive tense: I *was reading.* He *was reading.*

- **The** *-ing* **verb form must have a helping verb to be complete:**
  She playing the tuba. (*incorrect*)
  She *is playing* the tuba. (*correct*)

- **The present progressive tense shows that an action is in progress now:**
  Aunt Belle *is waxing* her van.

- **The present progressive tense can also show that an action will take place in the future:**
  Later today, Aunt Belle *is driving* us to the movies.

- **The past progressive tense shows that an action was in progress at a certain time in the past:**
  Aunt Belle *was waxing* her van when she heard thunder.

CHAPTER REVIEW

Proofread this paragraph for incomplete progressive verbs. Write the missing verbs above the lines.

(1) Scientists studying the role of human genes in everything from eye color and intelligence to the tendency to get heart disease. (2) Recently, a map of every gene in the human body—three billion elements in all—was completed by researchers of the Human Genome Project. (3) Scientists using this new information to find the genes that cause certain diseases. (4) Already, the map leading to cures and to other helpful discoveries, like finding bacteria that eat up oil spills and then die. (5) On the other hand, ethical problems arising. (6) Some insurance companies refusing to insure healthy people who carry certain genes. (7) In the future, will employers be allowed to use genetic tests the way some now use lie detectors or drug tests? (8) Will parents try to plan the physical traits or talents of their babies? (9) Because of questions like these, some people calling genetic research a Pandora's box, not a magic bullet.

EXPLORING ONLINE

<http://ww2.college-em.qc.ca/prof/epritchard/verblis9.htm> Interactive quiz: Practice progressive tense verbs as you visit old Montreal.

<http://college.cengage.com/devenglish> Visit the *Grassroots* 9/e student website for more exercises, quizzes, and live links to all websites mentioned in this chapter.

CHAPTER 12

Fixed-Form Helping Verbs and Verb Problems

PART A Defining and Spotting the Fixed-Form Helping Verbs

You already know the common—and changeable—helping verbs: *to have, to do,* and *to be.* Here are some helping verbs that do not change:

Fixed-Form Helping Verbs	
can	could
will	would
may	might
shall	should
must	

The fixed-form helping verbs do not change, no matter what the subject is. They always keep the same form.

PRACTICE 1

Fill in each blank with a fixed-form helping verb.

1. You _____ do it!

2. This _____ be the most exciting presidential debate ever held.

3. I _____ row while you watch for crocodiles.

4. Rico _____ go to medical school.

5. In South America, the elephant beetle _____ grow to twelve inches in length.

6. If the committee _____ meet today, we _____ have a new budget on time.

7. We _____ rotate the crops this season.

8. Violent films _____ cause children to act out violently.

9. You _____ have no difficulty finding a sales position.

10. Janice _____ teach users to do research on the Internet.

PART B   Using the Fixed-Form Helping Verbs

> (1) Al will stay with us this summer.
>
> (2) Susan can shoot a rifle well.

● *Will* is the fixed-form helping verb in sentence (1). What main verb does it help? _____

● *Can* is the fixed-form helping verb in sentence (2). What main verb does it help? _____

● Notice that *stay* and *shoot* are the simple forms of the verbs. They do not show tense by themselves.

When a verb has two parts—a fixed-form helping verb and a main verb—the main verb keeps its simple form.

PRACTICE 2

In the left column, each sentence contains a verb made up of some form of *to have* (the changeable helping verb) and a past participle (the main verb).

Each sentence in the right column contains a fixed-form helping verb and a blank. Write the form of the main verb from the left column that correctly completes each sentence.

	Have + Past Participle	Fixed-Form Helping Verb + Simple Form
EXAMPLES:	I have talked to him.	I may ___talk___ to him.
	She has flown to Ireland.	She will ___fly___ to Ireland.
	1. Irena has written a song.	1. Irena must _____ a song.
	2. We have begun.	2. We can _____ .

3. Joy has visited Graceland.

4. He has slept all day.

5. I have run three miles.

6. We have seen an eclipse.

7. It has drizzled.

8. Fred has gone on vacation.

9. Has he studied?

10. Della has been promoted.

3. Joy will _____ Graceland.

4. He could _____ all day.

5. I will _____ three miles.

6. We might _____ an eclipse.

7. It may _____ .

8. Fred could _____ on vacation.

9. Should he _____ ?

10. Della might _____ promoted.

PART C   Using CAN and COULD

(1) He says that I *can* use any tools in his garage.

(2) He said that I *could* use any tools in his garage.

● What is the tense of sentence (1)? _____

● What is the tense of sentence (2)? _____

● What is the helping verb in sentence (1)? _____

● What is the helping verb in sentence (2)? _____

● As you can see, *could* may be used as the past tense of *can*.

Present tense: Today, I *can* touch my toes.

Past tense: Yesterday, I *could* touch my toes.

Can **means** *am/is/are able.* **It may be used to show present tense.**

Could **means** *was/were able* **when it is used to show the past tense of** *can.*

(3) If I went on a diet, I *could* touch my toes.

(4) Rod wishes he *could* touch his toes.

● In sentence (3), the speaker *could* touch his toes *if* . . . Touching his toes is a possibility, not a certainty.

● In sentence (4), Rod *wishes* he *could* touch his toes, but probably he cannot. Touching his toes is a wish, not a certainty.

Could **also means** *might be able,* **a possibility, a wish, or a request.**

PRACTICE 3

Fill in the present tense helper *can* or the past tense helper *could,* whichever is needed. To determine whether the sentence is in the present or the past, look at the other verbs in the sentence or look for words like *now* and *yesterday.*

1. When I am rested, I _____ study for hours.

2. When I was rested, I _____ study for hours.

3. George insists that he _____ play the trumpet.

4. George insisted that he _____ play the trumpet.

5. A year ago, Zora _____ jog for only five minutes at a time.

6. Now Zora _____ jog for nearly an hour at a time.

7. If you're so smart, how come you _____ never find your own socks?

8. If you were so smart, how come you _____ never find your own socks?

9. When the air was clear, you _____ see the next town.

10. When the air is clear, you _____ see the next town.

PRACTICE 4

Circle either *can* or *could.*

1. Sue thinks that she (can, could) carry a tune.

2. Yesterday, we (can, could) not go to the town meeting.

3. I wish I (can, could) pitch like Pedro Martinez.

4. You should meet Tony: he (can, could) lift a two-hundred-pound weight.

5. Everyone I meet (can, could) do a cartwheel.

6. Until the party, everyone thought that Harry (can, could) cook.

7. She (can, could) ice skate better now than she (can, could) last year.

8. On the night that Smithers disappeared, the butler (can, could) not be found.

9. When my brother was younger, he (can, could) name every car on the road.

10. I hope that the snow leopards (can, could) survive in captivity.

PRACTICE 5

On a separate paper, write five sentences using *can* to show present tense and five sentences using *could* to show past tense.

PART D   Using WILL and WOULD

(1) You know you *will* do well in that class.

(2) You knew you *would* do well in that class.

- Sentence (1) says that *you know* now (present tense) that you *will* do well in the future. *Will* points to the future from the present.
- Sentence (2) says that *you knew* then (past tense) that you *would* do well after that. *Would* points to the future from the past.

Would **may be used as the past tense of** *will,* **just as** *could* **may be used as the past tense of** *can.*

(3) *If* you studied, you *would* pass physics.

(4) Juanita wishes she *would* get an A in French.

- In sentence (3), the speaker *would* pass physics *if* . . . Passing physics is a possibility, not a certainty.
- In sentence (4), Juanita *wishes* she *could* get an A, but this is a wish, not a certainty.

Would **can also express a possibility, a wish, or a request.**

PRACTICE 6

Fill in the present tense *will* or the past tense *would.*

1. The meteorologist predicts that it _____ snow on Friday.
2. The meteorologist predicted that it _____ snow on Friday.
3. Hernan said that he _____ move to Colorado.
4. Hernan says that he _____ move to Colorado.
5. Roberta thinks that she _____ receive financial aid.
6. Roberta thought that she _____ receive financial aid.
7. I _____ marry you if you propose to me.
8. Unless you stop adding salt, no one _____ want to eat that chili.
9. Hugo thinks that he _____ be a country and western star someday.
10. Because she wanted to tell her story, she said that she _____ write an autobiography.

PRACTICE 7

Circle either *will* or *would.*

1. You (will, would) find the right major once you start taking courses.
2. When the house is painted, you (will, would) see how lovely the old place looks.
3. Yolanda wishes that her neighbor (will, would) stop raising ostriches.
4. The instructor assumed that everyone (will, would) improve.
5. They insisted that they (will, would) pick up the check.
6. The whole town assumed that they (will, would) live happily ever after.
7. When we climb the tower, we (will, would) see for miles around.

8. If I had a million dollars, I (will, would) buy a big house on the ocean.

9. Your flight to Mars (will, would) board in fifteen minutes.

10. Because we hated waiting in long lines, we decided that we (will, would) shop somewhere else.

PART E Writing Infinitives

Every verb can be written as an **infinitive.** An infinitive has two parts: *to* + the simple form of the verb—*to kiss, to gaze, to sing, to wonder, to help.* Never add endings to the infinitive form of a verb: no *-ed,* no *-s,* no *-ing.*

> (1) Erin has *to take* a course in clinical dental hygiene.
>
> (2) Neither dictionary seems *to contain* the words I need.

● In sentences (1) and (2), the infinitives are *to take* and *to contain.*

● *To* is followed by the simple form of the verb: *take, contain.*

Don't confuse an infinitive with the preposition *to* followed by a noun or a pronoun.

> (3) Robert spoke *to Sam.*
>
> (4) I gave the award *to her.*

● In sentences (3) and (4), the preposition *to* is followed by the noun *Sam* and the pronoun *her.*

● *To Sam* and *to her* are prepositional phrases, not infinitives.*

PRACTICE 8

Find the infinitives in the following sentences and write them in the blanks at the right.

Infinitive

EXAMPLE: Many people don't realize how hard it is to write a funny essay.

_____to write_____

1. Our guests started to leave at midnight.

_____

2. Barbara has decided to run for mayor.

_____

3. Hal has to get a B on his final exam, or he will not transfer to Wayne State.

_____

4. It is hard to think with that radio blaring!

_____

5. The man wanted to buy a silver watch to give to his son.

_____

*For more work on prepositions, see Chapter 6, Part C, and Chapter 22.

PRACTICE 9

Write an infinitive in each blank in the following sentences. Use any verb that makes sense. Remember that the infinitive is made up of *to* plus the simple form of the verb.

1. They began _____ in the cafeteria.

2. Few people know how _____ well.

3. Would it be possible for us _____ again later?

4. He hopes _____ an operating-room nurse.

5. It will be easy _____ _____ .

PART F   Revising Double Negatives

The most common **negatives** are *no, none, not, nowhere, no one, nobody, never,* and *nothing.*

The negative *not* is often joined to a verb to form a contraction: *can't, didn't, don't, hasn't, haven't,* and *won't,* for example.

However, a few negatives are difficult to spot. Read these sentences:

> (1) There are hardly any beans left.
>
> (2) By noon, we could scarcely see the mountains on the horizon.

● The negatives in these sentences are *hardly* and *scarcely.*

● They are negatives because they imply that there are *almost* no beans left and that we *almost couldn't* see the mountains.

Use only one negative in each idea. The **double negative** is an error you should avoid.

> (3) **Double negative:** I *can't* eat *nothing.*

● There are two negatives in this sentence—*can't* and *nothing*—instead of one.

● Double negatives cancel each other out.

To revise a double negative, simply drop one of the negatives.

> (4) **Revised:** I *can't* eat anything.
>
> (5) **Revised:** I can eat *nothing.*

● In sentence (4), the negative *nothing* has been changed to the positive *anything.*

● In sentence (5), the negative *can't* has been changed to the positive *can.*

When you revise double negatives that include the words *hardly* and *scarcely,* keep those words and change the other negatives to positives.

(6) **Double negative:** They couldn't hardly finish their papers on time.

● The two negatives are *couldn't* and *hardly.*

(5) **Revised:** They could hardly finish their papers on time.

● Change *couldn't* to *could.*

PRACTICE 10

Revise the double negatives in the following sentences.

EXAMPLE: I don't have no more homework to do.
Revised: *I don't have any more homework to do.*

1. I can't hardly wait for Christmas vacation.

   Revised: _____

2. Ms. Chandro hasn't never been to Los Angeles before.

   Revised: _____

3. Fido was so excited that he couldn't scarcely sit still.

   Revised: _____

4. Nat won't talk to nobody until he's finished studying.

   Revised: _____

5. Yesterday's newspaper didn't contain no ads for large-screen television sets.

   Revised: _____

6. Alice doesn't have no bathing suit with her.

   Revised: _____

7. If Harold were smart, he wouldn't answer no one in that tone of voice.

   Revised: _____

8. Kylie claimed that she hadn't never been to a rodeo before.

   Revised: _____

9. Some days, I can't seem to do nothing right.

   Revised: _____

10. Umberto searched, but he couldn't find his gold bow tie nowhere.

    Revised: _____

PRACTICE 11

Writing Assignment

Review this chapter briefly. What part was most difficult for you? Write a paragraph explaining the difficult material to someone who is having the same trouble you had. Your purpose is to make the lesson crystal clear to him or her.

CHAPTER HIGHLIGHTS

- **Fixed-form verbs do not change, no matter what the subject is:**

    I *can.*

    He *can.*

    They *can.*

- **The main verb after a fixed-form helping verb keeps the simple form:**

    I will *sleep.*

    She might *sleep.*

    Sarita should *sleep.*

- **An infinitive has two parts, *to* + the simple form of a verb:**

    to drive

    to exclaim

    to read

- **Do not write double negatives:**

    I didn't order no soup. (*incorrect*)

    I didn't order any soup. (*correct*)

    They couldn't hardly see. (*incorrect*)

    They could hardly see. (*correct*)

CHAPTER REVIEW

Proofread the following essay for errors in fixed-form verbs, infinitives, and double negatives. Cross out each incorrect word and correct the error above the line.

Man of Honor

(1) According to public opinion polls, the most influential Hispanic American in the country is Edward James Olmos. (2) Olmos is someone who couldn't never be happy promoting only himself. (3) He has tried to setting an example for others through his choice of movie roles. (4) Olmos decided early in his career that he would not take no parts in *Rambo-* and *Terminator*-style movies just to get rich. (5) Instead, he wanted his life work to be something that he and his descendants will be proud of.

(6) As a result, his film projects have included *American Me*, an examination of gang members and life in prison. (7) Young people have told him that this film

convinced them that they should not have nothing to do with gangs. (8) Olmos is also famous for his portrayal of teacher Jaime Escalante in *Stand and Deliver*. (9) Other projects, from an anti–domestic violence documentary to a film about Brazilian political activist Chico Mendes called *The Burning Season*, aimed to educating the public.

(10) Olmos also hopes that he would change lives through his community activism. (11) He gives antidrug speeches. (12) In addition, Olmos visits public schools and promotes projects that help Latinos. (13) For example, he cofounded and now codirects the Los Angeles Latino International Film Festival. (14) The actor also supports the Latino Book and Family Festival and oversees Latino Public Broadcasting. (15) Olmos knows from experience that one person could make a difference.

Edward James Olmos as Commander Adama in the science fiction series *Battlestar Galactica*.

The Everett Collection.

EXPLORING ONLINE

<http://depts.gallaudet.edu/englishworks/exercises/exgrammar/modal01.htm>
Graded quiz: Help! Can you fix these verbs?

<http://www.bbc.co.uk/skillswise/words/grammar/texttypes/negatives/quiz.shtml>
Double negatives game: Try all three levels.

<http://college.cengage.com/devenglish> Visit the *Grassroots* 9/e student website for more exercises, quizzes, and live links to all websites mentioned in this chapter.

WRITING ASSIGNMENTS

As you complete each writing assignment, remember to perform these steps:

- Write a clear, complete topic sentence.

- Use freewriting, brainstorming, or clustering to generate ideas for the body of your paragraph, essay, or letter.

- Arrange your best ideas in a plan.

- Revise for support, unity, coherence, and exact language.

- Proofread for grammar, punctuation, and spelling errors.

Writing Assignment 1: *Tell a family story.* Many of us heard family stories as we were growing up—how our great-grandmother escaped from Poland, how Uncle Chester took his sister for a joy ride in the Ford when he was six. Assume that you have been asked to write such a story for a scrapbook that will be given to your grandmother on her eightieth birthday. Choose a story that reveals something important about a member of your family. As you revise, make sure that all your verbs are correct. Consider sharing your story online at a website that invites viewers to share their personal experiences. Try <http://story.hallmarkchannel.com/> or <http://www.ellisisland.org/Story/tellstory.asp>.

Writing Assignment 2: *Describe a giraffe (a person who sticks his or her neck out to help others).* In this unit, you might have read about Majora Carter, who vastly improved the quality of life for her South Bronx neighbors. Carter could be described as a "giraffe," a person who goes out of his or her way for the common good. Visit the Giraffe Heroes Project at <http://www.giraffe.org/>, read some of the stories, and study the nomination form. Do you know (or know of) a giraffe? Submit your own "Giraffe Sighting Report" by describing someone you know (in person or from word of mouth or the media) who deserves to be honored on this site.

Writing Assignment 3: *Describe a lively scene.* To practice choosing and using verbs, go where the action is—to a sports event, a busy store, a club, a public park, even the woods or a field. Observe carefully as you take notes and freewrite. Capture specific sounds, sights, colors, actions, and smells. Then write a description of what takes place, using lively verbs. Choose either present or past tense and make sure to use that tense consistently throughout.

Writing Assignment 4: *Describe a few intense moments.* Read paragraph A on page 169, which uses lively verbs to describe the saving of someone's life at a health club. This writer uses the present tense, as if the action is happening now. Describe some brief but dramatic event—the birth of a child, the opening of an important letter, the arrival of a blind date, or the reaction of the person to whom you just proposed. Decide whether present or past tense would be better, and choose varied, interesting verbs. As you revise, make sure the verbs are correct.

REVIEW

Transforming

A.   Rewrite this paragraph, changing every *I* to *she*, every *me* to *her*, and every *us* to *them*. Do not change any verb tenses. Be sure all verbs agree with their new subjects, and make any other necessary changes.

(1) I am at the gym, training a client. (2) A man near us gets off the treadmill and suddenly collapses onto the floor. (3) I know that I must act quickly. (4) I shout, "Call 911!" (5) I dash to the portable defibrillator on the wall, open the box, and remove the device. (6) I press the green start button and quickly tear off the unconscious man's T-shirt. (7) I place the two electrode pads on his chest and plug them into the machine. (8) The defibrillator analyzes the man's heartbeat to determine whether his heart needs to be shocked. (9) It does. (10) The machine charges itself and warns me not to touch the patient. (11) When I press the orange button, the machine delivers a jolt and then checks to see if the patient needs another. (12) One is enough. (13) The man's skin almost instantly turns from gray to pink, and he has a pulse. (14) When the paramedics arrive, they tell me that the defibrillator and I probably saved his life.

Marcel Alfonso, student

B.   Rewrite this paragraph, changing the verbs from present tense to past tense.

(1) It is the morning of August 29, 2005. (2) Hurricane Katrina churns over the warm waters of the Gulf of Mexico and bears down on the coasts of Louisiana and Mississippi. (3) When it makes landfall at 6:10 a.m., it is a monster storm, packing 125-mile-an-hour winds and dumping 10 to 15 inches of rain. (4) Hurricane-force winds rage 120 miles outward from its center. (5) In the city of New Orleans, the storm whips up huge waves in Lake Pontchartrain. (6) These waves slam into the levees around the city, causing the levees to break. (7) Lake water pours into the city and floods low-lying areas. (8) Winds and torrents rip down telephone and power lines, wash away streets and bridges, and level whole neighborhoods. (9) Many of the people still in their homes swim for their lives. (10) Others scramble to their rooftops, where they wait, sometimes in vain, for rescue. (11) One of the greatest disasters in U.S. history, Hurricane Katrina costs over $100 billion in

damages. (12) Far worse, it leaves over 1,800 people dead, shatters millions of lives, and raises deeply disturbing questions.

What story does this picture tell?

Photograph © Robert Polidori

Proofreading

The following essay contains both past tense errors and past participle errors. First, proofread for verb errors, underlining all the incorrect verbs. Then correct the errors above the lines. (You should find a total of thirteen errors.)

Protector of the Chimps

(1) Dr. Jane Goodall, DBE[*], has did more than anyone else to understand the lives of chimpanzees. (2) Always an animal lover, she was too poor to go to college to study animals. (3) She worked as a waitress until the age of twenty-five. (4) Then she fufilled a lifelong dream and gone to East Africa. (5) There she was thrilled by the beauty of the land and the wild animals.

(6) In Africa, she meet Louis Leakey, a famous naturalist. (7) Leakey recognize Goodall's curiosity, energy, and passion for the natural world. (8) He hired her for a six-month study of the wild chimpanzees in a national park in Tanzania. (9) Despite malaria, primitive living conditions, and hostile wildlife, this determined woman followed the activities of a group of chimps in the Gombe forest. (10) For months, she watch the chimps through binoculars. (11) She moved closer and closer until she eventually become part of their lives. (12) Dr. Goodall named the chimps and

[*]DBE: Dame of the British Empire, an honorary title in England, like "Knight."

recorded their daily activities. (13) She learned that chimps was capable of feeling happiness, anger, and pain. (14) They formed complex societies with leaders, politics, and tribal wars. (15) One of her most important discoveries were that chimps made and used tools. (16) Dr. Goodall expected to stay in Gombe for six months; instead she studied the chimps there for almost forty years. (17) Her studies lead to a totally new understanding of chimps, and she became world famous.

Jane Goodall communicates with a chimpanzee.

© The Jane Goodall Institute, www.janegoodall.org. / Photo © Michael Neugebauer.

(18) However, her life changed completely in 1986. (19) She attend a conference in Chicago, where she heard horrible stories about the fate of chimps outside Gombe. (20) She learned about the destruction of the forests and the wildlife of Africa. (21) From that day on, Dr. Goodall committed herself to education and conservation. (22) Since then, she has traveled, lectured, gave interviews, and met with people. (23) She established both the Jane Goodall Institute and a young people's group, Roots & Shoots, and is a UN Messenger of Peace. (24) These worldwide organizations have already carry out many important conservation and educational projects. (25) The author of remarkable books and the subject of inspiring television specials, Dr. Goodall is knowed for her total commitment to chimps and to a healthy natural world.

EXPLORING ONLINE

<http://www.janegoodall.org>

<http://www.worldwildlife.org> Visit the Jane Goodall Institute or the World Wildlife Federation to learn more about endangered species.

WRITERS' WORKSHOP

Tell a Family Story

A **narrative** tells a story. It presents the most important events in the story, usually in time order. Here, a student tells of her mother-in-law's inspiring journey to self-realization.

In your group or class, read this narrative essay aloud, if possible. As you read, underline any words or details that strike you as vivid or powerful.

Somebody Named Seeta

(1) Someone I deeply admire is my mother-in-law, Seeta, who struggled for years to become her best self. She was born in poverty on the sunny island of Trinidad. Seeta's father drank and beat his wife, and sadly, her mother accepted this lifestyle. Her parents did not believe in sending girls to school, so Seeta's daily chores began at 4:00 a.m. when she milked the cows. Then she fed the hens, scrubbed the house, cooked, and tended babies (as the third child in a family of ten children). During stolen moments, she taught herself to read. At age sixteen, this skinny girl with long black hair ran away from home.

(2) Seeta had nowhere to go, so her friend's family took her in. They believed in education, yet Seeta struggled for years to catch up and finish school. Even so, she calls this time her "foot in the door." She married my father-in-law and had four children, longing inside to become "somebody" someday. When their oldest was nine and the youngest two months, Seeta's husband died. She had to get a job fast. She cut sugar cane in the fields, wrapping her baby in a sheet on the ground. In the evenings, she hiked home to care for the other children. Word got around on the sugar estate that she was bringing a baby to work, so she was given a job indoors. All the while, Seeta stayed patient and hopeful that God would help her someday.

(3) In fact, after seven years, she moved with her children to America. She was so poor that she owned only one pot and one spoon. After she finished cooking, the children would all gather around the pot, and sitting on the floor, they passed the spoon from one to another. My mother-in-law got a job at a department store, selling by day and cleaning offices at night. All the time, in the back of her head, she wanted to be somebody. A plan was taking shape. Eight years ago, my mother-in-law enrolled at this college, first for her GED and then for a college degree. She graduated and became a registered nurse.

(4) When I first met Seeta, I thought she did not like me. Was I wrong! She was just checking me out to see what I was made of. Did I too have goals to be conquered? She taught me that patience is a virtue but that one should never give up. She told me that even in modern America where

women have their independence, she had to fight to hold on to hers. Today my mother-in-law is attending Lehman College at night for her master's degree in surgical nursing.

Rosalie Ramnanan, student

1. How effective is Rosalie Ramnanan's essay?

    _____ Clear thesis statement?   _____ Rich supporting details?

    _____ Logical organization?   _____ Effective conclusion?

2. Underline the thesis statement (main idea sentence) for the whole essay. The rest of the paper—a narrative—develops this idea.

3. Ramnanan uses different action verbs to help the reader see and hear the story, especially in paragraphs (1), (2), and (3). Can you identify them?

4. Why do you think the writer chose the title she did? How effective is it?

5. Proofread for grammar and spelling. Do you notice any error patterns (two or more errors of the same type) that this student should watch out for?

Writing and Revising Ideas

1. Tell an inspiring story about one or more of your family members.

2. Use narrative to develop this topic or thesis sentence: Poverty or difficult circumstances can make some people stronger and more ambitious.

For help writing your paragraph or essay, see Chapters 4 and 5. As you revise, make sure that your main idea is clear and that your paper explains it. To add punch to your writing as you revise, replace *is, was, has,* and *had* with action verbs whenever possible.

Joining Ideas Together

Too many short, simple sentences can make your writing sound monotonous. This unit will show you five ways to create interesting sentences. In this unit, you will

- Join ideas through *coordination* and *subordination*

- Spot and correct run-ons or comma splices

- Use semicolons and conjunctive adverbs correctly

- Join ideas with *who*, *which*, and *that*

- Join ideas by using *-ing* modifiers

Spotlight on Writing

Here, writer Brent Staples uses several methods of joining ideas as he describes his first passionate kiss (at least, *he* was passionate). If possible, read the paragraph aloud.

I stepped outside and pulled the door closed behind me, and in one motion encircled her waist, pulled her to me, and whispered breathlessly that I loved her. There'd been no rehearsing this; the thought, deed, and word were one. "You do? You love me?" This amused her, but that didn't matter, I had passion enough for the two of us. When I closed in for the kiss, she turned away her lips and offered me her cheek. I kissed it feverishly and with great force. We stood locked this way until I came up for air. Then she peeled me from her and went inside for the flour.

Brent Staples, *Parallel Time*

- Brent Staples mixes simple sentences with sentences that join ideas in different ways. Sentences 1, 2, and 5, for example, combine ideas in ways you will learn in this unit.

- How do you think the writer now feels about this incident from his youth? Does his tone seem angry, frustrated, or amused? Which sentences tell you?

 Writing Ideas

- *Your first crush or romantic encounter*
- *A time you discovered that a loved one's view of the relationship was very different from your view of it*

CHAPTER 13

Coordination

As a writer, you will sometimes want to join short, choppy sentences to form longer sentences. One way to join two ideas is to use a comma and a **coordinating conjunction**.

> (1) This car has many special features, and it costs less than $15,000.
>
> (2) The television picture is blurred, but we will watch the football game anyway.
>
> (3) She wants to practice her Italian, so she is going to Italy.

- Can you break sentence (1) into two complete and independent ideas or thoughts? What are they? Underline the subject and verb in each.

- Can you do the same with sentences (2) and (3)? Underline the subjects and verbs.

- In each sentence, circle the word that joins the two parts of the sentence together. What punctuation mark comes before that word?

- *And, but,* and *so* are called *coordinating conjunctions* because they coordinate, or join together, ideas. Other coordinating conjunctions are *for, nor, or,* and *yet*.

To join two complete and independent ideas, use a coordinating conjunction preceded by a comma.

Now let's see just how coordinating conjunctions connect ideas:

Coordinating Conjunctions		
and	*means*	in addition
but, yet	*mean*	in contrast
for	*means*	because
nor	*means*	not either
or	*means*	either, a choice
so	*means*	as a result

BE CAREFUL: *Then, also,* and *plus* are not coordinating conjunctions. By themselves, they cannot join two ideas.

> **Incorrect:** He studied, then he went to work.
>
> **Correct:** He studied, and then he went to work.

PRACTICE 1

Read these sentences for meaning. Then punctuate them correctly and fill in the coordinating conjunction that best expresses the relationship between the two complete thoughts. REMEMBER: Do you want to *add, contrast, give a reason, show a result,* or *indicate a choice*?

1. Every year, thousands of people travel into Nevada's blistering Black Rock Desert , *because* they want to participate in an amazing ritual.

2. They build and live in an experimental community called Black Rock City , *but* they tear it down completely just one week later.

3. The event is called the Burning Man Festival *because* on the final day, an eighty-foot-tall wooden figure of a man is set ablaze.

4. Each year there is a theme , *and* past themes have included time, fertility, outer space, and belief.

5. Everyone is encouraged to contribute something related to the theme , *so* participants experience artwork, costumes, foods, prayers, kite making, music, and other gifts from the heart.

6. People pay to get into the festival , *but* they then enter a volunteer and gift economy.

7. Commercial vendors are not allowed , *nor* can participants buy or sell anything using money.

8. People focus instead on giving something to the group , *for* the festival encourages "radical self-expression."

Two Burning Man participants frame the wooden statue of Burning Man, lit at the festival's end.

© Peter Menzel/
www.menzelphoto.com.

9. The event began in 1986 as a small gathering of friends on a San Francisco beach, ___yet___ today it has grown to include over 30,000 participants.

10. They might make the trip looking for a weeklong party, ___or___ they might be seeking a more satisfying way of life.

EXPLORING ONLINE

<http://www.burningman.com> Would you make a pilgrimage to Black Rock for this festival? If not, write down three reasons why you wouldn't. If you would attend, write about what you would hope to gain from the experience and what you would contribute to the community.

PRACTICE 2

Each of these thoughts is complete by itself, but you can join them together to make more interesting sentences. Combine pairs of these thoughts, using *and, but, for, nor, or, so,* or *yet,* and write six new sentences on the lines that follow. Punctuate correctly.

babies need constant supervision

Rico overcame his disappointment

in the 1840s, American women began to fight for the right to vote, *but*

I will write my essay at home tonight, *or*

the ancient Chinese valued peaches *and*

he decided to try again

they are the best Ping-Pong players on the block

you should never leave them by themselves

I will write it tomorrow in the computer lab,

they did not win that right until 1920

they can't beat my cousin from Cleveland

they believed that eating peaches made a person immortal

1. _Babies need constant supervision, so you should never leave them by themselves._

2. _Rico overcame his disappointment, so he decided to try again._

3. _In the 1840s, American women began to fight for the right to vote, but they did not win that right until 1920._

4. _I will write my essay at home tonight, or I will write tomorrow in the computer lab._

5. The ancient chinese valued peaches, and they believed that eating peaches made a person immortal.

6. They are the best Ping-Pong players on the block, but they can't beat my cousin from Cleveland.

PRACTICE 3

Finish these sentences by adding a second complete idea after the coordinating conjunction.

1. She often interrupts me, but _she's my best friend_

2. Yuri has lived in the United States for ten years, so _now he is move back to Paris_

3. Len has been married three times, and _she has three boys, and two girl_

4. I like owning a car, for _long time._

5. I like owning a car, but _the too spencif._

PRACTICE 4

On paper or on a computer, write seven sentences of your own, using each of the coordinating conjunctions—*and, but, for, nor, or, so,* and *yet*—to join two independent ideas. Punctuate correctly.

PRACTICE 5

Writing Assignment

Whether you are a teenager, a young adult, middle-aged, elderly, single, or part of a couple, there are characters in TV sitcoms who are supposed to represent you. Do these characters correctly portray the kind of person you are, or are you seeing one or more irritating exaggerations?

Write a letter of praise or complaint to a network that broadcasts one of these sitcoms. Make clear why you think a certain character does or does not correctly portray someone like you. Use examples and specific details. As you write, avoid choppy sentences by joining ideas with coordinating conjunctions.

CHAPTER HIGHLIGHTS

● **A comma and a coordinating conjunction join two independent ideas:**

The fans booed, *but* the umpire paid no attention.

| Independent idea | , and
, but
, for
, nor
, or
, so
, yet | independent idea. |

● **Note:** *Then*, *also*, and *plus* **are not coordinating conjunctions.**

CHAPTER REVIEW

Read this paragraph of short, choppy sentences. Then rewrite it, using different coordinating conjunctions to combine some pairs of sentences. Keep some short sentences for variety. Copy your revised paragraph on a fresh sheet of paper. Punctuate with care.

(1) In 1929, Alice Orr answered a want ad for bronco riders for a Wild West show. (2) She was hired immediately. (3) Her new job launched a remarkable career. (4) Orr became an international rodeo star. (5) She was an expert in every rodeo event. (6) Her specialty was saddle bronco riding. (7) That tough competition has since been dropped from women's rodeos. (8) Orr won four world championships in it. (9) Orr was also concerned about working conditions for rodeo competitors. (10) She helped establish a professional rodeo association. (11) In the 1940s, Orr and her husband put on rodeos themselves. (12) She would demonstrate her world-famous saddle bronco riding. (13) Orr retired from rodeos in her fifties. (14) She did movie stunt work until she was eighty. (15) When Alice Orr died in 1995 at the age of ninety-three, many people still remembered her as queen of the bronco riders.

EXPLORING ONLINE

<http://grammar.ccc.commnet.edu/grammar/quizzes/nova/nova1.htm>
Interactive quiz: Place commas in sentences with coordinating conjunctions.

<http://aliscot.com/bigdog/joiners.htm> Coordination tips from Big Dog.

<http://college.cengage.com/devenglish> Visit the *Grassroots* 9/e student website for more exercises, quizzes, and live links to all websites mentioned in this chapter.

Subordination

PART A **Defining and Using Subordinating Conjunctions**

PART B **Punctuating Subordinating Conjunctions**

PART A   Defining and Using Subordinating Conjunctions

Another way to join ideas together is with a **subordinating conjunction.**
Read this paragraph:

> A great disaster happened in 1857. The SS *Central America* sank. This steamship was carrying six hundred wealthy passengers from California to New York. Many of them had recently struck gold. Battered by a storm, the ship began to flood. Many people on board bailed water. Others prayed and quieted the children. Thirty hours passed. A rescue boat arrived. Almost two hundred people were saved. The rest died. Later, many banks failed. Three tons of gold had gone down with the ship.

This could have been a good paragraph, but notice how dull the writing is because the sentences are short and choppy.

Here is the same paragraph, rewritten to make it more interesting:

> A great disaster happened in 1857 *when* the SS *Central America* sank. This steamship was carrying six hundred wealthy passengers from California to New York. Many of them had recently struck gold. Battered by a storm, the ship began to flood. Many people on board bailed water *while* others prayed and quieted the children. *After* thirty hours passed, a rescue boat arrived. Almost two hundred people were saved *although* the rest died. Later, many banks failed *because* three tons of gold had gone down with the ship.

- Note that the paragraph now reads more smoothly and is more interesting because the following words were used to join some of the choppy sentences: *when, while, after, although,* and *because.*

- *When, while, after, although,* and *because* are part of a large group of words called *subordinating conjunctions.* As you can see from the paragraph, these conjunctions join ideas.

BE CAREFUL: Once you add a *subordinating conjunction* to an idea, that idea can no longer stand alone as a complete and independent sentence. It has become a subordinate or dependent idea; it must rely on an independent idea to complete its meaning.*

(1) Because he is tired, <u>he has to take a breack.</u>

(2) As I left the room, <u>they stated the meetling</u>

(3) If you know Spanish, <u>you can work with those spanish people</u>

● Note that each of these ideas is dependent and must be followed by something else—a complete and independent thought.

● Sentence (1), for example, could be completed like this: Because he is tired, *he won't go out.*

● Add an independent idea to complete each dependent idea on the lines above.

Below is a partial list of subordinating conjunctions.

Common Subordinating Conjunctions

after	even though	when
although	if	whenever
as	since	where
as if	so that	whereas
as though	though	wherever
because	unless	whether
before	until	while

PRACTICE 1

Read these sentences for meaning. Then fill in the subordinating conjunction that best expresses the relationship between the two ideas.

1. <u>if</u> you are like most people, you resist admitting mistakes or hurtful actions.

2. <u>as though</u> it is commonly thought that apologizing shows weakness, an apology actually requires great strength.

3. A genuine apology is a powerful tool <u>because</u> it can repair damaged relationships, heal humiliation, and encourage forgiveness.

4. <u>if</u> we learn to apologize sincerely, psychologists say, we can prevent grudges, revenge, and a lot of pain.

5. _____ you apologize to someone, remember the key ingredients of a successful apology.

6. <u>Whether</u> you have hurt someone's feelings or betrayed that person, you must first admit your wrongdoing.

7. Specifically describe what you did <u>while</u> you reveal an understanding of your offense and its impact.

*For more work on sentence fragments of this type, see Chapter 7, Part C.

8. Say, for example, "I'm sorry for hurting you _because_ I criticized you in front of your friends."

9. _as_ you apologize, you must communicate remorse with both your words and your body language.

10. The other person will question your sincerity _unless_ you seem truly distressed and sorry.

11. _____ you admit your transgression, you should explain your actions.

12. For instance, "My behavior occurred _while_ I was feeling stressed (or tired, frustrated, angry)."

13. _before_ you end your apology, reassure the offended person.

14. Explain that you did not intend to wound him or her _____ you did so.

15. _____ it is difficult, an apology will be worth the effort.

PRACTICE 2

Now that you understand how subordinating conjunctions join thoughts together, try these sentences. Here you have to supply one idea. Make sure that the ideas you add have subjects and verbs.

1. The cafeteria food improved when _they changed the menu._

2. Because Damon and Luis both love basketball, _they whent to watch the match every afternoon._

3. If _she knows about the programme,_ Adolph plans to get legal advice.

4. I was repairing the roof while _I was on vecation_

5. Before _you start working,_ you should get all the facts.

PART B   Punctuating Subordinating Conjunctions

As you may have noticed in the preceding exercises, some sentences with subordinating conjunctions use a comma whereas others do not. Here is how it's done.

> (1) Because it rained very hard, we had to leave early.
>
> (2) We had to leave early because it rained very hard.

● Sentence (1) has a comma because the dependent idea comes before the independent idea.

| Because it rained very hard | , | we had to leave early. |

↓   ↓

Dependent idea   *,*   *independent idea.*

● Sentence (2) has no comma because the dependent idea follows the independent idea.

We had to leave early	because it rained very hard.

$\downarrow$ $\downarrow$

Independent idea   *dependent idea.*

Use a comma after a dependent idea; do not use a comma before a dependent idea.

PRACTICE 3

If a sentence is punctuated correctly, write *C* in the blank. If it is not, punctuate it correctly by adding a comma.

1. Whenever Americans get hungry, they want to eat quickly. ___

2. When McDonald's opened in 1954 it started a trend that continues today. ___

3. Whether you are talking about pizza or hamburgers, fast food is big business—earning more than $110 billion a year. ___

4. Fast food is appealing because it is cheap, tasty, and—of course—fast. ___

5. While it has many advantages, fast food also presents some health hazards. ___

6. Although the industry is booming many people are worried about the amount of fat in fast foods. ___

7. Whereas some nutritionists recommend eating only thirty-five grams of fat a day, you often eat more than that in just one fast-food meal. ___

8. If you order a Burger King Double Whopper with cheese, you take in a whopping sixty-three grams of fat. ___

9. That goes up to sixty-seven fat grams whenever you devour a McDonald's Big Mac, large fries, and chocolate shake. ___

10. Now some fast-food restaurants are claiming to serve low-fat items so that they can attract health-conscious customers. ___

11. However, you still must pay attention to the ingredients, if you want to make sure that your meal is healthy. ___

12. For example, most grilled or roasted chicken sandwiches are relatively low in fat before they are slathered with mayonnaise and special sauces. ___

13. Because just one tablespoon of mayonnaise or salad dressing contains eleven fat grams these tasty toppings add gobs of extra fat and calories. ___

14. Although they might taste delicious cheese and cheese sauces also add surprising quantities of fat to a meal. ___

15. When you next order your favorite fast food don't forget to say, "Hold the sauce!" ___

© New Yorker Collection 1988 Tom Cheney from cartoonbank.com. All Rights Reserved.

PRACTICE 4

Combine each pair of sentences by using a subordinating conjunction. Write each combination two ways: once with the subordinating conjunction at the beginning of the sentence and once with the subordinating conjunction in the middle of the sentence. Punctuate correctly.

EXAMPLE: Marriage exists in all societies.
Every culture has unique wedding customs.

Although marriage exists in all societies, every culture has unique wedding

customs.

Every culture has unique wedding customs although marriage exists in all

societies.

1. Young couples in India marry.
The ceremony may last for days.

As young couples in India marry, the ceremony may last for days.

Young couples in India marry, but the ceremony may last for days.

2. The wedding takes place at the bride's home.
Everyone travels to the groom's home for more celebrating.

Since the wedding takes place at the bride's home, Everyone travels to the groom's home for more celebrating

3. They are often included in Korean wedding processions.
   Ducks mate for life.

   _____

   _____

   _____

   _____

4. Iroquois brides gave grain to their mothers-in-law.
   Mothers-in-law gave meat to the brides.

   _____

   _____

   _____

   _____

5. The food was exchanged.
   The bride and groom were considered married.

   _____

   _____

   _____

   _____

6. The tradition went out of style.
   Finnish brides and grooms used to exchange wreaths.

   _____

   _____

   _____

   _____

7. The bride, groom, and bridal party dance special dances.
   A Zulu wedding is not complete.

   _____

   _____

   _____

   _____

8. The bride dances wildly and gloriously.
   She stabs at imaginary enemies with a knife.

   _____

   _____

   _____

9. The wedding ring is a very old symbol.
   The elaborate wedding cake is even older.

   _____

   _____

   _____

   _____

10. The ring symbolizes the oneness of the new couple.
    The cake represents fertility.

    _____

    _____

    _____

    _____

PRACTICE 5

Now try writing sentences of your own. Fill in the blanks, being careful to punctuate correctly. Do not use a comma before a dependent idea.

1. _____ because

   _____ .

2. Although _____

   _____ .

3. _____ whenever

   _____ .

4. Unless _____

   _____ .

PRACTICE 6

Writing Assignment

Imagine that you are a teacher planning a lesson on courtesy for a class of young children. Use a personal experience, either positive or negative, to illustrate your point. Brainstorm, freewrite, or cluster to generate details for the lesson. Then write what—and how—you plan to teach. Keeping in mind that you are trying to reach young children, make sure that the significance of the experience you will describe is clear. Join ideas together with subordinating conjunctions, being careful about punctuation.

   Form small groups to discuss one another's lessons. Which are most convincing? Why? Would children learn more from examples of good behavior or from examples of bad behavior?

CHAPTER HIGHLIGHTS

- **A subordinating conjunction joins a dependent idea and an independent idea:**

    When I registered, all the math courses were closed.

    All the math courses were closed *when* I registered.

- **Use a comma after a dependent idea.**

    After
    Because
    Before
    If
    Since
    Unless
    When
    While

    dependent idea, independent idea.

- **Do not use a comma before a dependent idea.**

    Independent idea

    after
    because
    before
    if
    since
    unless
    when
    while

    dependent idea.

CHAPTER REVIEW

Read this paragraph of short, choppy sentences. Then revise it by making changes above the lines, using different subordinating conjunctions to combine pairs of sentences. Keep some short sentences for variety. Punctuate with care.

(1) Jacob Lawrence was a great American painter, *while* a powerful teller of stories on canvas. (2) Young Jacob *When* joined his mother in Harlem in 1930. (3) *he* He began to paint the people around him. (4) Luckily, he found excellent art classes in Harlem. (5) The big art academies often excluded blacks then. (6) He was only 23. (7) *When* He gained fame for his sixty-picture *Migration Series*. (8) A New York gallery *While* displayed these paintings. (9) No major commercial gallery had showcased an African American artist before. (10) The *Migration Series* depicts southern blacks journeying north to find work after World War I. (11) The paintings show people

searching for a better life. (12) Lawrence's work portrays the poverty and prejudice the migrants endured. (13) He also wanted viewers of his work "to experience the beauty of life." (14) During his long career, Lawrence painted many more energetic canvases and series. (15) His work reminds us that we are all migrants. (16) We are always on the move. (17) We are seeking something more.

EXPLORING ONLINE

See Lawrence's paintings at the Whitney Museum of Art online.
    <http://www.whitney.org/jacoblawrence/> Click on "Jacob Lawrence's Art."
    Describe your favorite painting to someone who has never seen it. More
    writing ideas appear under "Explore" and "Tell Your Own Story."

Brownstones, 1958, by
Jacob Lawrence.
Courtesy of Clark Atlanta University
Art Collections.

EXPLORING ONLINE

<http://grammar.ccc.commnet.edu/grammar/quizzes/indep_clause_quiz.htm>
    Interactive clause line-up: I.D. the independent or dependent clauses.

<http://web2.uvcs.uvic.ca/elc/studyzone/330/grammar/subcon.htm>
    Explanation of subordination followed by interactive practice sets.

<http://college.cengage.com/devenglish> Visit the *Grassroots* 9/e student website
    for more exercises, quizzes, and live links to all websites mentioned in this
    chapter.

CHAPTER 15

Avoiding Run-Ons and Comma Splices

Now that you have had practice in joining ideas together, here are two errors to watch out for: the **run-on** and the **comma splice.**

> **Run-on:** Herb talks too much nobody seems to mind.

- There are two complete ideas here: *Herb talks too much* and *nobody seems to mind.*
- A *run-on* incorrectly runs together two complete ideas without using a conjunction or punctuation.

> **Comma splice:** Herb talks too much, nobody seems to mind.

- A *comma splice* incorrectly joins two complete ideas with a comma but no conjunction.

Here are three ways to correct a run-on and a comma splice.

1. **Write two separate sentences, making sure that each is complete.**

> Herb talks too much. Nobody seems to mind.

2. **Use a comma and a coordinating conjunction** (*and, but, for, nor, or, so, yet*).*

> Herb talks too much, *but* nobody seems to mind.

3. **Use a subordinating conjunction** (for example, *although, because, if, since,* or *when*).**

> *Although* Herb talks too much, nobody seems to mind.

---

*For more work on coordinating conjunctions, see Chapter 13.
**For more work on subordinating conjunctions, see Chapter 14.

Cher Prov, ꃮ

PRACTICE 1

Many of these sentences contain run-ons or comma splices. If a sentence is correct, write *C* in the right-hand column. If it contains a run-on or a comma splice, write either *RO* or *CS*. Then correct the error in any way you wish. Use each method at least once.

EXAMPLE:

Because a   *addictions,*
A number of celebrities have admitted their addictions public aware-

ness of addiction has increased.   *RO*

1. Many famous people have struggled with alcoholism or drug abuse

   some have overcome those problems.   *C*

2. Often politicians, athletes, and actors hide their addiction and their

   recovery, they do not want to risk ruining their careers.   *C*

3. Other celebrities are forced to go public in their battles with alcohol or

   drugs.   *C*

4. A few feel that their struggles may help others, they want to act as

   positive role models.   *C*

5. One such person was Betty Ford, a former first Lady with her family's

   help, she became sober at age sixty.   *RO*

6. Her recovery was successful she agreed to help several friends create

   a treatment center in Rancho Mirage, California.   *RO*

7. At the Betty Ford Center, celebrities like Kelsey Grammer and Keith

   Urban as well as everyday people receive support for their new way

   of life.   *C*

8. Treatment centers now exist around the country the problem of addiction

   seems to be increasing, especially among the young.   *CS*

9. For example, Drew Barrymore was famous at age six for her role in the

   film *E.T.* by age nine she was addicted to drugs and alcohol. *CS*

10. Forced into rehab at age thirteen, Drew was able to get her acting career

    back on track.   *C*

11. Former child star Jodie Sweetin went public with her addiction to

    crystal methamphetamine her recovery story helped others face this

    devastating problem.   *RO*

12. Actors Robert Downey Jr. and Matthew Perry likewise developed addictions getting treatment helped them stay on top in their profession. _RO_

13. Legendary athlete and NBA coach John Lucas went through detox, turned his life around, and now helps athletes recover. _C_

14. Alcohol and drugs might seem glamorous, especially to the young, they can destroy relationships, careers, and self-esteem. _CS_

15. Millions of Americans are affected, when someone returns from substance abuse, his or her triumph can encourage others to seek help. _CS_

PRACTICE 2

Correct each run-on or comma splice in two ways. Be sure to punctuate correctly.

EXAMPLE:

Technology will change the way we shop will we like the new way?

a. Technology will change the way we shop. Will we like the new way?

b. Technology will change the way we shop, but will we like the new way?

1. For instance, you want to purchase a car, you may walk up to an outdoor booth.

   a. _for instance, you want to purchase a car_

   b. _____

2. You select the options on a computer screen, you press an order entry key.

   a. _____

   b. _____

3. A factory assembles your car it is later delivered to your local dealer.

   a. _____

   b. _____

4. You go to a store to buy jeans, none are on the shelf.

    a. _____

    _____

    b. _____

    _____

5. Instead, you look at different styles onscreen you make your choice.

    a. _____

    _____

    b. _____

    _____

6. Taking measurements is not new now they can be taken by a three-dimensional camera.

    a. _____

    _____

    b. _____

    _____

7. Your measurements have been taken electronically your jeans will fit perfectly.

    a. _____

    _____

    b. _____

    _____

8. Your selection and measurements are transmitted to a factory your jeans are made to order.

    a. _____

    _____

    b. _____

    _____

9. You want to experiment with changing your hairstyle, a computer screen will show you with long, short, or differently colored hair.

    a. _____

    _____

    b. _____

    _____

10. You can leave the way you came in you can leave with a new look.

a. _____

_____

b. _____

_____

PRACTICE 3

Writing Assignment

A letter of application, which is a vital job-search tool, always includes a paragraph that summarizes the applicant's qualifications for a particular job. Write a summary of your work experience, beginning with your very first job and moving in chronological order from that job to your current job. Include both paid and volunteer positions. For each job, provide your dates of employment and a brief description of your major responsibilities. A letter of application must be error-free, so proofread it carefully. Exchange papers with a classmate and check each other's work.

CHAPTER HIGHLIGHTS

Avoid run-ons and comma splices:

Her house faces the ocean the view is breathtaking. (*run-on*)

Her house faces the ocean, the view is breathtaking. (*comma splice*)

Use these techniques to avoid run-ons and comma splices:

● **Write two complete sentences.**

Her house faces the ocean. The view is breathtaking.

● **Use a coordinating conjunction.**

Her house faces the ocean, *so* the view is breathtaking.

● **Use a subordinating conjunction.**

Because her house faces the ocean, the view is breathtaking.

CHAPTER REVIEW

Run-ons and comma splices are most likely to occur in paragraphs or longer pieces of writing. Proofread each of the following paragraphs for run-ons and comma splices. Correct them in any way that makes sense: make two separate sentences, add a coordinating conjunction, or add a subordinating conjunction. Make your corrections above the lines. Punctuate with care.

A. (1) Many people are creating personal pages on social networking websites like Facebook, MySpace, and Friendster, these sites offer an enjoyable way to make new friends with common interests. (2) Yet surprising numbers of people post intimate, extreme, or even invented information about themselves. (3) They might think that their new online identities will be fun, hip, or outrageous they probably do not realize that their peers are not the only ones visiting their sites. (4) College admissions officials and potential employers now routinely view the personal pages of promising applicants these pages often provide additional information. (5) For example, one recruiter for a tutoring company was shocked, she checked a young job applicant's page on the Facebook site. (6) The candidate had posted detailed descriptions of his love of late-night partying and drinking. (7) He had illustrated his descriptions with explicit photographs, one picture showed him apparently passed out. (8) The recruiter questioned both the behavior and the judgment of a person who would post this kind of information, he declined to hire the applicant.

B. (1) Skateboarder Tony Hawk has not only dramatically changed his sport, he also has contributed to the popularity of all extreme sports. (2) The wholesome Hawk is responsible for cleaning up skateboarding's early reputation as the pastime of rebels and hoodlums now it's an acceptable, mainstream activity. (3) Hawk is also famous for defying the laws of physics to create amazing new aerial acrobatics. (4) In 1999, at the age of thirty-one, he was the first skater ever to complete a 900, this is a 360-degree spin done two-and-a-half times in midair. (5) As a result, he is called "the Michael Jordan of skateboarding." (6) Today, although he has retired from competition, he performs in exhibitions all over the country surveys of young people reveal that he is more popular than Shaquille O'Neal or Tiger Woods. (7) Hawk's fame has created a huge interest in skateboarding. (8) In 2005, 10.3 million Americans six years old or older played baseball, 11.4 million skateboarded. (9) Today, these young athletes roll into skate parks that have sprung up all over the country, thanks to Hawk's influence.

C. (1) What do you do every night before you go to sleep and every morning when you wake up? (2) You probably brush your teeth, most people in the United States did not start brushing their teeth until after the 1850s. (3) People living in the nineteenth century did not have toothpaste, Dr. Washington Wentworth Sheffield developed a tooth-cleaning substance, which soon became widely available. (4) With the help of his son, this Connecticut dentist changed our daily habits by making the first toothpaste it was called Dr. Sheffield's Creme Dentifrice. (5) The product was not marketed cleverly enough, the idea of using toothpaste caught on slowly. (6) Then toothpaste was put into tin tubes everyone wanted to try this new product. (7) Think of life without tubes of mint-flavored toothpaste then thank Dr. Sheffield for his idea.

D. (1) The first semester of college is difficult for many students they must take on many new responsibilities. (2) For instance, they must create their own schedules. (3) New students get to select their courses in addition, they have to decide when they will take them. (4) Students also must purchase their own textbooks, colleges do not distribute textbooks each term as high schools do. (5) No bells ring to announce when classes begin and end students are supposed to arrive on time. (6) Furthermore, many professors do not call the roll they expect students to attend classes regularly and know the assignments. (7) Above all, new students must be self-disciplined. (8) No one stands over them telling them to do their homework or to visit the writing lab for extra help, they must balance the temptation to have fun and the desire to build a successful future.

E. (1) Languages are disappearing in countries on every continent. (2) North America has two hundred Native American languages, only about fifty now have more than a thousand speakers. (3) The Celtic languages of northwestern Europe also have been declining for many generations. (4) The death of languages is most noticeable in isolated communities in Asia and Australia, however. (5) A different language is spoken in each tiny community sometimes only ten people speak it.

(6) In such small communities, a whole language can die if one village perishes. (7) When Westerners explored a rain forest in Venezuela in the 1960s they

carried a flu virus into a tiny community. (8) The virus killed all the villagers, their language disappeared with them. (9) However, most languages fade out when a smaller community comes into close contact with a larger, more powerful one, people begin to use the "more important" language. (10) A language that gives better access to education, jobs, and new technology usually prevails over a native mother tongue.

(11) According to scholars who study languages, almost half of the world's 6,500 languages are in danger of extinction. (12) That statistic represents more than the loss of specific languages, every language represents a way of looking at the world. (13) Whenever a language disappears, we lose a unique point of view. (14) No other language can really take its place.

 EXPLORING ONLINE

<http://chompchomp2.com/csfs01/csfs01.htm> Interactive quiz-contest: Find comma splices or run-ons (called fused sentences here).

<http://grammar.ccc.commnet.edu/grammar/quizzes/nova/nova4.htm> Interactive quiz: Find and fix the run-ons in these sentences.

<http://college.cengage.com/devenglish> Visit the *Grassroots* 9/e student website for more exercises, quizzes, and live links to all websites mentioned in this chapter.

CHAPTER 16

Semicolons and Conjunctive Adverbs

PART A Defining and Using Semicolons

PART B Defining and Using Conjunctive Adverbs

PART C Punctuating Conjunctive Adverbs

PART A Defining and Using Semicolons

So far you have learned to join ideas together in two ways.

Coordinating conjunctions (*and, but, for, nor, or, so, yet*) can join ideas:

> (1) This is the worst food we have ever tasted, *so* we will never eat in this restaurant again.

Subordinating conjunctions (for example, *although, as, because, if,* and *when*) also can join ideas:

> (2) *Because* this is the worst food we have ever tasted, we will never eat in this restaurant again.

Another way to join ideas is with a **semicolon:**

> (3) This is the worst food we have ever tasted; we will never eat in this restaurant again.

A *semicolon* **joins two related independent ideas without a conjunction; do not capitalize the first word after a semicolon.**

Use the semicolon for variety. In general, use no more than one or two semicolons in a paragraph.

PRACTICE 1

Each independent idea below is the first half of a sentence. Add a semicolon and a second complete idea, one that can stand alone.

EXAMPLE: Ken was a cashier at Food City *; now he manages the store.*

1. My cat spotted a mouse _____

   _____

2. The garage became an art studio *hi was fill with ompaint*

   _____

3. Beatrice has an unlisted phone number *only her mam com use it*

   _____

4. I felt sure someone had been in the room *She can c...*

   _____

5. Roslyn's first car had a stick shift *she doesn't how to dhive it*

   _____

BE CAREFUL: Do not use a semicolon between a dependent idea and an independent idea.

> Although he is never at home, he is not difficult to reach at the office.

● You cannot use a semicolon in this sentence because the first idea (*although he is never at home*) cannot stand alone.

● The word *although* requires that another idea be added in order to make a complete sentence.

PRACTICE 2

Which of these ideas can be followed by a semicolon and an independent thought? Check them (✔).

1. When Molly peered over the counter _____

2. The library has installed new computers _____

3. After he finishes cleaning the fish _____

4. She suddenly started to laugh _____

5. My answer is simple _____

6. I cannot find my car keys _____

7. The rain poured down in buckets _____

8. Before the health fair is over _____

9. Unless you arrive early _____

10. Because you understand, I feel better _____

Now copy the sentences you have checked, add a semicolon, and complete each sentence with a second independent idea. You should have checked sentences 2, 4, 5, 6, 7, and 10.

2. _____

4. _____

5. _____

6. _____

7. _____

10. _____

PRACTICE 3

Proofread for incorrect semicolons or capital letters. Make your corrections above the lines.

(1) The Swiss Army knife is carried in the pockets and purses of millions of travelers, campers, and just plain folks. (2) Numerous useful gadgets are folded into its famous red handle; These include knife blades, tweezers, scissors, toothpick, screwdriver, bottle opener, fish scaler, and magnifying glass. (3) Because the knife contains many tools; it is also carried by explorers, mountain climbers, and astronauts. (4) Lives have been saved by the Swiss Army knife. (5) It once opened the iced-up oxygen system of someone climbing Mount Everest; It saved the lives of scientists stranded on an island who used the tiny saw on the knife to cut branches for a fire. (6) The handy Swiss Army knife was created for Swiss soldiers in 1891; and soon became popular all over the world. (7) It comes in many models and colors many people prefer the classic original. (8) The Swiss Army knife deserves its reputation for beautiful design and usefulness; a red one is on permanent display in New York's famous Museum of Modern Art.

PART B   Defining and Using Conjunctive Adverbs

Another excellent method of joining ideas is to use a semicolon and a special kind of adverb. This special adverb is called a **conjunctive adverb** because it is part *conjunction* and part *adverb*.

(1) (a) He received an *A* on his term paper; *furthermore,*
    (b) the instructor exempted him from the final.

● *Furthermore* adds idea (b) to idea (a).

● The sentence might have been written, "He received an *A* on his term paper, *and* the instructor exempted him from the final."

● However, *furthermore* is stronger and more emphatic.

● Note the punctuation.

(2) (a) Luzette has never studied finance; *however,*
    (b) she plays the stock market like a pro.

● *However* contrasts ideas (a) and (b).

● The sentence might have been written, "Luzette has never studied finance, *but* she plays the stock market like a pro."

● However, the word *however* is stronger and more emphatic.

● Note the punctuation.

(3) (a) The complete dictionary weighs thirty pounds; *therefore,*
    (b) I bring my pocket edition to school.

● *Therefore* shows that idea (a) is the cause of idea (b).

● The sentence might have been written, "*Because* the complete dictionary weighs thirty pounds, I bring my pocket edition to school."

● However, *therefore* is stronger and more emphatic.

● Note the punctuation.

A *conjunctive adverb* **may be used with a semicolon only when both ideas are independent and can stand alone.**

Here are some common conjunctive adverbs and their meanings:

Common Conjunctive Adverbs

consequently	*means*	as a result
furthermore	*means*	in addition
however	*means*	in contrast
instead	*means*	in place of
meanwhile	*means*	at the same time
nevertheless	*means*	in contrast
otherwise	*means*	as an alternative
therefore	*means*	for that reason

Conjunctive adverbs are also called **transitional expressions.** They help the reader see the transitions, or changes in meaning, from one idea to the next.

PRACTICE 4

Add an idea after each conjunctive adverb. The idea you add must make sense in terms of the entire sentence, so keep in mind the meaning of each conjunctive adverb. If necessary, refer to the chart.

EXAMPLE: Several students had questions about the final; therefore, _they stayed_

after class to chat with the instructor.

1. Aunt Bessie did a handstand; meanwhile, _____

_____

2. Anna says whatever is on her mind; consequently, _she mind offend people_

_____

3. I refuse to wear those red cowboy boots again; furthermore, _I would never_

wear that hat

4. Travis is a good role model; otherwise, _I not be here today_

_____

5. Kim wanted to volunteer at the hospital; however, _she did not have_

off

6. My mother carried two bulky pieces of luggage off the plane; furthermore,

she has her grand daughter

7. I have many chores to do today; nevertheless, _I still_

_____

8. The gas gauge on my car does not work properly; therefore, _I_

_____

PART C Punctuating Conjunctive Adverbs

Notice the punctuation pattern:

Complete idea; conjunctive adverb, complete idea.

● The conjunctive adverb is preceded by a semicolon.
● It is followed by a comma.

PRACTICE 5

Punctuate these sentences correctly.

1. Many people think that art is serious rather than fun however they might change their minds if they could see a Cow Parade.

2. For this public art event, a city's artists decorate identical, life-size sculptures of cows consequently each cow becomes a humorous artistic work.

3. In the Chicago and New York Cow Parades, the finished art objects were anything but dull and reserved instead they were wildly creative.

4. Each artist picked a character or idea to portray furthermore; he or she gave that special bovine a fitting name.

5. For example, one cow was painted with stars and stripes to resemble our country's flag consequently its name was "Americow the Beautiful."

6. Dark-eyed "Cowapatra" was decorated like the Queen of the Nile meanwhile "Moozart" wore the red velvet coat and white wig of that famous composer.

7. "Prima Cowlerina" posed in a pink tutu and four toe shoes, and "Cownt Dracula" had fangs therefore even blasé city dwellers paused to admire them.

8. Many cows were decorated with a famous work of art consequently they had names like "Picowso," "Mootisse," or "Vincent Van Cogh."

9. People seem to love meeting a plaster cow dressed in hip hop clothing or covered with gumdrops on a city street meanwhile urban work and play can go on as usual.

10. Each event concludes with an auction of the cows to benefit charity therefore a Cow Parade not only brings art to the public but also raises money for a good cause.

Lady Cowdiva, New York Cow Parade.

Courtesy Cow Parade Holdings Corp.

PRACTICE 6

Combine each set of sentences into one, using a conjunctive adverb. Choose a conjunctive adverb that expresses the relationship between the two ideas. Punctuate with care.

1. (a) Marilyn fell asleep on the train.

   (b) She missed her stop.

   Combination: _____

   _____

2. (a) Last night Channel 20 televised a special about gorillas.

   (b) I did not get home in time to see it.

   Combination: _____

   _____

3. (a) Roberta writes to her nephew every month.

   (b) She sends a gift with every letter.

   Combination: _____

   _____

4. (a) It takes me almost an hour to get to school each morning.

   (b) The scenery makes the drive a pleasure.

   Combination: _____

   _____

5. (a) Luke missed work on Monday.

   (b) He did not proofread the quarterly report.

   Combination: _____

   _____

BE CAREFUL: Never use a semicolon and a conjunctive adverb when the conjunctive adverb does not join two independent ideas.

(1) *However,* I don't climb mountains.

(2) I don't, *however,* climb mountains.

(3) I don't climb mountains, *however.*

● Why aren't semicolons used in sentences (1), (2), and (3)?

● These sentences contain only one independent idea; therefore, a semicolon cannot be used.

Never use a semicolon to join two ideas if one of the ideas is subordinate to the other.

(4) If I climbed mountains, *however*, I would hike in the Rockies.

● Are the two ideas in sentence (4) independent?

● *If I climbed mountains* cannot stand alone as an independent idea; therefore, a semicolon cannot be used.

PRACTICE 7

Writing Assignment

Many people find that certain situations make them nervous or anxious—for example, giving a speech or meeting strangers at a social gathering. Have you ever conquered such an anxiety yourself or even learned to cope with it successfully?

Write to someone who has the same fear you have had; encourage him or her with your success story, explaining how you managed the anxiety. Describe what steps you took.

Use one or two semicolons and at least one conjunctive adverb in your paper. Make sure that you are joining together two independent ideas.

CHAPTER HIGHLIGHTS

● **A semicolon joins two independent ideas:**

I like hiking; she prefers fishing.

● **Do not capitalize the first word after a semicolon.**

| *Independent idea* | ; | *independent idea.* |

● **A semicolon and a conjunctive adverb join two independent ideas:**

We can't go rowing now; *however,* we can go on Sunday.

Lou earned an 83 on the exam; *therefore,* he passed physics.

| *Independent idea* | ; consequently,
; furthermore,
; however,
; instead,
; meanwhile,
; nevertheless,
; therefore, | *independent idea.* |

● **Use a semicolon *only* when the conjunctive adverb joins two independent ideas:**

I wasn't sorry; however, I apologized. (*two independent ideas*)

I apologized, however. (*one independent idea*)

If you wanted to go, however, you should have said so. (*one dependent idea + one independent idea*)

CHAPTER REVIEW

Proofread the following paragraph for semicolon errors, conjunctive adverb errors, and punctuation errors. Correct each error above the line.

(1) Perhaps you have seen a sleek circular symbol consisting of two connected teardrop shapes, one white and one black. (2) This is the Chinese symbol Yin Yang. (3) According to ancient Chinese philosophy, we live in a world of opposites consequently the world contains female and male, dark and light, cold and hot, yin and yang. (4) Yin and yang represent contrasting life forces however the symbol shows us a harmony of opposites that underlies the universe. (5) On the one hand, yin is any force that is feminine, soft, receptive, hidden, cool, and dark, thus; the dark part of the symbol represents yin. (6) Yang, on the other hand, describes any force that is masculine, hard, aggressive, open, hot, and light, therefore, the light part of the symbol represents yang. (7) However, the Yin Yang symbol also contains a dot of black in the white area and a dot of white in the black area. (8) These dots remind us that nothing is simply black or white everything contains an element of the opposing force. (9) For example, all people are a mix of yin and yang qualities, whatever their gender. (10) The whole symbol seems to say that we know pleasure because we have felt pain, beauty because we have seen ugliness, and love because we have known its opposite.

EXPLORING ONLINE

<http://owl.english.purdue.edu/handouts/grammar/g_commacompEX1.html>
Paper-and-pencil quiz: Does each sentence require a comma or a semicolon?

<http://grammar.ccc.commnet.edu/grammar/cgi-shl/quiz.pl/run-ons_add1.htm>
Interactive quiz: Click the sentence that corrects the run-on or comma splice.

<http://college.cengage.com/devenglish> Visit the *Grassroots* 9/e student website for more exercises, quizzes, and live links to all websites mentioned in this chapter.

Relative Pronouns

CHAPTER 17

PART A Defining and Using Relative Pronouns

PART B Punctuating Ideas Introduced by WHO, WHICH, or THAT

PART A   Defining and Using Relative Pronouns

To add variety to your writing, you sometimes may wish to use **relative pronouns** to combine two sentences.

> (1) My grandfather is eighty years old.
>
> (2) He collects stamps.

● Sentences (1) and (2) are grammatically correct.

● They are so short, however, that you may wish to combine them.

> (3) My grandfather, who is eighty years old, collects stamps.

● Sentence (3) is a combination of (1) and (2).

● *Who* has replaced *he*, the subject of sentence (2). *Who* introduces the rest of the idea, *is eighty years old*.

● *Who* is called a *relative pronoun* because it *relates* "is eighty years old" to "my grandfather."*

BE CAREFUL: An idea introduced by a relative pronoun cannot stand alone as a complete and independent sentence. It is dependent; it needs an independent idea (like "My grandfather collects stamps") to complete its meaning.

Here are some more combinations:

> (4) He gives great singing lessons.
>
> (5) All his pupils love them.
>
> (6) He gives great singing lessons, *which* all his pupils love.

---

*For work on subject-verb agreement with relative pronouns, see Chapter 8, Part G.

(7) I have a large dining room.

(8) It can seat twenty people.

(9) I have a large dining room *that* can seat twenty people.

● As you can see, *which* and *that* can also be used as relative pronouns.

● In sentence (6), what does *which* relate or refer to? _____

● In sentence (9), what does *that* relate or refer to? _____

When *who, which,* and *that* are used as relative pronouns, they usually come directly after the words they relate to.

My grandfather, who . . .

. . . singing lessons, which . . .

. . . dining room that . . .

BE CAREFUL: *Who, which,* and *that* cannot be used interchangeably.

Who **refers to people.**

Which **refers to things.**

That **refers to people or things.**

PRACTICE 1

Combine each set of sentences into one sentence. Make sure to use *who, which,* and *that* correctly.

EXAMPLE: a. The garden is beginning to sprout.

b. I planted it last week.

Combination: The garden that I planted last week is beginning to sprout.

1. a. My uncle is giving me diving lessons.

b. He was a state champion.

Combination: My uncle, who is giving me diving Lesson, who was a state champion.

2. a. Our marriage ceremony was quick and sweet.

b. It made our nervous parents happy.

Combination: Our marriage ceremony, which was quick and sweet, who made our nervous parents happy.

3. a. The manatee is a sea mammal.

b. It lives along the Florida coast.

Combination: the manatee, that is a sea mammal who lives along the florida coast.

4. a. Donna bought a new backpack.

b. The backpack has thickly padded straps.

Combination: _The backpack which_ _____

_____

5. a. This walking tour has thirty-two stops.
   b. It is a challenge to complete.

Combination: _that has_ _____

_____

6. a. Hockey is a fast-moving game.
   b. It often becomes violent.

Combination: _who often_ _____

_____

7. a. Andrew Jackson was the seventh U.S. president.
   b. He was born in South Carolina.

Combination: _who_ _____

_____

8. a. At the beach, I always use sunscreen.
   b. It prevents burns and lessens the danger of skin cancer.

Combination: _which pre_ _____

_____

PART B   Punctuating Ideas Introduced by WHO, WHICH, or THAT

Ideas introduced by relative pronouns can be one of two types, **restrictive** or **non-restrictive.** Punctuating them must be done carefully.

Restrictive _you need the comma_

> Never eat peaches _that are_ green.

- A _relative clause_ has (1) a subject that is a relative pronoun and (2) a verb.
- What is the relative clause in the sentence in the box? _____
- Can you leave out _that are green_ and still keep the basic meaning of the sentence?
- No! You are not saying _don't eat peaches_; you are saying don't eat _certain kinds_ of peaches—_green_ ones.
- Therefore, _that are green_ is _restrictive_; it restricts the meaning of the sentence.

A _restrictive clause_ **is not set off by commas; it is necessary to the meaning of the sentence.**

Nonrestrictive

My guitar, *which is a Martin*, was given to me as a gift.

● In this sentence, the relative clause is _____ .
● Can you leave out *which is a Martin* and still keep the basic meaning of the sentence?
● Yes! *Which is a Martin* merely adds a fact. It does not change the basic idea of the sentence, which is *my guitar was given to me as a gift*.
● Therefore, *which is a Martin* is *nonrestrictive*; it does not restrict or change the meaning of the sentence.

A *nonrestrictive clause* **is set off by commas; it is not necessary to the meaning of the sentence.**

Note: *Which* is often used as a nonrestrictive relative pronoun.

PRACTICE 2

Punctuate correctly. Write a *C* next to each correct sentence.

1. People who need help are often embarrassed to ask for it.   C
2. Ovens that clean themselves are the best kind.   C
3. Paint that contains lead can be dangerous to children.   C
4. The anaconda which is the largest snake in the world, can weigh 550 pounds.   ___
5. Edward's watch which tells the time and the date was a gift from his wife.   ___
6. Carol who is a flight attendant has just left for Pakistan.
7. Joel Upton who is a dean of students usually sings in the yearly talent show.   ___
8. Exercise that causes severe exhaustion is dangerous.   C

PRACTICE 3

Complete each sentence by completing the relative clause.

EXAMPLE: Boxing is a sport that *upsets me* _____ .

1. My aunt, who _____, rescued a cat last week.
2. A family that _____ can solve its problems.
3. I never vote for candidates who _____ .
4. This T-shirt, which _____, was a gift.
5. Paris, which _____, is an exciting city to visit.
6. James, who _____, just enlisted in the Air Force.

7. I cannot resist stores that _____ .

8. This company, which _____ , provides health benefits and retirement plans for employees.

PRACTICE 4

On paper or on a computer, write four sentences using restrictive relative clauses and four using nonrestrictive relative clauses. Punctuate with care.

PRACTICE 5

Writing Assignment

In a small group, discuss a change that would improve life in your neighborhood—a new traffic light or more police patrols, for instance. Your task is to write a flier that will convince neighbors that this change is important; your purpose is to win them over to your side. The flier might note, for instance, that a child was killed at a certain intersection or that several burglaries could have been prevented. Each group member should write his or her own flier, including two sentences with relative pronouns and correct punctuation. Then read the fliers aloud; decide which are effective and why. Finally, exchange papers and check for correct relative pronoun use.

CHAPTER HIGHLIGHTS

- **Relative pronouns (*who*, *which*, and *that*) can join two independent ideas:**

    We met Krizia Stone, *who* runs an advertising agency.

    Last night, I had a hamburger *that* was too rare.

    My favorite radio station, *which* is WQDF, plays mostly jazz.

- **Restrictive relative clauses change the meaning of the sentence. They are not set off by commas:**

    The uncle *who is helping me through college* lives in Texas.

    The car *that we saw Ned driving* was not his.

- **Nonrestrictive relative clauses do not change the meaning of the sentence. They are set off by commas:**

    My uncle, *who lives in Texas,* owns a supermarket.

    Ned's car, *which is a 1992 Mazda,* was at the repair shop.

CHAPTER REVIEW

Proofread the following paragraph for relative pronoun errors and punctuation errors. Correct each error above the line.

(1) Charles Anderson is best known as the trainer of the Tuskegee Airmen who were the first African-American combat pilots. (2) During a time when African

Seven of the famous African-American pilots of World War II, the Tuskegee Airmen.

Bettmann/CORBIS.

Americans were prevented from becoming pilots, Anderson was fascinated by planes. (3) He learned about flying from books. (4) At age twenty-two, he bought a used plane which, became his teacher. (5) Eventually he met someone, who helped him become an expert flyer. (6) Battling against discrimination, Anderson became the first African American to earn an air transport pilot's license. (7) He and another pilot made the first round-trip flight across America by black Americans. (8) In 1939, Anderson started a civilian pilot training program at Tuskegee Institute in Alabama. (9) One day Eleanor Roosevelt, which was first lady at the time insisted on flying with him. (10) Soon afterward, Tuskegee Institute was chosen by the Army Air Corps for a special program. (11) Anderson who was chief flight instructor gave America's first African-American World War II pilots their initial training. (12) During the war, the Tuskegee Airmen showed great skill and heroism which were later recognized by an extraordinary number of honors and awards.

EXPLORING ONLINE

<http://grammar.ccc.commnet.edu/grammar/quizzes/which_quiz.htm> Interactive quiz: Choose *who, which,* or *that.*

<http://www.dailygrammar.com/256to260.shtml> Graded quiz: Combine sentences with *who, which,* or *that* (here called adjective) clauses.

<http://college.cengage.com/devenglish> Visit the *Grassroots* 9/e student website for more exercises, quizzes, and live links to all websites mentioned in this chapter.

-ING Modifiers

PART A Using -ING Modifiers

PART B Avoiding Confusing Modifiers

PART A Using -ING Modifiers

Another way to join ideas together is with an **-ing modifier**, or **present participle**.

> (1) Beth was learning to ski. She broke her ankle.
>
> (2) Learning to ski, Beth broke her ankle.

- It seems that *while* Beth was learning to ski, she had an accident. Sentence (2) emphasizes this time relationship and also joins two short sentences in one longer one.

- In sentence (2), *learning* without its helping verb, *was*, is not a verb. Instead, *learning to ski* refers to or modifies *Beth,* the subject of the new sentence.

> Learning to ski, Beth broke her ankle.

- Note that a comma follows the introductory *-ing* modifier, setting it off from the independent idea.

PRACTICE 1

Combine the two sentences in each pair, using the *-ing* modifier to connect them. Drop unnecessary words. Draw an arrow from the *-ing* word to the word or words to which it refers.

EXAMPLE: Tom was standing on the deck. He waved good-bye to his family.

Standing on the deck, Tom waved good-bye to his family.

1. Kyla was searching for change. She found her lost earring.

_____

2. The children worked all evening. They completed the jigsaw puzzle.

   _____

3. They were hiking cross-country. They made many new friends.

   _____

4. She was visiting Santa Fe. She decided to move there.

   _____

5. You are loading your camera. You spot a grease mark on the lens.

   _____

6. Seth was mumbling to himself. He named the fifty states.

   _____

7. Judge Smithers was pounding his gavel. He called a recess.

   _____

8. The masons built the wall carefully. They were lifting huge rocks and cementing them in place.

   _____

   _____

PART B   Avoiding Confusing Modifiers

Be sure that your *-ing* modifiers say what you mean!

> (1) Hanging by the toe from the dresser drawer, Joe found his sock.

● Probably the writer did not mean that Joe spent time hanging by his toe. What, then, was hanging by the toe from the dresser drawer?

● *Hanging* refers to the *sock*, of course, but the order of the sentence does not show this. We can clear up the confusion by turning the ideas around.

> Joe found his sock hanging by the toe from the dresser drawer.

Read your sentences in Practice 1 to make sure the order of the ideas is clear, not confusing.

> (2) Visiting my cousin, our house was robbed.

- Does the writer mean that *our house* was visiting my cousin? To whom or what, then, does *visiting my cousin* refer?

- *Visiting* seems to refer to *I*, but there is no *I* in the sentence. To clear up the confusion, we would have to add or change words.

Visiting my cousin, I learned that our house was robbed.

PRACTICE 2

Rewrite the following sentences to clarify any confusing *-ing* modifiers.

1. Biking and walking daily, Cheryl's commuting costs were cut.

   Rewrite: _____

2. Leaping from tree to tree, Professor Fernandez spotted a monkey.

   Rewrite: _____

3. Painting for three hours straight, the bathroom and the hallway were finished by Theresa.

   Rewrite: _____

4. My son spotted our dog playing soccer in the schoolyard.

   Rewrite: _____

5. Lying in the driveway, Tonya discovered her calculus textbook.

   Rewrite: _____

PRACTICE 3

On paper or on a computer, write three sentences of your own, using *-ing* modifiers to join ideas.

PRACTICE 4

Writing Assignment

Some people feel that much popular music degrades women and encourages drug abuse and violence. Others feel that popular songs expose many of the social ills we suffer from today. What do you think?

Prepare to take part in a debate to defend or criticize popular music. Your job is to convince the other side that your view is correct. Use specific song titles and artists as examples to support your argument. Use one or two *-ing* modifiers to join ideas together. Remember to punctuate correctly.

CHAPTER HIGHLIGHTS

- **An *-ing* modifier can join two ideas:**

    (1) Sol was cooking dinner.

    (2) He started a small fire.

    (1) + (2) *Cooking* dinner, Sol started a small fire.

- **Avoid confusing modifiers:**

    I finally found my cat riding my bike. (*incorrect*)

    Riding my bike, I finally found my cat. (*correct*)

CHAPTER REVIEW

Proofread the following paragraph for comma errors and confusing modifiers. Correct each error above the line.

(1) What happened in the shed behind Patrick O'Leary's house to start the Great Chicago Fire of 1871? (2) No one knows for sure. (3) Smoking in the shed some people say the fire was started by careless boys. (4) In another story, poker-playing youngsters accidentally kicked over an oil lamp. (5) The blame, however, usually is placed on Mrs. O'Leary's cow. (6) At 8:45 p.m., swinging a lantern at her side Mrs. O'Leary went out to milk the unruly cow. (7) The cow tipped the lantern switching its tail. (8) Recalling the incident Mrs. Nellie Hayes branded the cow theory "nonsense." (9) In fact, she said that the O'Learys' neighbors were having a party on the hot night of October 7. (10) Looking for some fresh milk a thirsty guest walked into the shed and dropped a lighted candle along the way. (11) Whatever happened, the fire was the greatest calamity of nineteenth-century America. (12) Killing three hundred people and destroying more than three square miles of buildings it left ninety thousand people homeless.

EXPLORING ONLINE

<http://grammar.ccc.commnet.edu/grammar/cgi-shl/quiz.pl/modifier_quiz.htm>
Are your modifiers misplaced? Take this quiz and improve your skills.

<http://college.cengage.com/devenglish> Visit the *Grassroots* 9/e student website for more exercises, quizzes, and live links to all websites mentioned in this chapter.

WRITING ASSIGNMENTS

As you complete each writing assignment, remember to perform these steps:

● Write a clear, complete topic sentence.

● Use freewriting, brainstorming, or clustering to generate ideas for the body of your paragraph, essay, or letter.

● Arrange your best ideas in a plan.

● Revise for support, unity, coherence, and exact language.

● Proofread for grammar, punctuation, and spelling errors.

Writing Assignment 1: *Post your thoughts online.* Many websites and blogs invite viewers to respond by posting their comments or opinions. Find a blog or website forum that focuses on a topic you find interesting, such as music, sports, health/fitness, politics, the media, art, or technology. Select a site you already know and like, or find one in a list of the best websites (<http://www .100bestwebsites.org/>) or blogs (<http://blogs.botw.org/>). Then, contribute your thoughts or feedback. For example, you could post your thoughts about a favorite television show at <http://www.televisionwithoutpity.com/>, contribute to a spiritual discussion at <http://www.beliefnet.com/boards/index.asp>, or comment on current events at <http://www.cnn.com/exchange/ireports/topics/index.html>. Use as many techniques for joining ideas as you can, and proofread for run-ons and comma splices.

Writing Assignment 2: *Be a witness.* You have just witnessed a fender-bender involving a car and an ice cream truck. No one was hurt, but the insurance company has asked you to write an eyewitness report. First, visualize the accident and how it occurred. Then jot down as many details as possible to make your description of the accident as vivid as possible. Use subordinating conjunctions that indicate time (*when, as, before, while,* and so on) to show the order of events. Use as many techniques for joining ideas as you can, being careful about punctuation. Proofread for run-ons and comma splices.

Writing Assignment 3: *Evaluate so-called reality TV shows.* A newspaper has asked readers to respond to the question "Has reality television gone too far?" Think about the latest reality programs—*Survivor, Fear Factor*, and similar shows in which contestants are often humiliated and forced to do bizarre things. State whether reality TV has, or has not, gone too far. Then explain why you feel this way, using vivid details and examples from one or more programs to support your point. Use as many techniques for joining ideas as you can; proofread for run-ons and comma splices.

Writing Assignment 4: *React to a quotation.* From the "Work and Success" section of the Quotation Bank at the end of this book, choose a quotation that you strongly agree or disagree with. For instance, do you think it is true that "most of us are looking for a calling, not a job" or that "money is like manure"? In your first sentence, repeat the entire quotation, explaining whether you do or do not agree with it. Then brainstorm, freewrite, or cluster to generate examples and facts supporting your view. Use your own or other people's experiences to strengthen your argument. Use as many techniques for joining ideas as you can. Proofread for run-ons and comma splices.

REVIEW

Five Useful Ways to Join Ideas

In this unit, you have combined simple sentences by means of a **coordinating conjunction,** a **subordinating conjunction,** a **semicolon,** and a **semicolon** and **conjunctive adverb.** Here is a review chart of the sentence patterns discussed in this unit.

Coordination

Option 1   *Independent clause*   { , and / , but / , for / , nor / , or / , so / , yet }   *independent clause.*

Option 2   *Independent clause*   ;   *independent clause.*

Option 3   *Independent clause*   { ; consequently, / ; furthermore, / ; however, / ; indeed, / ; in fact, / ; moreover, / ; nevertheless, / ; then, / ; therefore, }   *independent clause.*

Subordination

Option 4   *Independent clause*   { after / although / as (as if) / because / before / if / since / unless / until / when(ever) / whereas / while }   *dependent clause.*

Option 5   { After / Although / As (as if) / Because / Before / If / Since / Unless / Until / When(ever) / Whereas / While }   *dependent clause, independent clause.*

Proofreading

The student composition below has been changed to contain run-ons, comma splices, and misused semicolons. Proofread for these errors. Then correct them above the lines in any way you choose. (You should find eight errors.)

Managing Time in College

(1) When I started college, time was a problem. (2) I was always desperately reading an assignment just before class or racing to get to work on time. (3) The stress became too much. (4) It took a while now I know how to manage my time. (5) The secret of my success is flexible planning.

(6) At the beginning of each semester, I mark a calendar with all the due dates for the term these include deadlines for assignments, papers, and tests. (7) I also write in social events and obligations, therefore; I know at a glance when I need extra time during the next few months.

(8) Next, I make out a model weekly study schedule. (9) First, I block in the hours when I have to sleep, eat, work, go to class, and tend to my family then I decide what time I will devote to study and relaxation. (10) Finally, I fill in the times I will study each subject, making sure I plan at least one hour of study time for each hour of class time. (11) Generally, I plan some time just before or after a class that way I can prepare for a class or review my notes right after a lecture.

(12) In reality, I don't follow this schedule rigidly, I vary it according to the demands of the week and day. (13) In addition, I spend more time on my harder subjects and less time on the easy ones. (14) I also try to study my harder subjects in the morning; when I am most awake.

(15) I find that by setting up a model schedule but keeping it flexible, I can accomplish all I have to do with little worry. (16) This system may not help everyone, it has certainly worked for me.

Jesse Rose, student

Combining

Read each pair of sentences below to determine the relationship between them. Then join each pair in *two* different ways, using the conjunctions shown. Punctuate correctly.

1. The tide had not yet come in.
   We went swimming.

   (although) _____

   _____

   (but) _____

   _____

2. Michael enjoys drinking coffee.
   He needs to limit his caffeine intake.

   (yet) _____

   _____

   (nevertheless) _____

   _____

3. Alexis plays the trumpet very well.
   She hopes to have her own band someday.

   (and) _____

   _____

   (furthermore) _____

   _____

4. The lecture starts in five minutes.
   We had better get to our seats.

   (because) _____

   _____

   (so) _____

   _____

5. He knows how to make money.
   He doesn't want to start another company.

   (although) _____

   _____

   (however) _____

   _____

Revising

Read through this essay of short, choppy sentences. Then revise it, combining some sentences. Use one coordinating conjunction, one subordinating conjunction, and any other ways you have learned to join ideas together. Keep some short sentences for variety. Make your corrections above the lines, and punctuate with care.

Control Your Credit

(1) One-fourth of all Americans want to get out of debt. (2) Many college students are among them (3) These students graduate. (4) They owe more than $2,000 in credit-card debt. (4) Good credit habits can be learned. (5) You may have abused your plastic and gotten into trouble. (6) You might be using credit cards for the first time. (7) You can develop three habits to help control your credit-card debt.

(8) First, have and carry just one credit card. (9) Using two or more can quickly lead to overspending. (10) Choose your card wisely. (11) Some cards are better than others. (12) The best card offers the lowest interest rate. (13) It should not charge an annual fee.

(14) A second good habit is to use a credit card only as a last resort. (15) Whenever possible, use cash, a debit card, or a check. (16) Save your credit cards for true emergencies. (17) When cash is low, don't grab a card. (18) Reduce spending instead. (19) Experts also offer this rule of thumb: "If you can eat it or drink it, don't charge it!"

(20) Finally, get in the habit of thinking of credit cards as just another form of cash. (21) You never let your charges exceed your available funds. (22) You will be able to pay your full balance each month. (23) As a result, you'll avoid expensive interest charges that only increase your debt.

(24) You develop good credit card habits. (25) You will stay in control of debt. (26) It will not take control of you.

WRITERS' WORKSHOP

Describe a Detour off the Main Highway

When a writer really cares about a subject, often the reader will care too. In your group or class, read this student's paragraph, aloud if possible. As you read, underline any words or details that strike you as vivid or powerful.

> Sometimes detours off the main highway can bring wonderful surprises, and last week this happened to my husband and me. On the Fourth of July weekend, we decided to drive home the long way, taking the old dirt farm road. Pulling over to admire the afternoon light gleaming on a field of wet corn we saw a tiny farm stand under a tree. No one was in sight, but a card table covered with a red checkered cloth held pints of tomatoes, jars of jam, and a handwritten price list. Next to these was a vase full of red poppies and tiny American flags. We bought tomatoes, leaving our money in the tin box stuffed with dollar bills. Driving home we both felt so happy—as if we had been given a great gift.
>
> *Kim Lee, student*

1. How effective is Kim Lee's paragraph?

   _____ Clear topic sentence?   _____ Rich supporting details?

   _____ Logical organization?   _____ Effective conclusion?

2. Discuss your underlinings with one another, explaining as specifically as possible why a particular word or sentence is effective. For instance, the "red poppies and tiny American flags" are so exact that you can see them.

3. This student supports her topic sentence with a single *example*, one brief story told in detail. If you were to support the same topic sentence, what example from your own life might you use?

4. The concluding sentence tells the reader that she and her husband felt they had been given "a great gift." Do you think that the gift was being trusted to be honest?

5. Proofread for grammar and spelling. Do you notice any error patterns (two or more errors of the same type) that this student should watch out for?

> About her writing process, Kim Lee says:
>
> I wrote this paper in my usual way—I sort of plan, and then I freewrite on the subject. I like freewriting—I pick through it for certain words or details, but of course it is also a mess. From my freewriting I got "light gleaming on a field of wet corn" and the last sentence, about the gift.

Writing and Revising Ideas

1. Develop the topic sentence "Sometimes detours off the main highway can bring wonderful [disturbing] surprises."

2. Write about a time when you were trusted or distrusted by a stranger. What effect did this have on you?

As you plan your paragraph, try to angle the subject toward something that interests *you*—chances are, it will interest your readers too. Consider using one good example to develop your paragraph. As you revise, make sure that the body of your paragraph perfectly fits the topic sentence.

Choosing the Right Noun, Pronoun, Adjective, Adverb, or Preposition

Choosing the right *form* of many words in English can be tricky. This unit will help you avoid some common errors. In this unit, you will

- Learn about singular and plural nouns
- Choose correct pronouns
- Use adjectives and adverbs correctly
- Choose the right prepositions

Spotlight on Writing

Here, two researchers set forth new findings about happiness. If possible, read the paragraph aloud.

In study after study, four traits characterize happy people. First, especially in individualistic Western cultures, they like themselves. They have high self-esteem and usually believe themselves to be more ethical, more intelligent, less prejudiced, better able to get along with others, and healthier than the average person. Second, happy people typically feel personal control. Those with little or no control over their lives—such as prisoners, nursing home patients, severely impoverished groups or individuals, and citizens in totalitarian regimes—suffer lower morale and worse health. Third, happy people are usually optimistic. Fourth, most happy people are extroverted. Although one might expect that introverts would live more happily in the serenity of their less stressed . . . lives, extroverts are happier—whether alone or with others.

David G. Myers and Ed Diener, "The Pursuit of
Happiness," *Scientific American*

- This well-organized paragraph tells us that happy people think they are "more *ethical*, more *intelligent*, less *prejudiced*, better *able* . . ., and *healthier* . . ." Do you know why these words—adjectives—are correct as written?

- If you don't know the meaning of the words *extrovert* and *introvert*, look them up. Which refers to you?

 Writing Ideas

- *Analyze how happy you are, based on the four traits mentioned above.*

- *Describe an extrovert or an introvert you have observed.*

CHAPTER 19

Nouns

PART A Defining Singular and Plural

PART B Signal Words: Singular and Plural

PART C Signal Words with OF

PART A Defining Singular and Plural

A **noun** names a person, a place, a thing, or an idea. Nouns may be singular or plural.

Singular **means one.** *Plural* **means more than one.**

Singular	Plural
a reporter	the reporters
a pear	the pears
the couch	the couches

● Nouns usually add -*s* or -*es* to form the plural.

Some nouns form their plurals in other ways. Here is a partial list:

Singular	Plural
child	children
foot	feet
goose	geese
man	men
mouse	mice
tooth	teeth
woman	women

Many nouns ending in -*f* or -*fe* change their endings to -*ves* in the plural:

Singular	Plural
half	halves
knife	knives

leaf	leaves
life	lives
scarf	scarves
shelf	shelves
wife	wives
wolf	wolves

Add *-es* to most nouns that end in *o*:

echo + *es* = echoes	potato + *es* = potatoes
hero + *es* = heroes	veto + *es* = vetoes

● Here are some exceptions to memorize:

pianos	solos
radios	sopranos

Other nouns do not change at all to form the plural. Below is a partial list:

Singular	Plural
deer	deer
fish	fish
moose	moose
sheep	sheep

Hyphenated nouns usually form plurals by adding *-s* or *-es* to the first word:

Singular	Plural
brother-in-law	brothers-in-law
maid-of-honor	maids-of-honor
mother-to-be	mothers-to-be
runner-up	runners-up

If you are ever unsure about the plural of a noun, check a dictionary. For example, if you look up the noun *woman* in the dictionary, you will find an entry like this:

woman / women

The first word listed, *woman,* is the singular form of the noun; the second word, *women,* is the plural. Some dictionaries list the plural form of a noun only if the plural is unusual. If no plural is listed, the noun probably adds *-s* or *-es.*

PRACTICE 1

Make the following nouns plural.* If you are not sure of a particular plural, check the charts on the previous pages.

Singular	Plural	Singular	Plural
1. notebook	_____	11. brother-in-law	_____
2. hero	_____	12. technician	_____
3. man	_____	13. shelf	_____
4. half	_____	14. potato	_____
5. bridge	_____	15. mouse	_____
6. deer	_____	16. child	_____
7. runner-up	_____	17. flight	_____
8. woman	_____	18. wife	_____
9. radio	_____	19. place	_____
10. tooth	_____	20. maid-of-honor	_____

REMEMBER: **Do not add an -s to words that form plurals by changing an internal letter or letters. For example, the plural of** *man* **is** *men,* **not** *mens;* **the plural of** *woman* **is** *women,* **not** *womens;* **the plural of** *foot* **is** *feet,* **not** *feets.*

PRACTICE 2

Proofread the following paragraph for incorrect plural nouns. Cross out the errors and correct them above the lines.

(1) Many peoples consider Glacier National Park the jewel of the National Park Service. (2) Its many mountains, glaciers, waterfalls, blue-green lake, and amazing wildlifes are in the remote Rocky Mountains in the northwest corner of Montana. (3) Several road take visitors into the park, especially Going-to-the-Sun Road, which clings to the mountainside and offers spectacular, stomach-churning views. (4) At Logan Pass—6,646 foot high—the road crosses the Continental Divide. (5) From this line along the spine of the Rocky, all river flow either west to the Pacific Ocean, south to the Gulf, or east. (6) Because Glacier is truly a wilderness park, it is best seen by hikers, not drivers. (7) Most men, woman, and childs who hike the park's 700 miles of trails come prepared—with hats, long-sleeved shirts, and on their feets, proper hiking shoes. (8) Their equipments includes bottled water and, just in case, bear spray. (9) Glacier has a large population of grizzly bears, which can weigh up to 1,400 pounds, have four-inch claws, and dislike surprises. (10) Besides grizzlies, one might glimpse mountain lions,

*For help with spelling, see Chapter 31.

wolfs, black bear, white mountain goats, moose, bighorn sheeps, elk, and many smaller mammals. (11) Salmon, trouts, and other fishs swim the ice-cold rivers and lakes. (12) Scientist worry that the glaciers are melting too quickly, but Glacier Park remains a treasure.

EXPLORING ONLINE

<http://www.nps.gov/parks.html> Visit the National Park Service website. Click on the long list of parks that the public can visit and select one (Glacier National Park or some other) that you might like to learn about. Read, explore, and jot down any writing—or travel—ideas.

PART B   Signal Words: Singular and Plural

A *signal word* **tells you whether a singular or a plural noun usually follows.**
These **signal words** tell you that a *singular noun* usually follows:

Signal Words

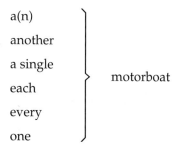

These signal words tell you that a *plural noun* usually follows:

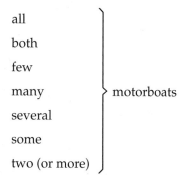

PRACTICE 3

In the blank following each signal word, write either a singular or a plural noun. Use as many different nouns as you can think of.

EXAMPLES: a single *stamp* _____

   most *fabrics* _____

1. a(n) _____   3. few _____

2. some _____   4. nine _____

5. one _____   9. a single _____

6. all _____   10. every _____

7. each _____   11. both_____

8. another _____   12. many _____

PRACTICE 4

Read the following essay for incorrect singular or plural nouns following signal words. Cross out the errors and correct them above the lines.

The Best Medicine

(1) Many researcher believe that laughter is good for people's health. (2) In fact, some doctor have concluded that laughter actually helps patients heal faster. (3) To put this theory into practice, several hospital have introduced humor routines into their treatment programs. (4) One programs is a children's clown care unit that operates in seven New York City hospitals. (5) Thirty-five clown from the Big Apple Circus go to the hospitals three times every weeks. (6) Few child can keep from laughing at the "rubber chicken soup" and "red nose transplant" routines.

(7) Although the program hasn't been studied scientifically, many observer have witnessed its positive effects. (8) However, some specialist are conducting strictly scientific research on health and laughter. (9) One study, carried out at Loma Linda University in California, has shown the positive effects of laughter on the immune system. (10) Another tests, done at the College of William and Mary in Virginia, has confirmed the California findings. (11) Other studies in progress are suggesting that all physiological system may be affected positively by laughter. (12) Finally, research also is backing up a claims made by Norman Cousins, author of the book *Anatomy of an Illness*. (13) While he was fighting a life-threatening diseases, Cousins maintained that hearty laughter took away his pain. (14) Several recent study have shown that pain does become less intense when the sufferer responds to comedy.

PRACTICE 5

On paper or on a computer, write three sentences using signal words that require singular nouns. Then write three sentences using signal words that require plural nouns.

PART C   Signal Words with OF

Many signal words are followed by *of . . .* or *of the. . . .* Usually, these signal words are followed by a *plural* noun (or a collective noun) because you are really talking about one or more from a larger group.*

many of the
a few of the   } houses are . . .
lots of the

one of the
each of the   } houses is . . .

BE CAREFUL: The signal words *one of the* and *each of the* are followed by a *plural* noun, but the verb is *singular* because only the signal word (*one, each*) is the real subject.**

(1) *One* of the apples *is* spoiled.

(2) *Each* of the trees *grows* quickly.

● In sentence (1), *one* is the subject, not *apples*.

● In sentence (2), *each* is the subject, not *trees.*

PRACTICE 6

Fill in your own nouns in the following sentences. Use a different noun in each sentence.

1. Many of the _____ enrolled in Chemistry 202.

2. Larry lost one of his _____ at the beach.

3. This is one of the _____ that everyone liked.

4. Each of the _____ carried a sign.

5. You are one of the few _____ who can do somersaults.

6. Few of the _____ produced calves.

PRACTICE 7

Write five sentences, using the signal words with *of* provided in parentheses. Use a different noun in each sentence.

EXAMPLE: (many of those . . .) _____ I planted many of those flowers myself.

1. (one of my . . .) _____

_____

———————

*For more work on collective nouns, see Chapter 20, Part C.
**For more work on this type of construction, see Chapter 8, Part G.

2. (many of the . . .) _____

_____

3. (lots of the . . .) _____

_____

4. (each of these . . .) _____

_____

5. (a few of your . . .) _____

_____

PRACTICE 8

Read the following paragraph for correct plural nouns after signal words with *of*. Cross out the errors and correct them above the lines.

(1) In 1782, the bald eagle became the national symbol of the United States. (2) Sadly, over the years, many of these magnificent bird suffered destruction of their habitat, poisoning of their food sources, and illegal extermination by farmers, ranchers, and hunters. (3) By the 1960s, these majestic raptors were declared an endangered species. (4) Today, however, eagles are back in American skies, thanks to some of the new recovery method used by wildlife specialists. (5) In one such method, scientists remove each of the egg from a wild eagle's nest and place it in

Eagle puppet feeding a three-day-old bald eaglet.

Grant Heilman Photography, Inc.

an incubator. (6) Baby eagles must not attach themselves to people, so all of the hatchling are fed first with tweezers and later with eagle puppets. (7) In this way, they learn to recognize Mom and Dad. (8) Protected and well fed, lots of the chick grow strong enough to be placed in the nests of adult eagles. (9) Instinct kicks in, and the adults adopt and raise the chicks as their own. (10) Today, many of our wild eagle got their start in eaglet nurseries.

PRACTICE 9

Writing Assignment

For some families, shopping—whether for food, clothing, or a computer—is a delightful group outing, a time to be together and share. For other families, it is an ordeal, a time of great stress, with arguments about what to purchase and how much to spend.

Describe a particularly enjoyable or awful family shopping experience. Your first sentence might read, "Shopping for _____ was (is) a(n) _____ experience." Explain what made it so good or so bad: Was it what you were shopping for or where you were shopping? Were there arguments? Why?

Check your work for the correct use of singular and plural nouns. Be especially careful of nouns that follow signal words.

CHAPTER HIGHLIGHTS

- **Most plural nouns are formed by adding** *-s* or *-es* **to the singular noun:**
    job/jobs   watch/watches

- **Some plurals are formed in other ways:**
    child/children   woman/women   wolf/wolves

- **Some nouns ending in** *o* **add** *-es*; **others add** *-s*:
    echo/echoes   solo/solos

- **Some nouns have identical singular and plural forms:**
    fish/fish   equipment/equipment

- **Hyphenated nouns usually add** *-s* or *-es* **to the first word:**
    father-in-law/fathers-in-law

- **Signal words, with and without** *of*, **indicate whether a singular or a plural noun usually follows:**
    another musician   *many of the* musicians

CHAPTER REVIEW

Proofread the following essay for incorrect singular and plural nouns. Cross out the errors and correct them above the lines.

The Effects of Alcohol on Pregnancy

(1) All mother-to-bes who drink alcohol run the risk of harming an innocent children. (2) When a pregnant women takes a drink, the alcohol goes straight from her bloodstream into the bloodstream of her child. (3) When she has several drink, the blood-alcohol level of her child rises as high as her own.

(4) Newborns can be harmed by alcohol in many way. (5) Some infant are born addicted to alcohol. (6) Other children are born mentally retarded. (7) In fact, most doctor believe that exposure to alcohol before birth is one of the major cause of mental retardation. (8) In the worst cases, babies are born with a disease called fetal alcohol syndrome. (9) These unfortunate children not only are mentally retarded but also can have many physical deformity. (10) In milder cases, the children's problems don't show up until they go to school. (11) For instance, they may have poor memories and short attention spans. (12) Later, they may have trouble holding a jobs.

(13) Too many young life have been ruined before birth because of alcohol consumption. (14) All unborn child need and deserve a chance to have a healthy, normal futures. (15) If you are a women who is expecting a baby, stop drinking alcohol now!

EXPLORING ONLINE

<http://a4esl.org/q/h/vf004-bp.html> Interactive quiz: Click on the correct singular or plural.

<http://grammar.ccc.commnet.edu/grammar/noun_exercise2.htm> Art Class! Study Bruegel's famous painting and hunt for nouns.

<http://college.cengage.com/devenglish> Visit the *Grassroots* 9/e student website for more exercises, quizzes, and live links to all websites mentioned in this chapter.

Pronouns

PART A   Defining Pronouns and Antecedents

Pronouns take the place of or refer to nouns or other pronouns. The word or words that a pronoun refers to are called the **antecedent** of the pronoun.

> (1) *Bob* said that *he* was tired.

- *He* refers to *Bob.*
- *Bob* is the antecedent of *he.*

> (2) *Sonia* left early, but I did not see *her* until later.

- *Her* refers to *Sonia.*
- *Sonia* is the antecedent of *her.*

> (3) *Robert and Tyrone* have been good friends ever since *their* college days.

- *Their* refers to *Robert and Tyrone.*
- *Robert and Tyrone* is the antecedent of *their.*

A pronoun must agree with its antecedent. In sentence (1), the antecedent *Bob* requires the singular, masculine pronoun *he*. In sentence (2), the antecedent *Sonia* requires the singular, feminine pronoun *her*. In sentence (3), the antecedent *Robert and Tyrone* requires the plural pronoun *their*.

PRACTICE 1

In each of the following sentences, circle the pronoun. In the columns on the right, write the pronoun and its antecedent as shown in the example.

	Pronoun	Antecedent
EXAMPLE:		
Susan B. Anthony promoted women's rights before (they) were popular.	they	rights
1. Susan B. Anthony deserves praise for her accomplishments.	her	Susan
2. Anthony became involved in the antislavery movement because of her principles.	her	An
3. She helped President Lincoln develop his plans to free the slaves during the Civil War.	she	president
4. Eventually, Anthony realized that women wouldn't be fully protected by law until they could vote.	they	women
5. When Anthony voted in the presidential election of 1872, she was arrested.	She	Anthony
6. She was found guilty and given a $100 fine, but she refused to pay it.	it	fine
7. The judge did not sentence Anthony to jail because a sentence would have given her grounds for an appeal.	Judge	Anthony
8. If the Supreme Court had heard her appeal, it might have ruled that women had the right to vote.	her	women
9. Audiences in England and Germany showed their appreciation of Anthony's work with standing ovations.	their	
10. Unfortunately, women in the United States had to wait until 1920 before they could legally vote.		women

PRACTICE 2

Read this paragraph for meaning; then circle each pronoun you find and write its antecedent above the pronoun.

(1) In 1935, a Hungarian journalist got tired of the ink blotches his fountain pen made. (2) So László Biro and his brother developed a pen with a rolling ball at

the point. (3) It wrote without making blotches. (4) Their pen wasn't the first ballpoint, but it was the first one that worked well. (5) The new pens got a big boost during World War II. (6) Pilots needed a pen they could use at high altitudes. (7) Only ballpoints did the job. (8) In 1945, a department store in New York City introduced these pens to its shoppers. (9) The store sold ten thousand ballpoints the first day. (10) They cost $12.50 each! (11) Today, people buy almost two *billion* ballpoints a year, for as little as ten cents apiece.

PART B   Referring to Indefinite Pronouns

Indefinite pronouns do not point to a specific person.

anybody
anyone
each
everybody
everyone   Indefinite pronouns are usually *singular*.
no one   A pronoun that refers to an indefinite
nobody   pronoun should also be singular.
somebody
someone

(1) *Everyone* should do what *he* or *she* can to help.

● *Everyone* is a singular antecedent and must be used with the singular pronoun *he* or *she.*

(2) *Each* wanted to read *his* or *her* composition aloud.

● *Each* is a singular antecedent and must be used with the singular pronoun *his* or *her.*

(3) If *someone* smiles at you, give *him* or *her* a smile in return.

● *Someone* is a singular antecedent and must be used with the singular pronoun *him* or *her.*

In the past, writers used *he, his,* or *him* to refer to both men and women. Now, however, many writers use *he or she, his or her,* or *him or her.* Of course, if *everyone* is a woman, use *she* or *her;* if *everyone* is a man, use *he, his,* or *him.**

Someone left *her* purse in the classroom.

Someone left *his* wallet on the bus.

Someone left *his or her* glasses on the back seat.

———
*For more work on pronoun reference, see Chapter 24, "Consistent Person."

It is often best to avoid the repetition of *his or her* and *he or she* by changing the indefinite pronoun to a plural.

> (4) *Everyone* in the club agreed to pay *his or her* dues on time.
>
> *or*
>
> (5) The club *members* agreed to pay *their* dues on time.

PRACTICE 3

Fill in the blanks with the correct pronouns. Then write the antecedent of each pronoun in the column on the right.

Antecedent

EXAMPLE: Everyone should do ___his or her___ best.   ___everyone___

1. The average citizen *singul* does not take ___his___ right to vote seriously enough.   ___citizen___

2. If a person chooses a career in accounting, ___she___ must enjoy working with numbers.   ___person___

3. Each player gave ___her___ best in the women's basketball finals.   ___Player___

4. Anyone can learn to do research on the Internet if ___she___ will put the time into it.   ___Anyone___

5. Fred and Nina always do ___they___ housecleaning on Tuesday.   ___Fred and Nina___

6. Someone left ___his___ fingerprints on the windshield.   ___Someone___

7. The sales managers asked me to attend ___they___ meeting tomorrow.   ___managers___

8. Everyone should see ___her___ dentist at least once a year.   ___Everyone___

9. Nobody wanted to waste ___his___ money on a singing stapler.   ___Nobody___

10. Everybody is welcome to try ___his___ luck in the lottery.   ___Everboby___

PRACTICE 4

Some of the following sentences contain errors in pronoun reference. Revise the incorrect sentences. Write a *C* in the blank next to each correct sentence.

EXAMPLE: Everyone must provide ~~their~~ lunch.   ___

1. Somebody left their bag of popcorn on the seat.   ___

2. A child should not carry heavy items in his or her backpack.   ___

3. Everybody can take their choice of two dishes from column A and one from column B.   ___

4. No one works harder at their paramedic job than my brother-in-law. ___

5. Each state has their own flag. ___

6. Anyone can conquer his or her fear of speaking in public. ___

PRACTICE 5

On paper or on a computer, write three sentences using indefinite pronouns as antecedents.

PART C   Referring to Collective Nouns

Collective nouns imply more than one person but are generally considered *singular*. Here is a partial list:

Common Collective Nouns		
board	family	panel
class	flock	school
college	government	society
committee	group	team
company	jury	tribe

(1) The *jury* meets early today because *it* must decide on a verdict.

● *Jury* is a singular antecedent and is used with the singular pronoun *it*.

(2) *Society* must protect *its* members from violence.

● *Society* is a singular antecedent and is always used with the singular pronoun *it*.
● Use *it* or *its* when referring to collective nouns.
● Use *they* or *their* only when referring to collective nouns in the plural (*schools, companies,* and so forth).

PRACTICE 6

Write the correct pronoun in the blank. Then write the antecedent of the pronoun in the column on the right.

Antecedent

EXAMPLE: The committee sent ___its___ best recommendations to the president of the college.   _committee_

1. Wanda's company will have _____ annual picnic next week.   _____

2. The two teams picked up _____they_____ gloves and bats and walked off the field.   _____team_____

3. My high school class will soon have ___its___ tenth reunion.   _____h lass_____

4. The city is doing ___its___ best to build a new stadium.   _____city_____

5. Many soap operas thrive on _____ viewers' enjoyment of "a good cry."   _____

6. Each band has _____ guitar player and drummer.   _____bo_____

7. The panel made ___its___ report public.   _____panel_____

8. This college plans to train ___its___ student teachers in classroom management.   _____college_____

PRACTICE 7

Some of the following sentences contain errors in pronoun reference. Cross out the incorrect pronoun and write the correct pronoun above the line. Write a C in the blank next to each correct sentence.

EXAMPLES: The committee will present ~~their~~ *its* report today.   ___

The jury has reached its verdict.   _c_

1. The computer company retrains their employees for new jobs.   ___

2. Central Technical College wants to double their enrollment by 2008.   ___

3. That rock group has changed their name for the third time.   ___

4. The plumbing crew did its best to finish by 4 a.m.   ___

5. The gas company plans to move their headquarters again.   ___

6. The Robinson family held its yearly reunion last week.   ___

PRACTICE 8

On paper or on a computer, write three sentences using collective nouns as antecedents.

PART D   Referring to Special Singular Constructions

each of . . .
either of . . .
every one of . . .
neither of . . .
one of . . .

Each of these constructions is *singular*.
Pronouns that refer to them must also be singular.

> (1) *Each* of the women did *her* work.

- *Each* is a singular antecedent and is used with the singular pronoun *her.*
- Do not be confused by the prepositional phrase *of the women.*

> (2) *Neither* of the men finished *his* meal.

- *Neither* is a singular antecedent and is used with the singular pronoun *his.*
- Do not be confused by the prepositional phrase *of the men.*

> (3) *One* of the bottles is missing from *its* place.

- *One* is a singular antecedent and is used with the singular pronoun *its.*
- Do not be confused by the prepositional phrase *of the bottles.**

PRACTICE 9

Fill in the blanks with the correct pronouns. Then write the antecedent of each pronoun in the column on the right.

Antecedent

EXAMPLE: Each of my nephews did ___his___   ___each___
homework.

1. One of the hikers filled ___his___ canteen.   ___hikers___

2. Every one of the women scored high on ___her___   ___every one___
   entrance examination.

3. Each of the puzzles has ___its___ own solution.   ___each___

4. Either of them should be able to learn ___her___ lines
   before opening night.   ___Either___

5. One of my brothers does not have a radio in
   ___his___ car.   ___one___

6. Neither of the dental technicians has had ___her___
   lunch yet.   ___Neither___

7. Every one of the children sat still when ___his___
   photograph was taken.   ___Everyone___

8. Lin Li and her mother opened ___they___ boutique
   in 1998.   ___lin li and___

---

*For more work on these special constructions, see Chapter 8, Part G.

PRACTICE 10

Some of the following sentences contain errors in pronoun reference. Cross out the incorrect pronoun and write the correct pronoun above it. Write a *C* in the blank next to each correct sentence.

EXAMPLE: One of my uncles made ~~their~~ *his* opinion known. ___

1. One of the women at the hardware counter hasn't made their

   purchase yet. ___

2. Each of the birds has their distinctive mating ritual. ___

3. Most public speakers rehearse their speeches beforehand. ___

4. I hope that neither of the men will change their vote. ___

5. Both supermarkets now carry Superfizz Carrot Juice for their health-

   conscious customers. ___

6. Neither of the women bought their toe ring at Toes R Us. ___

7. One of the televisions was still in its box. ___

8. Each of my grandchildren has their own bedroom. ___

PRACTICE 11

On paper or on a computer, write three sentences that use special singular constructions as antecedents.

PART E   Avoiding Vague and Repetitious Pronouns

Vague Pronouns

Be sure that all pronouns *clearly* refer to their antecedents. Be especially careful of the pronouns *they* and *it*. If *they* or *it* does not refer to a *specific* antecedent, change *they* or *it* to the exact word you have in mind.

> (1) **Vague pronoun:** At registration, they said I should take Math 101.
>
> (2) **Revised:** At registration, an adviser said I should take Math 101.

● In sentence (1), who is *they*? The pronoun *they* does not clearly refer to an antecedent.

● In sentence (2), the vague *they* has been replaced by *an adviser.*

> (3) **Vague pronoun:** On the beach, it says that no swimming is allowed.
>
> (4) **Revised:** On the beach, a sign says that no swimming is allowed.

● In sentence (3), what is *it*? The pronoun *it* does not clearly refer to an antecedent.

● In sentence (4), the vague *it* has been replaced by *a sign.*

Repetitious Pronouns

Don't repeat a pronoun directly after its antecedent. Use *either* the pronoun *or* the antecedent—not both.

> (1) **Repetitious pronoun:** The doctor, she said that my daughter is in perfect health.

● The pronoun *she* unnecessarily repeats the antecedent *doctor,* which is right before it.

> (2) **Revised:** *The doctor* said that my daughter is in perfect health.
>
> *or*
>
> *She* said that my daughter is in perfect health.

● Use either *the doctor* or *she,* not both.

PRACTICE 12

Rewrite the sentences that contain vague or repetitious pronouns. If a sentence is correct, write *C.*

EXAMPLE: Dyslexia, it is a learning disorder that makes reading difficult.

Revised: _____ Dyslexia is a learning disorder that makes reading difficult. _____

1. Many dyslexic persons, they have achieved success in their chosen professions.

   Revised: _____

   _____

2. For example, Albert Einstein, he was dyslexic.

   Revised: _____

   _____

3. In his biography, it says that he couldn't interpret written words the way others could.

   Revised: ____ it _____

   _____

4. At his elementary school, they claimed that he was a slow learner.

   Revised: ____ employe _____

   _____

5. However, this slow learner, he changed the way science looked at time and space.

   Revised: _____

   _____

6. Even politics has had its share of dyslexic leaders.

   Revised: _____ Corect _____

7. American history, it teaches us that President Woodrow Wilson and Vice President Nelson Rockefeller, they were both dyslexic.

   Revised: _____

8. Authors can have this problem too; the well-known mystery writer Agatha Christie, she had trouble reading.

   Revised: _____

9. Finally, in several magazines, they report that both Jay Leno and Cher are dyslexic.

   Revised: _____

10. Cher, she wasn't able to read until she was eighteen years old.

    Revised: _____ no good _____

PART F   Using Pronouns as Subjects, Objects, and Possessives

Pronouns have different forms, depending on how they are used in a sentence. Pronouns can be *subjects* or *objects* or *possessives*. They can be in the *subjective case, objective case,* or *possessive case.*

Pronouns as Subjects

A pronoun can be the *subject* of a sentence:

> (1) *He* loves the summer months.
>
> (2) By noon, *they* had reached the top of the hill.

● In sentences (1) and (2), the pronouns *he* and *they* are subjects.

Pronouns as Objects

A pronoun can be the *object* of a verb:

> (1) Graciela kissed *him.*
>
> (2) Sheila moved *it* to the corner.

● In sentence (1), the pronoun *him* tells whom Graciela kissed.

● In sentence (2), the pronoun *it* tells what Sheila moved.

● These objects answer the questions *kissed whom?* and *moved what?*

A pronoun can also be the *object* of a preposition (a word like *to, for,* or *at*).*

(3) The umpire stood between *us.*

(4) Near *them,* the children played.

● In sentences (3) and (4), the pronouns *us* and *them* are the objects of the prepositions *between* and *near.*

Sometimes the prepositions *to* and *for* are understood, usually after words like *give, send, tell,* and *bring.*

(5) I gave *her* the latest sports magazine.

(6) Carver bought *him* a cowboy hat.

● In sentence (5), the preposition *to* is understood before the pronoun *her:* I gave *to* her . . .

● In sentence (6), the preposition *for* is understood before the pronoun *him:* Carver bought *for* him . . .

Pronouns That Show Possession

A pronoun can show *possession* or ownership.

(1) Bill took *his* report and left.

(2) The climbers spotted *their* gear on the slope.

● In sentences (1) and (2), the pronouns *his* and *their* show that Bill owns *his* report and that the climbers own *their* gear.

The chart below can help you review all the pronouns discussed in this part.

Pronoun Case Chart

	Singular Pronouns			Plural Pronouns		
	Subjective	Objective	Possessive	Subjective	Objective	Possessive
1st person:	I	me	my (mine)	we	us	our (ours)
2nd person:	you	you	your (yours)	you	you	your (yours)
3rd person:	he	him	his	they	them	their (theirs)
	she	her	her (hers)			
	it	it	its			

*See the list of prepositions on page 267.

PRACTICE 13

In the sentences below, underline the pronouns. Then, over each pronoun, write an *S* if the pronoun is in the subjective case, an *O* if it is in the objective case, and a *P* if it is in the possessive case.

Kiowa Dancer performing at a powwow.

AP Images.

EXAMPLE: Native American dancing has special significance for <u>us</u>. *[O]*

preposition

1. My brother Shadow Hawk and I represent our Kiowa tribe at many powwows, competing in the men's traditional dance category. *[subjec]* *[prossive]*

2. We wear costume pieces handed down to us from previous generations.

3. Each dancer wears a warrior's feather headdress, called a *roach*, and an impressive bustle of feathers tied to his back. *[prosesive]*

4. Because the bustles are made of sacred eagle feathers, spectators stand and remove their hats to show their reverence.

5. The steady drumbeat provides its rhythm for our movements.

6. This dance evolved from old forms of war dances, so we use it now to act out the story of a battle or a hunt.

7. Shadow Hawk interprets his story one way, and I interpret mine differently, so our movements are individually creative.

8. But we both begin by crouching low to the ground, looking for the tracks of the animal or the enemy.

9. The tempo of the drum increases, and he and I speed up our footwork to dramatize stalking our prey. *prose*

10. Acting out the dramatic final challenge means a lot to me because I can express with my movements the bravery, dignity, and pride that I feel. *subjective*

PART G Choosing the Correct Case After AND or OR

When nouns or pronouns are joined by *and* or *or,* be careful to use the correct pronoun case after the *and* or the *or.*

(1) **Incorrect:** *Bob* and *her* have to leave soon. *she has to*

● In sentence (1), the pronoun *her* should be in the *subjective case* because it is part of the subject of the sentence.

(2) **Revised:** *Bob* and *she* have to leave soon.

● Change *her* to *she.*

(3) **Incorrect:** The dean congratulated *Charles* and *I.* *them*

● In sentence (3), the pronoun *I* should be in the *objective case* because it is the object of the verb *congratulated.*

● The dean congratulated *whom*? The dean congratulated *me.*

(4) **Revised:** The dean congratulated *Charles* and *me.*

● Change *I* to *me.*

(5) **Incorrect:** Is that letter for *them* or *he*?

● In sentence (5), both objects of the preposition *for* must be in the *objective case.* What should *he* be changed to? _____

One simple way to make sure that you have the right pronoun case is to leave out the *and* or the *or,* and the word before it. You probably would not write these sentences:

(6) **Incorrect:** *Her* have to leave soon.
(7) **Incorrect:** The dean congratulated *I.*
(8) **Incorrect:** Is that letter for *he*?

These sentences look and sound strange, and you would know that they have to be corrected.

PRACTICE 14

In the sentences below, circle the correct pronoun in the parentheses. If the pronoun is a *subject*, use the *subjective case*. If the pronoun is the *object* of a verb or a preposition, use the *objective case*.

1. Frieda and I, me) were born in Bogotá, Colombia.

2. (We, Us) girls are determined to make an A on the next exam.

3. For (we, us), a swim in the ocean on a hot day is one of life's greatest joys.

4. If it were up to Angelo and (he, him, they would spend all their time snow skiing.

5. Our lab instructor expects Dan and (I, me) to hand in our report today.

6. I'm going to the movies tonight with Yolanda and (she, her).

7. The foreman chose Ellen and (they, them).

8. Between you and (I, me), I don't like spinach.

9. Robert and (they, them) have decided to go to Rocky Mountain National Park with Jacinto and (she, her).

10. Either (he, him) or (she, her) must work overtime.

PRACTICE 15

Revise the sentences in which the pronouns are in the wrong case. Write a *C* in the blank next to each sentence that is correct.

1. Annie and me enjoy going to the gym every day. ___

2. Her and me have tried every class, from kickboxing to spinning. ___

3. Between you and I, I favor hydroboxing, or kickboxing in water. ___

4. Us and our friends also use the pool for water aerobics. ___

5. On cold days, however, they and I prefer step classes to keep warm. ___

6. Stationary cycling sometimes feels boring to Annie and I. ___

7. On the other hand, it is a good time for she and I to daydream. ___

8. Annie favors body pump classes, but I think she likes the instructor. ___

9. I am not sure whether him or weightlifting makes her sweat so much. ___

10. Talking while we work out gives her and me mouth and jaw exercise too. ___

PART H   Choosing the Correct Case in Comparisons

Pronouns in comparisons usually follow *than* or *as.*

> (1) Ferdinand is taller *than* I.
>
> (2) These guidelines help you as much *as* me.

- In sentence (1), the comparison is completed with a pronoun in the subjective case, *I.*

- In sentence (2), the comparison is completed with a pronoun in the objective case, *me.*

> (1) Ferdinand is taller than I . . . (am tall).
>
> (2) These guidelines help you as much as . . . (they help) . . . me.

- A comparison is really a kind of shorthand that omits repetitious words.

By completing the comparison mentally, you can choose the correct case for the pronoun.

BE CAREFUL: The case of the pronoun you place after *than* or *as* can change the meaning of the sentence.

> (3) Diana likes Tom more than *I* . . . (more than *I* like him).
>
> *or*
>
> (4) Diana likes Tom more than *me* . . . (more than she likes *me*).

- Sentence (3) says that Diana likes Tom more than I like Tom.
- Sentence (4) says that Diana likes Tom more than she likes me.*

PRACTICE 16

Circle the correct pronoun in these comparisons.

1. You study more often than (I, me).

2. The movie scared us more than it did (he, him).

3. Diego eats dinner earlier than (I, me).

4. She ran a better campaign for the local school board than (he, him).

5. Stan cannot memorize vocabulary words faster than (he, him). *no*

6. The ringing of a telephone disturbs her more than it disturbs (they, them). *no*

7. They may think they are sharper than (she, her), but wait until they tangle with her and find out the truth. *no*

---

*For more work on comparisons, see Chapter 21, Part C.

8. I hate doing laundry more than (they, them).

9. Sometimes our children are more mature than (we, us).

10. Remembering birthdays seems easier for me than for (he, him).

PRACTICE 17

Revise only those sentences in which the pronoun after the comparison is in the wrong case. Write a *C* in the blank next to each correct sentence.

1. Ben learned to operate this program more slowly than us. ___

2. Jean can sing Haitian folk songs better than me. ___

3. Nobody, but nobody, can whistle louder than she. ___

4. Sarah was surprised that Joyce paid more than her for a ticket. ___

5. In a crisis, you can reach us sooner than you can reach them. ___

6. Before switching jobs, I wanted to know if Rose would be as good a

   supervisor as him. ___

7. The night shift suits her better than I. ___

8. Antoinette is six feet tall; no one on the loading dock is taller than her. ___

PRACTICE 18

On paper or on a computer, write three sentences using comparisons that are completed with pronouns. Choose each pronoun case carefully.

PART I   Using Pronouns with -SELF and -SELVES

Pronouns with *-self* and *-selves* are used in two ways.

(1) José admired *himself* in the mirror.

● In sentence (1), José did something to *himself*; he admired *himself*. In this sentence, *himself* is called a **reflexive pronoun.**

(2) The teacher *herself* thought the test was too difficult.

● In sentence (2), *herself* emphasizes the fact that the teacher—much to her surprise—found the test too hard. In this sentence, *herself* is called an **intensive pronoun.**

This chart will help you choose the right reflexive or intensive pronoun.

	Antecedent		Reflexive or Intensive Pronoun
Singular	I	_____	myself
	you	_____	yourself
	he	_____	himself
	she	_____	herself
	it	_____	itself
Plural	we	_____	ourselves
	you	_____	yourselves
	they	_____	themselves

Note that in the plural *-self* is changed to *-selves*.

PRACTICE 19

Write the correct reflexive or intensive pronoun in each sentence. Be careful to match the pronoun with the antecedent.

EXAMPLES: I should have stopped _____*myself*_____ .

Roberta _____*herself*_____ made this bracelet.

1. We built all the cabinets _ourselves_

2. He _____ was surprised to discover that he had a green thumb.

3. Did you give _yourself_ a party after you graduated?

4. Rick, look at _himself_ in the mirror!

5. Don't bother; Don and André will hang the pictures _____ .

6. The trainer _herself_ was amazed at the progress the athletes had made.

7. Sonia found _herself_ in a difficult situation.

8. These new lamps turn _itself_ on and off.

9. The oven cleans _itself_ .

10. Because he snores loudly, he wakes _himself_ up several times each night.

PRACTICE 20

On paper or on a computer, write three sentences, using either a reflexive or an intensive pronoun in each.

PRACTICE 21

Writing Assignment

In a small group, discuss the factors that seem absolutely necessary for a successful marriage or long-term relationship. As a group, brainstorm to identify four or five key factors.

Now imagine that a friend with very little experience has asked you for written advice about relationships. Each member of the group should choose just one of the factors and write a letter to this person. Explain in detail why this factor—for example, honesty or mutual respect—is so important to a good relationship.

Read the finished letters to one another. Which letters give the best advice or are the most convincing? Why? Exchange letters with a partner, checking for the correct use of pronouns.

CHAPTER HIGHLIGHTS

- **A pronoun takes the place of or refers to a noun or another pronoun:**

  Louise said that *she* would leave work early.

- **The word that a pronoun refers to is its antecedent:**

  I have chosen *my* seat for the concert.
  (*I* is the antecedent of *my*.)

- **A pronoun that refers to an indefinite pronoun or a collective noun should be singular:**

  Everyone had cleared the papers off *his* or *her* desk.

  The *committee* will give *its* report Friday.

- **A pronoun after *and* or *or* is usually in the subjective or objective case:**

  Dr. Smythe and *she* always work as a team. (*subjective*)

  The bus driver wouldn't give the map to Ms. Tallon or *me*.
  (*objective*)

- **Pronouns in comparisons usually follow *than* or *as*:**

  Frank likes Sally more than *I*.
  (*subjective*: . . . more than I like Sally)

  Frank likes Sally more than *me*.
  (*objective*: . . . more than he likes me)

- **A pronoun ending in -*self* (singular) or -*selves* (plural) may be used as a reflexive or an intensive pronoun. A reflexive pronoun shows that someone did something to himself or to herself; an intensive pronoun is used for emphasis:**

  On his trip, Martin bought nothing for *himself*.

  The musicians *themselves* were almost late for the street fair.

CHAPTER REVIEW

Proofread the following essay for pronoun errors. Cross out any incorrect, vague, or repetitious pronouns and make your corrections above the lines. Use nouns to replace vague pronouns.

A New Beginning

(1) Martha Andrews, she was a good student in high school. (2) After graduation, she found a job as a bank teller to save money for college. (3) She liked her job because she knew her regular customers and enjoyed handling his or her business. (4) When she was nineteen, Patrick Kelvin, another teller, and her fell in love and married. (5) By the time she was twenty-two, she was the mother of three children. (6) Martha's plans for college faded.

(7) As her fortieth birthday approached, Martha began thinking about going to college to study accounting; however, she had many fears. (8) Would she remember how to study after so many years? (9) Would the younger students be smarter than her? (10) Would she feel out of place with them? (11) Worst of all, her husband, he worried that Martha would neglect him. (12) He thought that everyone who went to college forgot their family. (13) He also feared that Martha would be more successful than him.

(14) One of Martha's children, who attended college hisself, encouraged her. (15) With his help, Martha got the courage to visit Middleton College. (16) In the admissions office, they told her that older students were valued at Middleton. (17) Older students often enriched classes because he or she brought a wealth of life experiences with them. (18) Martha also learned that the college had a special program to help their older students adjust to school.

(19) Martha enrolled in college the next fall. (20) To their credit, her and her husband soon realized that they had made the right decision.

 ## EXPLORING ONLINE

<http://grammar.ccc.commnet.edu/grammar/cgi-shl/quiz.pl/pronouns_add2.htm>
Interactive quizzes: Choose the correct pronoun or verb.

<http://aliscot.com/bigdog/agrpa_exercise.htm> Take Big Dog's pronoun quiz to see how well you have mastered pronoun use.

<http://college.cengage.com/devenglish/> Visit the *Grassroots* 9/e student website for more exercises, quizzes, and live links to all websites mentioned in this chapter.

CHAPTER 21 Adjectives and Adverbs

PART A Defining and Writing Adjectives and Adverbs

Adjectives and adverbs are two kinds of descriptive words. An **adjective** describes a noun or a pronoun. It tells *which one, what kind,* or *how many.*

> (1) The *red* coat belongs to me.
>
> (2) He looks *healthy.*

● In sentence (1), the adjective *red* describes the noun *coat.*

● In sentence (2), the adjective *healthy* describes the pronoun *he.*

An **adverb** describes a verb, an adjective, or another adverb. Adverbs often end in *-ly.* They tell *how, to what extent, why, when,* or *where.*

> (3) Laura sings *loudly.*
>
> (4) My biology instructor is *extremely* short.
>
> (5) Lift this box *very* carefully.

● In sentence (3), *loudly* describes the verb *sings.* How does Laura sing? She sings *loudly.*

● In sentence (4), *extremely* describes the adjective *short.* How short is the instructor? *Extremely* short.

● In sentence (5), *very* describes the adverb *carefully*. How carefully should you lift the box? *Very* carefully.

PRACTICE 1

Complete each sentence with an appropriate adjective from the list below.

funny	orange	sarcastic	energetic
old	tired	bitter	little

1. Janet is _____.
2. He often wears a(n) _____ baseball cap.
3. _____ remarks will be his downfall.
4. My daughter collects _____ movie posters.
5. This coffee tastes _____.

PRACTICE 2

Complete each sentence with an appropriate adverb from the list below.

quietly	loudly	wildly	convincingly
madly	quickly	constantly	happily

1. The waiter _____ cleaned the table.
2. Mr. Huff whistles _____.
3. The lawyer spoke _____.
4. They charged _____ down the long hallway.
5. _____, he entered the rear door of the church.

Many adjectives can be changed into adverbs by adding an *-ly* ending. For example, *glad* becomes *gladly*, *thoughtful* becomes *thoughtfully*, and *wise* becomes *wisely*.

Be especially careful of the adjectives and adverbs in this list; they are easily confused.

Adjective	Adverb	Adjective	Adverb
awful	awfully	quiet	quietly
bad	badly	real	really
poor	poorly	sure	surely
quick	quickly		

(6) This chair is a *real* antique.

(7) She has a *really* bad sprain.

● In sentence (6), *real* is an adjective describing the noun *antique*.

● In sentence (7), *really* is an adverb describing the adjective *bad*. How bad is the sprain? The sprain is *really* bad.

PRACTICE 3

Change each adjective in the left-hand column into its adverb form.*

EXAMPLE: You are polite.   You answer _____politely_____.

Adjective	**Adverb**
1. She is honest.	1. She responds _____.
2. They are loud.	2. They sing _____.
3. It is easy.	3. It turns _____.
4. We are careful.	4. We decide _____.
5. He is creative.	5. He thinks _____.
6. She was quick.	6. She acted _____.
7. It is perfect.	7. It fits _____.
8. It is real.	8. It is _____ hot.
9. He is eager.	9. He waited _____.
10. We are joyful.	10. We watch _____.

PRACTICE 4

Circle the adjective or adverb form of the word in parentheses.

EXAMPLE: Lovers of nature argue (passionate, passionately) that we must protect the Galapagos Islands.

1. These (remote, remotely) islands lie in the Pacific Ocean six hundred miles off the coast of Ecuador.

2. They are (actual, actually) just piles of volcanic lava.

3. Nevertheless, they are home to (abundant, abundantly) wildlife.

4. For centuries, the Galapagos Islands remained (complete, completely) isolated and undisturbed by humans.

5. As a result, some (rare, rarely) animal species developed there.

6. For example, giant tortoises up to six feet long from head to tail lumber (slow, slowly) across the hills and beaches.

7. The world's only swimming iguanas (lazy, lazily) sun themselves on jet-black rocks.

8. The islands are also home to many (amazing, amazingly) birds.

9. Blue-footed boobies waddle (comic, comically) over the boulders.

10. Flightless cormorants, which live only in the Galapagos, dive (graceful, gracefully) into the sea, searching for eel and octopus.

11. Tiny Galapagos penguins, the only ones north of the equator, hop (easy, easily) into and out of the ocean.

_____
*If you have questions about spelling, see Chapter 31, Part E.

Giant Galapagos Islands Tortoise.

Wolfgang Kaehler/CORBIS.

12. During his voyage of 1831, Charles Darwin visited the Galapagos Islands and gathered evidence to support his (famous, famously) theory of natural selection.

13. Today, the islands are still the (perfect, perfectly) place for scientists to conduct research.

14. Ecotourists, too, are drawn to the (spectacular, spectacularly) scenery and (fabulous, fabulously) animals.

15. If we tread very (gentle, gently) on this fragile ecosystem, we might preserve it for future generations.

EXPLORING ONLINE

Using Google or your favorite search engine, look up "Galapagos, animals, birds" or "Galapagos, Darwin's voyage" to see pictures and learn more about these islands.

PRACTICE 5

Using paper or on a computer, write sentences using the following adjectives and adverbs: *quick/quickly, bad/badly, glad/gladly, real/really, easy/easily.*

EXAMPLES: (*cheerful*) You are cheerful this morning.
   (*cheerfully*) You make breakfast cheerfully.

PART B   A Troublesome Pair: GOOD/WELL

Unlike most adjectives, *good* does not add *-ly* to become an adverb; it changes to *well.*

(1) **Adjective:** Peter is a *good* student.

(2) **Adverb:** He writes *well*.

● In sentence (1), the adjective *good* describes or modifies *student*.

● In sentence (2), the adverb *well* describes or modifies *writes*.

Note, however, that *well* can be used as an adjective to mean *in good health*—for example, *He felt well after his long vacation.*

PRACTICE 6

Write either *good* or *well* in each blank.

EXAMPLE: Charles plays ball very _____*well*_____.

1. Lorelle is a _____ pilot.

2. She handles a plane _____.

3. How _____ do you understand virtual reality?

4. Pam knows my bad habits very _____.

5. It is a _____ thing we ran into each other.

6. Brian works _____ with other people.

7. How _____ or how badly did you do at the tryouts?

8. Were the cherry tarts _____ or tasteless?

9. Denzel Washington is not just a _____ actor; he's a great one.

10. These plants don't grow very _____ in the sunlight.

11. Carole doesn't look as though she takes _____ care of herself.

12. He asked _____ questions at the meeting, and she answered them _____.

PART C Writing Comparatives

(1) John is *tall*.

(2) John is *taller* than Mike.

● Sentence (1) describes John with the adjective *tall*, but sentence (2) *compares* John and Mike in terms of how tall they are: John is the *taller* of the two.

Taller **is called the** *comparative* **of** *tall*.

Use the comparative when you want to compare two people or things.

To Form Comparatives

Add *-er* to adjectives and adverbs that have *one syllable:**

short	shorter
fast	faster
thin	thinner

Place the word *more* before adjectives and adverbs that have *two or more syllables:*

foolish	more foolish
rotten	more rotten
happily	more happily

PRACTICE 7

Write the comparative form of each word. Either add *-er* to the word or write *more* before it. Never add both *-er* and *more!*

EXAMPLES: _____ fresh <u>er</u>_____

__<u>more</u>__ willing _____

1. _____ fast _____   5. _____ thick _____
2. _____ interesting _____   6. _____ modern _____
3. _____ hopeful _____   7. _____ valuable _____
4. _____ sweet _____   8. _____ cold _____

Here is one important exception to the rule that two-syllable words use *more* to form the comparative:

To show the comparative of two-syllable adjectives ending in *-y,* change the *y* to *i* and add *-er.***

cloudy	cloudier
sunny	sunnier

PRACTICE 8

Write the comparative form of each adjective.

EXAMPLE: happy _____<u>happier</u>_____

1. shiny _____   5. fancy _____
2. friendly _____   6. lucky _____
3. lazy _____   7. lively _____
4. easy _____   8. crazy _____

_____

*For questions about spelling, see Chapter 31, Part D.
**For questions about spelling, see Chapter 31, Part G.

PRACTICE 9

The following incorrect sentences use both *more* and *-er*. Decide which one is correct and write your revised sentences on the lines provided.

REMEMBER: Write comparatives with either *more* or *-er*—not both!

EXAMPLES: Jan is more younger than her brother.

Jan is younger than her brother.

I feel more comfortabler in this chair than on the couch.

I feel more comfortable in this chair than on the couch.

1. Her new boss is more fussier than her previous one.

2. The trail was more rockier than we expected.

3. The people in my new neighborhood are more friendlier than those in my old one.

4. Magda has a more cheerfuler personality than her sister.

5. I have never seen a more duller TV program than this one.

6. The audience at this theater is more noisier than usual.

7. His jacket is more newer than Rudy's.

8. If today is more warmer than yesterday, we'll picnic on the lawn.

PRACTICE 10

On paper or on a computer, write sentences using the comparative form of the following adjectives or adverbs: *dark, cloudy, fortunate, slowly, wet.*

EXAMPLE: (*funny*) This play is funnier than the one we saw last week.

PART D   Writing Superlatives

(1) Tim is the *tallest* player on the team.

(2) Juan was voted the *most useful* player.

● In sentence (1), Tim is not just *tall* or *taller than* someone else; he is the *tallest* of all the players on the team.

● In sentence (2), Juan was voted the *most useful* of all the players.

Tallest **and** *most useful* **are called** *superlatives.*

Use the superlative when you wish to compare more than two people or things.

To Form Superlatives

Add *-est* to adjectives and adverbs of *one syllable:*

short   shortest

Place the word *most* before adjectives and adverbs that have *two or more syllables:*

foolish   most foolish

Exception: With two-syllable adjectives ending in *-y*, change the *y* to *i* and add *-est.**

happy   happiest

PRACTICE 11

Write the superlative form of each word. Either add *-est* to the word or write *most* before it; do not do both.

EXAMPLES: _____ tall *est*_____

*most* ridiculous _____

1. _____ loud _____   6. _____ wild _____
2. _____ colorful _____   7. _____ practical _____
3. _____ brave _____   8. _____ frightening _____
4. _____ strong _____   9. _____ green _____
5. _____ brilliant _____   10. _____ hazy _____

PRACTICE 12

The following incorrect sentences use both *most* and *-est*. Decide which one is correct and write your revised sentences on the lines provided.

   REMEMBER: Write superlatives with either *most* or *-est*—not both!

EXAMPLES: Jane is the most youngest of my three children.

Jane is the youngest of my three children.

He is the most skillfulest guitarist in the band.

He is the most skillful guitarist in the band.

1. My nephew is the most thoughtfulest teenager I know.

   _____

2. Mercury is the most closest planet to the sun.

   _____

3. This baby makes the most oddest gurgling noises we have ever heard.

   _____

_____
*For questions about spelling, see Chapter 31, Part 6.

4. Jackie always makes us laugh, but she is most funniest when she hasn't had enough sleep.

_____

5. When I finally started college, I was the most eagerest student on campus.

_____

6. Ms. Dross raises the most strangest reptiles in her basement.

_____

7. This peach is the most ripest in the basket.

_____

8. He thinks that the most successfulest people are just lucky.

_____

PART E   Troublesome Comparatives and Superlatives

These comparatives and superlatives are some of the trickiest you will learn:

		Comparative	**Superlative**
Adjective:	good	better	best
Adverb:	well	better	best
Adjective:	bad	worse	worst
Adverb:	badly	worse	worst

PRACTICE 13

Fill in the correct comparative or superlative form of the word in parentheses. REMEMBER: *Better* and *worse* compare *two* persons or things. *Best* and *worst* compare three or more persons or things.

EXAMPLES: Is this report _____*better*_____ (good) than my last one?
(Here two reports are compared.)

It was the _____*worst*_____ (bad) movie I have ever seen.
(Of *all* movies, it was the *most* awful.)

1. He likes jogging _____ (well) than running.

2. I like country and western music _____ (well) of all.

3. Bob's motorcycle rides _____ (bad) now than it did last week.

4. That is the _____ (bad) joke Molly has ever told!

5. The volleyball team played _____ (badly) than it did last year.

6. He plays the piano _____ (well) than he plays the guitar.

7. The traffic is _____ (bad) on Fridays than on Mondays.

8. That was the _____ (bad) cold I have had in years.

9. Sales are _____ (good) this year than last.

10. Do you take this person for _____ (good) or for _____ (bad)?

PART F Demonstrative Adjectives: THIS/THAT and THESE/THOSE

This, that, these, and *those* are called **demonstrative adjectives** because they point out, or demonstrate, which noun is meant.

> (1) I don't trust *that* wobbly front wheel.
>
> (2) *Those* toys are not as safe as their makers claim.

- In sentence (1), *that* points to a particular wheel, the wobbly front one.

- In sentence (2), *those* points to a particular group of toys.

Demonstrative adjectives are the only adjectives that change to show singular and plural:

Singular	Plural
this book	these books
that book	those books

This and *that* are used before singular nouns; *these* and *those* are used before plural nouns.

PRACTICE 14

In each sentence, circle the correct form of the demonstrative adjective in parentheses.

1. (This, These) corn flakes taste like cardboard.

2. Mr. Lathorpe is sure (this, these) address is correct.

3. You can find (that, those) maps in the reference room.

4. Can you catch (that, those) waiter's eye?

5. I can't imagine what (that, those) gadgets are for.

6. We prefer (this, these) tennis court to (that, those) one.

7. The learning center is in (that, those) gray building.

8. (These, This) biography tells the story of Charles Curtis, the first Native American elected to the Senate.

PRACTICE 15

Writing Assignment

Sports figures and entertainers can be excellent role models. Sometimes, though, they can set bad examples and teach the wrong lessons. For example, some athletes and entertainers have been convicted of drug possession, spousal abuse, or assault.

Assume that you are concerned that your child or sibling is being negatively influenced by one of these figures. Write a "fan letter" to this person explaining the bad influence he or she is having on young people—in particular, on your child or sibling. Convince him or her that being in the spotlight is a serious responsibility and that a positive change in behavior could help many young fans.

Brainstorm, freewrite, or cluster to generate ideas and examples to support your concern. Check your letter for the correct use of adjectives and adverbs.

CHAPTER HIGHLIGHTS

- **Most adverbs are formed by adding *-ly* to an adjective:**

    quick/quickly   bright/brightly   *but* good/well

- **Comparative adjectives and adverbs compare two persons or things:**

    I think that Don is *happier* than his brother.
    Laura can balance a checkbook *more quickly* than I can.

- **Superlative adjectives and adverbs compare more than two persons or things:**

    Last night, Ingrid had the *worst* headache of her life.
    That was the *most carefully* prepared speech I have ever heard.

- **The adjectives *good* and *bad* and the adverbs *well* and *badly* require special care in the comparative and the superlative:**

    good/better/best
    bad/worse/worst

    well/better/best
    badly/worse/worst

- **Demonstrative adjectives can be singular or plural:**

    this/that (chair)
    these/those (chairs)

CHAPTER REVIEW

Proofread these paragraphs for adjective and adverb errors. Cross out the errors and correct them above the lines.

A. (1) The Hubble Space Telescope is the world's famousest telescope and one of

the most important in history. (2) Launched into space in 1990, it orbits regular

around the Earth and takes incredibly photographs. (3) Named for astronomer

Dr. Edwin Hubble, it carries real sensitive equipment that captures more better and

sharp images than Earth-based telescopes do. (4) This extreme detailed pictures of planets, galaxies, nebulas, and black holes have helped scientists solve age-old riddles, such as the age of the universe. (5) Hubble has helped find new galaxies and the most old planet known—3 billion years. (6) Many people log on to the Hubble website every day just to gaze at beautiful close-ups of Mars or brilliantly gas towers rising from a nebula. (7) For them, viewing the universe through Hubble's eyes is inspirational, even spiritually. (8) In 2013, NASA plans to let the Hubble telescope burn up in Earth's atmosphere. (9) Some say that its demise won't be the baddest thing that could happen because plans to launch an even more big telescope are already under way.

The Hubble Telescope orbiting in space.

EXPLORING ONLINE

<http://hubblesite.org/> Go to the Hubble website, click on Gallery, and take notes as you look at the images. Why do you think so many people log on to gaze? Why do some call the pictures "spiritual"?

B.   (1) One of the real inspirational stories of recent years is the story of Lance Armstrong. (2) In 1993, Armstrong became the World Cycling champion. (3) In 1999, he won the 2,287-mile Tour de France, the world's most greatest bike race. (4) Between those two events, however, he won something that was even more importanter.

   (5) In 1996, Lance Armstrong was diagnosed with testicular cancer. (6) The cancer spread to his brain, abdomen, and lungs. (7) He was given only a 40 percent

chance of surviving and even worser odds of ever returning to biking. (8) According to his doctors, however, he approached his cancer with the same skills he used for competitive sports: discipline, persistence, sacrifice. (9) Armstrong courageous went through brain surgery and incredibly painful chemotherapy, but he also continued training. (10) Two years later, he became only the second American to win the twenty-one-day Tour de France. (11) More stronger than ever, Armstrong finished seven minutes and thirty-seven seconds ahead of his most nearest competitor. (12) Astonishingly enough, he went on to win the Tour de France the following year and an Olympic bronze medal in 2000.

(13) Although some people believe that cancer is the worstest thing that can happen, Armstrong maintains that cancer is the most best thing that ever happened to him. (14) In his book, *It's Not about the Bike,* he writes that without those disease he would not have married or had a child. (15) When you face death, he says, your focus becomes really clear.

 EXPLORING ONLINE

<http://www.dailygrammar.com/066to070.shtml> Five tests with answers: Choose the correct adjective or adverb.

<http://depts.gallaudet.edu/esl/compsuperl.htm> Practice with hints and answers: Write the correct comparatives or superlatives.

<http://college.cengage.com/devenglish/> Visit the *Grassroots* 9/e student website for more exercises, quizzes, and live links to all websites mentioned in this chapter.

Prepositions

PART A Defining and Working with Prepositional Phrases

PART B Troublesome Prepositions: IN, ON, and LIKE

PART C Prepositions in Common Expressions

PART A Defining and Working with Prepositional Phrases

A **preposition** is a word like *at, from, in,* or *of.* Below is a partial list of common prepositions:*

Common Prepositions

about	beside	off
above	between	on
across	by	over
after	during	through
against	except	to
along	for	toward
among	from	under
around	in	until
at	into	up
before	like	with
behind	of	without

A preposition is usually followed by a noun or pronoun. The noun or pronoun is called the **object** of the preposition. Together, the preposition and its object are called a **prepositional phrase.**

Here are some prepositional phrases:

Prepositional Phrase	=	Preposition	+	Object
after the movie		after		the movie
at Kean College		at		Kean College
beside them		beside		them
between you and me		between		you and me

---

*For more work on prepositions, see Chapter 6, Part C.

The preposition shows a relationship between the object of the preposition and some other word in the sentence. Below are some sentences with prepositional phrases:

(1) Ms. Kringell arrived *at noon.*

(2) A man *in a gray suit* bought three lottery tickets.

(3) The huge moving van sped through the tunnel.

● In sentence (1), the prepositional phrase *at noon* tells when Ms. Kringell arrived. It describes *arrived.*

● In sentence (2), the prepositional phrase *in a gray suit* describes how the man was dressed. It describes *man.*

● What is the prepositional phrase in sentence (3)? _____

Which word does it describe? _____

PRACTICE 1

Underline the prepositional phrases in the following sentences.

1. Bill collected some interesting facts about human biology.

2. Human eyesight is sharpest at midday.

3. In extreme cold, shivering produces heat, which can save lives.

4. A pound of body weight equals 3,500 calories.

5. Each of us has a distinguishing odor.

6. Fingernails grow fastest in summer.

7. One of every ten people is left-handed.

8. The human body contains approximately ten pints of blood.

9. Beards grow more rapidly than any other hair on the human body.

10. Most people with an extra rib are men.

PART B Troublesome Prepositions: IN, ON, and LIKE

IN/ON for Time

Use *in* before seasons of the year, before months not followed by specific dates, and before years that do not include specific dates.

(1) *In the summer,* some of us like to lie around in the sun.

(2) No classes will meet *in January.*

(3) Rona was a student at Centerville Business School *in 2004.*

Use *on* before days of the week, before holidays, and before months if a date follows.

> (4) *On Thursday*, the gym was closed for renovations.
>
> (5) The city looked deserted *on Christmas Eve*.
>
> (6) We hope to arrive in Burlington *on October 3*.

IN/ON for Place

In means *inside of.*

> (1) My grandmother slept *in the spare bedroom*.
>
> (2) The exchange student spent the summer *in Sweden*.

On means *on top of* or *at a particular place.*

> (3) The spinach pie *on the table* is for tonight's book discussion group meeting.
>
> (4) Dr. Helfman lives *on Marblehead Road*.

LIKE

Like is a preposition that means *similar to*. Therefore, it is followed by an object (usually a noun or a pronoun).

> (1) *Like you*, I prefer watching films on DVD rather than going to a crowded movie theater.

Do not confuse *like* with *as* or *as if*. *As* and *as if* are subordinating conjunctions.* They are followed by a subject and a verb.

> (2) *As the instructions explain*, insert flap B into slit B before folding the bottom in half.
>
> (3) Robert sometimes acts *as if he has never made a mistake*.

PRACTICE 2

Fill in the correct prepositions in the following sentences. Be especially careful when using *in*, *on*, and *like*.

1. To celebrate America's one hundredth birthday, _____ July 4, 1876, the French decided to give a special statue _____ their "sister country."

2. Sculptor Frederic-Auguste Bartholdi sailed _____ America, seeking support _____ the ambitious project.

---

*For more work on subordinating conjunctions, see Chapter 14.

3. Bartholdi was awed _____ America's vastness as he traveled _____ redwood forests, _____ prairies, and _____ mountains.

4. _____ Egypt he had seen huge monuments _____ the pyramids and the Sphinx, and he wanted to honor liberty _____ a structure as majestic as those.

5. His monument would be so big that visitors would be able to walk _____ it and climb _____ a staircase _____ its top.

6. Funded _____ the French, Bartholdi finally built his statue _____ a woman raising her torch _____ the sky.

7. _____ many delays, a newspaper urged American citizens to help pay for the statue's base; money poured _____ , and the base was erected _____ Bedloe's Island _____ New York Harbor.

8. The Statue of Liberty was not shipped _____ France _____ America _____ 1885, and then it took six months to mount her _____ the foundation.

9. One million people and hundreds of ships gathered _____ the rain and fog to see the statue unveiled _____ October 28, 1886.

10. Today, Lady Liberty still rises 305 feet _____ the harbor, lighting the darkness _____ her torch and symbolizing freedom _____ the globe.

 EXPLORING ONLINE

To learn more, look up "Statue of Liberty" on your favorite search engine. Can you answer these questions? 1. What famous person designed the metal skeleton, or scaffolding, that holds up Lady Liberty? 2. In how many pieces was the Statue of Liberty shipped from France?

PART C   Prepositions in Common Expressions

Prepositions often are combined with other words to form certain expressions—groups of words, or phrases, in common use. These expressions can sometimes be confusing. Below is a list of some troublesome expressions. If you are in doubt about others, consult a dictionary.

Common Expressions with Prepositions

Expression	Example
acquainted with	He became *acquainted with* his duties.
addicted to	I am *addicted to* chocolate.
agree on (a plan)	They finally *agreed on* a sales strategy.
agree to (another's proposal)	Did she *agree to* their demands?
angry about or at (a thing)	The subway riders are *angry about* (or *at*) the delays.
angry with (a person)	The manager seems *angry with* Jake.

Common Expressions with Prepositions (*continued*)

apply for (a position)	You should *apply for* this job.
approve of	Does he *approve of* the proposed budget?
consist of	The plot *consisted of* both murder and intrigue.
contrast with	The red lettering *contrasts* nicely *with* the gray stationery.
convenient for	Is Friday *convenient for* you?
correspond with (write)	My daughter *corresponds with* a pen pal in India.
deal with	How do you *deal with* friends who always want to borrow your notes?
depend on	He *depends on* your advice.
differ from (something)	A diesel engine *differs from* a gasoline engine.
differ with (a person)	On that point, I *differ with* the medical technician.
different from	His account of the accident is *different from* hers.
displeased with	She is *displeased with* all the publicity.
fond of	We are all *fond of* Sam's grandmother.
grateful for (something)	Jim was *grateful for* the two test review sessions.
grateful to (someone)	We are *grateful to* the plumber for repairing the leak on Sunday.
identical with	This watch is *identical with* hers.
interested in	George is *interested in* modern art.
interfere with	Does the party *interfere with* your study plans?
object to	She *objects to* the increase in the state sales tax.
protect against	This vaccine *protects* people *against* the flu.
reason with	Don't *reason with* a hungry pit bull.
reply to	Did the newspaper editor *reply to* your letter?
responsible for	Omar is *responsible for* marketing.
shocked at	We were *shocked at* the damage to the buildings.
similar to	That popular song is *similar to* another one I know.
specialize in	The shop *specializes in* clothing for large men.
succeed in	Gandhi *succeeded in* freeing India from British rule.
take advantage of	Let's *take advantage of* that two-for-one paperback book sale.
worry about	I no longer *worry about* my manager's moods.

PRACTICE 3

Circle the correct expressions in these sentences.

1. Most people need time to adjust to a new environment that (differs with, differs from) what is familiar and comfortable.

2. For example, entering a new college or country requires that a person (deal with, deal in) strange sights, customs, and values.

3. The difficulty of the adjustment period (depends on, depends with) the individual.

4. The process of cultural adjustment (consists in, consists of) four predictable stages.

5. During the enjoyable "honeymoon stage," a person is (interested on, interested in) the new place.

6. He or she settles in and gets (acquainted with, acquainted to) the new surroundings.

7. In the second stage, however, the excitement wears off, and the person might (worry of, worry about) not fitting in.

8. In this "conflict stage," people struggle to understand behaviors and expectations (different from, different with) those in their native country or hometown.

9. In the third, so-called "critical stage," some (take advantage on, take advantage of) the opportunity and immerse themselves in the foreign culture.

10. Others feel (displeased with, displeased in) their experience and spend more time with people who share their customs.

11. During the final stage, the "recovery stage," those who (deal about, deal with) their experience as an adventure usually begin to feel more at ease.

12. They (succeed on, succeed in) adapting to their new home.

PRACTICE 4

Writing Assignment

A friend or relative of yours has come to spend a holiday week in your city. He or she has never been there before and wants advice on sightseeing. In complete sentences, write directions for one day's sightseeing. Make sure to explain why you think this person would enjoy visiting each particular spot.

Organize your directions according to time order—that is, what to do first, second, and so on. Use transitional expressions like *then, after,* and *while* to indicate time order. Be especially careful when using the prepositions *in* and *on.* Try to work in a few of the expressions listed in Part C.

CHAPTER HIGHLIGHTS

- Prepositions are words like *at, from, in,* and *of.* A prepositional phrase contains a preposition and its object:

  The tree *beneath my window* has lost its leaves.

- Be careful of the prepositions *in, on,* and *like:*

  I expect to graduate *in* June.
  I expect to graduate *on* June 10.

  The Packards live *in* Tacoma.
  The Packards live *on* Farnsworth Avenue.

  Like my father, I am a Dodgers fan.

- Prepositions are often combined with other words to form fixed phrases:

  convenient for, different from, reason with

CHAPTER REVIEW

Proofread this essay for preposition errors. Cross out the errors and correct them above the lines.

Listening for Life Among the Stars

(1) On the film *Contact,* actress Jodie Foster plays a scientist searching for intelligent life at the universe. (2) Foster's character is not real. (3) However, she is very similar of Dr. Jill Tarter, research director at SETI, the Search for Extraterrestrial Intelligence Institute. (4) Dr. Tarter and her team listen for radio signals sent off outer space because such signals might prove that life exists among the stars.

(5) Dr. Tarter earned her degrees across engineering and physics upon the 1960s and 1970s. (6) After completing her education, she worked for the space agency. (7) Then she heard off a new program specializing on the search for life at space. (8) Dr. Tarter was greatly interested of this exciting program. (9) Since then, she has spent more hours gazing onto a telescope than anyone else under the planet.

(10) To scan even bigger areas of space, Dr. Tarter led the development of the Allen Telescope Array on California. (11) This group of telescopes searches twenty-four

hours a day for communications from deep space. (12) Dr. Tarter is also raising funds for build a radio telescope ten times more powerful than any used today. (13) She hopes that soon astronauts will install a radio telescope in the moon. (14) Dr. Tarter maintains a sense of humor around her unusual career. (15) When people tease her of her search of "little green men," she laughingly replies at these skeptics that she might find "big blue women" instead.

EXPLORING ONLINE

<http://a4esl.org/q/h/vm/prepos01.html> Interactive quiz: Select the right prepositions for each sentence.

<http://a4esl.org/q/j/ck/mc-prepositions.html> Test your preposition intuition with this 52-question quiz.

<http://www.eslcafe.com/quiz/prep1.html> Visit the ESL café and test your preposition use.

<http://college.cengage.com/devenglish/> Visit the *Grassroots* 9/e student website for more exercises, quizzes, and live links to all websites mentioned in this chapter.

WRITING ASSIGNMENTS

As you complete each writing assignment, remember to perform these steps:

- Write a clear, complete topic sentence.
- Use freewriting, brainstorming, or clustering to generate ideas for the body of your paragraph, essay, or speech.
- Arrange your best ideas in a plan.
- Revise for support, unity, coherence, and exact language.
- Proofread for grammar, punctuation, and spelling errors.

Writing Assignment 1: *Imagine yourself going global.* Have you ever imagined leaving your familiar culture in the United States to study, work, or volunteer abroad? If you could live for one year anywhere in the world, where would you go and to what task or cause would you devote yourself? Would you want to focus on doing humanitarian work or on developing your knowledge, career, or language skills? Describe your dream destination and the work you would want to do there. Proofread for the correct use of nouns, pronouns, adjectives, adverbs, and prepositions.

Writing Assignment 2: *Explain your job.* Explain what you do—your duties and responsibilities—to someone who knows nothing about your kind of work but is interested in it. In your first sentence, sum up the work you do. Then name the equipment you use and tell how you spend an average working day. Explain the rewards and drawbacks of your job. Finally, proofread for the correct use of nouns, pronouns, adjectives, adverbs, and prepositions.

Writing Assignment 3: *Give an award.* When we think of awards, we generally think of awards for the most home runs or the highest grade average. However, Cal Ripken Jr. of the Baltimore Orioles became famous because he played in a record number of consecutive games. In other words, his award was for *showing up,* for *being there,* for *constancy.* Write a speech for an awards dinner in honor of someone who deserves recognition for this kind of constancy. Perhaps your parents deserve the award, or your spouse, or the law enforcement officer on the beat in your neighborhood. Be specific in explaining why this person deserves the award. You might try a humorous approach. Proofread your speech for the correct use of nouns, pronouns, adjectives, adverbs, and prepositions.

Writing Assignment 4: *Discuss your future.* Imagine yourself ten years from now; how will your life be different? Pick one major way in which you expect it will have changed. You may want to choose a difference in your income, your marital status, your idea of success, or anything else that is important to you. Your first sentence should state this expected change. Then explain why this change will be important to you. Proofread for the correct use of nouns, pronouns, adjectives, adverbs, and prepositions.

REVIEW

Proofreading

Proofread the following essay for the incorrect use of nouns, pronouns, adjectives, adverbs, and prepositions. Cross out errors and correct them above the lines. (You should find twenty-six errors.)

The Last Frontier

(1) When the government of Brazil opened the Amazon rain forest for settlement on the 1970s, they created the last frontier on earth. (2) Many concerned man and woman everywhere now fear that the move has been a disasters for the land and for the people.

(3) The most large rain forest in the world, the Amazon rain forest has been hit real hard. (4) The government built highways to make it more easy for poor people to get to the land, but the roads also made investors interested to the forest. (5) Lumber companies chopped down millions of tree. (6) Ranchers and settlers theirselves burned the forest to make room for cattle and crops. (7) All this activities have taken their toll: in one area, which is the size of Colorado, three-quarters of the rain forest has already been destroyed. (8) Many kinds of plants and animals have been lost forever.

(9) As the rain forest itself, the Indians who live there are threatened by these wholesale destruction. (10) Ranchers, miners, loggers, and settlers have moved onto Indian lands. (11) Contact with the outside world has changed the Indians' traditional way of life. (12) A few Indian tribe have made economic and political gains; many tribes have totally disappeared, however.

(13) Many of the settler are not doing very good either. (14) People have poured into the region too rapid, and the government is unable to provide the needed services. (15) Small villages have become crowded cities, diseases (especially malaria) have spread, and lawlessness is common. (16) Worse of all, the soil beneath the rain forest is not fertile. (17) After a few years, the settlers' land, it is worthless. (18) As the settlers go into debt, businesses take advantage for the situation by buying land quick and exploiting it bad.

(19) Can the situation in the rain forest improve? (20) Although the Brazilian government has been trying to preserve those forest, thousands of fires are still set

every year to clear land for cattle grazing, planting, and building. (21) On the more hopeful side, however, scientists have discovered fruits in the rain forest that are extreme high in vitamins and proteins. (22) Those fruits would be much better crops for the rain forest than the corn, rice, and beans that farmers are growing there now. (23) The world watches nervous. (24) Will the Earth's preciousest rain forest survive?

Transforming

Change the subject of this paragraph from singular (*the hybrid*) to plural (*hybrids*), changing every *the car* to *cars*, every *it* to *they*, and so forth. Make all necessary verb and other changes. Write your revisions above the lines.

(1) The hybrid automobile is gaining popularity worldwide, especially in the United States, Europe, and Japan. (2) It is powered by a combination of gasoline and a rechargeable electric battery instead of gasoline alone. (3) Admirers of the hybrid like its excellent gas mileage and the fact that it is less polluting than conventional cars. (4) Although a hybrid car, truck, or SUV will not solve our global warming problem, it will help reduce the emission of gases harmful to our environment. (5) In the future, this vehicle may be supplanted by a car powered by hydrogen fuel cells or other technologies. (6) But for now, it is probably the most environmentally friendly car on the road.

WRITERS' WORKSHOP

Tell How Someone Changed Your Life

Strong writing flows clearly from point to point so that a reader can follow easily. In your class or group, read this essay, aloud if possible. As you read, pay special attention to organization.

Stephanie

(1) There are many people who are important to me. However, the most important person is Stephanie. Stephanie is my daughter. She has changed my life completely. She has changed my life in a positive way.

(2) Stephanie is only five years old, but she has taught me the value of education. When I found out that I was pregnant, my life changed in a positive way. Before I got pregnant, I didn't like school. I went to school just to please my mom, but I wasn't learning anything. When I found out that I was pregnant, I changed my mind about education. I wanted to give my baby the best of this world. I knew that without a good education, I wasn't going anywhere, so I decided to get my life together.

(3) Stephanie taught me not to give up. I remember when she was trying to walk, and she fell down. She didn't stop but kept on going until she learned how to walk.

(4) In conclusion, you can learn a lot from babies. I learned not to give up. Stephanie is the most important person in the whole world to me. She has changed me in the past, and she will continue to change me in the future.

Claudia Huezo, student

1. How effective is this essay?

   _____ Clear thesis statement?   _____ Good support?

   _____ Logical organization?   _____ Effective conclusion?

2. Claudia Huezo has organized her essay very well: introduction and thesis statement, two supporting paragraphs, conclusion. Is the main idea of each supporting paragraph clear? Does each have a good topic sentence?

3. Is each supporting paragraph developed with enough facts and details? If not, what advice would you give the writer for revising, especially for reworking paragraph (3)?

4. This student has picked a wonderful subject and writes clearly—two excellent qualities. However, did you find any places where short, choppy, or repetitious sentences could be improved?

If so, point out one or two places where Huezo might cross out or rewrite repetitious language (where she says the same thing twice in the same words). Point out one or two places where she might combine short sentences for variety.*

5. Proofread for grammar and spelling. Do you spot any error patterns this student should watch out for?

Writing and Revising Ideas

1. Tell how someone changed your life.

2. Discuss two reasons why education is (is not) important.

Before you write, plan or outline your paragraph or essay so that it will be clearly organized (see Chapter 3, Part E, and Chapter 4, Part B). As you revise, pay special attention to the order of ideas and to clear, concise writing without needless repetition (see Chapter 4, Part C).

---

*Cross out paragraph 2, sentence 2, and paragraph 4, sentence 2. Combine paragraph 4, sentences 2 and 3. Combine paragraph 2, sentences 4 and 5.

Revising for Consistency and Parallelism

This unit will teach you some easy but effective ways to add style to your writing. In this unit, you will

- Make sure your verbs and pronouns are consistent

- Use a secret weapon of many writers—parallel structure

- Vary the lengths and types of your sentences

280

Spotlight on Writing

This writer uses balanced sentences to make her point about date rape. If possible, read her paragraph aloud.

Women charge that date rape is the hidden crime; men complain it is hard to prevent a crime they can't define. Women say it isn't taken seriously; men say it is a concept invented by women who like to tease but not take the consequences. Women say the date-rape debate is the first time the nation has talked frankly about sex; men say it is women's unconscious reaction to the excesses of the sexual revolution. Meanwhile, men and women argue among themselves about the "gray area" that surrounds the whole murky arena of sexual relations, and there is no consensus in sight.

Nancy Gibbs, "When Is It Rape?" *Time*

- This writer presents the differing ideas of many men and women by balancing their points of view in sentence after sentence, a technique you will learn in this unit.

- Note that she increases the force of the paragraph by placing the topic sentence last.

 Writing Ideas

- *Date rape*

- *Another issue on which men and women may disagree*

CHAPTER 23 Consistent Tense

Consistent tense means using the same verb tense whenever possible within a sentence or paragraph. As you write and revise, avoid shifting from one tense to another—for example, from present to past—without a good reason for doing so.

(1) **Inconsistent tense:**	We *were* seven miles from shore. Suddenly, the sky *turns* dark.
(2) **Consistent tense:**	We *were* seven miles from shore. Suddenly, the sky *turned* dark.
(3) **Consistent tense:**	We *are* seven miles from shore. Suddenly, the sky *turns* dark.

- The sentences in (1) begin in the past tense with the verb *were* but then shift into the present tense with the verb *turns.* The tenses are inconsistent because both actions are occurring at the same time.

- The sentences in (2) are consistent. Both verbs, *were* and *turned,* are in the past tense.

- The sentences in (3) are also consistent. Both verbs, *are* and *turns,* are in the present tense.

Of course, you should use different verb tenses in a sentence or paragraph if they convey the meaning you want to express.

(4) Two years ago, I *wanted* to be a chef, but now I *am studying* forestry.

- The verbs in sentence (4) accurately show the time relationship: In the past, I *wanted* to be a chef, but now I *am studying* forestry.

As you proofread your papers for tense consistency, ask yourself: Have I unthinkingly moved from one tense to another, from past to present, or from present to past?

282

PRACTICE 1

Underline the verbs in these sentences. Then correct any tense inconsistencies above the line.

EXAMPLE: As soon as I get out of bed, I did fifty pushups.
                                    got (above "get")

or

As soon as I get out of bed, I did fifty pushups.
                                    do (above "did")

1. We were walking near the lake when a large moose appears just ahead.

2. When Bill asks the time, the cab driver told him it was after six.

3. The woman on the red bicycle was delivering newspapers while she is enjoying the morning sunshine.

4. Dr. Choi smiled and welcomes the next patient.

5. The Oklahoma prairie stretches for miles, flat and rusty red. Here and there, an oil rig broke the monotony.

6. They were strolling down Main Street when the lights go out.

7. My cousins questioned me for hours about my trip. I describe the flight, my impressions of Paris, and every meal I ate.

8. We started cheering as he approaches the finish line.

9. If Terry takes short naps during the day, she didn't feel tired in the evening.

10. Yesterday, we find the book we need online. We ordered it immediately.

11. Whenever I attempt the tango, I am looking goofy, not sexy.

12. My roommate saves money for three years and then took the trip of a lifetime to Vietnam and Cambodia.

13. An afternoon protein shake can provide an energy boost and kept a person from overeating later in the day.

14. As Cal opens the door, we all broke into song.

PRACTICE 2

Writing Assignment

Suppose that you have been asked for written advice on what makes a successful family. Your adult child, an inexperienced friend, or a sibling has asked you to write down some words of wisdom on what makes a family work. Using your own family as an example, write your suggestions for making family life as nurturing, cooperative, and joyful as possible. You may draw on your family's experience to give examples of pitfalls to avoid or of positive behaviors and attitudes. Revise for consistent tense.

CHAPTER HIGHLIGHTS

- **In general, use the same verb tense within a sentence or a paragraph:**

    She *sings* beautifully, and the audience *listens* intently.

    or

    She *sang* beautifully, and the audience *listened* intently.

- **However, at times different verb tenses are required because of meaning:**

    He *is* not *working* now, but he *spent* sixty hours behind the counter last week.

CHAPTER REVIEW

Read each of these paragraphs for consistent tense. Correct any inconsistencies by changing the tense of the verbs. Write your corrections above the lines.

A.   (1) Self-confidence is vital to success both in childhood and in adulthood. (2) With self-confidence, children knew that they are worthwhile and that they have important goals. (3) Parents can teach their children self-confidence in several ways. (4) First, children needed praise. (5) When they drew, for example, parents can tell them how beautiful their drawings are. (6) The praise lets them know they had talents that other people admire. (7) Second, children required exposure to many different experiences. (8) They soon found that they need not be afraid to try new things. (9) They realized that they can succeed as well at chess as they do at basketball. (10) They discovered that a trip to a museum to examine medieval armor is fascinating or that they enjoy taking a class in pottery. (11) Finally, it was very important to treat children individually. (12) Sensitive parents did not compare their children's successes or failures with those of their brothers or sisters, relatives, or friends. (13) Of course, parents should inform children if their behavior or performance in school needs improvement. (14) Parents helped children do better, however, by showing them how much they have accomplished so far and by suggesting how much they can and will accomplish in the future.

B.   (1) Like many ancient Greek myths, the story of Narcissus provided psychological insight and vocabulary still relevant today. (2) Although Narcissus was a mere mortal, this conceited young man believes himself to be as handsome as the gods. (3) Many young women fall in love with him, including a pretty nymph* named Echo. (4) When Narcissus rejected her affections, Echo sinks into heartbreak. (5) She faded into the landscape until the only thing left is the echo of her voice. (6) The youth's outrageous vanity infuriated the goddess Nemesis.** (7) She decides to teach Narcissus a lesson and dooms him to fall in love with his own image. (8) As he passed by Echo's pond, he glimpses himself in the water and falls in love with his own reflection. (9) For days, Narcissus lay lovesick on the bank, pining hopelessly for his own eyes, lips, and curls, until he dies. (10) From the ashes of his funeral pyre grows a white flower now known as the narcissus. (11) The story of this arrogant young man also gave modern psychology the term *narcissist,* a person so admiring of himself that he cannot love others.

Narcissus, 1597–1599, as imagined by the painter Caravaggio. Oil on canvas, 110 × 92 cm. What would a twenty-first-century Narcissus look like?

Photo credit: Scala/Art Resource, NY.

---

*nymph: a minor nature goddess
**Nemesis: goddess of divine vengeance and retribution

C.   (1) Last summer, we visited one of the world's oddest museums, the home of someone who never existed. (2) Early one afternoon, we walked along the real Baker Street in London, England. (3) Suddenly, it looms in front of us: number 221B, Mrs. Hudson's boarding house, home of the famous but fictitious detective Sherlock Holmes. (4) Once inside the perfect reproduction of Holmes' rooms, we are astonished to find all of Holmes' belongings, including his violin, his walking stick, and his chemistry set. (5) We learn that the founders of the museum had searched the country for Victorian objects and furniture like those in the Holmes stories. (6) They succeed beyond any Sherlock Holmes fan's wildest dreams. (7) They locate a Persian slipper like the one in which Holmes' stored pipe tobacco. (8) They even uncover a gold and emerald tie pin like the one Queen Victoria gave Holmes. (9) The museum also had quarters for Holmes' friend and assistant, Dr. Watson. (10) For him, the founders buy nineteenth-century medical supplies and surgical instruments. (11) After we return home that summer, I reread several Sherlock Holmes stories. (12) In my mind's eye, I see Holmes' rooms and belongings more vividly than ever before. (13) Of course, Holmes would have predicted that. (14) "Elementary," he would have said.

 EXPLORING ONLINE

<http://owl.english.purdue.edu/handouts/grammar/g_tensecEX1.html> Here are three exercises in tense consistency. Hone your skills.

<http://college.cengage.com/devenglish/> Visit the *Grassroots* 9/e student website for more exercises, quizzes, and live links to all websites mentioned in this chapter.

Consistent Person

Consistent person means using the same person or personal pronoun throughout a sentence or a paragraph. As you write and revise, avoid confusing shifts from one person to another. For example, don't shift from *first person* (*I, we*) or *third person* (*he, she, it, they*) to *second person* (*you*).*

(1) **Inconsistent person:**	College *students* soon see that *you* are on *your* own.
(2) **Consistent person:**	College *students* soon see that *they* are on *their* own.
(3) **Consistent person:**	In college, *you* soon see that *you* are on *your* own.

- Sentence (1) shifts from the third person plural *students* to the second person *you* and *your.*

- Sentence (2) uses the third person plural consistently. *They* and *their* now clearly refer to *students.*

- Sentence (3) is also consistent, using the second person *you* and *your* throughout.

PRACTICE 1

Correct any inconsistencies of person in these sentences. If necessary, change the verbs to make them agree with any new subjects. Make your corrections above the lines.

EXAMPLE: Each hiker should bring ~~your~~ his or her own lunch.

1. Belkys treats me like family when I visit her. She always makes you feel at home.

---

*For more work on pronouns, see Chapter 20.

2. I love to go dancing. You can exercise, work off tension, and have fun, all at the same time.

3. If a person has gone to a large high school, you may find a small college a welcome change.

4. When Lee and I drive to work at 6 a.m., you see the city waking up.

5. Every mechanic should make sure they have a good set of tools.

6. People who want to buy cars today are often stopped by high prices. You aren't sure how to get the most for your money.

7. Do each of you have his or her own e-mail address?

8. Many people mistakenly think that your vote doesn't really count.

9. A teacher's attitude affects the performance of their students.

10. It took me three years to decide to enroll in college; in many ways, you really didn't know what you wanted to do when you finished high school.

11. Each person should seek a type of exercise that you enjoy.

12. The students in my CSI class were problem solvers; he loved a challenge.

13. If that is your heart's desire, she should pursue it.

PRACTICE 2

Writing Assignment

In small groups, write as many endings as you can think of for this sentence: "You can (cannot) tell much about a person by . . ." You might write, "the way he or she dresses," "the way he or she styles his or her hair," or "the kind of movies he or she likes." Each group member should write down every sentence.

Then let each group member choose one sentence and write a short paragraph supporting it. Use people in the news or friends as examples to prove your point. As you write, be careful to use the first, second, or third person correctly. When everyone is finished, exchange papers, checking each other's work for consistent person.

CHAPTER HIGHLIGHTS

● **Use the same personal pronoun throughout a sentence or a paragraph:**

> When *you* apply for a driver's license, *you* may have to take a written test and a driving test.

> When a *person* applies for a driver's license, *he or she* may have to take a written test and a driving test.

CHAPTER REVIEW

Correct the inconsistencies of person in these paragraphs. Then make any other necessary changes. Write your corrections above the lines.

A. (1) When exam time comes, do you become anxious because you aren't sure how to study for tests? (2) They may have done all the work for their courses, but you still don't feel prepared. (3) Fortunately, he can do some things to make taking tests easier. (4) They can look through the textbook and review the material one has underlined. (5) You might read the notes you have taken in class and highlight or underline the main points. (6) A person can think about some questions the professor may ask and then try writing answers. (7) Sometimes, they can find other people from your class and form a study group to compare class notes. (8) The night before a test, they shouldn't drink too much coffee. (9) They should get a good night's sleep so that your mind will be as sharp for the exam as your pencil.

B. (1) The sport of mountain biking began in northern California in the 1970s. (2) Some experienced cyclists began using his or her old one-speed fat-tire bikes to explore dirt roads and trails. (3) You began by getting car rides up one of the mountains and pedaling their bikes down. (4) Then they began cycling farther up the mountain until he and she were pedaling to the top. (5) Those cyclists eventually started designing bikes to fit our sport. (6) By the end of the 1970s, road bike manufacturers decided you would join the action. (7) By the mid-1980s, mountain biking had become a national craze, and sales of mountain bikes were exceeding sales of road bikes.

(8) Today, mountain bikers pay about $1,000 for bikes that have everything we need for riding on rough trails: front-wheel shock absorbers, twenty-four gears that shift easily, a lightweight frame, flexible wheels, and even a full-suspension frame. (9) Cyclists ride your bikes everywhere; some of their favorite places are South Dakota's Badlands, Colorado's ski resorts, and Utah's Canyonlands National Park. (10) You compete in mountain bike races all over the world. (11) To top this off, in 1996 some of you competed in the first Olympic mountain bike race, outside Atlanta, Georgia. (12) The course, which had tightly spaced trees and large rocks, included steep climbs and sharp descents with surprise jumps. (13) What were those early "inventors" thinking as he and she watched that first Olympic race?

EXPLORING ONLINE

<http://www.powa.org/content/view/246/108/1/5/> Review and complete Activity 4.16: Rewrite the paragraph in consistent first person (*I* or *we*) and then in third person (*he/she* or *they*).

<http://college.cengage.com/devenglish/> Visit the *Grassroots* 9/e student website for more exercises, quizzes, and live links to all websites mentioned in this chapter.

Parallelism

CHAPTER 25

PART A Writing Parallel Constructions

PART B Using Parallelism for Special Effects

PART A Writing Parallel Constructions

Which sentence in each pair sounds better to you?

> (1) Jennie is an artist, spends time at athletics, and flies planes.
>
> (2) Jennie is *an artist, an athlete,* and *a pilot.*
>
> (3) He slowed down and came sliding. The winning run was scored.
>
> (4) He *slowed* down, *slid,* and *scored* the winning run.

● Do sentences (2) and (4) sound smoother and clearer than sentences (1) and (3)?

● Sentences (2) and (4) balance similar words or phrases to show similar ideas.

This technique is called *parallelism* **or** *parallel structure.* **The italicized parts of (2) and (4) are** *parallel.* **When you use parallelism, you repeat similar grammatical constructions in order to express similar ideas.**

● In sentence (2), can you see how *an artist, an athlete,* and *a pilot* are parallel? All three words in the series are singular nouns.

● In sentence (4), can you see how *slowed, slid,* and *scored* are parallel? All three words in the series are verbs in the past tense.

Now let's look at two more pairs of sentences. Note which sentence in each pair contains parallelism.

> (5) The car was big, had beauty, and it cost a lot.
>
> (6) The car was *big, beautiful,* and *expensive.*
>
> (7) They raced across the roof, and the fire escape is where they came down.
>
> (8) They raced *across the roof* and *down the fire escape.*

● In sentence (6), how are *big, beautiful,* and *expensive* parallel words?

● In sentence (8), how are *across the roof* and *down the fire escape* parallel phrases?

_____

Certain special constructions require parallel structure:

(9) The room is *both* light *and* cheery.

(10) You *either* love geometry *or* hate it.

(11) Tanya *not only* plays the guitar *but also* sings.

(12) Richard would *rather* fight *than* quit.

Each of these constructions has two parts:

both . . . and	not only . . . but also
(n)either . . . (n)or	rather . . . than . . .

The words, phrases, or clauses following each part must be parallel:

light . . . cheery	plays . . . sings
love . . . hate	fight . . . quit

Parallelism is an excellent way to add smoothness and power to your writing. Use it in pairs or in a series of ideas, balancing a noun with a noun, an *-ing* verb with an *-ing* verb, a prepositional phrase with a prepositional phrase, and so on.

PRACTICE 1

Circle the element that is *not* parallel in each list.

EXAMPLE: blue
red
(colored like rust)
purple

1. rowing
   jogging
   runner
   lifting weights

2. my four dogs
   out the door
   across the yard
   under the fence

3. painting the kitchen
   cans of paint
   several brushes
   one roller

4. persistent
   strong-willed
   work
   optimistic

5. opening his mouth to speak
   toward the audience
   smiling with anticipation
   leaning against the table

6. music shops
   clothing stores
   buying a birthday present
   electronics shops

7. dressed for the office
   laptop computer
   leather briefcase
   cellular phone

8. We shop for fruits at the market.
   We buy enough food to last a week.
   We are baking a cake tonight.
   We cook special meals often.

PRACTICE 2

Rewrite each sentence, using parallelism to accent the similar ideas.

EXAMPLE: Do you believe that gratitude and feeling happy are related?
Rewrite: _Do you believe that gratitude and happiness are related?_

1. Many people believe that they will be happy once they have money, they are famous, married to a spouse, or working at a good job.

   Rewrite: _____

   _____

2. Psychologist Martin Seligman found that gratitude is a key ingredient of happiness, and the "gratitude visit" was his invention.

   Rewrite: _____

   _____

3. First, you think of a person who was truly helpful to you, and then a "gratitude letter" is written by you to that person.

   Rewrite: _____

   _____

4. In this letter, explain sincerely and with specifics why you are grateful.

   Rewrite: _____

   _____

5. Then visit this person and reading your letter aloud.

   Rewrite: _____

   _____

6. According to Seligman, the ritual is moving, powerful, and there is a lot of emotion.

   Rewrite: _____

   _____

7. Seligman says people feel happier if they focus on the positive aspects of the past rather than being negative.

   Rewrite: _____

   _____

8. Gratitude visits, he believes, increase how intense, the length, and the frequency of positive memories.

   Rewrite: _____

   _____

9. In addition, they tend to inspire the receivers of thanks to become giving of thanks.

   Rewrite: _____

   _____

10. One gratitude visit leads to another, creating a chain of appreciation and also to make everyone feel more content.

    Rewrite: _____

    _____

PRACTICE 3

Fill in the blanks in each sentence with parallel words or phrases of your own. Be creative. Take care that your sentences make sense and that your parallels are truly parallel.

EXAMPLE: I feel _____ rested _____ and _____ happy _____.

1. Ethan's favorite colors are _____ and

   _____.

2. The day of the storm, we _____, and they

   _____.

3. Her attitude was strange. She acted as if _____and

   as if _____.

4. I like people who _____ and who

   _____.

5. Some married couples _____, whereas others

   _____.

6. Harold _____, but I just

   _____.

7. To finish this project, work _____ and

   _____.

8. _____ and _____ relax

   me.

9. We found _____, _____,

   and_____ on the beach.

10. They might want to _____ or to

    _____.

PART B   Using Parallelism for Special Effects

By rearranging the order of a parallel series, you can sometimes add a little drama or humor to your sentences. Which of these two sentences is more dramatic?

(1) Bharati is a wife, a mother, and a black belt in karate.

(2) Bharati is a wife, a black belt in karate, and a mother.

● If you chose sentence (1), you are right. Sentence (1) saves the most surprising item—*a black belt in karate*—for last.

● Sentence (2), on the other hand, does not build suspense but gives away the surprise in the middle.

You can also use parallelism to set up your readers' expectations and then surprise them with humor.

> (3) Mike Hardware was the kind of private eye who didn't know the meaning of the word *fear*, who could laugh in the face of danger and spit in the eye of death—in short, a moron with suicidal tendencies.

● Clever use of parallelism made this sentence a winner in the Bulwer-Lytton Contest. Every year, contestants make each other laugh by inventing the first sentence of a bad novel.

PRACTICE 4

On paper or on a computer, write five sentences of your own, using parallel structure. In one or two of your sentences, arrange the parallel elements to build toward a dramatic or humorous conclusion. For ideas, look at Practice 3, but create your own sentences.

PRACTICE 5

Writing Assignment

Write a one-paragraph newspaper advertisement to rent or sell your house or apartment. Using complete sentences, let the reader know the number of rooms, their size, and their appearance, and explain why someone would be happy there. Emphasize your home's good points, such as "lots of light" or "closet space galore," but don't hide the flaws. If possible, minimize them while still being honest.

You may want to begin with a general description such as "This apartment is a plant lover's dream." Be careful, though: if you describe only the good features or exaggerate, readers may think, "It's too good to be true." Use parallel structure to help your sentences read more smoothly.

CHAPTER HIGHLIGHTS

● **Parallelism balances similar words or phrases to express similar ideas:**

> He left the gym *tired, sweaty,* and *satisfied.*

> Tami not only *finished the exam in record time* but also *answered the question for extra credit.*

> To celebrate his success, Roger *took in a show, went to a dance,* and *ate a late dinner.*

CHAPTER REVIEW

This essay contains both correct and faulty parallel constructions. Revise the faulty parallelism. Write your corrections above the lines.

Chinese Medicine in the United States

(1) When diplomatic relations between the United States and mainland China were restored in 1972, acupuncture was one import that sparked America's imagination and made people interested. (2) In the United States today, the most popular form of Chinese medicine is acupuncture.

(3) Acupuncture involves the insertion of thin, sterile, made of stainless steel needles at specific points on the body. (4) Chinese medical science believes that the *chi,* or life force, can be redirected by inserting and by the manipulation of these needles. (5) They are inserted to just below the skin and are either removed quickly or leave them in for up to forty minutes. (6) In addition, the acupuncturist can twirl them, heat them, or charging them with a mild electrical current. (7) Acupuncture can reduce pain for those suffering from allergies, arthritis, backache, or with a toothache. (8) It also has helped in cases of chronic substance abuse, anxiety, and for depressed people.

(9) Chinese medicine has grown in popularity and become important in America. (10) Thirty-five schools in the United States teach Chinese acupuncture. (11) Forty-four states have passed laws that regulate or for licensing the practice of acupuncture. (12) Since 1974, the federal government has authorized several studies of acupuncture's effectiveness and how reliable it is. (13) Although research has failed to explain how acupuncture works, it has confirmed that it does work. (14) The studies also suggest that acupuncture should continue to be tested and using it.

EXPLORING ONLINE

<http://grammar.ccc.commnet.edu/grammar/cgi-shl/quiz.pl/parallelism_quiz.htm>
Interactive quiz: Click on the sentence that uses parallelism correctly.

<http://grammar.ccc.commnet.edu/grammar/quizzes/niu/niu10.htm>
Interactive quiz: Which sentence in each group has parallelism errors?

<http://college.cengage.com/devenglish/> Visit the *Grassroots* 9/e student website for more exercises, quizzes, and live links to all websites mentioned in this chapter.

WRITING ASSIGNMENTS

As you complete each writing assignment, remember to perform these steps:

● Write a clear, complete topic sentence.

● Use freewriting, brainstorming, or clustering to generate ideas for the body of your paragraph, essay, or speech.

● Arrange your best ideas in a plan.

● Revise for support, unity, coherence, and exact language.

● Proofread for grammar, punctuation, and spelling errors.

Writing Assignment 1: *Pay a gratitude visit.* Experts like Dr. Martin Seligman claim that people who let themselves feel and express gratitude are happier than people who do not. Do your own research. 1. Pick a person who has been kind or helpful to you but whom you have never properly thanked. 2. Write a letter to this person, discussing specifically, in concrete terms, why you feel grateful to him or her. 3. Arrange a visit to the object of your gratitude and—in person—read your letter aloud. 4. Then write a one-paragraph report on how the two of you felt about the experience. Are the experts right? Revise for consistent tense and person; use parallelism to make your sentences read smoothly.

Writing Assignment 2: *Send an e-mail of praise or complaint to a company.* What recent purchase either pleased you or disappointed you? Use a search engine to find the website of this product's manufacturer. Locate the Contact Us or Customer Support page of the website, and write an e-mail that explains specifically what you like or dislike about the product. Before you click Send, proofread for the correct use of nouns, pronouns, adjectives, adverbs, and prepositions. Be sure to print a copy or send one to your instructor.

Writing Assignment 3: *Take a stand on date rape.* In a group with classmates, read aloud and discuss Nancy Gibbs's powerful paragraph on date rape on page 281. Do you agree with her that the sexes often have different views on this topic? Do you know someone who has experienced date rape or anyone who has been accused of it? On your own, jot down ideas and narrow the subject to one aspect that interests you. Plan and write a paragraph or short essay. Revise carefully for consistency and parallelism.

Writing Assignment 4: *Review a restaurant.* You have been asked to review the food, service, and atmosphere at a local restaurant. Your review will appear in a local newspaper and will have an impact on the success or failure of this eating establishment. Tell what you ordered, how it tasted, and why you would or would not recommend this dish. Note the service: was it slow, efficient, courteous, rude, or generally satisfactory? Is the restaurant one in which customers can easily carry on a conversation, or is there too much noise? Is the lighting good or poor? Include as much specific detail as you can. Revise for consistent tense and person.

6

REVIEW

Proofreading

A.   We have changed this student's composition so that it contains inconsistent tenses and faulty parallelism. Proofread for these errors, and correct them above the lines. (You should find fourteen errors.)

My Thoughts on Failure

(1) What brought me to this college was my dream of becoming a physician's assistant. (2) When I arrive on campus, I already had good study habits. (3) I know that my curriculum required hard work, and some of the subject matter was tedious and difficult to learn. (4) I also knew that biology was one of the hardest subjects. (5) But one day, my first thoughts of failure sneak into my brain when I overhear other students talking about Biology 23. (6) They said the course was so hard that few students last term even pass it. (7) Soon I heard testimonials from students who either fail Bio 23 or withdrew because they were failing. (8) I begin to doubt my own abilities. (9) What if I fail, too? (10) I need the course to achieve my dream.

(11) I realized that I am scaring myself with negative thoughts. (12) Instead, I focused on my goal of becoming a physician's assistant. (13) I pushed all my fears to the back of my mind and registered for Bio 23. (14) Once I enter the class, I study all the material day and night. (15) I took every pop quiz and test and poured my best effort into every assignment. (16) In the end, I pass with a B. (17) This experience increased my self-confidence because I turn my fear into victory by trying.

Jacqueline Dixon, student

B.   Proofread the following essay for inconsistent person and faulty parallelism. Correct the errors above the lines. (You should find thirteen errors.)

True Colors

(1) One day in 1992, the life of Californian John Box changed radically for the second time. (2) That day, John drove four hours to buy a new wheelchair that would allow you to play tennis. (3) Years before, a motorcycle accident had left both his legs paralyzed, but John refused to surrender his love of sports. (4) Instead, he turned anger into being determined. (5) Now a weekend wheelchair athlete, John wanted a better, lighter chair, and one that was faster. (6) When he arrived at

Copyright © Heinle, Cengage Learning. All rights reserved.

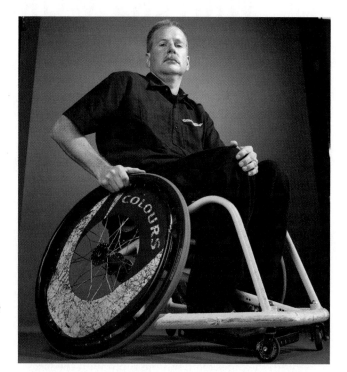

John Box, wheelchair athlete and founder of Colours Wheelchair.

Michael Grecco/Getty Exclusive.

the wheelchair manufacturer, however, the salespeople ignored him as if his disability made him invisible.

(7) Back home, furious and feeling frustration, John and his brother Mike decided to design one's own sports wheelchair. (8) The result inspired them to start a company and name her Colours. (9) Colours Wheelchair sells high-performance chairs with edgy names like Hammer, Avenger, Swoosh, and one is called Boing. (10) John Box, the company's president, hires other "wheelers," and he or she often contribute new product ideas. (11) The company also sponsors seventy-five wheelchair athletes. (12) In fact, fourteen-year-old Aaron Fotheringham, a wheelchair skateboarder, recently became the first human to perform a somersault flip in a wheelchair.

(13) Today John Box and his brother not only want to expand his or her successful company but also in educating the public about disability. (14) "A person doesn't lose their personality by becoming disabled," declares John. (15) The disabled, he says, can be funny, brilliance, pregnant, competing, sexy, or none of the above, just like everyone else.

 EXPLORING ONLINE

Visit the Colours Wheelchair website and examine the photos, video, and presentation of disabled people. What is the message this website is sending? Do these images of the disabled differ from other images you have seen?

WRITERS' WORKSHOP

Shift Your Audience and Purpose

Playing with the idea of audience and purpose can produce some interesting writing—such as writing to your car to persuade it to keep running until finals are over. Likewise, writing as if you are someone else can be a learning experience.

In your class or group, read this unusual essay, aloud if possible.

A Fly's-Eye View of My Apartment

(1) Hey, are you guys ready? Today is Armageddon!* When you enter this door, remember, you're not getting out alive. She's a pretty tough lady. Oh, and don't forget to eat all you can. The kids are always dropping crumbs. You can make it through the night if you stay on the ceilings. Whatever you do, stay out of the peach room that is always humid. Once the door is shut, you're trapped. Try not to be noticed on the cabinets in the room where the smells come from. There is nothing interesting in the room with the big screen, but the room with the large bed can be rather stimulating if you stay on the walls.

(2) She won't get tired of us until about 6 p.m.; that is usually around dinnertime. She switches around, using different swatters, so you never really know what to look for. When you hear the gospel music, start looking out. She gets an enormous amount of energy from this music, and her swats are accurate, which means they're deadly. It kills me how she becomes so baffled about how we get in since she has screens on the windows. Little does she know that it's every time she opens the front door.

(3) Well, I think she's ready to leave for work. I hear the lock. To a good life, fellows. See you in heaven—and remember to give her hell!

Tanya Peck, student

1. How effective is Tanya Peck's essay?

   _____ Interesting subject?   _____ Good supporting details?

   _____ Logical organization?   _____ Effective conclusion?

2. This writer cleverly plays with the notions of speaker, audience, and purpose. Who is Peck pretending to be as she writes? Whom is she addressing and for what purpose?

3. The writer/speaker refers to the "pretty tough lady" of the house. Who is that lady? How do you know?

———————
*Armageddon: a final battle between forces of good and evil.

4. Peck divides her essay into two main paragraphs and a brief conclusion. Because of her unusual subject, the paragraphs do not have topic sentences. However, does each paragraph have a clear main idea? What is the main idea of paragraph (1)? of paragraph (2)?

5. Underline any details or sentences that you especially liked—for example, in paragraph (2), the clever idea that the fly realizes that gospel music (for some mysterious reason) energizes the woman with the swatter. Can you identify the rooms described in paragraph (1)?

6. The essay concludes by playing with the terms *heaven* and *hell*. Do you find this effective—or offensive? Are these words connected to *Armageddon* in the introduction? How?

7. Proofread for any grammar or spelling errors.

Writing and Revising Ideas

1. Write a _____'s-eye view (dog, cat, flea, canary, goldfish, ant, roach) of your home.

2. Describe an important moment in history as if you were there.

Before you write, read about audience and purpose in Chapter 1, Part B. Prewrite and plan to get an engaging subject. As you revise, pay special attention to keeping a consistent point of view; really try to imagine what that person (or other creature) would say in those circumstances.

Mastering Mechanics

Even the best ideas may lose their impact if the writer doesn't know how to capitalize and punctuate correctly. In this unit, you will

- Learn when—and when not—to capitalize

- Recognize when—and when not—to use commas

- Find out how to use apostrophes

- Learn how to quote the words of others in your writing

Spotlight on Writing

Correct punctuation adds to the power of this writer's humorous look at a serious subject. If possible, read his paragraph aloud.

My daughter, Olivia, who just turned three, has an imaginary friend whose name is Charlie Ravioli. Olivia is growing up in Manhattan, and so Charlie Ravioli has a lot of local traits: he lives in an apartment "on Madison and Lexington," he dines on grilled chicken, fruit, and water, and having reached the age of seven and a half, he feels, or is thought, "old." But the most peculiarly local thing about Olivia's imaginary playmate is this: he is always too busy to play with her. She holds her toy cell phone up to her ear, and we hear her talk into it. "Ravioli? It's Olivia . . . It's Olivia. Come and play? OK. Call me. Bye." Then she snaps it shut and shakes her head. "I always get his machine," she says. Or she will say, "I spoke to Ravioli today." "Did you have fun?" my wife and I ask. "No. He was busy working. On a television" (leaving it up in the air if he repairs electronic devices or has his own talk show).

Adam Gopnik, "Bumping Into Mr. Ravioli," *The New Yorker*

- This writer describes his daughter's imaginary playmate as someone too busy to play! Why do you think Olivia has invented a playmate like Ravioli? Where did she learn about cell conversations, phone machines, and busyness?

- Does this paragraph point out a modern problem? If so, is it a big-city problem or a problem that exists in many places? What is the solution?

 Writing Ideas

- *Taking time to play*

- *A time when "child's play" taught you something important*

Capitalization

Here are the basic rules of capitalization:

1. nationality, race, language, religion	*Capitalize* →	American, African American, French, Latino, Protestant, Jewish, Catholic, Muslim, Buddhist, and so forth

● This group is *always capitalized*.

2. names of persons, countries, states, cities, places, streets, bodies of water, and so forth	*Capitalize* → *but* →	Bill Morse, New Zealand, Texas, Denver, Golden Gate Bridge, Jones Street, Pacific Ocean, and so forth
		a person, a country, a large state, a city, a bridge, an ocean, and so forth

● If you name a specific person, state, city, street, or body of water, *capitalize;* if you don't, use small letters.

3. buildings, organizations, institutions	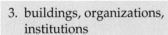 *Capitalize* → *but* →	Art Institute of Chicago, Apollo Theater, National Council of La Raza, Johnson City Library, Smithson University, and so forth
		a museum, a famous theater, an activist group, a library, an old school, and so forth

● If you name a specific building, group, or institution, *capitalize;* if you don't, use small letters.

4. historical events, periods, documents	*Capitalize* → *but* →	the Spanish-American War, the Renaissance, the Constitution, and so forth
		a terrible war, a new charter, and so forth

● If you name a specific historical event, period, or document, *capitalize;* if you don't, use small letters.

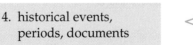

5. months, days, holidays June, Monday, the Fourth of July, and so forth

summer, fall, winter, spring

● *Always capitalize* months, days, and holidays; use small letters for the seasons.

6. professional and civil titles Dr. Smith, Professor Greenstein, Judge Alvarez, and so forth

the doctor, the professor, the judge, and so forth

● If you name the doctor, judge, and so forth, *capitalize;* if you don't, use small letters.

7. family names Uncle Xavier, Grandmother Stein, Cousin Emma, Mother, Grandfather, and so forth

an uncle, the grandmother, our cousin, my mother, and so forth

● If you name a relative or use *Mother, Father, Grandmother,* or *Grandfather* as a name, *capitalize;* however, if one of these words is preceded by the word *a, an,* or *the,* a possessive pronoun, or an adjective, use a small letter.

8. brand names Greaso hair oil, Quick drafting ink, and so forth

● *Capitalize* the brand name but not the type of product.

9. geographic locations the East, the Northwest, the South, and so forth

east on the boulevard

● If you mean a geographic location, *capitalize;* if you mean a direction, use small letters.

10. academic subjects Mathematics 51, Sociology 11, English Literature 210, and so forth

a tough mathematics course, an A in sociology, a course in English literature, and so forth

● If you use the course number, *capitalize;* if you don't, use small letters. Remember to capitalize languages and countries, however.

| 11. titles of books, poems, plays, films | Capitalize → | *Pride and Prejudice,* "Ode to a Bat," *Fences, Women on the Edge of a Nervous Breakdown,* and so forth |

● *Capitalize* the first letter of words in titles except for *a, an,* and *the;* prepositions; and coordinating conjunctions. However, always capitalize the first letter of the *first* and *last* words of the title.

PRACTICE 1

Capitalize where necessary.

EXAMPLE: Dr. richard carmona went from high school dropout to Surgeon
              General of the united states.

1. Richard carmona grew up in a poor puerto rican family in harlem, new york.

2. He started skipping classes in middle school and dropped out of dewitt clinton high school at age seventeen.

3. Carmona worked at dull, low-paying jobs until a conversation with a young man on leave from the u.s. army changed his life.

4. This soldier inspired him to join the military in 1967, and Carmona soon found himself working as a medic in vietnam.

5. He joined the green berets, earning two purple hearts for his brave service.

6. Carmona returned to america determined to become a doctor, so he enrolled at bronx community college.

7. He says that he owes his career to that college and to several of its professors—including michael steuerman and richard kor, who inspired him to succeed.

8. Carmona went on to earn degrees in biology and chemistry; he attended medical school at the university of california, graduating first in his class in three years instead of four.

9. Even after becoming a trauma surgeon and professor at the university of arizona, he continued to use his military training and knowledge of special operations.

10. This crime-fighting doctor joined the SWAT team for the pima county sheriff's department in 1986.

11. Carmona made headlines in 1992 when he dangled out of a helicopter to rescue a person stranded on the side of a cliff, an event that inspired a television movie.

12. In 1999, he stopped at a traffic accident in tucson, arizona; saw a hostage taker holding a woman at gunpoint; and shot the suspect.

13. Less than a year after the terrorist attacks of september 11, 2001, president george w. bush selected dr. carmona for the country's top medical post, noting his knowledge of law enforcement, bioterrorism, and emergency preparedness.

14. The second latino to be named to the u.s. post, surgeon general Carmona thanked the president in both spanish and english.

15. Senator john mccain said in the u.s. congress that carmona is "the embodiment of the american dream."

PRACTICE 2

Writing Assignment

Is your vacation usually a disaster or a success? Describe a particularly memorable vacation—either bad or good—in which you learned something about how to plan or enjoy a vacation.

In your first sentence, tell what you learned. Explain what went right and what went wrong. Be sure to name the places you visited and the sights you saw. You will probably want to arrange events in time order. Proofread for correct capitalization.

CHAPTER HIGHLIGHTS

- **Capitalize nationalities, languages, races, and religions:**
    Asian, French, Caucasian, Baptist

- **Capitalize specific countries, states, cities, organizations, and buildings:**
    Belgium, Utah, Akron, United Nations, the White House

- **Capitalize months, days, and holidays, but not seasons:**
    November, Friday, Labor Day, summer

- **Capitalize professional titles only when a person is named:**
    Mayor Gomez, the mayor, Superintendent Alicia Morgan

- **Capitalize brand names, but not the type of product:**
    Dawn dishwashing detergent

- **Capitalize geographic locations, but not directions:**
    the West, west of the city

- **Capitalize academic subjects only when they are followed by a course number:**
    History 583, psychology

- **Capitalize titles of books, poems, plays, and films:**
    House on Mango Street, "The Raven," *Rent*, *The Perfect Storm*

CHAPTER REVIEW

Proofread the following essay for errors in capitalization; correct the errors above the lines.

The Strange Career of Deborah Sampson

(1) Few Soldiers have had a stranger army career than Deborah Sampson. (2) Sampson disguised herself as a man so that she could fight in the revolutionary war. (3) Born on december 17, 1760, she spent her early years in a Town near plymouth, massachusetts. (4) Her Father left his large family, however, and went to sea when Sampson was seven years old. (5) After living with a Cousin and then with the widow of a Minister, sampson became a servant in a wealthy family.

(6) Household tasks and hard outdoor work built up her physical strength. (7) She was taller than the average Man and more muscular than the average Woman. (8) Therefore, she was able to disguise herself successfully. (9) Sampson enlisted in the continental army on may 20, 1782, under the name of robert shurtleff.

(10) Sampson fought in several Battles and was wounded at least twice. (11) One story says that she took a bullet out of her own leg with a penknife to avoid seeing a Doctor. (12) However, after the surrender of the british, Sampson's regiment was sent to philadelphia, where she was hospitalized with a high fever and lost consciousness. (13) At the Hospital, dr. Barnabas Binney made the discovery that ended Sampson's army life. (14) She was honorably discharged by general henry knox at west point on october 28, 1783.

(15) Officially female again, Sampson returned to Massachusetts and eventually married a Farmer named benjamin gannett. (16) The story of Sampson's adventures spread; in 1797, a book titled *the female review* was published about her. (17) When Sampson decided to earn money by telling her own story, she became the first american woman to be paid as a Public Speaker. (18) She gave her first talk at the federal street theatre in boston in march 1802 and toured until september. (19) Her health was poor, however, and she could not continue her appearances.

(20) In 1804, paul revere, who was a neighbor of the gannetts, wrote to a member of the united states congress. (21) He asked for a pension for this Soldier who had never been paid and was still suffering from her war wounds. (22) Congress granted deborah sampson gannett a pension of four dollars a month.

(23) Deborah Sampson died in sharon, Massachusetts, in april 1827. (24) Her story inspired the People of her own time and continues to inspire People today. (25) Two plays have been written about her: *she was there* and *portrait of deborah*. (26) On veterans day in 1989, a life-size bronze statue was dedicated in front of the sharon public library to honor her.

EXPLORING ONLINE

<http://grammar.ccc.commnet.edu/grammar/cgi-shl/par_numberless_quiz.pl/caps _quiz.htm> Interactive quiz: Capitalize as needed.

<http://www.dailygrammar.com/311to315.shtml> Four short quizzes: Practice your capitalization skills.

<http://college.cengage.com/devenglish/> Visit the *Grassroots* 9/e student website for more exercises, quizzes, and live links to all websites mentioned in this chapter.

Commas

The comma is a pause. It gives your reader a chance to stop for a moment to think about where your sentence has been and where it is going, and to prepare to read on.

Although this chapter will cover basic uses of the comma, always keep this generalization in mind: If there is no reason for a comma, leave it out!

PART A   Commas After Items in a Series

(1) I like apples, oranges, and pears.

● What three things do I like? _____, _____, and
_____

Use commas to separate three or more items in a series.

(2) We will walk through the park, take in a film, and visit a friend.

● What three things will we do? _____,
_____, and _____

(3) She loves to explore new cultures sample different foods and learn foreign languages.

● In sentence (3), what are the items in the series?

_____ , _____ ,

and _____

● Punctuate sentence (3).

However, if you want to join three or more items with *and* **or** *or* **between the items, do not use commas.**

(4) She plays tennis *and* golf *and* softball.

● Note that commas are not used in sentence (4).

PRACTICE 1

Punctuate these sentences correctly.

1. I can't find my shoes my socks or my hat!

2. Sylvia Eric and James have just completed a course in welding.

3. Over lunch, they discussed new accounts marketing strategy and motherhood.

4. Frank is in Florida Bob is in Brazil and I am in the bathtub.

5. On Sunday, we repaired the porch cleaned the basement and shingled the roof.

6. The exhibit will include photographs diaries and love letters.

7. Spinning kickboxing and Tai Chi have become very popular recently.

8. Paula hung her coat on the hook Henry draped his jacket over her coat and Sonia threw her scarf on top of the pile.

PRACTICE 2

On paper or on a computer, write three sentences, each containing three or more items in a series. Punctuate them correctly.

PART B Commas After Introductory Phrases

(1) By the end of the season, our local basketball team will have won thirty games straight.

● *By the end of the season* introduces the sentence.

An introductory phrase is usually followed by a comma.

(2) On Thursday we left for Hawaii.

However, a very short introductory phrase, like the one in sentence (2), need not be followed by a comma.

PRACTICE 3

Punctuate these sentences correctly. One sentence is already punctuated correctly.

1. During the rainstorm we huddled in a doorway.

2. Every Saturday at 9 p.m. she carries her telescope to the roof.

3. After their last trip Fred and Nita decided on separate vacations.

4. The first woman was appointed to the U.S. Supreme Court in 1981.

5. By the light of the moon we could make out a dim figure.

6. During the coffee break George reviewed his psychology homework.

7. In the deep end of the pool he found three silver dollars.

8. In almost no time they had changed the tire.

PRACTICE 4

On paper or on a computer, write three sentences using introductory phrases. Punctuate them correctly.

PART C   Commas for Direct Address

> (1) Bob, you must leave now.
>
> (2) You must, Bob, leave now.
>
> (3) You must leave now, Bob.
>
> (4) Don't be surprised, old buddy, if I pay you a visit very soon.

● In sentences (1), (2), and (3), *Bob* is the person spoken to; he is being *addressed directly*.

● In sentence (4), *old buddy* is being *addressed directly*.

The person addressed directly is set off by commas wherever the direct address appears in the sentence.

PRACTICE 5

Circle the person or persons directly addressed, and punctuate the sentences correctly.

1. I am happy to inform you Mr. Forbes that you are the father of twins.

2. We expect to return on Monday Miguel.

3. It appears my friend that you have won two tickets to the opera.

4. Get out of my roast you mangy old dog.

5. Tom it's probably best that you sell the old car at a loss.

6. If I were you Hilda I would wait to make the phone call until we are off the highway.

7. Bruce it's time you learned to operate the lawn mower!

8. I am pleased to announce ladies and gentlemen that Madonna is our surprise guest tonight.

PRACTICE 6

On paper or on a computer, write three sentences using direct address. Punctuate them correctly.

PART D Commas to Set Off Appositives

(1) The Rialto, a new theater, is on Tenth Street.

● *A new theater* describes *the Rialto*.

(2) An elderly man, my grandfather walks a mile every day.

● What group of words describes *my grandfather*? _____

(3) They bought a new painting, a rather beautiful landscape.

● What group of words describes *a new painting*?

_____

● *A new theater, an elderly man,* and *a rather beautiful landscape* are called *appositives*.

An *appositive* is usually a group of words that renames a noun or pronoun and gives more information about it. The appositive can appear at the beginning, middle, or end of a sentence. An appositive is usually set off by commas.

PRACTICE 7

Circle the appositive, and punctuate the sentences correctly.

1. That door the one with the X on it leads backstage.

2. A short man he decided not to pick a fight with the basketball player.

3. Hassim my friend from Morocco will be staying with me this week.

4. My nephew wants to go to Mama's Indoor Arcade a very noisy place.

5. George Eliot a nineteenth-century novelist was a woman named Mary Ann Evans.

6. A very close race the election for mayor wasn't decided until 2 a.m.

7. On the Fourth of July my favorite holiday my high school friends get together for an all-day barbecue.

8. Dr. Simpson a specialist in tribal music always travels with a digital recorder.

PRACTICE 8

On paper or on a computer, write three sentences using appositives. Punctuate them correctly.

PART E Commas for Parenthetical Expressions

(1) By the way, I think that you're beautiful.

(2) I think, by the way, that you're beautiful.

(3) I think that you're beautiful, by the way.

● *By the way* modifies or qualifies the entire sentence or idea.

● It is called a **parenthetical expression** because it is a side remark, something that could be placed in parentheses: *(By the way) I think that you're beautiful.*

Set off a parenthetical expression with commas.

Below is a partial list of parenthetical expressions:

as a matter of fact	in fact
believe me	it seems to me
I am sure	it would seem
I assure you	to tell the truth

PRACTICE 9

Circle the parenthetical expressions in the sentences below; then punctuate them correctly.

1. Believe me Sonia has studied hard for her driver's test.

2. He possesses it would seem an uncanny gift for gab.

3. It was I assure you an accident.

4. To tell the truth I just put a treadmill in your basement.

5. Her supervisor by the way will never admit when he is wrong.

6. A well-prepared résumé as a matter of fact can help you get a job.

7. He is in fact a black belt.

8. To begin with you need a new carburetor.

PRACTICE 10

On paper or on a computer, write three sentences using parenthetical expressions. Punctuate them correctly.

PART F   Commas for Dates

> (1) I arrived on Monday, March 20, 2004, and found that I was in the wrong city.

● Note that commas separate the different parts of the date.

● Note that a comma follows the last item in the date.

> (2) She saw him on Wednesday and spoke with him.

However, a one-word date (*Wednesday* or *1995*) preceded by a preposition (*in, on, near,* or *from,* for example) is not followed by a comma unless there is some other reason for it.

PRACTICE 11

Punctuate these sentences correctly. Not every sentence requires additional punctuation.

1. By Tuesday October 6 he had outlined the whole history text.

2. Thursday May 8 is Hereford's birthday.

3. She was born on January 9 1985 in a small Iowa town.

4. He was born on July 4 1976 the two-hundredth anniversary of the Declaration of Independence.

5. Do you think we will have finished the yearbook by May?

6. On January 24 1848 James Wilson Marshall found gold in California.

7. My aunt is staying with us from Tuesday to Friday.

8. Charles Schulz's final *Peanuts* comic strip was scheduled for February 13 2000 the day on which he died.

PRACTICE 12

On paper or on a computer, write three sentences using dates. Punctuate them correctly.

PART G   Commas for Addresses

> (1) We just moved from 11 Landow Street, Wilton, Connecticut, to 73 James Street, Charleston, West Virginia.

● Commas separate different parts of an address.

● A comma generally follows the last item in an address, usually a state (*Connecticut*).

(2) Julio Perez *from* Queens was made district sales manager.

However, a one-word address preceded by a preposition (*in, on, at, near,* or *from,* for example) is not followed by a comma unless there is another reason for it.

(3) Julio Perez, Queens, was made district sales manager.

Commas are required to set off a one-word address if the preposition before the address is omitted.

PRACTICE 13

Punctuate these sentences correctly. Not every sentence requires additional punctuation.

1. Their address is 6 Great Ormond Street London England.

2. Seattle Washington faces the Cascade Mountains.

3. That package must be sent to 30 West Overland Street Phoenix Arizona.

4. We parked on Marble Lane, across the street from the bowling alley.

5. His father now lives in Waco Texas but his sister has never left Vermont.

6. How far is Kansas City Kansas from Independence Missouri?

7. The old watch factory at 43 North Oak Street Scranton Pennsylvania has been condemned by the building inspector.

8. Foster's Stationery 483 Heebers Street Plainview sells special calligraphy pens.

PRACTICE 14

On paper or on a computer, write three sentences using addresses. Punctuate them correctly.

PART H   Commas for Coordination and Subordination

Chapters 13 and 14 cover the use of commas with coordinating and subordinating conjunctions. Below is a brief review.

(1) Enzio enjoys most kinds of music, but heavy metal gives him a headache.

(2) Although the weather bureau had predicted rain, the day turned out bright and sunny.

(3) The day turned out bright and sunny although the weather bureau had predicted rain.

- In sentence (1), a comma precedes the coordinating conjunction *but,* which joins together two independent ideas.

- In sentence (2), a comma follows the dependent idea because it precedes the independent idea.

- Sentence (3) does not require a comma because the independent idea precedes the subordinate one.

Use a comma before coordinating conjunctions—*and, but, for, nor, or, so,* or *yet*— that join two independent ideas.

Use a comma after a dependent idea only when the dependent idea precedes the independent one; do not use a comma if the dependent idea follows the independent one.

PRACTICE 15

Punctuate correctly. Not every sentence requires additional punctuation.

EXAMPLE: Because scrapped cars create millions of tons of ~~waste~~ *waste,* recycling auto parts has become an important issue.

1. Today new cars are made from many old parts and manufacturers are trying to increase the use of recycled materials from old cars.

2. Scrapped cars can be easily recycled because they consist mostly of metals.

3. After these cars are crushed magnets draw the metals out of them.

4. However, the big problem in recycling cars is the plastic they contain.

5. Although plastic can be recycled the average car contains about twenty different kinds of plastic.

6. Separating the different types of plastic takes much time but companies are developing ways to speed up the process.

7. Still, new cars need to be made differently before recycling can truly succeed.

8. Their parts should detach easily and they should be made of plastics and metals that can be separated from each other.

9. As we develop more markets for the recycled auto parts new cars may soon be 90 percent recycled and recyclable.

10. Our environment will benefit and brand-new cars will really be more than fifty years old!

PRACTICE 16

On paper or on a computer, write three sentences, one with a coordinating conjunction, one beginning with a subordinating conjunction, and one with the subordinating conjunction in the middle.

PRACTICE 17

Writing Assignment

We live in what is often called "the age of invention" because of rapid advances in technology, communication, and medicine. Which modern invention has meant the most to you *personally,* and why? You might choose something as common as disposable diapers or as sophisticated as a special feature of a personal computer.

In the first sentence, name the invention. Then, as specifically as possible, discuss why it means so much to you. Proofread for the correct use of commas.

CHAPTER HIGHLIGHTS

- **Commas separate three or more items in a series:**

    He bought a ball, a bat, and a fielder's glove.

- **Unless it is very short, an introductory phrase is followed by a comma:**

    By the end of January, I'll be in Australia.

- **Commas set off the name of a person directly addressed:**

    I think, Aunt Betty, that your latest novel is a winner.

- **Commas set off appositives:**

    My boss, the last person in line in the cafeteria, often forgets to eat lunch.

- **Commas set off parenthetical expressions:**

    My wife, by the way, went to school with your sister.

- **Commas separate the parts of a date or an address, except for a one-word date or an address preceded by a preposition:**

    On April 1, 1997, I was in a terrible blizzard.

    I live at 48 Trent Street, Randolph, Michigan.

    She works in Tucson as a plumber.

- **A comma precedes a coordinating conjunction that joins two independent ideas:**

    We had planned to see a movie together, but we couldn't agree on one.

- **If a dependent idea precedes the independent idea, it is followed by a comma; if the independent idea comes first, it is not followed by a comma:**

    Although I still have work to do, my project will be ready on time.

    My project will be ready on time although I still have work to do.

CHAPTER REVIEW

Proofread the following essay for comma errors—either missing commas or commas used incorrectly. Correct the errors above the lines.

Treetop Crusader

(1) On December 18, 1999 Julia Butterfly Hill's feet touched ground for the first time in more than two years. (2) She had just climbed down from the top, of an ancient tree in Humboldt County California. (3) The tree a thousand-year-old redwood was named Luna. (4) Hill had climbed 180 feet up Luna on December 10 1997 for what she thought would be a protest of two or three weeks.

(5) Hill's action was intended to stop Pacific Lumber a division of the Maxxam Corporation from cutting down old-growth forests. (6) The area immediately next to Luna, had already been stripped of trees. (7) Because nothing was left to hold the soil to the mountain a huge part of the hill had slid into the town of Stafford California. (8) Many homes had been destroyed.

(9) During her long tree-sit, Hill endured incredible hardships. (10) For more than two years she lived on a tiny platform eighteen stories off the ground. (11) El Niño storms almost destroyed her with ferocious winds razor-sharp rain and numbing cold. (12) She once wore two pairs of socks booties two pairs of thermal ski pants two thermal shirts a wool sweater two windbreakers a raincoat gloves and two hats to keep from freezing to death during a storm. (13) In addition to enduring nature's hardships Hill withstood life-threatening torment from the logging company. (14) She was harassed by helicopters various sieges and interference with receiving supplies. (15) Of course she also endured loneliness sometimes paralyzing fear and always deep sorrow for the destruction around her.

(16) Only twenty-three at the beginning of her tree-sit Hill eventually became both world famous and very knowledgeable about ancient forests. (17) At the top of Luna she used a cell phone a pager and a daily engagement planner. (18) She was trying to protect the tree itself to slow down all logging in the area and to raise public awareness. (19) She gave hundreds of phone interviews and answered hundreds of letters.

Julia Hill and Luna.
Shaun Walker/OtterMedia.com.

(20) Hill's action was dramatically successful; Luna was eventually saved from destruction. (21) When Hill returned to normal life she wrote a book *The Legacy of Luna: The Story of a Tree, a Woman, and the Struggle to Save the Redwoods.* (22) Julia Butterfly Hill is now a writer a poet and an activist. (23) She is a frequent speaker at environmental conferences she helped found the Circle of Life Foundation for preserving all life and she has received many honors and awards.

EXPLORING ONLINE

<http://owl.english.purdue.edu/handouts/interact/g_commaessEX1.html>
Interactive quiz: Where have all the commas gone?

<http://grammar.ccc.commnet.edu/grammar/quizzes/comma_quiz.htm>
Interactive quiz: Add commas to this basketball essay and score!

<http://college.cengage.com/devenglish/> Visit the *Grassroots* 9/e student website for more exercises, quizzes, and live links to all websites mentioned in this chapter.

Apostrophes

PART A Using the Apostrophe for Contractions

A contraction combines two words into one.

> do + not = don't
>
> should + not = shouldn't
>
> I + have = I've

● Note that an apostrophe (') replaces the omitted letters: "o" in *don't* and *shouldn't* and "ha" in *have*.

BE CAREFUL: *Won't* is an odd contraction because it cannot be broken into parts in the same way the previous contractions can.

> will + not = won't

PRACTICE 1

Write these words as contractions.

1. you + are = _____
2. who + is = _____
3. was + not = _____
4. they + are = _____
5. can + not = _____
6. it + is = _____
7. I + am = _____
8. will + not = _____

PRACTICE 2

Proofread this paragraph for incorrect or missing apostrophes in contractions. Write each corrected contraction above the lines.

(1) For musicians and music lovers in the twenty-first century, its a small world. (2) Musicians whove grown up in Asia, for instance, arent influenced by just Asian musical traditions anymore. (3) Hip-hops a perfect example of musical globalization. (4) Its inspired musicians all over the world, something the first American rappers couldnt have foreseen. (5) Many hip-hop artists in other countries, however, dont like the focus on money and sex in much of American hip-hop. (6) For example, Korean performers like Jo PD and Drunken Tiger are proud that theyre forces for social justice. (7) Many hip-hop stars from New Zealand are Pacific Islanders or Maori tribal people whove developed world-class skills and fight oppression with music. (8) In Senegal, politically active rappers claim that theyre responsible for toppling an oppressive government in the 2000 elections. (9) Some Latin-American hip-hop stars also have embraced a lifestyle thats committed to social justice. (10) Brazilian rappers, for example, do'nt perform just music; they also perform community service, teaching youth wholl spread the word about social change, music, and art.

PRACTICE 3

On paper or a computer, write five sentences using an apostrophe in a contraction.

PART B Defining the Possessive

A *possessive* is a word that shows that someone or something owns someone or something else.

PRACTICE 4

In the following phrases, who owns what?

EXAMPLE: "The hat of the man" means _____the man owns the hat_____ .

1. "The camera of Judson" means _____ .

2. "The hopes of the people" means _____ .

3. "The thought of the woman" means _____ .

4. "The trophies of the home team" means _____ .

5. "The ideas of that man" means _____ .

PART C Using the Apostrophe to Show Possession (in Words That Do Not Already End in -*S*)

| (1) the hands of my father | becomes | (2) my father's hands |

- In phrase (1), who owns what? _____
- In phrase (1), what is the *owner word*? _____
- How does the owner word show possession in phrase (2)?

  _____

- Note that what is owned, *hands,* follows the owner word.

If the *owner word* **(possessive) does not end in** -*s,* **add an apostrophe and an** -*s* **to show possession.**

PRACTICE 5

Change these phrases into possessives with an apostrophe and an -*s.* (Note that the owner words do not already end in -*s.*)

EXAMPLE: the friend of my cousin = _____*my cousin's friend*_____

1. the eyes of Rona = _____
2. the voice of the coach = _____
3. the ark of Noah = _____
4. the technology of tomorrow = _____
5. the jacket of someone = _____

PRACTICE 6

Add an apostrophe and an -*s* to show possession in these phrases.

1. Judy briefcase
2. the diver tanks
3. Murphy Law
4. Bill decision
5. somebody umbrella

6. everyone dreams
7. your daughter sandwich
8. last month prices
9. that woman talent
10. anyone guess

PRACTICE 7

On paper or on a computer, write five sentences. In each, use an apostrophe and an -*s* to show ownership. Use owner words that do not already end in -*s.*

PART D   Using the Apostrophe to Show Possession (in Words That Already End in -*S*)

> (1) the uniforms of the pilots   becomes   (2) the pilots' uniforms

- In phrase (1), who owns what? _____
- In phrase (1), what is the *owner word*? _____
- How does the owner word show possession in phrase (2)?

  _____

- Note that what is owned, *uniforms*, follows the owner word.

  If the *owner word* **(possessive) ends in** -*s*, **add an apostrophe after the** -*s* **to show possession.***

PRACTICE 8

Change these phrases into possessives with an apostrophe. (Note that the owner words already end in -*s*.)

EXAMPLE: the helmets of the players =   _____*the players' helmets*_____

1. the farm of my grandparents = _____

2. the kindness of my neighbors = _____

3. the dunk shots of the basketball players = _____

4. the music of The Smashing Pumpkins = _____

5. the trainer of the horses = _____

PRACTICE 9

Add either '*s* or ' to show possession in these phrases. BE CAREFUL: Some of the owner words end in -*s* and some do not.

1. the models faces

2. the model face

3. the pilot safety record

4. the children room

5. the runner time

6. Boris radio

7. my niece CDs

8. your parents anniversary

9. the men locker room

10. three students exams

11. several contestants answers

12. Mr. Jones band

_____

*Some writers add an '*s* to one-syllable proper names that end in -*s*: *James's book*.

PRACTICE 10

Rewrite each of the following pairs of short sentences as *one* sentence by using a possessive.

EXAMPLE: Joan has a friend. The friend comes from Chile.
Joan's friend comes from Chile.

1. Rusty has a motorcycle. The motorcycle needs new brakes.

   _____

2. The nurses had evidence. The evidence proved that the doctor was not careless.

   _____

3. Ahmad has a salary. The salary barely keeps him in peanut butter.

   _____

4. Lee has a job. His job in the Complaint Department keeps him on his toes.

   _____

5. José has a bad cold. It makes it hard for him to sleep.

   _____

6. Jessie told a joke. The joke did not make us laugh.

   _____

7. John Adams had a son. His son was the first president's son to also become president of the United States.

   _____

   _____

8. My sisters have a daycare center. The daycare center is open seven days a week.

   _____

9. The twins have a goal. Their goal is to learn synchronized swimming.

   _____

10. Darren has a thank-you note. The thank-you note says it all.

    _____

PRACTICE 11

Proofread this paragraph. Above the lines, correct any missing or incorrectly used apostrophes in possessives. BE CAREFUL: some owner words end in -s and some do not.

(1) Apple Computers' founder, Steven Jobs, is one of the industrys greatest innovators—and survivors. (2) Jobs first position, in the 1970s, was designing computer games for Atari. (3) Then he saw a friends' home-built computer. (4) Jobs convinced this friend, Steve Wozniak, to go into business with him. (5) At first, the partners built computers in the Jobs familys garage. (6) Their companys name came from the story of Isaac Newton, who supposedly formulated his great theory

of gravity when he watched an apple fall from a tree. (7) The mens' small computers were a huge success. (8) In 1984, they launched the Macintosh, which simplified peoples interactions with their computers by replacing typed commands with clicks. (9) But then, Job's luck changed. (10) After some poor management decisions, he was fired by Apples' board of directors. (11) Despite public failure, he started over. (12) Ironically, his new company was bought by Apple ten years later. (13) As Apple's leader once again, Jobs soon captured consumer's attention with his revolutionary iPod music player and iTunes software. (14) This mans' success flows not just from farsighted ideas but from a willingness to learn failures lessons and begin again.

PRACTICE 12

On paper or on a computer, write six sentences that use an apostrophe to show ownership—three using owner words that do not end in -s and three using owner words that do end in -s.

BE CAREFUL: Apostrophes show possession by nouns. As the following chart indicates, possessive pronouns do not have apostrophes.

Possessive Pronouns	
Singular	**Plural**
<u>my</u> book, <u>mine</u>	<u>our</u> book, <u>ours</u>
<u>your</u> book, <u>yours</u>	<u>your</u> book, <u>yours</u>
<u>his</u> book, <u>his</u>	<u>their</u> book, <u>theirs</u>
<u>her</u> book, <u>hers</u>	
<u>its</u> book, <u>its</u>	

Do not confuse *its* (possessive pronoun) with *it's* (contraction for *it is* or *it has*) or *your* (possessive pronoun) with *you're* (contraction for *you are*).*

REMEMBER: Use apostrophes for contractions and possessive nouns only. Do not use apostrophes for plural nouns (*four marbles*), verbs (*he hopes*), or possessive pronouns (*his, hers, yours, its*).

PRACTICE 13

Writing Assignment

Assume that you are writing to apply for a position as a teacher's aide. You want to convince the school principal that you would be a good teacher, and you decide to do this by describing a time when you taught a young child—your own child, a younger sibling, or a friend's child—to do something new.

In your topic sentence, briefly state who the child was and what you taught him or her. What made you want to teach this child? Was the experience easier or harder than you expected? How did you feel afterward? Proofread for the correct use of apostrophes.

---

*See Chapter 32 for work on words that look and sound alike.

CHAPTER HIGHLIGHTS

- **An apostrophe can indicate a contraction:**

  We're glad you could come.
  They *won't* be back until tomorrow.

- **A word that does not end in** *-s* **takes an** *'s* **to show possession:**

  Is that *Barbara's* coat on the sofa?
  I like *Clint Eastwood's* movies.

- **A word that ends in** *-s* **takes just an** *'* **to show possession:**

  That store sells *ladies'* hats with feathers.
  I depend on my *friends'* advice.

CHAPTER REVIEW

Proofread this paragraph for apostrophe errors—missing apostrophes and apostrophes used incorrectly. Correct the errors above the lines.

The Magic Fastener

(1) Its hard to remember the world without Velcro. (2) Shoelaces had to be tied; jackets' had to be zipped and did'nt make so much noise when they were loosened. (3) We have a Swiss engineers' curiosity to thank for todays changes. (4) On a hunting trip in 1948, Georges de Mestral became intrigued by the seedpods that clung to his clothing. (5) He knew that they we're hitching rides to new territory by fastening onto him, but he could'nt tell how they were doing it. (6) He examined the seedpods to find that their tiny hooks were catching onto the threads of his jacket. (7) The idea of Velcro was born, but the actual product wasnt developed overnight. (8) It took eight more years' before Georges de Mestrals invention was ready for the market. (9) Today, Velcro is used on clothing, on space suits, and even in artificial hearts. (10) Velcro can not only help keep a skier warm but can also save a persons' life.

EXPLORING ONLINE

<http://owl.english.purdue.edu/handouts/interact/g_apostEX1.html>
Interactive quizzes: Choose the correct word for the sentence.

<http://depts.gallaudet.edu/englishworks/exercises/exgrammar/GUPets2.htm>
"Gallaudet Pets—graded *S* practice": Choose singular, plural, or possessive.

<http://college.cengage.com/devenglish> Visit the *Grassroots* 9/e student website for more exercises, quizzes, and live links to all websites mentioned in this chapter.

CHAPTER 29

Direct and Indirect Quotations

PART A Defining Direct and Indirect Quotations

PART B Punctuating Simple Direct Quotations

PART C Punctuating Split Quotations

PART D Ending Direct Quotations

PART A Defining Direct and Indirect Quotations

> (1) John said that he was going.
>
> (2) John said, "I am going."

● Which sentence gives the *exact words* of the speaker, John?

_____

● Why is sentence (2) called a *direct quotation*?

_____

● Why is sentence (1) called an *indirect quotation*?

_____

● Note that the word *that* introduces the *indirect quotation*.

PRACTICE 1

Write *D* in the blank at the right if the sentence uses a *direct quotation*. Write *I* in the blank at the right if the sentence uses an *indirect quotation*.

1. She said that she was thirsty. ____

2. Rita asked, "Which is my laptop?" ____

3. Ruth insisted that one turkey would feed the whole family. ____

4. The students shouted, "Get out of the building! It's on fire!" ____

5. "This is silly," she said, sighing. ____

6. I suggested that Rod's future was in the catering business. ____

328

PART B Punctuating Simple Direct Quotations

Note the punctuation:

> (1) Rafael whispered, "I'll always love you."

- Put a comma before the direct quotation.
- Put quotation marks around the speaker's exact words.
- Capitalize the first word of the direct quotation.
- Put the period *inside* the end quotation marks.

  Of course, the direct quotation may come first in the sentence:

> (2) "I'll always love you," Rafael whispered.

- List the rules for a direct quotation written like the sentence above:

  _____

  _____

  _____

PRACTICE 2

Rewrite these simple direct quotations, punctuating them correctly.

1. He yelled answer the phone!

    Rewrite: _____

2. The usher called no more seats in front.

    Rewrite: _____

3. My back aches she repeated dejectedly.

    Rewrite: _____

4. Examining the inside cover, Bob said this book was printed in 1879.

    Rewrite: _____

5. A bug is doing the backstroke in my soup the man said.

    Rewrite: _____

PART C Punctuating Split Quotations

Sometimes one sentence of direct quotation is split into two parts:

> (1) "Because it is 2 a.m.," he said, "you had better go."

- *He said* is set off by commas.
- The second part of the quotation—*you had better go*—begins with a small letter because it is part of one directly quoted sentence.

(2) "Because it is 2 a.m. . . . you had better go."

A direct quotation can also be broken into separate sentences:

(3) "It is a long ride to San Francisco," he said. "We should leave early."

● Because the second part of the quotation is a separate sentence, it begins with a capital letter.
● Note the period after *said*.

BE CAREFUL: If you break a direct quotation into separate sentences, be sure that both parts of the quotation are complete sentences.

PRACTICE 3

Rewrite these split direct quotations, punctuating them correctly.

1. Before the guests arrive she said let's relax.

   Rewrite: _____

2. Don't drive so fast he begged I get nervous.

   Rewrite: _____

3. Although Mort is out shellfishing Fran said his hip boots are on the porch.

   Rewrite: _____

4. Being the youngest in the family she said has its advantages.

   Rewrite: _____

5. This catalog is fantastic the clerk said and you can have it for free.

   Rewrite: _____

PRACTICE 4

On paper or on a computer, write three sentences using split quotations.

PART D   Ending Direct Quotations

A sentence can end in any of three ways:
● with a period (.)
● with a question mark (?)
● with an exclamation point (!)

The period is *always* placed inside the end quotation marks:

(1) He said, "My car cost five thousand dollars."

The question mark and the exclamation point go before or after the quotation marks—depending on the sense of the sentence.

> (2) He asked, "Where are you?"
>
> (3) Did he say, "I am thirty-two years old"?
>
> (4) She yelled, "Help!"

● The question mark in sentence (2) is placed before the end quotation marks because the direct quotation is a question.

● The question mark in sentence (3) is placed after the end quotation marks because the direct quotation itself *is not a question.*

Note that sentence (2) can be reversed:

> (5) "Where are you?" he asked.

● Can you list the rules for the exclamation point used in sentence (4)?

_____

_____

Note that sentence (4) can be reversed:

> (6) "Help!" she yelled.

PRACTICE 5

Rewrite these direct quotations, punctuating them correctly.

1. Barbara asked is that your Humvee.

   Rewrite: _____

2. Did Shenoya make the team he inquired.

   Rewrite: _____

3. Be careful with that mirror she begged the movers.

   Rewrite: _____

4. The truck driver shouted give me a break.

   Rewrite: _____

5. Did she say I wouldn't give my social security number to that telemarketer?

   Rewrite: _____

PRACTICE 6

Writing Assignment

Write a note to someone with whom you have had an argument. Your goal is to get back on friendly terms with this person. In your first sentence, state this goal, asking for his or her open-minded attention. Then tell him or her why you think a misunderstanding occurred and explain how you think conflict might be avoided in the future. Refer to the original argument by using both direct and indirect quotations. Check for the correct use of quotation marks; be careful with *all* punctuation.

CHAPTER HIGHLIGHTS

- **A direct quotation requires quotation marks:**

  Benjamin Franklin said, "There never was a good war or a bad peace."

- **Both parts of a split quotation require quotation marks:**

  "It isn't fair," she argued, "for us to lose the money for the after-school programs."

- **When a direct quotation is split into separate sentences, begin the second sentence with a capital letter:**

  "It's late," he said. "Let's leave in the morning."

- **Always place the period inside the end quotation marks:**

  He said, "Sometimes I talk too much."

- **A question mark or an exclamation point can be placed before or after the end quotation marks, depending on the meaning of the sentence:**

  She asked, "Where were you when we needed you?"

  Did she say, "Joe looks younger without his beard"?

CHAPTER REVIEW

Proofread this essay for direct and indirect quotations. Punctuate the quotations correctly and make any other necessary changes above the lines.

Satchel Paige

(1) Some people say that the great pitcher Leroy Paige was called Satchel because of his big feet. (2) Paige himself said I got the nickname as a boy in Mobile before my feet grew. (3) He earned money by carrying bags, called satchels, at the railroad station. (4) I figured out a way to make more money by carrying several

bags at a time on a pole he said. (5) Other boys began shouting at him that he looked like a satchel tree. (6) The name stuck.

(7) Unfortunately, for most of Paige's long pitching career, major league baseball excluded African-American players. (8) However, Satchel Paige pitched impressively in the black leagues and in tours against white teams. (9) In 1934, he won a thirteen-inning, one-to-nothing pitching duel against the white pitcher Dizzy Dean and a team of major league all-stars. (10) My fast ball admitted Dean looks like a change of pace alongside of that little bullet old Satchel shoots up to the plate!

(11) After Jackie Robinson broke the major league color barrier in 1948, Satchel Paige took his windmill windup to the Cleveland Indians. (12) He became the oldest rookie in major league history. (13) Some people said that he was too old, but his record proved them wrong. (14) His plaque in the Baseball Hall of Fame reads he helped pitch the Cleveland Indians to the 1948 pennant.

(15) Satchel Paige pitched off and on until he was sixty years old. (16) When people asked how he stayed young, he gave them his famous rules. (17) Everyone remembers the last one. (18) Don't look back he said. (19) Something might be gaining on you.

EXPLORING ONLINE

<http://www.dailygrammar.com/371to375.shtml> Practice with answers: Place quotation marks and capitalize correctly.

<http://grammar.ccc.commnet.edu/grammar/quizzes/quotes_quiz.htm> Challenging interactive quiz: Think hard and punctuate.

<http://college.cengage.com/devenglish/> Visit the *Grassroots* 9/e student website for more exercises, quizzes, and live links of all websites mentioned in this chapter.

CHAPTER 30

Putting Your Proofreading Skills to Work

Proofreading is the important final step in the writing process. After you have planned and written a paragraph or an essay, you must **proofread,** carefully checking each sentence for correct grammar, punctuation, and capitalization. Proofreading means applying everything you have learned in Units 2 through 7. Is every sentence complete? Do all your verbs agree with their subjects? Have you mistakenly written any comma splices or sentence fragments?

This chapter gives you the opportunity to practice proofreading skills in real-world situations. As you proofread the paragraphs and essays that follow, you must look for any—and every—kind of error, just as you would in the real world of college or work. The first five practices tell you what kinds of errors to look for. If you have trouble, go back to the chapters listed and review the material. The final practices, however, give you no clues at all, so you must put your proofreading skills to the real-world test.

PRACTICE 1

Proofread this paragraph, correcting any errors above the lines. (You should find seventeen individual errors.) To review, see these chapters:

Chapter 10	past participle verb errors
Chapter 15	run-on sentences and comma splices
Chapter 19	errors in forming plural nouns
Chapter 22	preposition errors

(1) Bono is an unusual superstar. (2) Instead of going in shopping spree and polishing his ego, he travels the world, using his fame to empower others. (3) Bono

334

was born Paul Hewson at Ireland. (4) Young friends there nicknamed him *Bonovox*, which means "good voice" in Latin. (5) The *vox* was dropped, *bono* stuck. (6) Bono became the lead singer of the Irish rock band U2. (7) Using music to send a message of love and peace, U2 has sell more than 100 million album worldwide and has won fourteen Grammy Awards. (8) Yet perhaps Bono's greatest influence is not the sound of his voice crooning U2 songs under the heads of fans. (9) Rather, it is his work for human beings on need. (10) Bono has use his celebrity to turn the media's attention to Africa, where the lives of millions are being destroy by AIDS and starvation. (11) Frightening numbers of African child are already AIDS orphans, social structures in Africa are breaking down. (12) Bono urges the United States and other nations to relieve the crippling debt of African nations, one of the factor that keeps them unable to afford AIDS drugs and prevention programs. (13) He has work with former president Clinton, Oprah, and others to make the love he sings about become reality. (14) Bono has received many award for this humanitarian work he was even nominate for the Nobel Peace Prize.

PRACTICE 2

Proofread this paragraph, correcting any errors above the lines. (You should find fifteen individual errors.) To review, see these chapters:

Chapter 7   sentence fragments

Chapter 9   past tense errors

Chapter 23   tense consistency

Chapter 26   capitalization errors

(1) Flying is so common. (2) That many people take it for granted. (3) They often see jets, helicopters, and airplanes in the sky and give them little thought. (4) However, what would people think. (5) If they seen a human being flying through the air? (6) In july, 2003, Felix baumgartner flied across the english Channel without using an engine, something that had never been done before. (7) His amazing flight begun high above England. (8) When he jumped from an airplane at 30,000 feet. (9) He is wearing a parachute, of course, but his other piece of special equipment was a six-foot-wide wing strapped to his back. (10) Even though he was falling very quickly, the wing let him fly forward at 220 miles per hour. (11) He needs to fly

twenty-two miles to get to France, and he arrived over that country with 4,000 feet remaining. (12) After using the wing to slow himself down. (13) He opened his parachute and landed. (14) The entire flight lasts just six minutes. (15) People who want to experience this kind of flying can use the Skyray. (16) Which is similar to the special wing Baumgartner used to fly across the English channel. (17) Of course, to use this wing, you have to wear a parachute and jump out of an airplane. (18) Nevertheless, Skyray is bringing humans closer to the dream of flying like eagles.

PRACTICE 3

Proofread this paragraph, correcting any errors above the lines. (You should find sixteen individual errors.) To review, see these chapters:

Chapter 7	sentence fragments
Chapter 10	past participle verb errors
Chapter 15	run-ons and comma splices
Chapters 19 and 28	plural and possessive errors

(1) Christiane Amanpour is one of the most respected foreign correspondents in the world, but she calls herself an "accidental journalist." (2) Because she never intended to become one. (3) Her native Iran had no freedom of the press, journalism did not interest her. (4) Christiane attended high school in England. (5) Then the revolution in Iran brought chaos to her family, her fathers money was froze, the families fund were very tight. (6) Christianes' sister dropped out of journalism college in London, Christiane took her place for the sole reason of saving the tuition money. (7) Soon she was hook on reporting. (8) After graduating from the University of Rhode Island, she applied for a job at a new cable station. (9) Called CNN. (10) She longed to write news story's and go overseas but was mock by her boss, who said she didn't have the right looks and that her name was difficult to pronounce. (11) Amanpour worked hard and hid her frustration with doing routine task. (12) Like bringing people coffee. (13) Every time a new job opened at CNN, she applied for it. (14) Her big break was being send to Germany and the Gulf War. (15) With gunfires and rockets around her, she reported the news with intelligence and heart. (16) Today Amanpour says it is not so bad that some people "always try to knock your dreams." (17) This gives you the chance, she believes, to prove that you are strong enough to keep going.

PRACTICE 4

Proofread this paragraph, correcting any errors above the lines. (You should find twenty individual errors.) To review, see these chapters:

Chapter 7   sentence fragments

Chapter 8   subject/verb agreement errors

Chapter 27   comma errors

Chapter 28   apostrophe errors

(1) Every spring and summer, storm chaser's spreads out across the Midwestern part of the United States known as Tornado Alley. (2) Armed with video cameras maps and radios. (3) These lovers of violent weather follows huge weather systems called supercells, which sometimes produces tornadoes. (4) On a good day, a storm chaser may find a supercell. (5) And get close enough to film the brief, destructive life of a tornado. (6) Some joins the storm-chasing tours offered every summer by universities or private companies. (7) Others learn what they can from Internet websites and sets off on their own to hunt tornadoes. (8) Storm chasing can be very dangerous. (9) A large tornado spins winds between 125 and 175 mph, tearing roofs off houses ripping limbs from trees, and overturning cars. (10) The greatest danger comes from airborne branches boards shingles and glass hurtling through the air like deadly weapons. (11) Even if a supercell don't spawn tornadoes. (12) It often

Storm chasers confront a deadly twister in Tornado Alley.

©Carsten Peter/National Geographic Image Collection.

produces winds over 50 mph, heavy rain, large hail, and intense lightning. (13) Most storm chasers avoids these risks by racing out of a tornados' path before it gets too close. (14) Despite or perhaps because of these dangers, dramatized in the 1996 movie *Twister*. (15) Storm chasing remains popular. (16) Fans claim that few things in life matches the thrill of discovering a tornado and witnessing the power of nature.

PRACTICE 5

Proofread this paragraph, correcting any errors above the lines. (You should find seventeen individual errors.) To review, see these chapters:

Chapter 20	pronoun agreement errors
Chapter 21	adjective/adverb errors
Chapter 26	capitalization errors
Chapter 27	comma errors

(1) A secret society called SSSSH is gaining agents across the country. (2) To become a secret agent, one must simply perform a well deed for someone else without taking credit for it or letting them know who did it. (3) The group was inspired by a young Ohioan named hal reichle (pronounced "Rike-el"), a graduate of hiram college who had a habit of quiet helping people. (4) After Hal's death in a helicopter crash during the gulf War some friends started paying tribute to the fallen soldier by "pulling Reichles." (5) That is, they would do small or large good deeds, leaving only a card that said, "You are the recipient of an anonymously good deed done in the name of Hal Reichle." (6) The group called themselves SSSSH, or Secret Society of Serendipitous* Service to Hal. (7) After several newspapers wrote about the secret society, schoolchildren and people in other states began to pull Reichles theirselves. (8) If an agent wants to report, they can write about the deed performed—without a signature or return address, of course—to Hal Reichle, P.O. Box 375 Hiram ohio 44234. (9) A friend of Hal's whom claimed to know only that SSSSH exists but nothing more said that the goal of the organization is a simple one: increasing goodness in the world.

_____
*serendipitous: unexpectedly lucky

PRACTICE 6

Proofread this essay, correcting any errors above the lines.

Crime-Fighting Artist

(1) Jeanne Boylan helps capture Americas most wanted criminals but she's not a police officer or a detective. (2) Instead, she is an artist who draws the faces of suspects, base only on her gentle conversations with victim's and eyewitnesses. (3) Her portraits are so lifelike and accurate that she has became famous for drawing nearly mirror images of criminals. (4) Boylan's sketches often leads to arrests. (5) She drew the Unabomber in his sunglasses and hooded sweatshirt, the kidnapper-murderer of twelve-year-old Polly Klaas, and Timothy McVeigh. (6) Who bombed Oklahoma City's Federal Building. (7) Once doubtful, FBI officials and police now calls on Boylan in almost every major case.

(8) Boylan decided to become a sketch artist after she was the victim of a crime. (9) The police, following standard procedure, asked her to describe her attackers' faces, then they showed her mug shots of criminals. (10) Hoping that she would recognize the suspects. (11) Boylan sensed that this was the wrong approach to help her mind remember. (12) She realized that the authorities leading questions—questions like "Did he have a moustache? Was he wearing glasses?"—clutter the victim's mind with details that might not be true. (13) At the same time, the

Boylan's sketch (left) and a photo of the Unabomber, Ted Kaczynski.

AP Images.

subconscious mind is trying to avoid reliving a traumatic experience consequently, memories easily become distorted.

(14) Boylan developed a very different method for coaxing images from victims and witnesses. (15) What distinguishes her method from others, she says, is that she *listens.* (16) She takes her time. (17) Talking for hours with eyewitnesses to a crime. (18) She does not pressure them to recall the color of a suspect's eyes or what the shape of his nose was. (19) Instead, she asks about their daily lives and interests, here and there asking nonleading questions about what they saw. (20) Slowly and careful, she guides people back through their confusion and pain to the moment when they seen or felt something that they desperately want to forget. (21) She asks them to describe whole shapes, forms, and textures rather than specific details. (22) She sometimes gives children Play-Doh to mold as they explore their memories. (23) As they draw closer and closer to the terrifying images seared into their minds. (24) Boylan watches, listens, and sketching. (25) "What people see," she says, "is evidence as fragile and valuable as a fingerprint. (26) And it should be protected with as much care."

(27) Many have claimed that Boylan's method, a blend of art, psychology, and human compassion, are a unique gift. (28) Boylan insists, though, that her technique can be teach. (29) "What I do is no great mystery she says. (30) "It has to do with allowing someone the freedom and the time to remember. (31) It has to do with the human heart."

PRACTICE 7

Proofread this essay, correcting any errors above the lines.

Quiet, Please!

(1) America is loud. (2) Horns and sirens pierces the air, car stereos pump out loud music. (3) Cell phones rings, shriek, or trumpets the owner's noise of choice. (4) Construction equipments, lawnmowers, and leaf blowers buzz and roar into the public space. (5) Restaurant and movie theater manager's often seem to link loudness with cultural cool. (6) Sounds are measured in decibels, with the human voice measuring about 60 decibels, the sound of a car is about 80 decibels.

Notes

(7) According to the U.S. Environmental Protection Agency, 70 decibels is a safe daily average. (8) Here is the problem: the level of noise that many of us hear every day are far above this.

(9) The sound of a food blender, for example, measures 90 decibels. (10) Many leaf blower exceed 115 decibels, and a jet taking off is 120 decibels of ear-blasting noise. (11) All of this racket are taking it's toll on us both physically and in psychological ways. (12) According to the American Speech-Language-Hearing Association (ASHA), 28 million U.S. citizens have already suffer hearing loss from too much noise. (13) Furthermore, loud noise raises blood pressure increases stress hormone levels, and deprives us of sleep. (14) Noise pollution also increases aggression and even violence and harms concentration and learning. (15) One study found that New york children in classrooms that faced the train tracks were almost a year behind children taught in more quieter parts of the same school.

(16) In Europe, noise pollution has been taken serious for years. (17) Now in the United States, organizations like the Noise Pollution Clearinghouse is trying to raise awareness of the problem and promote solutions. (18) Members of this organization believes that just as smoke or toxins in the air are not acceptable, neither is loud noise. (19) They are working for new laws. (20) To enforce our right to peace and quiet.

CHAPTER HIGHLIGHTS

- **Know your error patterns.** *Most writers don't make hundreds of errors; they make the same few errors over and over again!* By now, you should know the kinds of errors you tend to make. This knowledge is an important tool for improving your writing and your college performance. Do you tend to write fragments or leave the –*ed*s off certain verbs? Then pay special attention to these problems as you proofread.

- **Know where to find help.** Find expert help for erasing your error patterns in this book, at the Web links listed at the end of each chapter, and on the *Grassroots* student website. You can also search the OWLs you have book-marked or type your search words—for example, "comma splices, explanation, practice"—into a search engine like Google. In addition, visit your college's writing lab to discover what writing help is offered there.

EXPLORING ONLINE

<http://owl.english.purdue.edu/handouts/general/gl_edit.html> Proofreading guide

<http://depts.gallaudet.edu/englishworks/writing/proofread.html> Punctuation and grammar review

<http://college.cengage.com/devenglish> Visit the *Grassroots* 9/e student website for more exercises, quizzes, and live links to all websites mentioned in this chapter.

WRITING ASSIGNMENTS

As you complete each writing assignment, remember to perform these steps:

- Write a clear, complete topic sentence.
- Use freewriting, brainstorming, or clustering to generate ideas for the body of your paragraph, essay, letter, or commercial.
- Arrange your best ideas in a plan.
- Revise for support, unity, coherence, and exact language.
- Proofread for grammar, punctuation, and spelling errors.

Writing Assignment 1: *Discuss an unusual friendship.* Have you ever had or witnessed a truly unusual friendship—for instance, between two people many years apart in age, between people from different social worlds who bonded because of a shared hobby or problem, or between a human being and an animal? Select one such unusual friendship and capture its essence in writing. How did the friendship start? What do you think bonded the two friends? Be as specific as possible so that the reader will understand this special relationship. Proofread carefully for correct use of capitals, commas, apostrophes, and quotation marks.

Writing Assignment 2: *Write a letter to compliment or to complain.* Write a letter to a store manager or a dean, to praise an especially helpful salesperson or a particularly good teacher. If you are not feeling complimentary, write the opposite: a letter of complaint about a salesperson or an instructor. State your compliment or complaint, describing what occurred and explaining why you are pleased or displeased. Remember, how well your letter is written will contribute to the impression you make. Proofread carefully for the correct use of capitals, commas, apostrophes, and quotation marks.

Writing Assignment 3: *Create a print ad.* You and several classmates considering careers in advertising have been asked to create a print ad for a magazine, newspaper, or billboard. You must sell one product or idea of your choice—anything from a brand of jeans to a cell phone to a good cause, like recycling or becoming a foster parent. Your goal is to capture people's attention with a strong picture and then persuade them with a few well-chosen words. Sketch and draft your ad; don't let punctuation errors get in the way of your message. For online help step by step, visit this website: <http://adbusters.org/spoofads/printad/>.

Writing Assignment 4: *Revise a quotation.* Pick a quotation from the Quotation Bank at the end of this book, and alter it to express something new. For example, you might want to change "Insanity is hereditary—you get it from your children" to "Insanity is learned—you get it from going to school." Be as serious or as humorous as you would like. Prove that your quotation is valid, arguing from your own or others' experience. Proofread carefully for the correct use of capitals, commas, apostrophes, and quotation marks.

REVIEW

Proofreading

A.   Proofread the following business letter for incorrect or missing capitals, commas, apostrophes, and quotation marks. Correct all errors above the lines. (You should find thirty-one individual errors.)

99 somers street

Northfield, ohio 44056

january 11, 2008

weird walts Discount Store

Main office

akron, Ohio 44313

Dear sir or Madam:

On january 5, 2008 I ordered a Panasonic forty-two-inch plasma flat-panel television with a remote control from your store at 1101 Lakeland avenue medina ohio. The model number is TH42PX20UP. When your delivery man brought the set to my home yesterday, he seemed impatient. He urged me to sign before I had a chance to open the box unpack it or examine the equipment. In fact, he said, "Listen, buddy Ive got five more deliveries, and Im out of here whether you open the box or not. To my dismay I later discovered that the hand-held remote control was missing.

Please send me this remote control immediately. I purchased this panasonic in time to use it at my Super-bowl party. Obviously, my friends and I need the remote control. For years now I have been a loyal customer of Weird Walts and will appreciate your prompt attention to this matter. thank you.

Sincerely your's,

Milton rainford

B. Proofread the following essay for incorrect or missing capitals, commas, apostrophes, and quotation marks. Correct the errors above the lines. (You should find thirty-eight individual errors.)

The Liberator of South America

(1) One day in 1805 Simón Bolívar made a vow. (2) He vowed that he wouldnt rest until South America was free from spanish oppression. (3) This promise changed his life and Latin-American history (4) Bolívar surprisingly enough spent the first twenty-two years of his life as a rich aristocrat. (5) When he died at fifty-seven he was known as the george Washington of south america.

(6) Bolívar was born in caracas, Venezuela on July 24 1783. (7) after he became an orphan at the age of nine his uncle provided him with a tutor Simón Rodriguez (8) A fierce patriot Rodriguez wanted South American's to rule themselves. (9) However young Simón Bolívar was'nt very interested in his tutors ideas about independence. (10) Bolívars uncle sent Simón to europe to help further the young mans education. (11) during his travels in Spain, Bolívar realized that Latin America was destined to be independent of Spain.

(12) Bolívar returned to Venezuela and joined those fighting Spain. (13) His troops were defeated but Bolívar would not admit to failure. (14) In a famous letter that he wrote in 1814, he declared, "the bonds that unite us to Spain have been cut". (15) Finally, the tide turned against Spain. (16) The spaniards were driven out of Colombia Venezuela Ecuador Peru, and Bolivia (17) Bolívar, leader of much of South America wanted to unite the people under one government. (18) His idea may have been a good one yet each area preferred to become a separate nation. (19) Although his plan for a united country failed Bolívar is still remembered as South Americas greatest hero.

WRITERS' WORKSHOP

Explain a Cause or an Effect

Examining causes and effects is a useful skill, both in college and at work. This student's thoughtful essay looks at the effects of school pressure to "speak like an American." In your group or class, read it aloud if possible. As you read, pay attention to the causes and effects he describes.

In America, Speak Like an American

(1) Many teachers tell immigrant students to lose their accents and "speak like an American." They mean well. They want the children to succeed. However, this can also encourage children to be ashamed of who they are and give up their heritage.

(2) When I was in fourth grade, I was sent to a class for "speech imperfections." Apparently, I had a Spanish accent. The class wasn't so bad, it taught us to say "chair" instead of "shair" and "school" instead of "eschool." It was so important for me to please the teacher, I did practically everything she asked. She told us things like "The bums on the street have accents, that's why they're not working." I abandoned my roots and my culture and embraced "America." I learned about Stonewall Jackson and William Shakespeare. Soon Ponce de León and Gonzalo de Barca were just memories at the back of my mind. I listened to country music and rock because this was "American."

(3) I can't remember when it happened, but suddenly I found myself listening to Spanish love songs. They were great! They were so sincere, the lyrics were beautiful. While turning the radio dial one day, I stopped at a Hispanic radio station. It was playing salsa. "Holy smokes," I thought to myself. All the instruments were synchronized so tightly. The horn section kept accenting the singer's lines. All of a sudden, my hips started swaying, my feet started tapping, and I stood up. And then the horror. I couldn't dance to this music, I had never learned how. There I was, a Puerto Rican boy, listening to Puerto Rican music, but unable to dance the typical Puerto Rican way.

(4) Anger flared through me as I remembered my fourth grade teacher. I was also upset with my parents, in their zeal to have me excel, they kept me from my roots as a first-generation Hispanic American. But that was years ago. I have searched for my Latin heritage. I've found beautiful music,

> wonderful literature, and great foods. I now associate with "my people" as well as with everyone else, and I am learning the joys of being Sam Rodriguez, Puerto Rican.
>
> *Sam Rodriguez, student*

1. How effective is Sam Rodriguez's essay?

   _____ Clear main idea?   _____ Good supporting details?

   _____ Logical organization?   _____ Effective conclusion?

2. Does the essay have a *thesis statement*, one sentence that states the main idea of the entire essay? Which sentence is it?

3. In paragraph (2), the writer says that he "abandoned [his] roots." In his view, what caused him to do this?

4. Underline the lines and ideas you find especially effective and share them with your group or class. Try to understand exactly why you like a word or sentence. For example, in paragraph (3), we can almost experience the first time the writer really *hears* salsa—the instruments, the horns accenting the singer's lines, his tapping feet and swaying hips.

5. As the writer gets older, he realizes he has lost too much of his heritage. At first he is angry (short-term effect), but what long-term effect does this new understanding have on him?

6. What order does this writer follow throughout the essay?

7. This fine essay is finished and ready to go, but the student makes the same punctuation error five different times. Can you spot and correct the error pattern that he needs to watch out for?

Writing and Revising Ideas

1. What does it mean to "become American"?

2. Write about something important that you gave up and explain why you did so.

Plan carefully, outlining your paragraph or essay before you write. State your main idea clearly and plan your supporting ideas or paragraphs. As you revise, pay special attention to clear organization and convincing, detailed support.

Improving Your Spelling

Some people are naturally better spellers than others, but anyone can *become* a better speller. In this unit, you will

- Master six basic spelling rules

- Learn to avoid common look-alike/sound-alike errors

Spotlight on Writing

No spelling errors mar this writer's memory of summer mornings years ago. If possible, read the paragraph aloud.

Summer, when I was a boy in Brooklyn, was a string of <u>intimacies</u>, a sum of small knowings, and almost none of them cost money. Nobody ever <u>figured</u> out a way to charge us for morning, and morning then was the <u>beginning</u> of everything. I was an altar boy in the years after the war, up in the morning before most other people for the long walk to the church on the hill. And I would watch the sun rise in Prospect Park—first a rumor, then a <u>heightened</u> light, something unseen and immense melting the hard, early darkness; then suddenly there was a molten ball, <u>screened</u> by the trees, about to climb to a scalding noon. The sun would dry the dew on the grass of the park, soften the tar, bake the rooftops, brown us on the <u>beaches</u>, make us sweat, force us out of the tight small flats of the tenements.

Pete Hamill, "Spaldeen Summers"

- Through his choice and arrangement of words, this writer helps us see and feel the park at sunrise. He also has avoided the six most common types of spelling errors. The underlined words are all spelled correctly. If you don't know why, read on.

 Writing Ideas

- *Morning in a particular place (a desert, a suburb, an all-night bar, a mountaintop, and so forth)*

- *An experience of "awe" or wonder*

CHAPTER 31 Spelling

PART A Suggestions for Improving Your Spelling

One important ingredient of good writing is accurate spelling. No matter how interesting your ideas are, your writing will not be effective if your spelling is incorrect.

Tips for Improving Your Spelling

1. **Look closely at the words on the page.** Use any tricks you can to remember the right spelling. For example, "Argument has no *e* because I lost the *e* during an argument" or "*Believe* has a *lie* in it."

2. **Use a dictionary.** Even professional writers frequently check spelling in a dictionary. As you write, underline the words you are not sure of and look them up when you write your final draft. If locating words in the dictionary is a real problem for you, consider a "poor speller's dictionary." Ask your professor to recommend one.

3. **Use a spell checker.** If you write on a computer, make a habit of using the spell checker. See Part B for tips and cautions about spell checkers.

4. **Keep a list of the words you misspell.** Look over your list whenever you can and keep it handy as you write.

5. **Look over corrected papers for misspelled words** (often marked *sp*). Add these words to your list. Practice writing each word three or four times.

6. **Test yourself.** Have a friend dictate words from your list or from this chapter or use flash cards; computerized flash cards can be helpful.

7. **Review the basic spelling rules explained in this chapter.** Take time to learn the material; don't rush through the entire chapter all at once.

8. **Study the spelling list on page 359,** and test yourself on those words.

9. **Read through Chapter 32, "Look-Alikes/Sound-Alikes,"** for commonly confused words (*their, there,* and *they're,* for instance). The practices in that chapter will help you eliminate some common spelling errors from your writing.

PART B Computer Spell Checkers

If you write on a computer, always run the spell checker as part of your proofreading process. A spell checker picks up certain spelling errors and gives you alternatives for correcting them. Your program might also highlight misspelled words as you write.

What a spell checker cannot do is *think*. If you have written one correctly spelled word instead of another—*if* for *it,* for example—the spell checker cannot bring that error to your attention. If you have written *then* for *than,* the spell checker cannot help.* To find such errors, you must always proofread your paper *after* running the spell checker.

PRACTICE 1

In a small group, read this poem, which "passed" spell check. Above the lines, correct the errors that the spell checker missed.

My righting is soup eerier

Too yore pay purr this thyme.

Iran my SA threw spell check,

Each sill able an rime.

Two bad, ewe awe full righters,

Fore ewe probe lee en vee me.

My verb all cents muss bee immense,

four aye right sew quick lee.

Eye donut kneed a textbook.

I through it inn the lake.

The pro fey sore rote big read Marx.

Their muss bee sum miss take!

PART C Spotting Vowels and Consonants

To learn some basic spelling rules, you must know the difference between vowels and consonants. See the chart on the following page.

---

*For questions about words that sound the same but are spelled differently, check Chapter 32, "Look-Alikes/Sound-Alikes."

The **vowels** are *a, e, i, o,* and *u.*

The **consonants** are *b, c, d, f, g, h, j, k, l, m, n, p, q, r, s, t, v, w, x,* and *z.*

The letter *y* can be either a vowel or a consonant, depending on its sound:

happy	shy
young	yawn

● In both *happy* and *shy, y* is a vowel because it has a vowel sound: an *ee* sound in *happy* and an *i* sound in *shy.*

● In both *young* and *yawn, y* is a consonant becauses it has the consonant sound of *y.*

PRACTICE 2

Write *V* for vowel or *C* for consonant in the space over each letter. Be careful of the *y.*

EXAMPLE:
$$\frac{C}{s}\ \frac{C}{t}\ \frac{V}{a}\ \frac{C}{r}\ \frac{C}{r}\ \frac{V}{y}$$

1. ___ ___ ___ ___ ___
   t h e r e

3. ___ ___ ___ ___
   r e l y

5. ___ ___ ___ ___ ___ ___
   h i d d e n

2. ___ ___ ___ ___
   j u m p

4. ___ ___ ___ ___
   y a m s

6. ___ ___ ___ ___ ___ ___
   s i l v e r

PART D Doubling the Final Consonant (in Words of One Syllable)

When you add a suffix, or ending, that begins with a vowel (like *-ed, -ing, -er, -est*) to a word of one syllable, double the final consonant *if* the last three letters of the word are consonant-vowel-consonant, or *cvc.*

mop + ed = mopped	swim + ing = swimming
burn + er = burner	thin + est = thinnest

● *Mop, swim,* and *thin* all end in *cvc;* therefore, the final consonants are doubled.

● *Burn* does not end in *cvc;* therefore, the final consonant is not doubled.

PRACTICE 3

Which of the following words double the final consonant? Check to see whether the word ends in *cvc.* Double the final consonant if necessary; then add the suffixes *-ed* and *-ing.*

	Word	Last Three Letters	-ed	-ing
EXAMPLES:	drop	cvc	dropped	dropping
	boil	vvc	boiled	boiling
1.	plan	_____	_____	_____
2.	brag	_____	_____	_____

3. dip   _____   _____   _____

4. sail   _____   _____   _____

5. stop   _____   _____   _____

PRACTICE 4

Which of the following words double the final consonant? Check for *cvc*. Then add the suffixes *-er* or *-est*.

Word	Last Three Letters	-er	-est
EXAMPLES: hot	cvc	hotter	hottest
cool	vvc	cooler	coolest
1. tall	_____	_____	_____
2. short	_____	_____	_____
3. fat	_____	_____	_____
4. slim	_____	_____	_____
5. wet	_____	_____	_____
6. quick	_____	_____	_____

PART E   Doubling the Final Consonant (in Words of More Than One Syllable)

When you add a suffix that begins with a vowel to a word of more than one syllable, double the final consonant *if*

(1) the last three letters of the word are *cvc,* **and**

(2) the accent or stress is on the *last* syllable.

> begin + ing = beginning
>
> patrol + ed = patrolled

● *Begin* and *patrol* both end in *cvc*.

● In both words, the stress is on the last syllable: *be-gin´, pa-trol´*. (Pronounce the words aloud and listen for the correct stress.)

● Therefore, *beginning* and *patrolled* double the final consonant.

> gossip + ing = gossiping
>
> visit + ed = visited

● *Gossip* and *visit* both end in *cvc*.

● However, the stress is **not** on the last syllable: *gos´-sip, vis´-it*.

● Therefore, *gossiping* and *visited* do not double the final consonant.

PRACTICE 5

Which of the following words double the final consonant? First, check for *cvc*. Then check for the final stress and add the suffixes *-ed* and *-ing*.

Word	Last Three Letters	-ed	-ing
EXAMPLES: repel	*cvc*	repelled	repelling
enlist	*vcc*	enlisted	enlisting
1. occur			
2. happen			
3. polish			
4. commit			
5. offer			
6. prefer			
7. exit			
8. travel			
9. wonder			
10. omit			

PRACTICE 6

Which words in parentheses double the final consonant? First, check for *cvc*. Then add the suffixes *-ed* and *-ing*. In words of two or more syllables, check for the final stress.

Martial Artist Jackie Chan

(1) Jackie Chan, the martial arts film star and director, _____ long
                                                            (work + ed)
and hard for his success in movies. (2) When he was a child, his parents

_____ him in the Peking Opera Academy. (3) Unlike Western opera,
(enroll + ed)
Chinese opera is like a circus that features acrobats, jugglers, and contortionists.

(4) Throughout his film career, Chan has _____ on the tumbling and
                                          (depend + ed)
gymnastic skills he learned at the academy. (5) When he graduated, however,

Chinese opera was out of fashion, and he was _____ to take a job
                                              (compel + ed)

_____ stunts in martial arts films. (6) He _____ small parts in
(perform + ing)   (obtain + ed)
two of Bruce Lee's films and much larger parts in many other, unsuccessful

pictures.

(7) Following Lee's death, a producer _____ that Jackie Chan
                                          (hope + ed)
would be the new Bruce Lee and signed him to a multipicture contract. (8) After

more unsuccessful films, Chan _____ to himself that he was
                                    (admit + ed)
_____ nowhere. (9) He considered _____ from the movies.
  (get + ing)   (retire + ing)
(10) By a stroke of luck, another producer _____ him to star in the mar-
                                              (ask + ed)
tial arts comedy *Snake in the Eagle's Shadow.* (11) Instead of trying to turn Chan into

a poor copy of Bruce Lee, this producer _____ him to create a comic un-
                                            (permit + ed)
derdog character. (12) The film was a huge success in Asia, and audiences

_____ more martial arts films _____ the comically gifted Chan.
  (demand + ed)   (star + ing)
     (13) Once Chan was a hit in the Far East, he _____ his break into the
                                                     (plan + ed)
American film industry. (14) After he had a worldwide crossover hit with *Rumble*

in the Bronx in 1994, Chan _____ making films in Asia and announced
                                 (stop + ed)
that he _____ Hollywood. (15) Since then, films like *Rush Hour, Shang-*
          (prefer + ed)
hai Noon, Shanghai Knights, and *The Medallion* have drawn huge audiences with

the _____ combination of laughs and _____ moves. (16) In
      (win + ing)   (astonish + ing)
fact, Chan has been _____ "a human special effect."
                       (proclaim + ed)

PART F   Dropping or Keeping the Final *E*

**When you add a suffix that begins with a vowel (like *-able, -ence,* or *-ing*), drop
the final** *e.*

**When you add a suffix that begins with a consonant (like *-less, -ment,* or *-ly*),
keep the final** *e.*

> write + ing = writing   pure + ity = purity

● *Writing* and *purity* both drop the final *e* because the suffixes *-ing* and *-ity* begin
   with vowels.

> hope + less = hopeless   advertise + ment = advertisement

● *Hopeless* and *advertisement* keep the final *e* because the suffixes *-less* and *-ment*
   begin with consonants.

   Here are some exceptions to memorize:

argument	courageous	knowledgeable	simply
awful	judgment	manageable	truly

PRACTICE 7

Add the suffix shown to each word.

EXAMPLES: come + ing =   _____coming_____

come + ness =   _____rudeness_____

1. blame + less = _____
2. guide + ance = _____
3. debate + ing = _____
4. motive + ation = _____
5. sincere + ly = _____
6. desire + able = _____
7. argue + ment = _____
8. home + less = _____
9. response + ible = _____
10. rejoice + ing = _____
11. awe + ful = _____
12. manage + er = _____
13. judge + ment = _____
14. fame + ous = _____
15. grieve + ance = _____
16. arrange + ing = _____

PART G   Changing or Keeping the Final Y

When you add a suffix to a word that ends in -*y*, change the *y* to *i* if the letter before the *y* is a consonant.
   Keep the final *y* if the letter before the *y* is a vowel.

happy + ness = happiness   delay + ed = delayed

● The *y* in *happiness* is changed to *i* because the letter before the *y* is a consonant, *p*.
● However, the *y* in *delayed* is not changed to *i* because the letter before it is a vowel, *a*.

When you add -*ing* to words ending in *y*, always keep the *y*.

copy + ing = copying   delay + ing = delaying

Here are some exceptions to memorize:

day + ly = daily   pay + ed = paid

lay + ed = laid   say + ed = said

When the final *y* is changed to *i*, add -*es* instead of -*s*.

fly + es = flies   candy + es = candies

marry + es = marries   story + es = stories

PRACTICE 8

Add the suffix shown to each of the following words.

EXAMPLES: vary + ed = _____varied_____

buy + er = _____buyer_____

1. cry + ed = _____
2. mercy + ful = _____
3. worry + ing = _____
4. say + ed = _____
5. juicy + er = _____

6. enjoy + able = _____
7. clumsy + ness = _____
8. wealthy + est = _____
9. day + ly = _____
10. merry + ly = _____

PRACTICE 9

Add the suffixes in parentheses to each word.

1. lively   (er)   _____
            (est)   _____
            (ness) _____
2. beauty   (fy)   _____
            (ful)   _____
            (es)   _____
3. healthy (er)   _____
            (est)   _____
            (ly)   _____

4. study   (es)   _____
            (ous)   _____
            (ing)   _____
5. busy   (ness) _____
            (er)   _____
            (est)   _____
6. try   (es)   _____
            (ed)   _____
            (al)   _____

PRACTICE 10

Add the suffix shown to each word in parentheses. Write the correctly spelled word in each blank.

Winter Blues

(1) Although Kim _____ to ignore her feelings, she always felt
(try + ed)
_____, _____, _____, and _____ during
(hungry + er) (sleep + er) (angry + er) (lonely + er)
the winter months. (2) As part of her _____, she went about her
(deny + al)
_____ as usual, but she knew that she no longer found life as
(busy + ness)
_____ as before.
pleasure + able

(3) Then one day she read a _____ magazine article about a medical
(fascinate + ing)
condition called *seasonal affective disorder*, or *SAD*. (4) Kim _____ saw
(immediate + ly)
the _____ between her yearly mood changes and the symptoms that
(similarity + es)

people with SAD _____. (5) She learned that winter SAD is a kind of
                 (display + ed)

depression triggered _____ by lack of _____ to light—by in-
                     (primary + ly)   (expose + ure)

sufficient sunshine, inadequate indoor light at home or work, or even by

_____ cloudy weather.
(mercy + lessly)

        (6) _____, Kim discovered that three or four kinds of treatment are
            (Happy + ly)

available. (7) The most severe cases—people who sleep more than fourteen hours

a day and still feel _____, for example—are usually cured by light ther-
                     (fatigue + ed)

apy given in a clinic or at home under a doctor's care. (8) Taking medication,

_____, or _____ one's diet often brings _____ re-
(exercise + ing)   (change + ing)   (notice + able)

lief. (9) Kim did some research on the Web and found a list of SAD clinics,

_____, and support. (10) Attending a light-therapy clinic near her
(guide + ance)

home, she soon experienced her _____ winter in years.
                                (healthy + est)

PART H   Choosing *IE* or *EI*

Write *i* before *e*, except after *c*, or in any *ay* sound like *neighbor*:

> niece, believe, conceive, weigh

● *Niece* and *believe* are spelled *ie*.

● *Conceive* is spelled *ei* because of the preceding *c*.

● *Weigh* is spelled *ei* because of its *ay* sound.

**However, words with a *shen* sound are spelled with an *ie* after the *c*: ancient,
*conscience, efficient, sufficient.***

Here are some exceptions to memorize:

| either | height | seize | their |
| foreign | neither | society | weird |

PRACTICE 11

Pronounce each word out loud. Then fill in the blanks with either *ie* or *ei*.

1. f __ __ ld	6. s __ __ ze	11. effic __ __ nt
2. w __ __ ght	7. rec __ __ ve	12. v __ __ n
3. n __ __ ther	8. br __ __ f	13. th __ __ r
4. w __ __ rd	9. h __ __ ght	14. for __ __ gn
5. ch __ __ f	10. ach __ __ ve	15. cash __ __ r

PART I   Commonly Misspelled Words

Below is a list of commonly misspelled words. They are words that you probably use daily in speaking and writing. Each word has a trouble spot, the part of the word that is often spelled incorrectly. The trouble spot is in bold type.

Two tricks to help you learn these words are (1) to copy each word twice, underlining the trouble spot, and (2) to copy the words on flash cards and have someone else test you. If possible, consult this list while or after you write.

1. across	20. embarrass	39. mathematics	58. reference
2. address	21. environment	40. meant	59. rhythm
3. answer	22. exaggerate	41. necessary	60. ridiculous
4. argument	23. familiar	42. nervous	61. separate
5. athlete	24. finally	43. occasion	62. similar
6. beginning	25. government	44. opinion	63. since
7. behavior	26. grammar	45. optimist	64. speech
8. calendar	27. height	46. particular	65. strength
9. career	28. illegal	47. perform	66. success
10. conscience	29. immediately	48. perhaps	67. surprise
11. crowded	30. important	49. personnel	68. taught
12. definite	31. integration	50. possess	69. temperature
13. describe	32. intelligent	51. possible	70. thorough
14. desperate	33. interest	52. prefer	71. thought
15. different	34. interfere	53. prejudice	72. tired
16. disappoint	35. jewelry	54. privilege	73. until
17. disapprove	36. judgment	55. probably	74. weight
18. doesn't	37. knowledge	56. psychology	75. written
19. eighth	38. maintain	57. pursue	

Personal Spelling List

In your notebook, keep a list of words that *you* misspell. Add words to your list from corrected papers and from the exercises in this chapter. First, copy each word as you misspelled it, underlining the trouble spot; then write the word correctly. Use the following form. Study your list often.

	As I Wrote It	**Correct Spelling**
1.	di*ssa*pointed	disappointed
2.	_____	_____
3.	_____	_____

PRACTICE 12

Writing Assignment

Success can be defined in many different ways. In a small group, discuss what the term *success* means to you. Is it a rewarding career, a happy family life, lots of money?

Now pick the definition that most appeals to you and write a paragraph explaining what success is. You may wish to use people in the news or friends to support your main idea. Proofread your work for accurate spelling, especially the words covered in this chapter. Finally, exchange papers and read each other's work. Did your partner catch any spelling errors that you missed?

CHAPTER HIGHLIGHTS

- **Double the final consonant in one-syllable words that end in** *cvc:*

    hop/hopped   swim/swimming

- **Double the final consonant in words of more than one syllable if they end in** *cvc* **and if the stress is on the last syllable:**

    begin/beginning   prefer/preferred

- **Keep the final** *e* **when adding a suffix that begins with a consonant:**

    hope/hopeful   time/timely

- **Drop the final** *e* **when adding a suffix that begins with a vowel:**

    hope/hoping   time/timer

- **Keep the final** *y* **when adding a suffix if the letter before the** *y* **is a vowel:**

    buy/buying   delay/delayed

- **Change the** *y* **to** *i* **when adding a suffix if the letter before the** *y* **is a consonant:**

    snappy/snappiest   pity/pitiful

- **Write** *i* **before** *e*, **except after** *c*, **or in any** *ay* **sound like** *neighbor:*

    believe, niece, *but* receive, weigh

- **Remember that there are exceptions to all of these rules. Check a dictionary whenever you are uncertain.**

CHAPTER REVIEW

Proofread this essay for spelling errors. Correct the errors above the lines.

A Precious Resource

(1) Many people have pleasant memorys of recieving their first library card or chooseing books for the first time at a local public library. (2) Widely recognized as a priceless resource, the public library is defined just as you might expect: a collection of books and other materials supported by the public for public use.

(3) Several New England towns claim the honor of contributeing the first public money for a library. (4) However, the first such library of meaningful size and influence—the first fameous public library—originated in Boston, Massachusetts, in 1854. (5) The Boston Public Library, with its useful refrence collection and its

The beautiful Library of Congress in Washington, D.C., offers the public an array of services and resources. Explore online at **http://www.loc.gov/index.html**.

© PictureNet/CORBIS.

policy of circulateing popular books, set the pattern for all public librarys subsequently created in the United States and Canada. (6) By the end of the nineteenth century, many state goverments were begining to raise taxes to support libraries. (7) They beleived that public libraries had an extremely importent role to play in helping people pursue knowlege and continue thier education. (8) Although public libaries today have much the same goal, they now offer a truely admireable number of resources and services. (9) These include story hours for children, book discussion clubs for adults, intresting lectures, art exhibits, literacy classes, and most recently, computer training and guideance.

(10) Technology, of course, has transformed the management of the public library as well as the way the library is used. (11) The biggest changes—today's computerized catalogs, searchable databases, and Internet access—would definately have gone beyond the wildest dreams of even the most commited early public libary supporters.

EXPLORING ONLINE

<http://grammar.ccc.commnet.edu/grammar/cgi-shl/quiz20.pl/spelling_quiz3.htm>
Interactive quiz: Add endings to these words.

<http://owl.english.purdue.edu/handouts/interact/g_spelieEX1.html> Is that *ei* or *ie*?

<http://college.cengage.com/devenglish> Visit the *Grassroots* 9/e student website for more exercises, quizzes, and live links to all websites mentioned in this chapter.

CHAPTER 32

Look-Alikes / Sound-Alikes

A/An/And

1. *A* **is used before a word beginning with a consonant or a consonant sound.**

   a man   *a* house   *a* union (the *u* in *union* is pronounced like the consonant *y*)

2. *An* **is used before a word beginning with a vowel (*a, e, i, o, u*) or a silent *h*.**

   an igloo   *an* apple   *an* hour (the *h* in *hour* is silent)

3. *And* **joins words or ideas together.**

   Edward *and* Brad are taking the same biology class.

   He is very honest, *and* most people respect him.

PRACTICE 1

Fill in *a*, *an*, or *and*.

1. Don Miller has used each summer vacation to try out _____ different career choice.

2. Last summer, he worked in _____ law office, filling in for _____ administrative assistant on leave.

3. One lawyer was impressed by how carefully Don worked _____ suggested that Don consider _____ law career.

4. Don returned to school in the fall _____ talked to his adviser about becoming _____ paralegal.

5. _____ paralegal investigates the facts of cases, prepares documents, _____ does other background work for lawyers.

6. With his adviser's help, Don found _____ course of study to prepare for this career.

7. Next summer, he hopes to work for _____ public interest law firm _____ to learn about environmental law.

8. He is happy to have found _____ interesting career _____ looks forward to making _____ difference.

362

Accept/Except

1. *Accept* **means "to receive."**

   Please *accept* my apologies.   I *accepted* his offer of help.

2. *Except* **means "other than" or "excluding."**

   Everyone *except* Ron thinks it's a good idea.

PRACTICE 2

Fill in forms of *accept* or *except*.

1. Did Steve _____ the collect call from his brother?

2. Mr. Francis will _____ the package in the mailroom.

3. All of our friends attended the wedding _____ Meg.

4. The athlete proudly _____ his award.

5. Every toddler _____ my daughter enjoyed the piñata party.

6. _____ for Jean, we all had tickets for the movie.

7. The tornado left every building standing _____ for the barn.

8. Everyone _____ Ranjan was willing to _____ the committee's decision.

Been/Being

1. *Been* **is the past participle form of** *to be*. *Been* **is usually used after the helping verb** *have,* **has, or** *had*.

   I *have been* to that restaurant before.

   She *has been* in Akron for ten years.

2. *Being* **is the** *-ing* **form of** *to be*. *Being* **is usually used after the helping verbs** *is,* *are, am, was,* **and** *were*.

   They *are being* helped by the salesperson.

   Rhonda *is being* courageous and independent.

PRACTICE 3

Fill in *been* or *being*.

1. The children have _____ restless all day.

2. What good films are _____ shown on television tonight?

3. We have _____ walking in circles!

4. I haven't _____ in such a good mood for a week.

5. This building is _____ turned into a community center.

6. His last offer has _____ on my mind all day.

7. Which elevator is _____ inspected now?

8. Because you are _____ honest with me, I will admit that I have _____ in love with you for years.

Buy/By

1. *Buy* **means "to purchase."**

   She *buys* new furniture every five years.

2. *By* **means "near," "before," or "by means of."**

   He walked right *by* and didn't say hello.

   By sunset, we had finished the harvest.

   We prefer traveling *by* bus.

PRACTICE 4

Fill in *buy* or *by.*

1. Did you _____ that computer, or did you rent it?

2. These tracks on the trail were made _____ a deer.

3. He stood _____ the cash register and waited his turn to _____ a cheeseburger.

4. She finds it hard to walk _____ a bookstore without going in to browse.

5. It's better to stick with your budget than to _____ that ten-seater couch.

6. Please answer this letter _____ October 10.

7. Pat trudged through the storm to _____ a Sunday paper.

8. The dishes _____ the sink need to be put away.

Fine/Find

1. *Fine* **means "good" or "well." It can also mean "a penalty."**

   He wrote a *fine* analysis of the short story.

   She paid a $10 *fine.*

2. *Find* **means "to locate."**

   I can't *find* my red suspenders.

PRACTICE 5

Fill in *fine* or *find.*

1. The library charges a large _____ for overdue videotapes.

2. As soon as we _____ your lost suitcase, we'll send it to you.

3. Can you _____ me one of these in an extra-large size?

4. Harold made a _____ impression on the assistant buyer.

5. By tonight, I will be feeling _____ .

6. My father gave me good advice: "When you _____ good friends, stick with them."

It's/Its

1. *It's* **is a contraction of** *it is* **or** *it has.* **If you cannot substitute** *it is* **or** *it has* **in the sentence, you cannot use** *it's.*

   It's a ten-minute walk to my house.   *It's* been a nice party.

2. *Its* **is a possessive and shows ownership.**

   The bear cub rolled playfully on *its* side.

   Industry must do *its* share to curb inflation.

PRACTICE 6

Fill in *it's* or *its.*

1. If _____ not too much trouble, drop the package off on your way home.

2. _____ been hard for him to accept the fact that he can no longer play ball.

3. The *Daily News* reporter was lucky because the jury reached _____ verdict just before her deadline.

4. _____ been a long time since I had a real vacation.

5. _____ a chocolate cake with your Social Security number in pink frosting.

6. My family is at _____ best when there is work to be done.

7. _____ impossible to open this window.

8. Although I hate shoveling the walk, I am happy _____ been a good year for winter sports.

9. _____ sad to see that seagull huddled in the sand.

10. If _____ not flying, perhaps _____ wing is hurt.

Know/Knew/No/New

1. *Know* **means "to have knowledge or understanding."** *Knew* **is the past tense of the verb** *to know.*

   Carl *knows* he has to finish by 6 p.m.

   The police officer *knew* the quickest route to the pier.

2. *No* **is a negative.**

   He is *no* longer dean of academic affairs.

3. *New* **means "fresh" or "recent."**

   I like your *new* belt.

PRACTICE 7

Fill in *know, knew, no,* or *new.*

1. We will need _____ wiring to handle those powerful air conditioners.

2. She didn't _____ the lid was loose.

3. I _____ I need to find _____ jokes because no one laughs when I tell my old ones.

4. Because she _____ the answer, she won a pool table and a popcorn machine.

5. Because you really _____ the _____ material, why don't you take the final early?

6. Charlene thinks there's _____ way we can do it, but I _____ we'll be speaking Italian by June.

7. Arnold _____ that he shouldn't have eaten that third dessert.

8. We have _____ way of knowing how well you scored on the civil service examination.

9. He didn't _____ whether the used equipment came with a guarantee.

10. I wish I _____ then what I _____ now.

Lose/Loose

1. *Lose* **means "to misplace" or "not to win."**

Be careful not to *lose* your way on those back roads.

George hates to *lose* at cards.

2. *Loose* **means "ill fitting" or "too large."**

That's not my size; it's *loose* on me.

PRACTICE 8

Fill in *lose* or *loose*.

1. Because the plug is _____ in the socket, the television keeps blinking on and off.

2. A professional team has to learn how to win and how to _____ gracefully.

3. If Irene doesn't tighten that _____ hubcap, she will _____ it.

4. I like wearing _____ clothing in the summer.

5. Before these pants shrank in the dryer, they were too _____ .

6. Act now, or you will _____ your opportunity to get that promotion.

7. She won't _____ those mittens again because I've clipped them onto her jacket.

8. I'm surprised you didn't _____ those _____ quarters.

Mine/Mind

1. *Mine* **is a possessive and shows ownership.**

This is your umbrella, but where is *mine*?

2. *Mind* **means "intelligence." It can also be a verb meaning "to object" or "to pay attention to."**

What's on your *mind*?   I don't *mind* if you come late.

PRACTICE 9

Fill in *mine* or *mind*.

1. Her road test is tomorrow; _____ was yesterday.

2. Will Doris _____ if we spend the evening talking about our days in boot camp?

3. Sherlock put his _____ to work and solved the mystery.

4. Please _____ your manners when we meet the king.

5. Please don't interrupt us; we really _____ when someone breaks our train of thought.

6. My _____ is made up; I want to switch my major from accounting to marketing.

7. Don't _____ him; he always snores in public.

8. "That toy is _____," whined Tim, "and I *do* _____ if you take it!"

Past/Passed

1. *Past* **is that which has already occurred; it is over with.**

His *past* work has been satisfactory.

Never let the *past* interfere with your hopes for the future.

2. *Passed* **is the past tense of the verb** *to pass.*

She *passed* by and nodded hello.

PRACTICE 10

Fill in *past* or *passed*.

1. He asked for the butter, but I absentmindedly _____ him the mayonnaise.

2. Forget about failures in the _____ and look forward to success in the future.

3. The police car caught up to the truck that had _____ every other car on the road.

4. I have _____ this same corner every Saturday morning for a year.

5. Wasn't that woman who just _____ us on a motorcycle your Aunt Sally?

6. In the _____, Frieda and Carolyn used to talk on the phone once a week.

7. Your _____ attendance record was perfect.

8. Don knew he had _____ the test, but he had never received such a high grade in the _____.

Quiet/Quit/Quite

1. *Quiet* **means "silent, still."**

The woods are *quiet* tonight.

2. *Quit* **means "to give up" or "to stop doing something."**

Last year, I *quit* smoking.

3. *Quite* **means "very" or "exactly."**

She was *quite* tired after playing soccer for two hours.

That's not *quite* right.

PRACTICE 11

Fill in *quiet*, *quit*, or *quite*.

1. When it comes to expressing her feelings, Tonya is _____ vocal.

2. I can't concentrate when my apartment is too _____.

3. Selling belly chains can be _____ amusing.

4. Please be _____; I'm trying to listen to the news.

5. If she _____ now, she will risk losing her vacation pay.

6. Dwight asked the crew to be absolutely _____ while the magicians performed.

7. Don't _____ when the going gets rough; just increase your efforts and succeed.

8. I have the general idea, but I don't _____ understand all the details.

9. This usually _____ library is now _____ noisy.

10. She _____ whistling when people in the line began to stare at her.

Rise/Raise

1. *Rise* **means "to get up by one's own power." The past tense of** *rise* **is** *rose*. **The past participle of** *rise* **is** *risen*.

   The sun *rises* at 6 a.m.

   Daniel *rose* early yesterday.

   He *has risen* from the table.

2. *Raise* **means "to lift an object" or "to grow or increase." The past tense of** *raise* **is** *raised*. **The past participle of** *raise* **is** *raised*.

   Raise your right hand.

   She *raised* the banner over her head.

   We *have raised* $1,000.

PRACTICE 12

Fill in forms of *rise* or *raise*.

1. When the moon _____, we'll be able to see the path better.

2. During the meeting, she _____ the possibility of a strike.

3. The jet _____ off the runway and roared into the clouds.

4. Bud would like to _____ early, but usually he wakes, turns over, and goes back to sleep.

5. Can you _____ corn in this soil?

6. He couldn't _____ from his chair because of the chewing gum stuck to his pants.

7. My boss has unexpectedly _____ my salary.

8. I felt foolish when I accidentally _____ my voice in the quiet concert hall.

9. The loaves of homemade bread have _____.

10. He _____ to his feet and shuffled out the door.

Sit/Set

1. *Sit* **means "to seat oneself." The past tense of** *sit* **is** *sat.* **The past participle of** *sit* **is** *sat.*

   Sit up straight!

   He *sat* down on the porch and fell asleep.

   She has *sat* reading that book all day.

2. *Set* **means "to place" or "to put something down." The past tense of** *set* **is** *set.* **The past participle of** *set* **is** *set.*

   Don't *set* your books on the dining room table.

   She *set* the package down and walked off without it.

   He had *set* the pot on the stove.

PRACTICE 13

Fill in forms of *sit* or *set.*

1. Marcy _____ her glasses on the seat next to her.

2. Please _____ there; the dentist will see you in ten minutes.

3. _____ the cans of paint in the corner, please.

4. My grandfather always _____ in that overstuffed, red-and-blue plaid chair.

5. Please _____ that box of clothes by the door.

6. _____ down, and let me _____ this Hawaiian feast before you.

7. I would have _____ your bracelet on the counter, but I was afraid someone might walk off with it.

8. We have always _____ in the first row, but tonight I want to

   _____ at the back of the auditorium.

Suppose/Supposed

1. *Suppose* **means "to assume" or "to guess." The past tense of** *suppose* **is** *supposed.* **The past participle of** *suppose* **is** *supposed.*

   Brad *supposes* that the teacher will give him an *A.*

   We all *supposed* she would win first prize.

   I had *supposed* Dan would win.

2. *Supposed* **means "should have"; it is followed by** *to.*

   He is *supposed* to meet us after class.

   You were *supposed* to wash and wax the car.

   REMEMBER: When you mean *ought* or *should,* always use the *-ed* ending—*supposed.*

PRACTICE 14

Fill in *suppose* or *supposed.*

1. How do you _____ he will get himself out of this mess?

2. My father-in-law was _____ to arrive last night.

3. I _____ I'll find my car keys in my other pants.

4. Why do you _____ that cereal is so expensive?

5. You are not _____ to open the presents until your birthday.

6. Diane was _____ to check the bus schedule.

7. Where do you _____ he bought that gold lamé shirt?

8. What are we _____ to do with these three-by-five-inch cards?

9. Frank _____ that Meredith would meet him for dinner.

10. I _____ Ron is willing to shovel the snow this time.

Their/There/They're

1. *Their* **is a possessive pronoun and shows ownership.**

They couldn't find *their* wigs.   *Their* children are charming.

2. *There* **indicates a location.**

I wouldn't go *there* again.   Put the lumber down *there*.

3. *There* **is also a way of introducing a thought.**

There is a fly in my soup.

There are two ways to approach this problem.

4. *They're* **is a contraction:** *they + are = they're.* **If you cannot substitute** *they are* **in the sentence, you cannot use** *they're.*

They're the best poems I have read in a long time.

If *they're* coming, count me in.

PRACTICE 15

Fill in *their, there,* or *they're.*

1. If you move over _____, I can get everyone into the picture.

2. _____ are three ways to mix paint, all of which are messy.

3. If _____ here, we can set out the food.

4. That is _____ hot air balloon way up _____.

5. _____ preparing for a hot, sticky summer.

6. Is _____ a faster route to Topeka?

7. _____ never on time when it comes to paying _____

   cell phone bills.

8. _____ products contain no sugar and no preservatives.

9. Is _____ a wrench in the toolbox?

10. Because _____ so quiet, I suppose _____ asleep.

Then/Than

1. *Then* **means "next" or "at that time."**

First, we went to the theater, and *then* we went for pizza.

I was a heavyweight boxer *then*.

2. *Than* **is used in a comparison.**

She is a better student *than* I.

PRACTICE 16

Fill in *then* or *than*.

1. Carlos works harder _____ anyone else in this office.

2. San Francisco has colder winters _____ San Diego.

3. Get your first paycheck; _____ think about moving into your own apartment.

4. It's often better to forgive someone _____ to carry a grudge.

5. If you receive straight *A*'s this semester, will you _____ apply for a scholarship?

6. You asked me a question and _____ interrupted me before I could answer.

7. This red convertible gets more miles to the gallon _____ any other car on the lot.

8. Now I'm ready for marriage; _____, I was confused.

Threw/Through

1. *Threw* **is the past tense of the verb** *to throw.*

Charleen *threw* the ball into the bleachers.

2. *Through* **means "in one side and out the other" or "finished."**

He burst *through* the front door laughing.

If you are *through* eating, we can leave.

PRACTICE 17

Fill in *threw* or *through*.

1. I went _____ my notes, but I couldn't find any reference to Guatemala.

2. He _____ the pillow on the floor and plopped down in front of the television.

3. Gail _____ her raincoat over her head and ran out into the storm.

4. You go _____ that door to get to the dean's office.

5. If you are _____ with that reference material, I would like to take a look at it.

6. We can always see _____ their tricks.

To/Too/Two

1. *To* **means "toward."**

We are going *to* the stadium.

2. *To* **can also be combined with a verb to form an infinitive.**

Where do you want *to go* for lunch?

3. *Too* **means "also" or "very."**

Roberto is going to the theater *too*.   They were *too* bored to stay awake.

4. *Two* **is the number 2.**

Ms. Palmer will teach *two* new accounting courses this term.

PRACTICE 18

Fill in *to, too,* or *two*.

1. If you want _____ enroll in college this fall, you will need _____ letters of recommendation.

2. It will be _____ awkward _____ leave the dinner before the dessert is served.

3. He likes _____ sing at parties _____ .

4. It's _____ early _____ go _____ the theater.

5. That dance step may be _____ advanced for me right now.

6. Belkys and I have _____ design _____ outfits by Friday if we want _____ enter the fashion competition.

7. We traveled _____ the Grand Canyon _____ try white-water rafting.

8. It's _____ much trouble to make my own salad dressing.

9. She _____ likes _____ watch professional wrestling.

10. We saw _____ undercover agents talking quietly _____ the bartender.

Use/Used

1. *Use* **means "to make use of." The past tense of** *use* **is** *used.* **The past participle of** *use* **is** *used.*

Why do you *use* a Palm Pilot?

He *used* the wrong paint in the bathroom.

I have *used* that brand of toothpaste myself.

2. *Used* **means "in the habit of" or "accustomed"; it is followed by** *to.*

I am not *used to* getting up at 4 a.m.   They got *used to* the good life.

REMEMBER: When you mean *in the habit of* or *accustomed,* always use the *-ed* ending—*used.*

PRACTICE 19

Fill in *use* or *used*.

1. Terry is _____ to long bus rides.

2. It may take a few days to get _____ to this high altitude.

3. Do you know how to _____ a digital camera?

4. Vera hopes to get _____ to her grumpy father-in-law.

5. Carlotta and Roland still _____ the laundromat on the corner.

6. We _____ the self-service pump; the gas was cheaper.

7. Feel free to _____ my telephone if you need to make a call.

8. You'll get _____ to it.

9. My grandmother does not _____ her e-mail account because she has never gotten _____ to it.

10. Never get _____ to failure; always expect success.

Weather/Whether

1. *Weather* **refers to atmospheric conditions.**

In June, the *weather* in Spain is lovely.

2. *Whether* **implies a question.**

Whether you pass is up to you.

PRACTICE 20

Fill in *weather* or *whether.*

1. Rainy _____ makes me lazy.

2. Be sure to tell the employment agency _____ you plan to take the job.

3. You never know _____ Celia will be happy or sad.

4. Good _____ always brings joggers to the park.

5. Flopsy didn't know _____ to eat the carrot or the lettuce first.

6. Please check to see _____ the printer needs a new ink cartridge.

7. The real estate agent must know by 10 a.m. _____ you intend to rent the house.

8. _____ the _____ cooperates or not, we're going to the beach.

Where/Were/We're

1. *Where* **implies place or location.**

Where have you been all day?   Home is *where* you hang your hat.

2. *Were* **is the past tense of** *are.*

We *were* on our way when the hurricane hit.

3. *We're* **is a contraction:** *we + are = we're.* **If you cannot substitute** *we are* **in the sentence, you cannot use** *we're.*

We're going to leave now.   Because *we're* in the city, let's go to the galleries.

PRACTICE 21

Fill in *where*, *were*, or *we're*.

1. The desk was emptied, but _____ not sure who did it.

2. _____ did you put the remote control?

3. Ted and Gloria _____ childhood sweethearts.

4. When you _____ in South America, _____ did your poodles stay?

5. Virginia is not _____ I was born.

6. The librarians _____ very helpful in showing us _____ to find the latest information.

7. _____ you surprised to learn that _____ commercial fishermen?

8. The clouds _____ blocking the sun in exactly the spot _____ we _____ sitting.

9. Everyone needs a peaceful hideaway, a place _____ he or she can be absolutely alone.

10. _____ _____ going, sir, is a question _____ not about to answer.

Whose/Who's

1. *Whose* **implies ownership and possession.**

   Whose term paper is that?

2. *Who's* **is a contraction of** *who is* **or** *who has.* **If you cannot substitute** *who is* **or** *who has,* **you cannot use** *who's.*

   Who's knocking at the window?

   Who's seen my new felt hat with the green bows?

PRACTICE 22

Fill in *whose* or *who's*.

1. _____ ready for an adventure?

2. _____ CDs are scattered all over the floor?

3. We found a puppy in the vacant lot, but we don't know _____ it is.

4. _____ that playing the saxophone?

5. He's a physician _____ diagnosis can be trusted.

6. Grace admires the late Marian Anderson, _____ singing always moved her.

7. I'm not sure _____ coming and _____ not.

8. _____ been eating all the chocolate chip cookies?

Your/You're

1. *Your* **is a possessive and shows ownership.**

   Your knowledge is astonishing!

2. *You're* **is a contraction:** *you + are = you're.* **If you cannot substitute** *you are* **in the sentence, you cannot use** *you're.*

   You're the nicest person I know.

PRACTICE 23

Fill in *your* or *you're*.

1. Is that _____ iPod or mine?

2. If _____ tired, take a nap.

3. Does _____ daughter like her new telescope?

4. I hope _____ teammates haven't forgotten the code words.

5. If _____ in a rush, we can mail _____ scarves to you.

6. _____ foreman was just transferred.

7. Please keep _____ Saint Bernard out of my rose garden.

8. _____ in charge of _____ finances from now on.

9. When _____ optimistic about life, everything seems to go right.

10. Let me have _____ order by Thursday; if it's late, _____ not likely to receive the merchandise in time for the holidays.

PRACTICE 24

Writing Assignment

Look back through this chapter and make a list of the look-alikes that most confuse you. List at least five pairs or clusters of words. Then use them all correctly in a paper about a problem on your campus or in your neighborhood (such as a lack of public parks or playgrounds, too much drug or alcohol use, or a gulf between computer haves and have-nots). Try to use every word on your look-alikes list and proofread to make sure you have spelled everything correctly.

CHAPTER HIGHLIGHTS

Some words look and sound alike. Below are a few of them:

● **it's/its**

It's the neatest room I ever saw.
Everything is in *its* place.

● **their/they're/there**

They found *their* work easy.
They're the best actors I have ever seen.
Put the lumber down *there*.

● **then/than**

I was a heavyweight boxer *then*.
He is a better cook *than* I.

● **to/too/two**

We are going *to* the stadium.
No one is *too* old to learn.
I bought *two* hats yesterday.

● **whose/who's**

Whose Italian dictionary is this?
I'm not sure *who's* leaving early.

● **your/you're**

Is *your* aunt the famous mystery writer?
You're due for a promotion and a big raise.

CHAPTER REVIEW

Proofread this essay for look-alike/sound-alike errors. Write your corrections above the lines.

Rapper with a Difference

(1) If you're concept of hip-hop music is gang fights, drugs, the fast life, and negative views of women, than perhaps you haven't heard of Wyclef Jean. (2) Like many rappers, Jean is committed to making music with powerful lyrics and driving rhythms. (3) However, this Haitian-born former Fugee sends a very different message and lives a quiter lifestyle than many hip-hop artists do.

Activist Wyclef Jean in concert.

(4) Unlike some hip-hop music—named "gangsta rap" for it's glorification of violence—Jean's songs celebrate nonviolence and understanding. (5) For example, in his fourth solo album, *The Preacher's Son*, Jean shares his vision of a peaceful world were everyone gets along. (6) He believes that if people can set and talk, they can work though almost anything. (7) Wyclef pleads for an end to dangerous feuds between rappers, such as the clashes between 50 Cent and Ja Rule, Jay-Z and Nas, and the passed rivalry, kept alive in music, between Tupac Shakur and Notorious B.I.G., both gunned down in there prime.

(8) Jean also differs from other rappers in his calm lifestyle. (9) While many hip-hop celebrities live the high life, traveling with bodyguards and a posse of companions, the down-to-earth Jean insists on strolling the streets by himself. (10) He says he does not want to become disconnected from reality buy cutting himself off from it. (11) So its not unusual to see Jean standing on a street corner talking with a homeless person or bonding with a young thug who tried to rob him moments before.

(12) Now Jean is been seen as a role model by a new generation of hip-hop artists and fans. (13) One of his passions is Clef's Kids, an after-school music program, for music is a vehicle to his higher goal of changing the world. (14) Jean's preacher father, now deceased, use to urge him to study theology, too which Jean replied, "I am just a messenger in a different way."

EXPLORING ONLINE

<http://grammar.ccc.commnet.edu/grammar/cgi-shl/quiz.pl/spelling_add1.htm>
Interactive quiz: Choose the correctly spelled word.

<http://owl.english.purdue.edu/handouts/interact/g_spelhomoEX1.html> Interactive quiz: Choose the correctly spelled word.

<http://a4esl.org/q/h/homonyms.html> Practice sound-alikes, like night/knight, that may confuse ESL students.

<http://college.cengage.com/devenglish> Visit the *Grassroots* 9/e student website for more exercises, quizzes, and live links to all websites mentioned in this chapter.

WRITING ASSIGNMENTS

As you complete each writing assignment, remember to perform these steps:

- Write a clear, complete topic sentence.
- Use freewriting, brainstorming, or clustering to generate ideas for the body of your paragraph, essay, letter, or review.
- Arrange your best ideas in a plan.
- Revise for support, unity, coherence, and exact language.
- Proofread for grammar, punctuation, and spelling errors.

Writing Assignment 1: *Express your opinion.* Write a letter to either a newspaper editor or an elected official (a mayor, governor, or senator, for example) in which you suggest one solution to a particular problem, such as illegal immigration or gun control. For topic ideas and information, visit Yahoo's directory of websites on current issues and causes at <http://dir.yahoo.com/Society_and_Culture/Issues_and_Causes/> or SpeakOut. com at <http://speakout.com/activism/issues/>. State your opinion in your topic sentence or thesis statement, and present at least three reasons in support of your opinion. Consider actually mailing your letter to the recipient, but not before you proofread for spelling errors that would weaken your writing.

Writing Assignment 2: *Solve a problem.* You have identified what you consider to be a problem in your place of employment. When you go to your supervisor, you are asked to write up your concerns and to suggest a solution. Begin first by describing the problem, and then give background information, including what you suspect are the causes of the problem. Then offer suggestions for solving it. End with some guidelines for evaluating the success of the changes. In your concluding sentence, thank your supervisor for his or her consideration of your letter. Don't let typos or mistaken look-alikes/sound-alikes detract from your ideas. Proofread for accurate spelling!

Writing Assignment 3: *Review a movie.* Your college newspaper has asked you to review a movie. Pick a popular film that you especially liked or disliked. In your first sentence, name the film and state whether you recommend it. Explain your evaluation by discussing two or three specific reasons for your reactions to the picture. Describe as much of the film as is necessary to make your point, but do not retell the plot. Proofread for accurate spelling. Consider posting your review at <http://www.movievine.com/> or <http://www.franksreelreviews.com/submit/submit.htm>.

Writing Assignment 4: *Describe a family custom.* Most families have customs that they perform together. These customs often help strengthen the bond that the members of the family feel toward each other. A custom might be eating Sunday dinner together, going to religious services, celebrating holidays in a special way, or even holding a family council to discuss difficulties and concerns. Write about a custom in your family that is especially meaningful. Of what value has this custom been to you or other members of the family? Proofread for accurate spelling.

REVIEW

Proofreading

The following essay contains a number of spelling and look-alike/sound-alike errors. First, underline the misspelled or misused words. Then write each correctly spelled word above the line. (You should find thirty-nine errors.)

Everyday Angel

(1) On January 2, 2007, construction worker Wesley Autry and his too young daugters were standing on a New York City subway platform waiting for the train. (2) Suddenly, a twenty-year-old student standing nearby suffered a siezure and tumbled onto the subway tracks. (3) Autry saw the headlights of an approaching train and realized that the young men was about to be run over right in front of the children. (4) Leapping onto the rails, Autry pulled the strugling student down into the shallow drainage ditch between the tracks and pined him their while one train and than another rumbled over them with about two inchs to spare. (5) The next day, national and international headlines proclaimed Autry to be an "angle," a "superman," a "hero," and "one in a million." (6) Autry explained simply, "I just tryed to do the right thing."

(7) But his action began a nationel arguement about how far one should go to help others. (8) People couldn't help wondering if they themselfs would make a similer split-second decision to risk they're own lives for a total stranger. (9) Was Autry's act truely a one-in-a-million occurence? (10) After all, pycologists and sociologists point out that people quiet often fail to act in a emergancy because of the "bystander effect." (11) Bystander effect is the tendency to do nothing in a crisis because one assumes that someone else will take any nesessary action.

(12) On the other hand, Autry's bravery inspirred people worldwide. (13) Some reconized his selfless deed buy giving him awards, scholarships for his children, cash, and free trips. (14) Others gained new confidence in they're own ability to peform a dareing rescue. (15) In one poll, most New Yorkers beleived that they would probly jump off a ferry boat to save a child who had fallen overboard, try to stop a mugger from steeling an elderly women's money, and even run into a

burning building to save someone traped inside. (16) Still others formed a grass-roots movment and established a new holiday in honor of Wesley Autry. (17) See Something/Do Something Day, now observed every year on Febuary 17, encourages people to stop been bystanders and start been everyday angels.

 EXPLORING ONLINE

<http://seesomethingdosomething.com/> Visit the See Something/Do Something website, read about others' good deeds, and post your own ideas about good deeds that you've done or seen.

WRITERS' WORKSHOP
Examine Positive (or Negative) Values

One good way to develop a paragraph or essay is by supporting the topic sentence or the thesis statement with three points. A student uses this approach in the following essay. In your group or class, read her work, aloud if possible.

Villa Avenue

(1) The values I learned growing up on Villa Avenue in the Bronx have guided me through thirty-five years and three children. Villa Avenue taught me the importance of having a friendly environment, playing together, and helping people.

(2) Villa Avenue was a three-block, friendly environment. I grew up on the middle block. The other ones were called "up the block" and "down the block." Mary's Candy Store was up the block. It had a candy counter and soda fountain on the left and on the right a jukebox that played three songs for twenty-five cents. My friends and I would buy candy, hang out, and listen to the Beatles and other music of the sixties. A little down from Mary's on the corner was Joey's Deli. When you walked into Joey's, different aromas would welcome you to a world of Italian delicacies. Fresh mozzarella in water always sat on the counter, with salami, pepperoni, and imported provolone cheese hanging above. On Sundays at Joey's, my father would buy us a black-and-white cookie for a weekly treat.

(3) On Villa Avenue, everyone helped everyone else. Everybody's doors were open, so if I had to go to the bathroom or needed a drink of water, I could go to a dozen different apartments. If my parents had to go somewhere, they would leave me with a friend. When people on the block got sick, others went to the store for them, cleaned for them, watched their kids, and made sure they had food to eat. If someone died, everyone mourned and pitched in to help with arrangements. When I reflect on those days, I realize that the way the mothers looked out for each other's children is like your modern-day play group. The difference is that our play area was "the block."

(4) The whole street was our playground. We would play curb ball at the intersection. One corner was home plate, and the other ones were the bases. Down the block where the street was wide, we would play Johnny on the Pony with ten to fifteen kids. On summer nights, it was kick the can or hide and seek. Summer days we spent under an open fire hydrant.

> Everyone would be in the water, including moms and dads. Sometimes the teenagers would go to my Uncle Angelo's house and get a wine barrel to put over the hydrant. With the top and bottom of the barrel off, the water would shoot twenty to thirty feet in the air and come down on us like a waterfall.
>
> *Loretta M. Carney, student*

1. How effective is Loretta Carney's essay?

   _____ Clear main idea?   _____ Good supporting details?

   _____ Logical organization?   _____ Effective conclusion?

2. What is the main idea of the essay? Can you find the thesis statement, one sentence that states this main idea?

3. The writer states that Villa Avenue taught her three values. What are they? Are these clearly explained in paragraphs 2, 3, and 4? Are they discussed in the same order in which the thesis statement presents them? If not, what change would you suggest?

4. Does this essay *conclude* or just stop? What suggestions would you make to the writer for a more effective conclusion?

5. Proofread Carney's essay. Do you see any error patterns that she should watch out for?

Writing and Revising Ideas

1. Describe a place or person that taught you positive (or negative) values.

2. Do places like Villa Avenue exist anymore? Explain why you do or do not think so.

See Chapter 5 for help with planning and writing. You might wish to present your topic with three supporting points, the way Loretta Carney does. As you revise, pay close attention to writing a good thesis sentence and supporting paragraphs that contain clear, detailed explanations.

Reading Selections and Quotation Bank

Unit 9 contains three parts:

- **Effective Reading: Strategies for the Writer**
  This introduction to the readings section gives tips on how to get the most out of your reading.

- **The Readings**
  Here you will find twenty readings on a range of interesting subjects. Discussion questions and writing assignments follow each reading.

- **Quotation Bank**
  This section contains a number of brief quotations for you to read and enjoy, be inspired by, and use in your writing.

Reading Selections

Effective Reading Strategies for the Writer

The reading selections that follow were chosen to interest you, inspire you, and make you think. Many deal with issues you face at college, at work, or at home. Your instructor may ask you to read a selection and be prepared to discuss it in class or to write a composition or journal entry about it. The more carefully you read these selections, the better you will be able to think, talk, and write about them. Below are eight strategies that can help you become a more active and effective reader.

1. **Preview the reading selection.** Before you begin to read, scan the whole article to get a sense of the author's main idea and supporting points. First read the title, headnote, and any subtitles; next, quickly read the first and last paragraphs. This should give you a fairly clear idea of the author's subject and point of view. Finally, skim the whole selection, looking for the main supporting ideas. Previewing will increase your enjoyment and understanding as you read.

2. **Underline important ideas.** It is easy to forget what you have read, even though you have recently read it. Underlining or highlighting what you consider the main ideas will help you later to remember and discuss what you have read. Some students number the main points in order to understand the development of the author's ideas.

3. **Write your reactions in the margins.** If you strongly agree or disagree with an idea, write *yes* or *no* next to it. Record other questions and comments also, as if you were having a conversation with the author. Writing assignments will often ask you to respond to a particular idea or situation in a selection. Having already noted your reactions in the margins will help you focus your thinking and your writing.

4. **Prepare questions.** You will occasionally come across material that you cannot follow. Reread the passage. If you still have questions, place a question mark in the margin to remind you to ask a classmate or the instructor for an explanation.

5. **Circle unfamiliar words.** If you come across a new word that makes it difficult to follow what the author is saying, look it up immediately, jot the definition in the margin, and go back to reading. If, however, you can sense the meaning from the context—how the word fits the sentence—just circle it and, when you have finished the selection, consult a dictionary.

6. **Note effective or powerful writing.** If a particular line strikes you as especially important or moving, underline or highlight it. You may wish later to quote it in your written assignment. Be selective, however, in what you mark. *Too much* annotation can make it hard to focus on what is important when you discuss the selection in class or write about it.

7. **Vary your pace.** Some selections can be read quickly because you already know a great deal about the subject or because you find the material simple and direct. Other selections may require you to read slowly, pausing between sentences. Guard against the tendency to skim when the going gets tough: more difficult material will usually reward your extra time and attention.

8. **Reread.** If you expect to discuss or write about a selection, one reading is usually not enough. Budget your time so you will be able to give the selection

a second or third reading. You will be amazed at how much more you can get from the selection as you reread. You may understand ideas that were unclear the first time around. In addition, you may notice significant new points and details: perhaps you will change your mind about ideas you originally agreed or disagreed with. Rereading will help you discuss and write more intelligently and will increase your reading enjoyment.

The following essay has been marked by a student. Your own responses to this essay would, of course, be different. Examining how this essay was annotated may help you annotate other selections in this book and read more effectively in your other courses.

Daring to Dream Big

DIANE SAWYER

I see her on TV—she's a top journalist.

I was seventeen years old, a high school senior in Louisville, Kentucky, representing my state in the 1963 America's Junior Miss competition in Mobile, Alabama.

A beauty contest?

In the midst of it all, there was one person who stood at the center—at least my psychological center—someone I viewed as an island in an ocean of anxiety. She was one of the judges, a well-known writer, a woman whose sea-gray eyes fixed on you with laser penetration. Her name was Catherine Marshall.

I like this comparison—my dad is my island.

During the rehearsal on the last day of the pageant, the afternoon before it would all end, several of us were waiting backstage when a pageant official said Catherine Marshall wanted to speak with us. We gathered around. Most of us were expecting a last-minute pep talk, but we were surprised.

Wow, this is interesting. Being a beauty queen is not enough.

She fixed her eyes upon us. "You have set goals for yourselves. I have heard some of them. But I don't think you have set them high enough. You have talent and intelligence and a chance. I think you should take those goals and expand them. Think of the most you could do with your lives. Make what you do matter. Above all, dream big."

Main idea? DREAM BIG.
Many of my friends don't set high goals for themselves. Do I?
Aspired = aimed

It was not so much an instruction as a dare. I felt stunned. This woman I admired so much was disappointed in us—not by what we were but by how little we aspired to be.

Good question: How would I answer it? Should I dream bigger?

I won the America's Junior Miss contest that year. I graduated in 1967 with a BA degree in English and a complete lack of inspiration about what I should do with it. I went to my father. "What is it that you enjoy doing most?" he asked.

"Writing," I replied slowly. "And working with people. And being in touch with what's happening in the world."

He thought for a moment. "Did you ever consider television?"

Marshall's speech really motivated Sawyer to act.

At that time there were few if any women journalists on television. The idea of being a pioneer in the field sounded like dreaming big. That's how I came to get up my nerve and go out to convince the news director at Louisville's WLKY-TV to let me have a chance.

revelation = discovery

He gave it to me. For the next two and a half years I worked as a combination weather and news reporter. Eventually, though, I began to feel restless. I'd wait for the revelation, the sign pointing in the direction of the Big Dream. What I didn't realize is what Catherine Marshall undoubtedly knew all along—that the dream is not the destination but the journey.

I never thought of it this way.

This story makes me think of the importance of good role models—a good writing topic?

Today I'm coeditor of CBS's *Sixty Minutes*. I keep a suitcase packed at all times so that I can fly out on assignment at a moment's notice. When I go out into the world, I can almost hear a wonderful woman prodding me with her fiery challenge to stretch farther and, no matter how big the dream, to dream a little bigger still. God, she seems to be saying, can forgive failure, but not failing to try.

I'm inspired! Should I go for it and be a dentist instead of a dental assistant?

A Homemade Education

MALCOLM X

Sometimes a book can change a person's life. In this selection, Malcolm X, the influential and controversial black leader who was assassinated in 1965, describes how, while he was in prison, a dictionary set him free.

It was because of my letters that I happened to stumble upon starting to acquire some kind of homemade education. ¹

I became increasingly frustrated at not being able to express what I wanted to convey in letters that I wrote, especially those to Mr. Elijah Muhammad.[1] In the street, I had been the most articulate hustler out there—I had commanded attention when I said something. But now, trying to write simple English, I not only wasn't articulate, I wasn't even functional. How would I sound writing in slang, the way I would *say* it, something such as, "Look, daddy, let me pull your coat about a cat. Elijah Muhammad—" ²

Many who today hear me somewhere in person, or on television, or those who read something I've said, will think I went to school far beyond the eighth grade. This impression is due entirely to my prison studies. ³

It had really begun back in the Charlestown Prison, when Bimbi first made me feel envy of his stock of knowledge. Bimbi had always taken charge of any conversation he was in, and I had tried to emulate[2] him. But every book I picked up had few sentences which didn't contain anywhere from one to nearly all of the words that might as well have been in Chinese. When I just skipped those words, of course, I really ended up with little idea of what the book said. So I had come to the Norfolk Prison Colony still going through only book-reading motions. Pretty soon, I would have quit even these motions, unless I had received the motivation that I did. ⁴

I saw that the best thing I could do was get hold of a dictionary—to study, to learn some words. I was lucky enough to reason also that I should try to improve my penmanship. It was sad. I couldn't even write in a straight line. It was both ideas together that moved me to request a dictionary along with some tablets and pencils from the Norfolk Prison Colony school. ⁵

> *"I saw that the best thing I could do was get hold of a dictionary—to study, to learn some words."*

I spent two days just riffling[3] uncertainly through the dictionary's pages. I'd never realized so many words existed! I didn't know *which* words I needed to learn. Finally, just to start some kind of action, I began copying. ⁶

In my slow, painstaking, ragged handwriting, I copied into my tablet everything printed on that first page, down to the punctuation marks. ⁷

I believe it took me a day. Then, aloud, I read back, to myself, everything I'd written on the tablet. Over and over, aloud, to myself, I read my own handwriting. ⁸

I woke up the next morning, thinking about those words—immensely proud to realize that not only had I written so much at one time, but I'd written words that I never knew were in the world. Moreover, with a little effort, I also could remember what many of these words meant. I reviewed the words whose meanings I didn't remember. Funny thing, from the dictionary first page right now, that "aardvark" springs to my mind. The dictionary had a picture of it, a long-tailed, long-eared burrowing African mammal, which lives off termites caught by sticking out its tongue as an anteater does for ants. ⁹

I was so fascinated that I went on—I copied the dictionary's next page. And the same experience came when I studied that. With every succeeding page, I also ¹⁰

---

1. Elijah Muhammad: founder of the Muslim sect Nation of Islam
2. emulate: copy
3. riffling: thumbing through

learned of people and places and events from history. Actually, the dictionary is like a miniature encyclopedia. Finally, the dictionary's A section had filled a whole tablet—and I went on into the B's. That was the way I started copying what eventually became the entire dictionary. It went a lot faster after so much practice helped me pick up handwriting speed. Between what I wrote in my tablet, and writing letters, during the rest of my time in prison I would guess I wrote a million words.

I suppose it was inevitable that as my word-base broadened, I could for the first time pick up a book and read and now begin to understand what the book was saying. Anyone who has read a great deal can imagine the new world that opened. Let me tell you something: from then until I left that prison, in every free moment I had, if I was not reading in the library, I was reading on my bunk. You couldn't have gotten me out of books with a wedge. Between Mr. Muhammad's teachings, my correspondence, my visitors—usually Ella and Reginald—and my reading of books, months passed without my even thinking about being imprisoned. In fact, up to then, I never had been so truly free in my life.

Discussion and Writing Questions

1. Malcolm X says that in the streets he had been the "most articulate hustler" of all, but that in writing English he "not only wasn't articulate, [he] wasn't even functional" (paragraph 2). What does he mean?

2. What motivated Malcolm X to start copying the dictionary? What benefits did he gain from doing this?

3. What does Malcolm X mean when he says that until he went to prison, he "never had been so truly free in [his] life" (paragraph 11)?

4. Have you ever seen the 1992 film *Malcolm X*? If so, do you think the film's prison scenes showed how strongly Malcolm X was changed by improving his writing skills?

Writing Assignments

1. Choose three entries on a dictionary page and copy them. Then describe your experience. What did you learn? Can you imagine copying the entire dictionary? How do you feel about what Malcolm X accomplished? Where do you think he got the motivation to finish the task?

2. Malcolm X's inner life changed completely because of the dictionary he copied. Write about a time when a book, a story, a person, or an experience changed your life.

3. Have you ever wished that you had a better vocabulary? Learning new words is a process that pays off quickly if you keep at it. For one week, learn and practice a new word every day, perhaps using the following useful vocabulary website with a year's worth of great words. Then write an evaluation of your experiment to share with the class. Go to <http://grammar.ccc.commnet.edu/grammar/definition_list.htm>.

Don't Share Your Life with Me

ELLEN GOODMAN

Now an essential feature of modern life, the cell phone helps us stay in touch with family and friends, conduct business, and get help in emergencies. But *Boston Globe* columnist Ellen Goodman argues that the cell phone's negative effects are spreading like a disease. Goodman's columns appear in 375 newspapers nationwide.

The flight ends, the ritual begins. Wheels down, cellphones up. Within seconds the woman standing behind me in a crowded airplane aisle has called her office and begun a cranky and noisy inquisition.[1] Has the memo gone out warning that "Ken was not a suitable candidate for trafficking director"?

Mind you, I don't know this woman. Nor do I know Ken. Nor do I know what a trafficking director is. But there she is, publicly sharing office gossip, not to mention Ken's future, with at least six people on either end of her substantial voice range.

This was by no means the only cell snippet[2] of a life story to come my way through the mobile airwaves—nor was it the most outrageous.

In just the past few weeks, there was the woman who got on the train in Boston with a shaky relationship—"I did *not* leave my things at your place on purpose"—and got off in New York with no relationship. There was the father in Cincinnati whose son's SAT scores—540 in math, 480 in English—were audibly not what he hoped for. There was the doctor in the grocery store discussing a CAT scan of a patient in Milwaukee. How do you spell adenocarcinoma?

By now we have all had little bits of dialogue float past us on the street. A *tête-a-tête*[3] is now a *tête-a-tous*.[4] What once was told in quiet now wafts[5] by any open ear. Cell stories have become the aural[6] equivalent of indecent exposure.

But this morning, with poor Ken's fate hanging in the airplane, my annoyance went on speed dial. It occurred to me that the line between what's public and what's private must have been inadvertently severed when the first phone line was disconnected from the wall.

Is it barely a generation since phones became mobile? Once the phone booth was the place where Clark Kent[7] could protect his privacy. Now cellphoners strip in public. And city folks who long ago cultivated a way of avoiding eye contact are now supposed to avoid ear contact.

Over the years, I have read and written my fair share of rants[8] against the ringing and the driving, and the rube[9] and the rude. I've applauded the quiet car on the train and the no-phone zone in the restaurant. I've been appalled[10] when cheery little sounds wafted over wedding bells and furtive[11] conversations took place in funerals.

Indeed, cell technology has metastasized[12] into all sorts of odd behavior. We now have people who perform running commentary on the minutiae[13] of their daily lives as they travel down a grocery line—"Honey, I'm at the avocados"—or round the corner. A favorite *New Yorker* cartoon tracks a cellphone narrator through three panels: "I'm boarding the train. I'm on the train. I'm leaving the train."

At the same time, it has cut down the number of small personal encounters that make strangers feel as if they inhabit the same world. It may not be a safety hazard to talk to one person while ordering coffee from another, but what was the woman's message to her hairstylist when she talked on the phone while he cut her hair? You're invisible?

"Once the phone booth was the place where Clark Kent could protect his privacy. Now cellphoners strip in public."

---

1. inquisition: interrogation; questioning
2. snippet: a small piece
3. *tête-a-tête:* French for a private conversation between two people
4. *tête-a-tous:* French for a conversation with everyone
5. wafts: floats or drifts
6. aural: related to the ear or hearing
7. Clark Kent: a fictional character who turned into Superman after ducking into a phone booth to shed his business suit
8. rants: angry speeches
9. rube: an unsophisticated person
10. appalled: horrified or disgusted
11. furtive: secretive
12. metastasized: spread like cancer cells from a primary tumor to other body parts
13. minutiae: small, trivial details

The diminished sense of place and the increased sense of anonymity have to- 11
gether transformed privacy. It is easier to hang your feelings or your son's SAT
scores out in public if the people around you are invisible.

Justice Louis Brandeis once famously described privacy as "the right to be let 12
alone." But Brandeis didn't have a cellphone. The original fear was that someone
would invade your space and dig into the personal details of your life. But what do
you call it when someone invades your space with the personal details of their life?

Discussion and Writing Questions

1. Do you own a cell phone? Are you in the habit of having conversations in public places? Does it bother you that others might be listening? Why or why not?

2. State the author's thesis in your own words. She develops her main idea with
   several personal examples. What are some of these? Can you think of examples
   from your own experience to share with the class?

3. In paragraph 9, Goodman writes that "cell technology has metastasized into all
   sorts of odd behavior." What does her choice of the word *metastasized* suggest?

4. Goodman complains that cell phones have "cut down the number of small personal encounters that make strangers feel as if they inhabit the same world"
   (paragraph 10). What does she mean? Can you give an example of such a small
   but meaningful encounter? If you agree with Goodman, is the cell phone the
   only device contributing to a sense of isolation, or are there others as well?

Writing Assignments

1. Goodman believes that people who conduct loud cell phone conversations "strip
   in public," treating others as "invisible." Has society become less considerate and
   more self-centered? What examples can you point to as evidence? Discuss your
   perception of the overall level of rudeness in this country, using observations
   from your own experience to support your main idea.

2. In your opinion, what should be the "rules of etiquette" for using cell phones
   in public? For instance, what places should always be off limits to cell phones? In
   what situations should people never answer or place a call? What kinds of topics should not be discussed within earshot of others? Create your own list of
   do's and don'ts for courteous cell phone use.

3. In her closing paragraph, the author quotes one famous definition of the word
   privacy. How do you define privacy? What behaviors would violate your definition of privacy?

Mrs. Flowers

MAYA ANGELOU

**Maya Angelou (born Marguerite Johnson) is one of America's best-loved poets and
the author of *I Know Why the Caged Bird Sings*. In this book, her life story, she tells of
being raped when she was eight years old. Her response to the traumatic experience
was to stop speaking. In this selection, Angelou describes the woman who eventually threw her a "life line."**

For nearly a year, I sopped around the house, the Store, the school and the 1
church, like an old biscuit, dirty and inedible. Then I met, or rather got to
know, the lady who threw me my first life line.

Does the woman in this painting by Romare Bearden look like your idea of Mrs. Flowers? What lines in the essay support your view?

IN THE GARDEN by Romare Bearden. Virginia Museum of Fine Arts, Richmond. Gift of Dr. Howard A. Parvan. Photo by Katherine Wetzel © Virginia Museum of Fine Arts./ Art © Romare Bearden Foundation/ Licensed by VAGA, New York, NY.

Mrs. Bertha Flowers was the aristocrat of Black Stamps. She had the grace of control to appear warm in the coldest weather, and on the Arkansas summer days it seemed she had a private breeze which swirled around, cooling her. She was thin without the taut[1] look of wiry people, and her printed voile[2] dresses and flowered hats were as right for her as denim overalls for a farmer. She was our side's answer to the richest white woman in town. 2

Her skin was a rich black that would have peeled like a plum if snagged, but then no one would have thought of getting close enough to Mrs. Flowers to ruffle her dress, let alone snag her skin. She didn't encourage familiarity. She wore gloves too. 3

I don't think I ever saw Mrs. Flowers laugh, but she smiled often. A slow widening of her thin black lips to show even, small white teeth, then the slow effortless closing. When she chose to smile on me, I always wanted to thank her. The action was so graceful and inclusively benign.[3] 4

She was one of the few gentlewomen I have ever known and has remained throughout my life the measure of what a human being can be. . . . 5

One summer afternoon, sweet-milk fresh in my memory, she stopped at the Store to buy provisions. Another Negro woman of her health and age would have been expected to carry the paper sacks home in one hand, but Momma said, "Sister Flowers, I'll send Bailey up to your house with these things." 6

She smiled that slow dragging smile. "Thank you, Mrs. Henderson. I'd prefer Marguerite though." My name was beautiful when she said it. "I've been meaning to talk to her, anyway." They gave each other age-group looks. 7

Momma said, "Well, that's all right then. Sister, go and change your dress. You going to Sister Flowers's." . . . 8

There was a little path beside the rocky road, and Mrs. Flowers walked in front swinging her arms and picking her way over the stones. 9

---

1. taut: tight, tense
2. voile: a light, semi-sheer fabric
3. benign: kind, gentle

She said, without turning her head, to me, "I hear you're doing very good school work, Marguerite, but that it's all written. The teachers report that they have trouble getting you to talk in class." We passed the triangular farm on our left, and the path widened to allow us to walk together. I hung back in the separate unasked and unanswerable questions. [10]

"Come and walk along with me, Marguerite." I couldn't have refused even if I wanted to. She pronounced my name so nicely. Or more correctly, she spoke each word with such clarity that I was certain a foreigner who didn't understand English could have understood her. [11]

"Now no one is going to make you talk—possibly no one can. But bear in mind, language is man's way of communicating with his fellow man and it is language alone which separates him from the lower animals." That was a totally new idea to me, and I would need time to think about it. [12]

"Your grandmother says you read a lot. Every chance you get. That's good, but not good enough. Words mean more than what is set down on paper. It takes the human voice to infuse[4] them with the shades of deeper meaning." [13]

I memorized the part about the human voice infusing words. It seemed so valid and poetic. [14]

She said she was going to give me some books and that I not only must read them. I must read them aloud. She suggested that I try to make a sentence sound in as many different ways as possible. [15]

"I'll accept no excuse if you return a book to me that has been badly handled." My imagination boggled at the punishment I would deserve if in fact I did abuse a book of Mrs. Flowers's. Death would be too kind and brief. [16]

The odors in the house surprised me. Somehow I had never connected Mrs. Flowers with food or eating or any other common experience of common people. There must have been an outhouse, too, but my mind never recorded it. [17]

The sweet scent of vanilla met us as she opened the door. [18]

"I made tea cookies this morning. You see, I had planned to invite you for cookies and lemonade so we could have this little chat. The lemonade is in the icebox." [19]

It followed that Mrs. Flowers would have ice on an ordinary day, when most families in our town bought ice late on Saturdays only a few times during the summer to be used in the wooden ice-cream freezers. [20]

She took the bags from me and disappeared through the kitchen door. I looked around the room that I had never in my wildest fantasies imagined I would see. Browned photographs leered or threatened from the walls and the white, freshly done curtains pushed against themselves and against the wind. I wanted to gobble up the room entire and take it to Bailey, who would help me analyze and enjoy it. [21]

"Have a seat, Marguerite. Over there by the table." She carried a platter covered with a tea towel. Although she warned that she hadn't tried her hand at baking sweets for some time, I was certain that like everything else about her the cookies would be perfect. [22]

They were flat round wafers, slightly browned on the edges and butter-yellow in the center. With the cold lemonade they were sufficient for childhood's lifelong diet. Remembering my manners, I took nice little lady-like bites off the edges. She said she had made them expressly for me and that she had a few in the kitchen that I could take home to my brother. So I jammed one whole cake in my mouth and the rough crumbs scratched the insides of my jaws, and if I hadn't had to swallow, it would have been a dream come true. [23]

As I ate she began the first of what we later called "my lessons in living." She said that I must always be intolerant of ignorance but understanding of illiteracy. That some people, unable to go to school, were more educated and even more intelligent than college professors. She encouraged me to listen carefully to what [24]

---

4. infuse: to fill or penetrate

country people called mother wit. That in those homely sayings was couched the collective[5] wisdom of generations.

When I finished the cookies she brushed off the table and brought a thick, small book from the bookcase. I had read *A Tale of Two Cities* and found it up to my standards as a romantic novel. She opened the first page and I heard poetry for the first time in my life. **25**

"It was the best of times and the worst of times . . ." Her voice slid in and curved down through and over the words. She was nearly singing. I wanted to look at the pages. Were they the same that I had read? Or were there notes, music, lined on the pages, as in a hymn book? Her sounds began cascading[6] gently. I knew from listening to a thousand preachers that she was nearing the end of her reading, and I hadn't really heard, heard to understand, a single word. **26**

"How do you like that?" **27**

It occurred to me that she expected a response. The sweet vanilla flavor was still on my tongue and her reading was a wonder in my ears. I had to speak. **28**

I said, "Yes ma'am." It was the least I could do, but it was the most also. **29**

"There's one more thing. Take this book of poems and memorize one for me. Next time you pay me a visit, I want you to recite." **30**

I have tried often to search behind the sophistication of years for the enchantment I so easily found in those gifts. The essence escapes but its aura[7] remains. To be allowed, no, invited, into the private lives of strangers, and to share their joys and fears, was a chance to exchange the Southern bitter wormwood[8] for . . . a hot cup of tea and milk with Oliver Twist.[9] **31**

I was liked, and what a difference it made. I was respected not as Mrs. Henderson's grandchild or Bailey's sister but for just being Marguerite Johnson. **32**

Childhood's logic never asks to be proved (all conclusions are absolute). I didn't question why Mrs. Flowers had singled me out for attention, nor did it occur to me that Momma might have asked her to give me a little talking to. All I cared about was that she had made tea cookies for *me* and read to *me* from her favorite book. It was enough to prove that she liked me. **33**

Discussion and Writing Questions

1. Angelou vividly describes Mrs. Flowers' appearance and style (paragraphs 2–5). What kind of woman is Mrs. Flowers? What words and details convey this impression?

2. What strategies does Mrs. Flowers use to reach out to Marguerite?

3. What does Marguerite's first "lesson in living" include (paragraph 24)? Do you think such a lesson could really help a young person live better or differently?

4. In paragraph 31, the author speaks of her enchantment at receiving gifts from Mrs. Flowers. Just what gifts did Mrs. Flowers give her? Which do you consider the most important gift?

Writing Assignments

1. Has anyone ever thrown you a life line when you were in trouble? Describe the problem or hurt facing you and just what this person did to reach out. What "gifts" did he or she offer you (attention, advice, and so forth)? Were you able to receive them?

---

5. collective: gathered from a group
6. cascading: falling like a waterfall
7. aura: a special quality or air around something or someone
8. wormwood: something harsh or embittering
9. Oliver Twist: a character from a novel by Charles Dickens

If you prefer, write about a time when you helped someone else. What seemed to be weighing this person down? How were you able to help?

2. Mrs. Flowers read aloud so musically that Marguerite "heard poetry for the first time in [her] life." Has someone ever shared a love—of a sport, gardening, or history, for example—so strongly that you were changed? What happened and how were you changed?

3. Many people have trouble speaking up—in class, at social gatherings, even to one other person. Can you express your thoughts and feelings as freely as you would like in most situations? What opens you up, and what shuts you up?

Beauty Is Not Just Smaller Than Life

LEONARD PITTS JR.

America's standard of female beauty, writes Leonard Pitts Jr., is now that "svelte look common to heroin addicts and supermodels." In this *Miami Herald* column, he examines this obsession and its consequences. For insightful commentary on American society, Pitts won the Pulitzer Prize in 2004.

"I wish I had a convenient theory for when and why womanly curves became a bad thing."

It may be the ultimate weight loss plan: no diet, no exercise, no surgery, no pills. Just a little digital wizardry. Point and click here, point and click there, and unwanted pounds melt magically away—from your photographed image, that is. 1

This is what the British edition of *GQ* magazine recently did, altering photographs of actress Kate Winslet—without her knowledge or permission, she says—to give her that svelte[1] look common to heroin addicts and supermodels. Winslet has responded angrily. "This is me," she says. "Like it or lump it. . . . I'm not a twig, and I refuse to be one. I'm happy with the way I am." 2

Let the church say amen. 3

Winslet, it should be pointed out, is not what we delicately describe as a "plus-sized woman." She's just a woman with womanly curves, some of which she displayed quite openly in her star-making turn as Rose in *Titanic*. 4

I wish I had a convenient theory for when and why womanly curves became a bad thing, wish I could explain our fascination with a kind of woman who does not, as a rule, exist in nature: stick legs, sunken cheeks, waist in to here, chest out to there. 5

It was not always thus. I mean, by those standards, sex symbols of an earlier era would never have heard the first wolf whistle. Marilyn Monroe was not, after all, a bean pole. And that famous pinup of Betty Grable,[2] which, we are told, inspired the GIs to go out and win World War II, did not show a woman who had missed many meals. 6

By contrast, a 1997 *Psychology Today* article reported on a researcher who had quantified[3] the fact that *Playboy* centerfolds and Miss America contestants—purported[4] icons[5] of feminine physical perfection—had been getting skinnier over the years. 7

Our perception of beauty has changed. And if you're wondering why that matters, it's because our girls are watching. Watching and learning from all this how it is they should be. Much of what they have learned has proven dangerous if not deadly to body and spirit. 8

---

1. svelte: slender
2. Betty Grable: a popular American movie star of the 1930s–1950s
3. quantified: put in numerical form
4. purported: supposed
5. icons: symbols

Fashion week in São Paolo, Brazil, where two anorexic models died in 2006. Whereas the average American woman wears a size 13, the average model wears a 2.

AP Images.

Approximately 5 million to 10 million women and girls (and 1 million boys and men) suffer from eating disorders—primarily anorexia and bulimia—which are sometimes fatal. That same *Psychology Today* recounted the results of a body image survey of 4,000 women and men. Almost 90 percent of the women wanted to lose weight. 9

Score one for pop culture. I mean, one of its primary functions is to make us dissatisfied with what we are, make us want what it is selling. Right now, it's selling the canard[6] that the average supermodel's body is achievable or even desirable for the average girl. And girls are getting sick, even dying, as a result. 10

There are those feminists who would argue that the solution is for men to stop objectifying[7] women, but their reasoning flies in the face of human nature. If somebody hadn't objectified somebody else, none of us would be here to argue about it. And anyone who doesn't think women fantasize about a masculine ideal has never seen a soap opera or romance novel. 11

I'm not out to stop—as if I could!—the endless mating dance of male and female. I'd just like to see something done to protect our girls and women from its more insidious[8] effects. Just like to see the gatekeepers of media become more conscientious about depicting the beauty of women and girls in all its dimensions. 12

Not just breasts, but brains, heart, humor, compassion, love. 13

It is a pipe dream, yes. So I guess those of us who care about such things will have to be satisfied with concentrating on those girls closest to us—our daughters, our nieces, our sisters and friends—and exhorting[9] them to value themselves for *all* the things they are. 14

I tell my adolescent daughter that there's going to come a day when someone will seek to evaluate her by the same cold, meat-market standards by which *GQ* evaluated Kate Winslet. I hope, when that day comes, she has enough love for herself to respond as Winslet did. 15

"This is me. Like it or lump it." 16

For the record, Kate: Like it. Like it a lot. 17

Discussion and Writing Questions

1. Pitts opens his essay by telling how the magazine *GQ* digitally altered photographs of Kate Winslet. Why do you think he starts this way? Is it an effective introduction?

---

6. canard: a false or misleading story
7. objectifying: regarding as an object
8. insidious: harmful in a hidden or sneaky way
9. exhorting: urging

2. In paragraphs 5–8, Pitts discusses America's changing ideal of female beauty from womanly curves to "stick legs and sunken cheeks." What examples of this shift does he give? Can you think of other examples?

3. What solution does Pitts propose to protect girls and women from the media's obsession with thinness (paragraphs 14–15)? Do you think this strategy will be effective? What else can be done to make young women value themselves for more than their physical appearance?

4. Do you agree that one of the main functions of pop culture is to "make us dissatisfied with what we are" (paragraph 10)? Why would this be so?

Writing Assignments

1. Have you or someone you know ever tried to achieve our society's beauty ideal, even got plastic surgery or developed an eating disorder? Tell the story of your own or someone else's quest for the perfect body.

2. Most of the world's societies actually prefer curvy or even plump women to skinny women. It is the Western world that celebrates the "svelte look common to heroin addicts and supermodels" (paragraph 2). Do you think that the majority's attitude is preferable to that of the Western world? Why?

3. Some photographers and editors alter photographs to manipulate the viewers' perceptions or "improve the shot." In your opinion, is this a problem? When does it become a problem? For examples, including the *GQ* Winslet cover, visit <http://www.frankwbaker.com/isbmag.htm> and <http://www.frankwbaker.com/isbnews.htm>.

Hot Dogs and Wild Geese

Firoozeh Dumas

More than 31 million people who live in the United States were born in other countries, and most of them did not speak English very well—or at all—when they first came here. As Iranian-born writer Firoozeh Dumas illustrates with her family's story, learning English is not only confusing but often downright hilarious. This essay appears in her recent book, *Funny in Farsi*.

Moving to America was both exciting and frightening, but we found great comfort in knowing that my father spoke English. Having spent years regaling[1] us with stories about his graduate years in America, he had left us with the distinct impression that America was his second home. My mother and I planned to stick close to him, letting him guide us through the exotic American landscape that he knew so well. We counted on him not only to translate the language but also to translate the culture, to be a link to this most foreign of lands. He was to be our own private Rosetta stone.[2]

Once we reached America, we wondered whether perhaps my father had confused his life in America with someone else's. Judging from the bewildered looks of store cashiers, gas station attendants, and waiters, my father spoke a version of English not yet shared with the rest of America. His attempts to find a "vater closet"[3] in a department store would usually lead us to the drinking fountain or the home

---

1. regaling: entertaining
2. Rosetta stone: carved stone tablet, the key to translating ancient Egyptian writing
3. "vater closet": *water closet*, the British term for *bathroom*

furnishings section. Asking my father to ask the waitress the definition of "sloppy Joe" or "Tater Tots" was no problem. His translations, however, were highly suspect. Waitresses would spend several minutes responding to my father's questions, and these responses, in turn, would be translated as "She doesn't know." Thanks to my father's translations, we stayed away from hot dogs, catfish, and hush puppies, and no amount of caviar[4] in the sea would have convinced us to try mud pie.

We wondered how my father had managed to spend several years attending school in America yet remain so utterly befuddled[5] by Americans. We soon discovered that his college years had been spent mainly in the library, where he had managed to avoid contact with all Americans except his engineering professors. As long as the conversation was limited to vectors,[6] surface tension, and fluid mechanics, my father was Fred Astaire[7] with words. But one step outside the scintillating[8] world of petroleum engineering and he had two left tongues.

My father's only other regular contact in college had been his roommate, a Pakistani who spent his days preparing curry. Since neither spoke English but both liked curries, they got along splendidly. The person who had assigned them together had probably hoped they would either learn English or invent a common language for the occasion. Neither happened.

My father's inability to understand spoken English was matched only by his efforts to deny the problem. His constant attempts at communicating with Americans seemed at first noble and adventurous, then annoying. Somewhere between his thick Persian accent and his use of vocabulary found in pre–World War II British textbooks, my father spoke a private language. That nobody understood him hurt his pride, so what he lacked in speaking ability, he made up for by reading. He was the only person who actually read each and every document before he signed it. Buying a washing machine from Sears might take the average American thirty minutes, but by the time my father had finished reading the warranties, terms of contracts, and credit information, the store was closing and the janitor was asking us to please step aside so he could finish mopping the floor.

> *"After searching fruitlessly for elbow grease, I asked the salesclerk for help."*

My mother's approach to learning English consisted of daily lessons with Monty Hall and Bob Barker.[9] Her devotion to *Let's Make a Deal* and *The Price Is Right*[10] was evident in her newfound ability to recite useless information. After a few months of television viewing, she could correctly tell us whether a coffeemaker cost more or less than $19.99. How many boxes of Hamburger Helper, Swanson's TV dinners, or Turtle Wax could one buy without spending a penny more than twenty dollars? She knew that, too. Strolling down the grocery aisle, she rejoiced in her celebrity sightings—Lipton tea! Campbell's tomato soup! Betty Crocker Rich & Creamy Frosting! Every day, she would tell us the day's wins and losses on the game shows. "He almost won the boat, but the wife picked curtain number two and they ended up with a six-foot chicken statue." The bad prizes on *Let's Make a Deal* sounded far more intriguing than the good ones. Who would want the matching La-Z-Boy recliners when they could have the adult-size crib and high-chair set?

My mother soon decided that the easiest way for her to communicate with Americans was to use me as an interpreter. My brother Farshid, with his schedule full of soccer, wrestling, and karate, was too busy to be recruited for this dubious[11] honor.

---

4. caviar: fancy fish eggs
5. befuddled: confused
6. vectors: mathematical quantities
7. Fred Astaire: American dancer and film star of the 1930s, 1940s, and 1950s
8. scintillating: sparkling, brilliant
9. Monty Hall and Bob Barker: early television game show hosts
10. *Let's Make a Deal* and *The Price Is Right*: television game shows of the 1960s and 1970s
11. dubious: doubtful, questionable

At an age when most parents are guiding their kids toward independence, my mother was hanging on to me for dear life. I had to accompany her to the grocery store, the hairdresser, the doctor, and every place else that a kid wouldn't want to go. My reward for doing this was the constant praise of every American we encountered. Hearing a seven-year-old translate Persian into English and vice versa made quite an impression on everyone. People lavished[12] compliments on me. "You must be very, very smart, a genius maybe." I always responded by assuring them that if they ever moved to another country, they, too, would learn the language. (What I wanted to say was that I wished I could be at home watching *The Brady Bunch*[13] instead of translating the qualities of various facial moisturizers.) My mother had her own response to the compliments: "Americans are easily impressed."

8   I always encouraged my mother to learn English, but her talents lay elsewhere. Since she had never learned English in school, she had no idea of its grammar. She would speak entire paragraphs without using any verbs. She referred to everyone and everything as "it," leaving the listener wondering whether she was talking about her husband or the kitchen table. Even if she did speak a sentence more or less correctly, her accent made it incomprehensible. "W" and "th" gave her the most difficulty. As if God were playing a linguistic[14] joke on us, we lived in "Vee-tee-er" (Whittier), we shopped at "Veetvood" (Whitwood) Plaza, I attended "Leff-ingvell" School, and our neighbor was none other than "Valter Villiams."

9   Despite little progress on my mother's part, I continually encouraged her. Rather than teach her English vocabulary and grammar, I eventually decided to teach her entire sentences to repeat. I assumed that once she got used to speaking correctly, I could be removed, like training wheels, and she would continue coasting. I was wrong.

10   Noticing some insects in our house one day, my mother asked me to call the exterminator. I looked up the number, then told my mother to call and say, "We have silverfish in our house." My mother grumbled, dialed the number, and said, "Please come rrright a-vay. Goldfeeesh all over dee house." The exterminator told her he'd be over as soon as he found his fishing pole.

11   A few weeks later, our washing machine broke. A repairman was summoned and the leaky pipe was quickly replaced. My mother wanted to know how to remove the black stain left by the leak. "Y'all are gonna hafta use some elbow grease," he said. I thanked him and paid him and walked with my mother to the hardware store. After searching fruitlessly[15] for elbow grease, I asked the salesclerk for help. "It removes stains," I added. The manager was called.

12   Once the manager finished laughing, he gave us the disappointing explanation. My mother and I walked home empty-handed. That, I later learned, is what Americans call a wild-goose chase.

13   Now that my parents have lived in America for thirty years, their English has improved somewhat, but not as much as one would hope. It's not entirely their fault; English is a confusing language. When my father paid his friend's daughter the compliment of calling her homely, he meant she would be a great housewife. When he complained about horny drivers, he was referring to their tendency to honk. And my parents still don't understand why teenagers want to be cool so they can be hot.

14   I no longer encourage my parents to learn English. I've given up. Instead, I'm grateful for the wave of immigration that has brought Iranian television, newspapers, and supermarkets to America. Now, when my mother wants to ask the grocer whether he has any more eggplants in the back that are a little darker and more firm, because the ones he has out aren't right for *khoresht bademjun*, she can do so in Persian, all by herself. And for that, I say hallelujah, a word that needs no translation.

---

12. lavished: heaped or poured
13. *The Brady Bunch*: an early 1970s television sitcom
14. linguistic: relating to language
15. fruitlessly: without success

Discussion and Writing Questions

1. Why was Dumas so sure that her father would guide the family easily through the mysteries of American life (paragraph 1)? Why was he, in fact, so little help (paragraph 2)? How do you guess that he translated the words *hot dogs, catfish, hush puppies,* and *mud pie* so that his family refused to eat these foods?

2. The author humorously describes the weird skills her mother learned by watching so much American television. What did the mother learn?

3. In paragraph 7, Dumas writes, "At an age when most parents are guiding their kids toward independence, my mother was hanging on to me for dear life." If a child of immigrants must serve as a translator for his or her parents, parent-child roles sometimes can be reversed. Is this a problem?

4. Dumas uses funny examples to show how confusing English can be. If English was not your first language, what words or aspects of American culture especially confused you? What was funniest (or most frustrating)?

Writing Assignments

1. The United States, with its many races and ethnic groups, has been called a "melting pot." In a group with several classmates, decide whether the United States is more like a *melting pot* (where various ingredients melt together into one soup or goo), a *salad* (where different ingredients are tossed together but keep their separate flavors), or a *grocery store shelf* (where many foods in sealed containers do not mix). Write a paper presenting your own ideas.

2. Have you ever found yourself in a place where you did not understand the "rules"? This place might be a new country, a new school, a new job, or the dinner table of your future in-laws. Describe the challenges you faced in this strange new world and tell how you dealt with them. Use humor if you wish.

3. Does your town have ethnic shops, markets, restaurants, or neighborhoods that you have never explored? Choose one place that you would like to learn more about and visit there, chat with people, and perhaps have something to eat. Take notes on the sights, sounds, smells, and details; then write a vivid account of your adventure.

A musician enjoys Miami's annual Calle Ocho festival, named after a street in the heart of Little Havana.

Tony Arruza/CORBIS.

My English

Julia Alvarez

When her family moved to the United States from the Dominican Republic, ten-year-old Julia Alvarez was uprooted from both her homeland and her native language, Spanish. In this essay, she discusses her childhood struggle to make English her own. Today, Alvarez is a gifted writer of poetry, fiction, and nonfiction—in English.

Mami and Papi used to speak it when they had a secret they wanted to keep from us children. We lived then in the Dominican Republic, and the family as a whole spoke only Spanish at home, until my sisters and I started attending the Carol Morgan School, and we became a bilingual family. Spanish had its many tongues as well. There was the castellano[1] of Padre Joaquín from Spain, whose lisp[2] we all loved to imitate. Then the educated español my parents' families spoke, aunts and uncles who were always correcting us children, for we spent most of the day with the maids and so had picked up their "bad Spanish." Campesinas,[3] they spoke a lilting,[4] animated campuno,[5] ss swallowed, endings chopped off, funny turns of phrases. 1

Besides all these versions of Spanish, every once in a while another strange tongue emerged from my papi's mouth or my mami's lips. What I first recognized was not a language, but a tone of voice, serious, urgent, something important and top secret being said, some uncle in trouble, someone divorcing, someone dead. *Say it in English so the children won't understand.* I would listen, straining to understand, thinking that this was not a different language but just another and harder version of Spanish. *Say it in English so the children won't understand.* From the beginning, English was the sound of worry and secrets, the sound of being left out. 2

Soon, I began to learn more English, at the Carol Morgan School. That is, when I had stopped gawking. The teacher and some of the American children had the strangest coloration: light hair, light eyes, light skin, as if Ursulina had soaked them in bleach too long, to' deteñio.[6] I did have some blond cousins, but they had deeply tanned skin, and as they grew older, their hair darkened, so their earlier paleness seemed a phase of their acquiring normal color. Just as strange was the little girl in my reader who had a *cat* and a *dog*, that looked just like un gatito y un perrito.[7] Her mami was *Mother* and her papi *Father*. Why have a whole new language for school and for books with a teacher who could speak it teaching you double the amount of words you really needed? 3

Butter, butter, butter, butter. All day, one English word that had particularly struck me would go round and round in my mouth and weave through all the Spanish in my head until by the end of the day, the word did sound like just another Spanish word. And so I would say, "Mami, please pass la mantequilla."[8] She would scowl and say in English, "I'm sorry, I don't understand. But would you be needing some butter on your bread?" 4

Why my parents didn't first educate us in our native language by enrolling us in a Dominican school, I don't know. Part of it was that Mami's family had a tradition of 5

> "See you later, alligator. *How wonderful to call someone an alligator and not be scolded for being disrespectful.*"

1. *castellano:* Castilian, the formal Spanish of Spain
2. lisp: a speech flaw (in English) in which the sounds "s" and "z" are pronounced *th*
3. *Campesinas:* peasants (Spanish)
4. lilting: lively and cheerful
5. *campuno:* Spanish with a peasant's accent, rural accent
6. to' deteñio: all faded, discolored
7. *un gatito y un perrito:* a kitten and a small dog (Spanish)
8. *mantequilla:* butter (Spanish)

sending the boys to the States to boarding school and college, and she had been one of the first girls to be allowed to join her brothers. At Abbot Academy, whose school song was our lullaby as babies ("Although Columbus and Cabot never heard of Abbot, it's quite the place for you and me"), she had become quite Americanized. It was very important, she kept saying, that we learn our English. She always used the possessive pronoun: *your* English, an inheritance we had come into and must wisely use. Unfortunately, my English became all mixed up with our Spanish.

Mix-up, or what's now called Spanglish, was the language we spoke for several years. There wasn't a sentence that wasn't colonized[9] by an English word. At school, a Spanish word would suddenly slide into my English like someone butting into line. Teacher, whose face I was learning to read as minutely[10] as my mother's, would scowl, but no smile played on her lips. Her pale skin made her strange countenance[11] hard to read, so that I often misjudged how much I could get away with. Whenever I made a mistake, Teacher would shake her head slowly, "In English, YU-LEE-AH, there's no such word as *columpio*. Do you mean a *swing*?"

I would bow my head, humiliated by the smiles and snickers of the American children around me. I grew insecure about Spanish. My native tongue was not quite as good as English, as if words like *columpio* were illegal immigrants trying to cross a border into another language. But Teacher's discerning[12] grammar-and-vocabulary-patrol ears could tell and send them back.

Soon I was talking up an English storm. "Did you eat an English parrot?" my grandfather asked one Sunday. I had just enlisted yet one more patient servant to listen to my rendition of "Peter Piper picked a peck of pickled peppers" at break-neck pace. "Huh?" I asked impolitely in English, putting him in his place. *Cat got your tongue? No big deal! So there! Take that! Holy Toledo!* (Our teacher's favorite "curse word.") *Go jump in the lake! Really dumb. Golly. Gosh.* Slang, clichés, sayings, hot-shot language that our teacher called, ponderously,[13] idiomatic[14] expressions. Riddles, jokes, puns,[15] conundrums.[16] *What is yellow and goes click-click? Why did the chicken cross the road? See you later, alligator.* How wonderful to call someone an alligator and not be scolded for being disrespectful. In fact, they were supposed to say back, *In a while, crocodile.*

When we arrived in New York, I was shocked. A country where everyone spoke English! These people must be smarter, I thought. Maids, waiters, taxi drivers, doormen, bums on the street, all spoke this difficult language. It took some time before I understood that Americans were not necessarily a smarter, superior race. It was as natural for them to learn their mother tongue as it was for a little Dominican baby to learn Spanish. It came with "mother's milk," my mother explained, and for a while I thought a mother tongue was a mother tongue because you got it from your mother's breast, along with proteins and vitamins.

But at the foot of those towering New York skyscrapers, I began to understand more and more—not less and less—English. In sixth grade, I had one of the first in a lucky line of great English teachers who began to nurture in me a love of language, a love that had been there since my childhood of listening closely to words. Sister Maria Generosa did not make our class interminably[17] diagram sentences

9. colonized: inhabited by settlers from elsewhere
10. minutely: carefully, in great detail
11. countenance: facial expression
12. discerning: perceptive
13. ponderously: heavily, awkwardly
14. idiomatic: peculiar to a particular language
15. puns: plays on words
16. conundrums: riddles or problems with no clear solution
17. interminably: endlessly

from a workbook or learn a catechism[18] of grammar rules. Instead, she asked us to write little stories imagining we were snowflakes, birds, pianos, a stone in the pavement, a star in the sky. What would it feel like to be a flower with roots in the ground? If the clouds could talk, what would they say? She had an expressive, dreamy look that was accentuated by the wimple[19] that framed her face.

Supposing, just supposing . . . My mind would take off, soaring into possibilities, a flower with roots, a star in the sky, a cloud full of sad, sad tears, a piano crying out each time its back was tapped, music only to our ears. 11

Sister Maria stood at the chalkboard. Her chalk was always snapping in two because she wrote with such energy, her whole habit shaking with the swing of her arm, her hand tap-tap-tapping on the board. "Here's a simple sentence: 'The snow fell.'" Sister pointed with her chalk, her eyebrows lifted, her wimple poked up. Sometimes I could see wisps of gray hair that strayed from under her headdress. "But watch what happens if we put an adverb at the beginning and a prepositional phrase at the end: 'Gently, the snow fell on the bare hills.'" 12

I thought about the snow. I saw how it might fall on the hills, tapping lightly on the bare branches of trees. Softly, it would fall on the cold, bare fields. On toys children had left out in the yard, and on cars and on little birds and on people out late walking on the streets. Sister Marie filled the chalkboard with snowy print, on and on, handling and shaping and moving the language, scribbling all over the board until English, those verbal gadgets, those tricks and turns of phrases, those little fixed units and counters, became a charged, fluid mass that carried me in its great fluent waves, rolling and moving onward, to deposit me on the shores of my new homeland. I was no longer a foreigner with no ground to stand on. I had landed in the English language. 13

Discussion and Writing Questions

1. What was the author's first childhood experience of the English language (paragraphs 1 and 2)? How did her perceptions change over time as she learned more English and moved to the United States?

2. Alvarez describes several different versions of Spanish. Do you speak more than one version of English? Describe any ways in which your language changes, depending on the situation or the people you are with. For example, do you speak differently with your friends at home than you do in a college class?

3. Why does the author believe that Sister Maria Generosa was a great English teacher (paragraph 10)? Do you agree with her opinion? Have you ever had a teacher who awakened your passion for a subject? What were some of that teacher's special qualities or methods?

4. If your native language is not English, how was your experience of learning English like or unlike that of Julia Alvarez? Alvarez loved certain English words. Did certain English expressions fascinate you, confuse you, or make you laugh?

Writing Assignments

1. Write a paragraph or essay called "My _____" (for example, "My Style," "My Excellent Study Habits," and so on) in which you discuss the process by which you mastered something and made it your own. You might describe how you learned to lose weight, conduct Internet searches, decorate a room, or master a difficult subject.

_____
18. catechism: a group of basic rules or beliefs
19. wimple: stiff cloth that is part of a nun's headwear

2. Do you think it's more (or less) important to be bilingual today than it was in the past? Write a composition in which you argue for (or against) learning a second language in addition to knowing English.

3. Do you (or does a member of your family, living or dead) have an interesting or humorous immigrant story? Tell that story, focusing, perhaps, on the journey to the United States or the months just after arrival. Prewrite to gather your best facts and details, and organize before you write. Consider submitting your work for publication on this website: <http://www.immigrantjourneys.com/>.

The Gift

COURTLAND MILLOY

Help sometimes comes from unexpected places. This newspaper story describes the generosity of a friend whose gift saved someone's life—and baffled most people who knew him. As you read, ask yourself how you would have acted in his place.

When Jermaine Washington entered the barbershop, heads turned and clippers fell silent. Customers waved and nodded, out of sheer respect. With his hands in the pockets of his knee-length, black leather coat, Washington acknowledged them with a faint smile and quietly took a seat. ¹

"You know who that is?" barber Anthony Clyburn asked in a tone reserved for the most awesome neighborhood characters, such as ball players and ex-cons. ²

A year and a half ago, Washington did something that still amazes those who know him. He became a kidney donor, giving a vital organ to a woman he described as "just a friend." ³

"They had a platonic¹ relationship," said Clyburn, who works at Jake's Barber Shop in Northeast Washington. "I could see maybe giving one to my mother, but just a girl I know? I don't think so." ⁴

Washington, who is 25, met Michelle Stevens six years ago when they worked for the D.C. Department of Employment Services. They used to have lunch together in the department cafeteria and chitchat on the telephone during their breaks. ⁵

"It was nothing serious, romance-wise," said Stevens, who is 23. "He was somebody I could talk to. I had been on the kidney donor waiting list for 12 months and I had lost all hope. One day, I just called to cry on his shoulder." ⁶

Stevens told Washington how depressing it was to spend three days a week, three hours a day, on a kidney dialysis machine.² She said she suffered from chronic fatigue and blackouts and was losing her balance and her sight. He could already see that she had lost her smile. ⁷

"I saw my friend dying before my eyes," Washington recalled. "What was I supposed to do? Sit back and watch her die?" ⁸

Stevens's mother was found to be suffering from hypertension³ and was ineligible to donate a kidney. Her 14-year-old sister offered to become a donor, but doctors concluded that she was too young. ⁹

Stevens's two brothers, 25 and 31, would most likely have made ideal donors because of their relatively young ages and status as family members. But both of them said no. ¹⁰

So did Stevens's boyfriend, who gave her two diamond rings with his apology. ¹¹

"'I had been on the kidney donor waiting list for 12 months and I had lost all hope. One day, I just called to cry on his shoulder.'"

---

1. platonic: nonromantic
2. kidney dialysis machine: a machine that filters waste material from the blood when the kidneys fail
3. hypertension: high blood pressure

"I understood," Stevens said. "They said they loved me very much, but they were just too afraid."   12

Joyce Washington, Jermaine's mother, was not exactly in favor of the idea, either. But after being convinced that her son was not being coerced,[4] she supported his decision.   13

The transplant operation took four hours. It occurred in April 1991, and began with a painful X-ray procedure in which doctors inserted a metal rod into Washington's kidney and shot it with red dye. An incision nearly 20 inches long was made from his groin to the back of his shoulder. After the surgery he remained hospitalized for five days.   14

Today, both Stevens and Washington are fully recovered. Stevens, a graduate of Eastern High School, is studying medicine at the National Educational Center. Washington still works for D.C. Employment Services as a job counselor.   15

"I jog and work out with weights," Washington said. "Boxing and football are out, but I never played those anyway."   16

A spokesman for Washington Hospital Center said the Washington-to-Stevens gift was the hospital's first "friend-to-friend" transplant. Usually, it's wife to husband, or parent to child. But there is a shortage of even those kinds of transplants. Today, more than 300 patients are in need of kidneys in the Washington area.   17

"A woman came up to me in a movie line not long ago and hugged me," Washington said. "She thanked me for doing what I did because no one had come forth when her daughter needed a kidney, and the child died."   18

About twice a month, Stevens and Washington get together for what they call a gratitude lunch. Since the operation, she has broken up with her boyfriend. Seven months ago, Washington got a girlfriend. Despite occasional pressure by friends, a romantic relationship is not what they want.   19

"We are thankful for the beautiful relationship that we have," Stevens said. "We don't want to mess up a good thing."   20

To this day, people wonder why Washington did it. To some of the men gathered at Jake's Barber Shop not long ago, Washington's heroics were cause for questions about his sanity. Surely he could not have been in his right mind, they said.   21

One customer asked Washington where he had found the courage to give away a kidney. His answer quelled[5] most skeptics[6] and inspired even more awe.   22

"I prayed for it," Washington replied. "I asked God for guidance and that's what I got."   23

Discussion and Writing Questions

1. A year and a half after Jermaine Washington donated a kidney to Michelle Stevens, his friends are still amazed by what he did. Why do they find his action so surprising?

2. Washington says, "What was I supposed to do? Sit back and watch her die?" (paragraph 8). Yet Stevens's brothers and her boyfriend did not offer to donate a kidney. Do you blame them? Do you understand them?

3. In what ways has Stevens's life changed because of Washington's gift? Consider her physical status, her social life, her choice of profession, her "gratitude lunches" with Washington, and so on.

4. According to Washington, where did he find the courage to donate a kidney? How did his action affect his standing in the community? How did it affect other aspects of his life?

---

4. coerced: pressured
5. quelled: quieted
6. skeptics: people who doubt or question

Writing Assignments

α 1. Have you ever been unusually generous—or do you know someone who was? Describe that act of generosity. Why did you—or the other person—do it? How did your friends or family react?

Bien

2. Do you have or does anyone you know have a serious medical condition? Describe the situation. How do or how can friends help? Can strangers help in any way?

3. Stevens and Washington do not have or want a romantic relationship. "We don't want to mess up a good thing," Stevens says (paragraph 20). Does romance "mess things up"? Write about a time when a relationship changed—either for better or for worse—because romance entered the picture.

Montgomery, Alabama, 1955

Rosa Parks

A refusal to give up her seat in a segregated bus pushed Rosa Parks into the spotlight of the civil rights movement. In this excerpt from *Rosa Parks: My Story*, the Medal of Freedom winner tells what really happened.

"The only tired I was, was tired of giving in."

When I got off from work that evening of December 1, I went to Court Square as usual to catch the Cleveland Avenue bus home.[1] I didn't look to see who was driving when I got on, and by the time I recognized him, I had already paid my fare. It was the same driver who had put me off the bus back in 1943, twelve years earlier. He was still tall and heavy, with red, rough-looking skin. And he was still mean-looking. I didn't know if he had been on that route before—they switched the drivers around sometimes. I do know that most of the time if I saw him on a bus, I wouldn't get on it. 1

I saw a vacant seat in the middle section of the bus and took it. I didn't even question why there was a vacant seat even though there were quite a few people standing in the back. If I had thought about it at all, I would probably have figured maybe someone saw me get on and did not take the seat but left it vacant for me. There was a man sitting next to the window and two women across the aisle. 2

The next stop was the Empire Theater, and some whites got on. They filled up the white seats, and one man was left standing. The driver looked back and noticed the man standing. Then he looked back at us. He said, "Let me have those front seats," because they were the front seats of the black section. Didn't anybody move. We just sat right where we were, the four of us. Then he spoke a second time: "Y'all better make it light on yourselves and let me have those seats." 3

The man in the window seat next to me stood up, and I moved to let him pass by me, and then I looked across the aisle and saw that the two women were also standing. I moved over to the window seat. I could not see how standing up was going to "make it light" for me. The more we gave in and complied,[2] the worse they treated us. 4

I thought back to the time when I used to sit up all night and didn't sleep and my grandfather would have his gun right by the fireplace, or if he had his one-horse wagon going anywhere, he always had his gun in the back of the wagon. People always say that I didn't give up my seat because I was tired, but that isn't true. I was not tired physically, or no more tired than I usually was at the end of a 5

---

1. home: Parks lived in Montgomery, the capital of Alabama, when racial segregation was legal.
2. complied: acted in accordance with the rules

working day. I was not old, although some people have an image of me as being old then. I was forty-two. No, the only tired I was, was tired of giving in.

The driver of the bus saw me still sitting there, and he asked was I going to stand up. I said, "No." He said, "Well, I'm going to have you arrested." Then I said, "You may do that." These were the only words we said to each other. I didn't even know his name, which was James Blake, until we were in court together. He got out of the bus and stayed outside for a few minutes, waiting for the police.   6

As I sat there, I tried not to think about what might happen. I knew that any-thing was possible. I could be manhandled or beaten. I could be arrested. People have asked me if it occurred to me then that I could be the test case the NAACP[3] had been looking for. I did not think about that at all. In fact, if I had let myself think too deeply about what might happen to me, I might have gotten off the bus. But I chose to remain.   7

Discussion and Writing Questions

1. How had Parks been treated on buses before this particular bus incident? How had she reacted before?

2. What does the bus driver mean by "make it light on yourselves" (paragraph 3)? What does Parks think about her seatmates' decision to stand up?

3. Paragraph 5 describes the actual moment of deliberation when Parks is decid-ing whether to stand up. What determined her decision? What factors were not important?

4. Why does the author conclude, "In fact if I had let myself think too deeply about what might happen to me, I might have gotten off the bus" (paragraph 7)? Parks takes full responsibility for her action, however. What two words indicate that?

Writing Assignments

1. Have you known someone who protested an injustice? What were the circum-stances? Describe the circumstances, along with your reaction. Then discuss how your view of the event has changed (or not changed) over time.

2. Parks maintains that the public's understanding of her motivation (she was old and tired) is simply not true. She thus draws attention to the difference be-tween how others may see us and how we see ourselves. Have you ever acted in a specific way, only to have others describe your actions differently? Write about your experience.

3. Do you have a complaint about college life? In a letter to your school newspa-per, try to imitate Parks's low-key style as you describe the problem and sug-gest a solution.

Quitting Hip-Hop

MICHAELA ANGELA DAVIS

Hip-hop music is "the talking drum of our time," declares Michaela angela Davis in this article for *Essence* magazine. She wonders, however, whether too many hip-hop artists are beating out the wrong kinds of messages. In this article, Davis shares her personal struggle with this question.

---

3. NAACP: National Association for the Advancement of Colored People

I am a 40-year-old fly girl.[1] My 13-year-old daughter, Elenni, and I often look for the same next hot thing—that perfect pair of jeans, a she's-gotta-have-it shoe, the ultimate handbag, and the freshest new sound in music, which is, more often than not, hip-hop. Though we are nearly three decades apart in age, we both feel that hip-hop is the talking drum of our time; it teaches us and represents us. But, just as some of our African ancestors sold their people to European slave traders for a few used guns and porcelain plates, it seems as if the images of women of color in much of today's hip-hop music have been sold off to a greedy industry for a few buckets of "ice"[2] and a stack of "cheese."[3]

Recently while watching a new video in which yet another half-dressed girl gyrated[4] and bounced, Elenni turned to me and asked, "Why can't that girl just have on a cute pair of jeans with a halter top? Why does she always have to have on booty shorts? And why can't she just dance instead of grinding on the hood of a car? What does that have to do with the song?" I had no easy answers. Although the images of the women were both demeaning and predictable, the beats were undeniably hot. Therein lies the paradox[5] at the heart of my beef with hip-hop: songs that make you bounce can carry a message far and wide, irrespective of what that message is. And far too often the message is that most young women of color are "bitches" or "hoes." I was backed into a corner, forced to choose between my love for hip-hop and my need to be respected and to pass the ideals of self-respect on to my daughter. No contest.

Look, I'm no finger-wagging conservative outsider. I was one of the founding editors of *Vibe*, the first national magazine dedicated to hip-hop music, style, and culture, so it's really hard for me to hate. I also worked as a fashion stylist, helping to create looks for everyone from LL Cool J to Mary J. Later I landed at *Honey*, a magazine for young urban women, and eventually became its editor-in-chief. I wouldn't have had my career if it weren't for hip-hop culture. And that goes for lots of black folks. In addition to its music, hip-hop has journalism, film, fashion, and other lucrative[6] by-products that have employed and empowered hundreds, if not thousands, of us. So clearly I'm not one of those out-of-touch mothers who won't listen to current music or who espouse[7] corny clichés like "In my day, we knew what real music was."

Today is my day, too. And the danger with what's currently going on in hip-hop is not as simple as a mere generation gap. Increasingly, the male-dominated industry tends to view women as moneymakers (as in the kind you shake). Few of us are in a position to be decision makers. As a result of this imbalance, many popular hip-hop CDs and videos feature a brand of violence and misogyny[8] that is as lethal as crack and as degrading as apartheid.[9] And though I would love to maintain my "flyest mom ever" status, my daughter's self-esteem and that of every young sister in the world is at risk. I'm willing to risk my public image to help recover theirs. If there's not a shift in how the hip-hop industry portrays women, then our 20-year relationship is officially O-V-E-R.

I've since found creative ways to deal with my daughter's dilemma and my heartbreaking breakup: I ask Elenni why she likes a song, then I suggest alternative artists who might have a similar vibe. We look for videos that feature more progressive acts like Floetry, Jean Grae, and Talib Kweli. We listen to classics such

"I was backed into a corner, forced to choose between my love for hip-hop and my need to be respected."

1. fly girl: slang for a pretty, stylish woman
2. "ice": slang for diamonds
3. "cheese": slang for money
4. gyrated: moved in a spiral
5. paradox: contradiction
6. lucrative: profitable
7. espouse: adopt or follow
8. misogyny: hatred of women
9. apartheid: the official policy of racial discrimination that existed in South Africa before 1994

as Public Enemy and MC Lyte, so she knows that hip-hop does have a positive history. We also participate in other urban-culture activities that affirm and satisfy us, like art exhibits, poetry slams, and yes, shoe shopping.

It's not going to be easy, leaving hip-hop behind. But I can no longer merely take what it dishes out and blame it on the boogie. The cost is just too great. 6

Discussion and Writing Questions

1. What does the author like and respect about hip-hop music? What does she strongly dislike about it? Specifically, what caused the author's "heartbreaking breakup" with hip-hop (paragraph 5)?

2. Do you listen to hip-hop? Do you agree with Davis that much of today's hip-hop is degrading to women and often violent? If so, what effects might this have on young women and young men? Does this message prevent both genders from "dreaming big," as Diane Sawyer urges (page 386)?

3. An effective argument establishes the credibility of both the writer and any experts whose opinions are included. Is this author a credible authority on the subject of hip-hop? Where in the essay does she reveal her credentials?

4. Hip-hop artists in countries like Korea, Senegal, and Brazil don't rap about money and sex, as many American performers do. Instead, they use their music to fight oppression and encourage social justice. Do you think that American hip-hop music would be as popular if it focused on similar subjects?

Writing Assignments

1. What kind of music do you enjoy? What do you like most about this style of music? What does it give you?

2. Michaela angela Davis, like most parents, wants to nurture her child's self-esteem and protect her from the negative messages of pop culture. Choose one gender, describe the risks faced by young men or women today, and describe the best way that parents can nurture and protect them.

3. In paragraph 3, Davis credits hip-hop with providing careers for many black people. How, in your opinion, has hip-hop music and culture *positively* affected America? Use specific examples and details to support your argument.

You Can Take This Job and . . . Well, It Might Surprise You

ANA VECIANA-SUAREZ

If you won a lottery jackpot, what would you do? Buy a house? Take a trip? Quit your job? Not so fast, cautions Ana Veciana-Suarez. According to this *Miami Herald* columnist, there are some very good reasons to keep right on working.

Have you heard about the part-time letter carrier who won the $183 million jackpot in Maryland? She will collect more than $76 million after state and federal taxes, making her one of the largest individual winners in U.S. lottery history. 1

And she bought the ticket on a *whim*.[1] 2

I read about Bernadette Gietka's good fortune just as I was about to begin a grueling[2] workday that consisted of catching up from vacation while juggling 3

---

1. whim: sudden impulse
2. grueling: difficult, exhausting

new assignments. She reminded me of all the other lottery winners I had heard about, lucky people made suddenly wealthy (and confused) by happenstance.[3] There was the California software consultant who had a $7 million winning ticket stuffed in her purse for two months. And one Nebraska couple who ended up buying the jackpot after the wife had had a bad day at work.

As my mother used to say, "*La suerte es loca y a cualquiera le toca.*" Luck is crazy 4
and it can touch anybody. (Believe me, it sounds better in Spanish.)

I'm not much of a player, and gambling, in one form or another, holds little attrac- 5
tion. Life itself, with its tribulations[4] and surprises, is risky enough for me. But belief in steady nose-to-the-grindstone economic growth has never stopped me from day-dreaming. So in a biting moment of anxiety, I schlepped[5] on over to the grocery store to buy a lottery ticket for the next drawing. You never know; you just never know.

Like most people, my friends and I entertain ourselves by coming up with 6
ways to spend money we don't have. (And money we do have.) It is one of those futile[6] exercises that, done right and not too flippantly,[7] can help you focus on priorities, what truly matters to you when money is taken out of the equation.

What would I do with a sudden windfall?[8] Take a trip. Buy a house on the 7
beach. Make sure my family is well taken care of. You know, the usual. I don't know if I would quit my job, however.

You would? Well, don't be so sure. Gietka, for one, plans to continue making 8
her rounds.

We complain about work, curse our bosses, practice Oscar-winning monologues[9] 9
to deliver when we finally walk out of the sweatshop, but most of us would keep punching that time clock. According to a recent Opinion Research Corporation poll, 70 percent of us would go right on working even if the fiscal gods smiled on us. In fact, we're so wedded to our jobs that only 5 percent would go on a vacation and 3 percent would actually splurge on shopping. I think I know why.

For better or for worse, work provides structure, imposes routine. It gives us an 10
identity. How many party conversations, after all, start with: "What do you do for a living?" Work is often social, the place we share stories about spouses and children and each other. Boardroom, factory, or cubicle, it is the prime venue[10] and source of juicy gossip.

But there's something more, too. Though we think we never have enough of it, 11
we also suspect, somewhere in the deep recesses[11] of our conniving,[12] greedy little hearts, that money, lots and lots of it, isn't all that it's cracked up to be. We nod know-ingly when we hear about co-workers who sue each other over lottery winnings. We tsk-tsk when news reports tell us about a couple splitting up over the winning num-bers. And we recognize, if only momentarily, that a weekly paycheck is paradoxi-cally[13] both enslaving and liberating. Just ask your unemployed neighbor.

My mother was right: crazy, fickle luck. It arrives in many guises[14] and some- 12
times in the shape of a pay stub.

"For better or for worse, work provides structure, imposes routine. It gives us an identity."

---

3. happenstance: accident or twist of fate
4. tribulations: troubles
5. schlepped: dragged or moved clumsily
6. futile: useless
7. flippantly: without much thought or care
8. windfall: unexpected good fortune
9. monologues: long speeches made by one person
10. venue: setting
11. recesses: interior spaces
12. conniving: scheming
13. paradoxically: seeming to go against common sense, yet true
14. guises: forms

Discussion and Writing Questions

1. Veciana-Suarez begins this article with three examples of recent lottery winners (paragraphs 1–3). Who are they? Do you think these winners' stories sum up the statement "Luck is crazy and it can touch anybody"?

2. Have you ever dreamed of winning the lottery? What would you do if you won $10 million? Explain why you would—or would not—quit your job.

3. What benefits of working, besides a paycheck, does the author discuss (paragraph 10)? Can you think of other benefits that a job provides? Do all jobs offer such benefits, or do only some jobs?

4. In paragraph 6, Veciana-Suarez says that daydreaming about how to spend lottery winnings "can help you focus on priorities, what truly matters to you when money is taken out of the equation." Is this true? List the three most important things you would do if you won $10 million. Does this list help you understand what truly matters to you?

Writing Assignments

1. The odds of winning a multimillion-dollar lottery are about one in 13.98 million, yet millions of people exchange their hard-earned cash for lottery tickets every week. Discuss the reasons why so many people play when the odds are so much against them. Use examples from your own or a friend's experience.

2. The author writes that "we suspect, somewhere in the deep recesses of our conniving, greedy little hearts, that money, lots and lots of it, isn't all that it's cracked up to be" (paragraph 11). What is more important than money? Write a composition in which you answer this question.

3. Describe three or four of the most important *benefits* of being employed. Draw on your own experiences or the experiences of people you know for examples or stories that support your points.

Papa, the Teacher

LEO BUSCAGLIA

Leo Buscaglia was the youngest of four children of Italian immigrants. In this selection, he describes how a father with only a fifth-grade education taught his children to respect—and even love—learning.

Papa had natural wisdom. He wasn't educated in the formal sense. When he was growing up at the turn of the century in a very small village in rural northern Italy, education was for the rich. Papa was the son of a dirt-poor farmer. He used to tell us that he never remembered a single day of his life when he wasn't working. The concept of doing nothing was never a part of his life. In fact, he couldn't fathom[1] it. How could one do nothing?

He was taken from school when he was in the fifth grade, over the protestations[2] of his teacher and the village priest, both of whom saw him as a young person with great potential for formal learning. Papa went to work in a factory in a nearby village, the very same village where, years later, he met Mama.

———
1. fathom: understand; get to the bottom of
2. protestations: objections

For Papa, the world became his school. He was interested in everything. He read all the books, magazines, and newspapers he could lay his hands on. He loved to gather with people and listen to the town elders and learn about "the world beyond" this tiny, insular[3] region that was home to generations of Buscaglias before him. Papa's great respect for learning and his sense of wonder about the outside world were carried across the sea with him and later passed on to his family. He was determined that none of his children would be denied an education if he could help it.

Papa believed that the greatest sin of which we were capable was to go to bed at night as ignorant as we had been when we awakened that day. The credo[4] was repeated so often that none of us could fail to be affected by it. "There is so much to learn," he'd remind us. "Though we're born stupid, only the stupid remain that way." To ensure that none of his children ever fell into the trap of complacency,[5] he insisted that we learn at least one new thing each day. He felt that there could be no fact too insignificant, that each bit of learning made us more of a person and insured us against boredom and stagnation.

So Papa devised a ritual. Since dinnertime was family time and everyone came to dinner unless they were dying of malaria, it seemed the perfect forum for sharing what new things we had learned that day. Of course, as children we thought this was perfectly crazy. There was no doubt, when we compared such paternal[6] concerns with other children's fathers, Papa was weird.

It would never have occurred to us to deny Papa a request. So when my brother and sisters and I congregated in the bathroom to clean up for dinner, the inevitable question was, "What did *you* learn today?" If the answer was "Nothing," we didn't dare sit at the table without first finding a fact in our much-used encyclopedia. "The population of Nepal is . . . ," etc.

Now, thoroughly clean and armed with our fact for the day, we were ready for dinner. I can still see the table piled high with mountains of food. So large were the mounds of pasta that as a boy I was often unable to see my sister sitting across from me. (The pungent[7] aromas were such that, over a half century later, even in memory they cause me to salivate.)

Dinner was a noisy time of clattering dishes and endless activity. It was also a time to review the activities of the day. Our animated conversations were always conducted in Piedmontese dialect[8] since Mama didn't speak English. The events we recounted, no matter how insignificant, were never taken lightly. Mama and Papa always listened carefully and were ready with some comment, often profound and analytical, always right to the point.

"That was the smart thing to do." "*Stupido*, how could you be so dumb?" "*Cosi sia*,[9] you deserved it." "*E allora*,[10] no one is perfect." "*Testa dura* ('hardhead'), you should have known better. Didn't we teach you anything?" "Oh, that's nice." One dialogue ended and immediately another began. Silent moments were rare at our table.

Then came the grand finale to every meal, the moment we dreaded most—the time to share the day's new learning. The mental imprint of those sessions still runs before me like a familiar film clip, vital and vivid.

"The greatest sin was to go to bed at night as ignorant as we had been when we awakened that day."

3. insular: like an island; isolated
4. credo: a statement of belief
5. complacency: a feeling of satisfaction or smugness
6. paternal: having to do with fathers
7. pungent: sharp, spicy
8. Piedmontese dialect: the language spoken in the Piedmont region of northwestern Italy
9. *Cosi sia:* Italian for "so be it"
10. *E allora:* Italian for "oh, well"

Papa, at the head of the table, would push his chair back slightly, a gesture that signified the end of the eating and suggested that there would be a new activity. He would pour a small glass of red wine, light up a thin, potent Italian cigar, inhale deeply, exhale, then take stock of his family. **11**

For some reason this always had a slightly unsettling effect on us as we stared back at Papa, waiting for him to say something. Every so often he would explain why he did this. He told us that if he didn't take time to look at us, we would soon be grown and he would have missed us. So he'd stare at us, one after the other. **12**

Finally, his attention would settle upon one of us. "*Felice*,"[11] he would say to me, "tell me what you learned today." **13**

"I learned that the population of Nepal is . . ." **14**

Silence. **15**

It always amazed me, and reinforced my belief that Papa was a little crazy, that nothing I ever said was considered too trivial for him. First, he'd think about what was said as if the salvation of the world depended upon it. **16**

"The population of Nepal. Hmmm. Well." **17**

He would then look down the table at Mama, who would be ritualistically fixing her favorite fruit in a bit of leftover wine. "Mama, did you know that?" **18**

Mama's responses were always astonishing and seemed to lighten the otherwise reverential atmosphere. "Nepal," she'd say. "Nepal? Not only don't I know the population of Nepal, I don't know where in God's world it is!" Of course, this was only playing into Papa's hands. **19**

"*Felice*," he'd say. "Get the atlas so we can show Mama where Nepal is." And the search began. The whole family went on a search for Nepal. This same experience was repeated until each family member had a turn. No dinner at our house ever ended without our having been enlightened by at least a half dozen such facts. **20**

As children, we thought very little about these educational wonders and even less about how we were being enriched. We couldn't have cared less. We were too impatient to have dinner end so we could join our less-educated friends in a rip-roaring game of kick the can. **21**

In retrospect, after years of studying how people learn, I realize what a dynamic educational technique Papa was offering us, reinforcing the value of continual learning. Without being aware of it, our family was growing together, sharing experiences, and participating in one another's education. Papa was, without knowing it, giving us an education in the most real sense. **22**

By looking at us, listening to us, hearing us, respecting our opinions, affirming our value, giving us a sense of dignity, he was unquestionably our most influential teacher. **23**

Discussion and Writing Questions

1. What does Buscaglia mean when he says that his father "wasn't educated in the formal sense" (paragraph 1)? In what way *was* his father educated?

2. How did Buscaglia's father and mother react to information that the children reported at dinnertime? How did their reaction affect Buscaglia as a child? As an adult?

3. Years later, Buscaglia realized that his father had offered the family "a dynamic educational technique" (paragraph 22). What does he mean?

4. What point does the author make by using the population of Nepal as an example in paragraph 14? Is it useful to know the population of Nepal? Why or why not?

---

11. *Felice: Felice* is Buscaglia's real first name. The name *Leo* was taken from his middle name, *Leonardo*.

Writing Assignments

1. Describe a typical dinnertime in your family as you were growing up. Was dinnertime a time for sharing? Fighting? Eating alone? What effect did this have on you? If you now live away from your birth family, are dinnertimes different?

2. Discuss your attitude toward education. Who or what shaped your point of view? Has your attitude changed since childhood? Why is education important?

3. Did *you* learn anything new today? If so, describe what you learned. If not, what got in the way of your learning?

Another Road Hog with Too Much Oink

DAVE BARRY

Humorist Dave Barry is the author of more than two dozen books, but he admits that not one of them contains useful information. Until 2005, his Pulitzer-Prize–winning humor column appeared in over 500 newspapers. In his spare time, Barry is a candidate for President of the United States. If elected, he promises to seek the death penalty for whoever made Americans install low-flow toilets. In the following essay, he takes on America's love of gigantic sport utility vehicles (SUVs).

If there's one thing this nation needs, it's bigger cars. That's why I'm excited that Ford is coming out with a new mound o' metal that will offer consumers even more total road-squatting mass than the current leader in the humongous[1]-car category, the popular Chevrolet Suburban Subdivision—the first passenger automobile designed to be, right off the assembly line, visible from the Moon.

I don't know what the new Ford will be called. Probably something like the "Ford Untamed Wilderness Adventure." In the TV commercials, it will be shown splashing through rivers, charging up rocky mountainsides, swinging on vines, diving off cliffs, racing through the surf, and fighting giant sharks hundreds of feet beneath the ocean surface—all the daredevil things that cars do in Sport Utility Vehicle Commercial World, where nobody ever drives on an actual road. In fact, the interstate highways in Sport Utility Vehicle Commercial World, having been abandoned by humans, are teeming[2] with deer, squirrels, birds, and other wildlife species that have fled from the forest to avoid being run over by nature seekers in multi-ton vehicles barreling through the underbrush at 50 miles per hour.

In the real world, of course, nobody drives sport utility vehicles in the forest, because when you have paid upward of $40,000 for a transportation investment, the last thing you want is squirrels pooping on it. No, if you want a practical "off-road" vehicle, you get yourself a 1973 American Motors Gremlin, which combines the advantage of not being worth worrying about with the advantage of being so ugly that poisonous snakes flee from it in terror.

In the real world, what people mainly do with their sport utility vehicles, as far as I can tell, is try to maneuver[3] them into and out of parking spaces. I base this statement on my local supermarket, where many of the upscale patrons drive Chevrolet Subdivisions. I've noticed that these people often purchase just a couple of items—maybe a bottle of diet water and a two-ounce package of low-fat dried carrot shreds—which they put into the back of their Subdivisions, which

"In the real world, of course, nobody drives a sport utility vehicle in the forest, because the last thing you want is squirrels pooping on it."

1. humongous: huge
2. teeming: filled
3. maneuver: move skillfully

*"We're not certain why they disappeared, but archeologists speculate
that it may have had something to do with their size."*

have approximately the same cargo capacity, in cubic feet, as Finland. This means
there is plenty of room left over back there in case, on the way home, these people
decide to pick up something else, such as a herd of bison.

Then comes the scary part: getting the Subdivision out of the parking space. 5
This is a challenge, because the driver apparently cannot, while sitting in the driver's
seat, see all the way to either end of the vehicle. I drive a compact car, and on a
number of occasions I have found myself trapped behind a Subdivision backing
directly toward me, its massive metal butt looming[4] high over my head, making
me feel like a Tokyo pedestrian looking up at Godzilla.[5]

I've tried honking my horn, but the Subdivision drivers can't hear me, because 6
they're always talking on cellular phones the size of Chiclets ("The Bigger Your
Car, the Smaller Your Phone," that is their motto). I don't know who they're talking to. Maybe they're negotiating with their bison suppliers. Or maybe they're
trying to contact somebody in the same area code as the rear ends of their cars, so
they can find out what's going on back there. All I know is, I'm thinking of carrying marine flares, so I can fire them into the air as a warning to Subdivision drivers that they're about to run me over. Although frankly I'm not sure they'd care if
they did. A big reason why they bought a sport utility vehicle is "safety," in the
sense of, "you, personally, will be safe, although every now and then you may
have to clean the remains of other motorists out of your wheel wells."

Anyway, now we have the new Ford, which will be *even larger* than the Subdi- 7
vision, which I imagine means it will have separate decks for the various classes
of passengers, and possibly, way up in front by the hood ornament, Leonardo
DiCaprio showing Kate Winslet[6] how to fly. I can't wait until one of these babies
wheels into my supermarket parking lot. Other motorists and pedestrians will try
to flee in terror, but they'll be sucked in by the Ford's powerful gravitational field
and become stuck to its massive sides like so many refrigerator magnets. They

---

4. looming: appearing to be huge and towering
5. Godzilla: a fictional monster that menaced cities in Japanese films
6. Leonardo DiCaprio, Kate Winslet: stars of the film *Titanic*

won't be noticed, however, by the Ford's driver, who will be busy whacking at the side of his or her head, trying to dislodge[7] his or her new cell phone, which is the size of a single grain of rice and has fallen deep into his or her ear canal.

And it will not stop there. This is America, darn it, and Chevrolet is not about to just sit by and watch Ford walk away with the coveted title of Least Sane Motor Vehicle. No, cars will keep getting bigger: I see a time, not too far from now, when upscale suburbanites will haul their overdue movies back to the video-rental store in full-size, 18-wheel tractor-trailers with names like The Vagabond.[8] It will be a proud time for all Americans, a time for us to cheer for our country. We should cheer loud, because we'll be hard to hear, inside the wheel wells.

Discussion and Writing Questions

1. What is Barry's point of view about huge sport utility vehicles (paragraph 1)? What lines tell you this? Barry often exaggerates to get a laugh and to make a point. Can you point to examples of this technique?

2. What passages or details in the essay do you find particularly funny? Look for experiences to which you relate, vivid word use, exaggerations, or lines that create humorous mental pictures.

3. In paragraph 6, Barry says that safety is a big reason why people claim to buy SUVs. Do you agree with their reasoning? What are some other reasons why so many Americans choose to drive giant vehicles?

4. Barry ends his essay with a prediction that American vehicles will get even bigger (paragraph 8). What does he predict will soon happen? Although the essay is humorous, it makes a serious point. Does the last line underscore this point?

Writing Assignments

1. Fill in the blank in this sentence: "If there's one thing this nation needs, it's _Bigger cars_" Then take a stand, perhaps humorous, as Barry has, about something else Americans crave: fancy cell phones, brand-name clothing, even plastic surgery. Or try a serious approach, arguing for more youth centers, "hybrid" automobiles, or some other goal.

2. Write a response to Dave Barry's criticisms of SUVs and their owners. Defend these vehicles by giving reasons why people *should* drive them. Take a humorous or serious approach, as you wish.

3. Barry suggests that we Americans like our possessions big. What are some other things, besides vehicles, that we continue to super-size? What do you think this trend reveals about Americans?

Stuff

RICHARD RODRIGUEZ

Do you—like many Americans—own a lot of stuff? Do the things you buy bring brief or lasting pleasure? San Francisco writer Richard Rodriguez wonders whether our relationship to material possessions sets us up for disappointment. Rodriguez is an editor at the *Pacific News* service; he has authored three books and numerous essays and articles.

---

7. dislodge: remove something stuck
8. vagabond: a wandering person

I come often to this huge building to do much of my shopping. It's called Costco. There are warehouse stores like this all over the country where you can buy most anything you need and you buy it in bulk, cheap.

A revolution is going on in American shopping habits. Two generations ago Americans went to their corner store where everyone knew the name of the man behind the counter and where toward the end of the month our grandmothers would ask to charge the milk and the bread. And then the suburbs created the supermarket with its Muzak[1] and its wide aisles and its 20 varieties of breakfast cereal. Now we don't go to the corner drugstore. Nor do we shop at a small nursery run by the lady who knows all about roses. We shop at places with names like Drug Barn and Plant World and Shoe Universe.

Every choice is available to us, and the prices are low, but no one knows your name and there is no Muzak. It's wonderful coming here to Costco. The well-to-do shop here along with immigrant families. Everyone's basket is full. You don't get a bottle of mineral water; you buy a case. You don't get a roll of toilet paper; you get a gigantic package that will last most families several months. You can buy tires at Costco, as well as Pampers and bananas. So people buy and buy and buy. And, yet, despite all the buying there is something oddly unmaterialistic about shopping in places plain as a warehouse.

We Americans often criticize ourselves for being materialistic. In fact, we take little pleasure in things, preferring to fill our lives with stuff. Only rarely do we dare a materialism that delights in the sensuality of the material world. In the 1950s, for example, we gave the world wonderful, wide-bodied cars with lots of chrome and fins like angels—the rare American instance of the materialism of the senses. We leave it, normally, to other cultures to teach us about materialism.

I remember years ago in London a friend of mine urging me to go into Fortnum and Mason's, the fancy food store, go in and buy just one piece of chocolate, he said, and think about that chocolate all day, and when you eat it tonight, eat it slowly, very slowly.

Americans don't eat slowly. We taught the world how to eat on the run, and we treasure food, convenience food, that doesn't take much thinking about, which is why in the end we don't have very much to say about the smell of a piece of chocolate.

To this day I remember the weight and the smells of the first books I ever owned. I can still remember the texture of paper in the first novel I ever got from the library. Now we can order our books on the Internet without first holding them in our hands or fingering the paper. Now Americans watch TV and order jewelry or dolls or whatever on the 24-hour shopping channels. People buy from catalogs without first trying the sweater on and testing its color against their skin.

There are no windows at Costco.

In an earlier, more sweetly materialistic America, our parents used to window shop. People would stop on a busy street, peer at the mannequins in the shop windows. Here in San Francisco there are still downtown department stores where one can see elaborate window displays, but who has the time to window shop?

Despite the many dollars we spend, I think we are less materialistic now than at any time in our history. We are not much interested in the shape of an orange or the weight of a book, or the dark scent of a chocolate. We buy appliances off a rack, and we throw them away when they no longer work. Nothing gets repaired in America. Nothing we own grows old. We buy in bulk. We are surrounded by choices. There is little we desire. We end up surrounded by stuff and regret. We take the huge bag of chocolates home, and we end up eating too many.

"We end up surrounded by stuff and regret."

---

1. Muzak: the name for easy-listening or "elevator" music played in retail stores and other companies

Discussion and Writing Questions

1. Why does Rodriguez begin his essay with the example about shopping at Costco? How do stores like Costco help prove his point about Americans and material things?

2. Do you agree with Rodriguez that other cultures can teach Americans about healthy materialism? What example does he provide as evidence? Can you think of other examples?

3. In your opinion, is it good or bad to be surrounded by too many choices? What are the advantages of having many choices? What are the advantages of having few choices?

4. In his famous poem "The World Is Too Much with Us," English poet William Wordsworth wrote that "getting and spending, we lay waste our powers." In other words, we squander our energy on making money and spending it. Do you agree? If so, what might humans be able to accomplish if we weren't spending so much time and effort on working and buying?

Writing Assignments

1. Describe a time when you immersed yourself in and truly savored a specific sensual experience—a moonlit swim, a delicious meal, a slow stroll down your favorite street, or the like. Describe this experience, including details about what you saw, smelled, tasted, touched, and heard.

2. Which of your possessions are crucial to your happiness? What things do you own now that you could live without? What possessions do you lack that you believe will make you happier?

3. In 1993, photographer Peter Menzel asked "statistically average" families in different countries to pose in front of their houses with every possession they owned. In a group with four of five classmates, carefully observe and discuss two of these families and their "stuff." From each family's home, location, and possessions, can you make any guesses about its values, daily life, or priorities? Is each family like or different from families you know?

A family from Bhutan and all its possessions.

© Peter Menzel/ www.menzelphoto.com.

A Japanese family and all its possessions.

© Peter Menzel/
www.menzelphoto.com.

In This Arranged
Marriage, Love Came Later

SHOBA NARAYAN

Although arranged marriages are common in many parts of the world, most Americans believe that the best marriages start with falling in love. In this essay, an American-educated journalist from India discusses her decision to let her family find her a husband.

We sat around the dining table, my family and I, replete[1] from yet another home-cooked South Indian dinner. It was my younger brother, Shaam, who asked the question. 1

"Shoba, why don't you stay back here for a few months? So we can try to get you married." 2

Three pairs of eyes stared at me across the expanse of the table. I sighed. Here I was, at the tail end of my vacation after graduate school. I had an airplane ticket to New York from Madras, India, in ten days. I had accepted a job at an artists' colony in Johnson, Vermont. My car, and most of my possessions, were with friends in Memphis. 3

"It's not that simple," I said. "What about my car . . . ?" 4

"We could find you someone in America," my dad replied. "You could go back to the States." 5

They had thought it all out. This was a plot. I glared at my parents accusingly. 6

Oh, another part of me rationalized, why not give this arranged-marriage thing a shot? It wasn't as if I had a lot to go back to in the States. Besides, I could always get a divorce. 7

Stupid and dangerous as it seems in retrospect,[2] I went into my marriage at twenty-five without being in love. Three years later, I find myself relishing my relationship with this brilliant, prickly man who talks about the yield curve and 8

---

1. replete: filled to satisfaction
2. in retrospect: looking back

derivatives,[3] who prays when I drive, and who tries valiantly to remember names like Giacometti, Munch, Kandinsky.[4]

My enthusiasm for arranged marriages is that of a recent convert. True, I grew up in India, where arranged marriages are common. My parents' marriage was arranged, as were those of my aunts, cousins, and friends. But I always thought I was different. I blossomed as a foreign fellow in Mount Holyoke College where individualism was expected and feminism encouraged. As I experimented with being an American, I bought into the American value system. [9]

I was determined to fall in love and marry someone who was not Indian. Yet, somehow, I could never manage to. Oh, falling in love was easy. Sustaining it was the hard part. [10]

Arranged marriages in India begin with matching the horoscopes of the man and the woman. Astrologers look for balance . . . so that the woman's strengths balance the man's weaknesses and vice versa. Once the horoscopes match, the two families meet and decide whether they are compatible. It is assumed that they are of the same religion, caste,[5] and social stratum.[6] [11]

While this eliminates risk and promotes homogeneity,[7] the rationale is that the personalities of the couple provide enough differences for a marriage to thrive. Whether or not this is true, the high statistical success rate of arranged marriages in different cultures—90 percent in Iran, 95 percent in India, and a similar high percentage among Hasidic Jews in Brooklyn, and among Turkish and Afghan Muslims—gives one pause. [12]

Although our families met through a mutual friend, many Indian families meet through advertisements placed in national newspapers. [13]

My parents made a formal visit to my future husband's house to see whether Ram's family would treat me well. My mother insists that "you can tell a lot about the family just from the way they serve coffee." The house had a lovely flower garden. The family liked gardening. Good. [14]

Ram's mother had worked for the United Nations on women's-rights issues. She also wrote humorous columns for Indian magazines. She would be supportive. She served strong South Indian coffee in the traditional stainless steel tumblers instead of china; she would be a balancing influence on my youthful radicalism. [15]

Ram's father had supported his wife's career even though he belonged to a generation of Indian men who expected their wives to stay home. Ram had a good role model. His sister was a pediatrician in Fort Myers. Perhaps that meant he was used to strong, achieving women. [16]

November 20, 1992. Someone shouted, "They're here!" My cousin Sheela gently nudged me out of the bedroom into the living room. [17]

"Why don't you sit down?" a voice said. [18]

I looked up and saw a square face and smiling eyes anxious to put me at ease. He pointed me to a chair. Somehow I liked that. The guy was sensitive and self-confident. [19]

He looked all right. Could stand to lose a few pounds. I liked the way his lips curved to meet his eyes. Curly hair, commanding voice, unrestrained laugh. To my surprise, the conversation flowed easily. We had a great deal in common, but his profession was very different from mine. He had an MBA from the University of Michigan and had worked on Wall Street before joining a financial consulting firm. [20]

Two hours later, Ram said, "I'd like to get to know you better. Unfortunately, I have to be back at my job in Connecticut, but I could call you every other day. No strings attached, and both of us can decide where this goes, if anywhere." [21]

"Stupid and dangerous as it seems in retrospect, I went into my marriage at twenty-five without being in love."

3. yield curve and derivatives: technical terms from finance
4. Giacometti, Munch, Kandinsky: great twentieth-century artists
5. caste: one of four social classes in India
6. stratum: level
7. homogeneity: sameness, similarity

I didn't dislike him. 22

He called ten days later. We talked about our goals, dreams, and anxieties. 23

"What do you want out of life?" he asked me one day. "Come up with five 24 words, maybe, of what you want to do with your life." His question intrigued me. "Courage, wisdom, change," I said, flippantly.[8] "What about you?"

"Curiosity, contribution, balance, family, and fun," he said. In spite of myself, I 25 was impressed.

One month later, he proposed and I accepted. Our extended honeymoon in 26 Connecticut was wonderful. On weekends, we took trips to Mount Holyoke, where I showed him my old art studio, and to Franconia Notch in New Hampshire, where we hiked and camped.

It was in Taos, New Mexico, that we had our first fight. Ram had arranged for a 27 surprise visit to the children's summer camp where I used to work as a counselor. We visited my old colleagues with their Greenpeace T-shirts and New Age commune mentality. Ram, with his clipped accent, neatly pressed clothes, and pleasant manners, was so different. What was I doing with this guy? On the car trip to the airport, I was silent. "I think, perhaps, we might have made a mistake," I said slowly. The air changed.

"Your friends may be idealistic, but they are escaping their lives, as are you," 28 he said. "We are married. Accept it. Grow up!"

He had never spoken to me this harshly before, and it hurt. I didn't talk to him 29 during the entire trip back to New York.

That fight set the pattern of our lives for the next several months. In the 30 evening, when Ram came home, I would ignore him or blame him for bringing me to Connecticut.

Two years into our marriage, something happened. I was ashamed to realize 31 that while I had treated Ram with veiled dislike, he had always tried to improve our relationship. I was admitted to the journalism program at Columbia, where, at Ram's insistence, I had applied.

Falling in love, for me, began with small changes. I found myself relishing a 32 South Indian dish that I disliked, mostly because I knew how much he loved it. I realized that the first thing I wanted to do when I heard some good news was to share it with him. Somewhere along the way, the "I love you, too" that I had politely parroted[9] in response to his endearments had become sincere.

My friends are appalled[10] that I let my parents decide my life partner; yet, the 33 older they get, the more intrigued they are. I am convinced that our successful relationship has to do with two words: tolerance and trust. In a country that emphasizes individual choice, arranged marriages require a familial web for them to work. For many Americans, that web doesn't exist.

As my friend Karen said, "How can I get my parents to pick out my spouse 34 when they don't even talk to each other?"

Discussion and Writing Questions

1. Why did the author agree to an arranged marriage?

2. What factors did her family consider as they matched her with a husband? Which of these factors do you think are important predictors of success in marriage? Which, if any, seem unimportant?

3. How did Shoba Narayan know, after two years, that she was falling in love? If you have ever fallen in love, how was your experience similar or different?

4. What might be the disadvantages, or even risks, of an arranged marriage?

---

8. flippantly: lightly, thoughtlessly
9. parroted: repeated mindlessly
10. appalled: shocked

Writing Assignments

1. Soon after they met, Ram asked Shoba what words she would choose to express what she wanted in life. She said, "Courage, wisdom, change." Ram chose "curiosity, contribution, balance, family, and fun." What three to five words would you select in answer to Ram's question? Choose your words carefully; then explain why each one is important to you.

2. Marriage in the United States usually occurs after two people "fall in love." Of course, more than 50 percent of marriages in this country end in divorce. Discuss three reasons why marriage that is based on first falling in love is or is not a good idea.

3. Would you consider letting your relatives pick your marriage partner? Take a stand, presenting the two or three most important reasons why you would or would not consider such a move.

Playing a Violin with Three Strings

JACK RIEMER

When Jack Riemer attended a concert by the famous violinist Itzhak Perlman, he and the rest of the audience felt lucky just to hear one of Perlman's dazzling musical performances. But then the unexpected happened. In this article for the *Houston Chronicle*, Riemer tells the story.

"We could hear it snap—it went off like gunfire across the room. There was no mistaking what that sound meant."

On November 18, 1995, Itzhak Perlman, the violinist, came on stage to give a concert at Avery Fisher Hall at Lincoln Center in New York City. Anyone who has ever been to a Perlman concert knows that getting on stage is no small achievement for him. 1

He was stricken with polio[1] as a child, and so he has braces on both legs and walks with the aid of two crutches. To see him walk across the stage one step at a time, painfully and slowly, is an unforgettable sight. He walks painfully, yet majestically,[2] until he reaches his chair. Then he sits down, slowly, puts his crutches on the floor, undoes the clasps on his legs, tucks one foot back, and extends the other foot forward. Then he bends down and picks up the violin, puts it under his chin, nods to the conductor, and proceeds to play. 2

By now, audience members are used to this ritual. They sit quietly while he makes his way across the stage to his chair. They remain reverently[3] silent while he undoes the clasps on his legs. They wait until he is ready to play. 3

But this time, something went wrong. Just as he finished the first few bars, one of the strings on his violin broke. We could hear it snap—it went off like gunfire across the room. There was no mistaking what that sound meant. There was no mistaking what he had to do. People who were there that night thought to themselves: "We figured that he would have to get up, put on the clasps again, pick up the crutches, and limp his way off stage—to either find another violin or else find another string for this one." 4

But he didn't. Instead, he waited a moment, closed his eyes, and then he played with such passion and such power and such purity as we had never heard before. Of course, anyone knows that it is impossible to play a symphonic[4] work with just 5

---

1. polio: a viral disease that disabled or killed many people until a polio vaccine was created in 1955
2. majestically: with greatness and dignity
3. reverently: with feelings of awe and respect
4. symphonic: meant for a large musical orchestra

three strings. I know that, and you know that, but that night Itzhak Perlman refused to know that. We could see him modulating,[5] changing, recomposing the piece in his head. At one point, it sounded like he was de-tuning the strings to get new sounds from them that they had never made before.

When he finished, there was an awesome silence in the room. And then people rose and cheered. There was an extraordinary outburst of applause from every corner of the auditorium. We were all on our feet, screaming and cheering, doing everything we could to show how much we appreciated what he had done.

He smiled, wiped the sweat from his brow, raised his bow to quiet us, and then he said, not boastfully, but in a quiet, pensive,[6] reverent tone, "You know, sometimes it is the artist's task to find out how much music he can still make with what he has left."

What a powerful line that is. It has stayed in my mind ever since I heard it. And who knows? Perhaps that is the definition of life—not just for artists but for all of us. Perhaps our task in this shaky, fast-changing, bewildering world in which we live is to make music, at first with all that we have, and then, when that is no longer possible, to make music with what we have left.

Discussion and Writing Questions

1. The first three paragraphs vividly describe Perlman as he walks onto the stage, sits, and prepares to play. What words or details especially capture the process? Why do you think the author devotes so many words to this description?

2. Why do you think the author compares the violin string's snapping to "gunfire" (paragraph 4)? What do the concertgoers expect to happen next? Why are they so amazed when instead Perlman improvises—when he changes the music in his head to fit his new situation?

3. Can you draw any conclusions about Perlman's personality or character from the description of his physical appearance, actions, and words? What does this man seem to believe is important?

4. In paragraph 8, what do you think Riemer means when he writes that perhaps Perlman's words apply to all of us—that our task "is to make music, at first with all that we have, and then, when that is no longer possible, to make music with what we have left"? Does this relate to you or to anyone you know?

Writing Assignments

1. Sometimes things that go wrong can lead us down new—and better—paths. Itzhak Perlman, for example, gave one of his most amazing performances after a violin string broke. Write about someone who has turned a loss, an illness, or a disability into a strength.

2. Discuss a memorable musical concert or performance that you attended—any kind of music, any number of performers. Think of an opening that will capture your readers' attention, perhaps describing in detail, as Riemer does, how the performer(s) came onstage. Then try to capture in words what made the performance so unforgettable.

3. Write about a time when you (or someone else) had to improvise under pressure. Think of a situation that did not go as you had planned—during work, college, or leisure time. What happened, and what did you do in response? Would you behave differently today?

---

5. modulating: adjusting or adapting
6. pensive: deeply thoughtful

One Man's Kids

DANIEL MEIER

A first-grade teacher describes his workday and reflects on his career—a career that crosses traditional gender boundaries. Daniel Meier raises questions for all of us to consider.

I teach first graders. I live in a world of skinned knees, double-knotted shoelaces, riddles that I've heard a dozen times, stale birthday cakes, hurt feelings, wandering stories, and one lost shoe ("and if you don't find it my mother'll kill me"). My work is dominated by six-year-olds. [1]

It's 10:45, the middle of snack, and I'm helping Emily open her milk carton. She has already tried the other end without success, and now there's so much paint and ink on the carton from her fingers that I'm not sure she should drink it at all. But I open it. Then I turn to help Scott clean up some milk he has just spilled onto Rebecca's whale crossword puzzle. [2]

While I wipe my milk- and paint-covered hands, Jenny wants to know if I've seen that funny book about penguins that I read in class. As I hunt for it in a messy pile of books, Jason wants to know if there is a new seating arrangement for lunch tables. I find the book, turn to answer Jason, then face Maya, who is fast approaching with a new knock-knock joke. After what seems like the tenth "Who's there?" I laugh and Maya is pleased. [3]

Then Andrew wants to know how to spell "flukes"[1] for his crossword. As I get to "u," I give a hand signal for Sarah to take away the snack. But just as Sarah is almost out the door, two children complain that "we haven't even had ours yet." I stop the snack mid-flight, complying with their request for graham crackers. I then return to Andrew, noticing that he has put "flu" for 9 Down, rather than 9 Across. It's now 10:50. [4]

My work is not traditional male work. It's not a singular[2] pursuit. There is not a large pile of paper to get through or one deal to transact. I don't have one area of expertise or knowledge. I don't have the singular power over language of a lawyer, the physical force of a construction worker, the command over fellow workers of a surgeon, the wheeling and dealing transactions of a businessman. My energy is not spent in pursuing, climbing, achieving, conquering, or cornering some goal or object. [5]

My energy is spent in encouraging, supporting, consoling, and praising my children. In teaching, the inner rewards come from without. On any given day, quite apart from teaching reading and spelling, I bandage a cut, dry a tear, erase a frown, tape a torn doll, and locate a long-lost boot. The day is really won through matters of the heart. As my students groan, laugh, shudder, cry, exult,[3] and wonder, I do too. I have to be soft around the edges. [6]

A few years ago, when I was interviewing for an elementary-school teaching position, every principal told me with confidence that, as a male, I had an advantage over female applicants because of the lack of male teachers. But in the next breath, they asked with a hint of suspicion why I chose to work with young children. I told them that I wanted to observe and contribute to the intellectual growth of a maturing mind. What I really felt like saying, but didn't, was that I loved helping a child learn to write her name for the first time, finding someone a new friend, or sharing in the hilarity of reading about Winnie the Pooh getting so stuck in a hole that only his head and rear show. [7]

---

1. flukes: the two divided ends of a whale's tail; also, strokes of luck or random accidents
2. singular: related to one thing; also, exceptional
3. exult: rejoice

I gave that answer to those principals, who were mostly male, because I thought they wanted a "male" response. This meant talking about intellectual matters. If I had taken a different course and talked about my interest in helping children in their emotional development, it would have been seen as closer to a "female" answer. I even altered my language, not once mentioning the word "love" to describe what I do indeed love about teaching. My answer worked; every principal nodded approvingly. 8

Some of the principals also asked what I saw myself doing later in my career. They wanted to know if I eventually wanted to go into educational administration. Becoming a dean of students or a principal has never been one of my goals, but they seemed to expect me, as a male, to want to climb higher on the career stepladder. So I mentioned that, at some point, I would be interested in working with teachers as a curriculum coordinator. Again, they nodded approvingly. 9

If those principals had been female instead of male, I wonder whether their questions, and my answers, would have been different. My guess is that they would have been. 10

At other times, when I'm at a party or a dinner and tell someone that I teach young children, I've found that men and women respond differently. Most men ask about the subjects I teach and the courses I took in my training. Then, unless they bring up an issue such as merit pay, the conversation stops. Most women, on the other hand, begin the conversation on a more immediate and personal level. They say things like "those kids must love having a male teacher" or "that age is just wonderful, you must love it." Then, more often than not, they'll talk about their own kids or ask me specific questions about what I do. We're then off and talking shop. 11

Possibly, men would have more to say to me, and I to them, if my job had more of the trappings and benefits of more traditional male jobs. But my job has no bonuses or promotions. No complimentary box seats at the ball park. No cab fare home. No drinking buddies after work. No briefcase. No suit. (Ties get stuck in paint jars.) No power lunches. (I eat peanut butter and jelly, chips, milk, and cookies with the kids.) No taking clients out for cocktails. The only place I take my kids is to the playground. 12

Although I could have pursued a career in law or business, as several of my friends did, I chose teaching instead. My job has benefits all its own. I'm able to bake cookies without getting them stuck together as they cool, buy cheap sewing materials, take out splinters, and search just the right trash cans for useful odds and ends. I'm sometimes called "Daddy" and even "Mommy" by my students, and if there's ever a lull in the conversation at a dinner party, I can always ask those assembled if they've heard the latest riddle about why the turkey crossed the road. (He thought he was a chicken.) 13

Discussion and Writing Questions

1. What, besides reading, writing, and 'rithmetic, is Meier teaching his first graders?

2. Why do so few men teach in elementary schools? What reasons does the author seem to offer?

3. Meier confesses that during job interviews he "even altered [his] language" (paragraph 8). What does he mean? Why did he do that?

4. In paragraph 11, the author observes that outside of school "men and women respond differently" to him. In what ways? How does Meier account for the differences?

Writing Assignments

1. Write a letter to the school principal nominating Meier for Teacher of the Year, or nominate a teacher from your own school history. In either case, discuss what you think makes a good teacher.

2. Do you have any experience in a nontraditional role—perhaps in a club, on a team, or on a job? What prompted you to cross traditional boundaries? How did the experience differ from your expectations? Write about your experience. Conclude with a reflection on how the experience changed, or didn't change, your views on traditional roles.

3. Meier suggests that work, to be rewarding, must provide benefits other than status and salary. Agree or disagree, using examples from your own experience.

The Hidden Life of Bottled Water

LIZA GROSS

Consumers buy more bottled water than ever, believing that they are satisfying their thirst with something healthy. In fact, they might be better off just turning on the tap, according to this writer for *Sierra*, a magazine devoted to conservation and the environment.

Americans used to turn on their faucets when they craved a drink of clear, cool water. Today, concerned about the safety of water supplies, they're turning to the bottle. Consumers spent more than $4 billion on bottled water last year, establishing the fount[1] of all life as a certifiably hot commodity. But is bottled really better?

You might think a mountain stream on the label offers some clue to the contents. But sometimes, to paraphrase Freud, a bottle is just a bottle. "Mountain water could be anything," warns Connie Crawley, a health and nutrition specialist at the University of Georgia. "Unless the label says it comes from a specific source, when the manufacturer says 'bottled at the source,' the source could be the tap."

Yosemite brand water comes not from a bucolic[2] mountain spring but from deep wells in the undeniably less picturesque Los Angeles suburbs, and Everest sells water drawn from a municipal source in Corpus Christi, Texas—a far cry from the pristine[3] glacial peaks suggested by its name. As long as producers meet the FDA's[4] standards for "distilled" or "purified" water, they don't have to disclose the source.

Even if the water does come from a spring, what's in that portable potable[5] may be *less* safe than what comes out of your tap. Bottled water must meet the same safety standards as municipal-system water. But while the EPA[6] mandates daily monitoring of public drinking water for many chemical contaminants, the FDA requires less comprehensive testing only once a year for bottled water. Beyond that, says Crawley, the FDA "usually inspects only if there's a complaint. Yet sources of bottled water are just as vulnerable to surface contamination as sources of tap water. If the spring is near a cattle farm, it's going to be contaminated."

Let's assume your store-bought water meets all the safety standards. What about the bottle? Because containers that sit for weeks or months at room temperature are ideal breeding grounds for bacteria, a bottle that met federal safety standards when it left the plant might have unsafe bacteria levels by the time you buy it. And because manufacturers aren't required to put expiration dates on bottles, there's no telling how long they've spent on a loading dock or on store shelves. (Bacteria also thrive on the wet, warm rim of an unrefrigerated bottle, so avoid

"Consumers spent more than $4 billion on bottled water last year, but is bottled really better?"

---

1. fount: source
2. bucolic: rural
3. pristine: pure
4. FDA's: Food and Drug Administration's
5. potable: a beverage that is safe to drink
6. EPA: Environmental Protection Agency

letting a bottle sit around for too long.) But even more troubling is what may be leaching[7] from the plastic containers. Scientists at the FDA found traces of bisphenol A—an endocrine[8] disruptor that can alter the reproductive development of animals—after 39 weeks in water held at room temperature in large polycarbonate containers (like that carboy[9] atop your office water cooler).

Wherever you get your water, *caveat emptor*[10] should be the watchword. If   6 you're simply worried about chlorine or can't abide its taste, fill an uncapped container with tap water and leave it in the refrigerator overnight; most of the chlorine will vaporize. If you know your municipal water is contaminated, bottled water can provide a safe alternative. But shop around. The National Sanitation Foundation (NSF) independently tests bottled water and certifies producers that meet FDA regulations and pass unannounced plant, source, and container inspections. And opt for glass bottles—they don't impart the taste and risks of chemical agents and they aren't made from petrochemicals.[11]

To get information on bottled-water standards—or to find out what's in the   7 water you buy—contact the Food and Drug Administration, (888) INFO-FDA, <http://www.fda.gov/>. For information on your tap water, called the EPA's Safe Drinking Water Hotline, (800) 426-4791, <http://www.epa.gov/safewater>.

Discussion and Writing Questions

1. Why might tap water be safer than bottled water?

2. Even if bottled water meets all safety standards, what other problems can affect its quality?

3. According to the author, how can consumers ensure that the bottled water they buy is, in fact, safe spring water?

4. What is the author suggesting about the American public and bottled water? What is she trying to accomplish by writing this article? Does she succeed?

Writing Assignments

1. Check a campus location that sells bottled water (vending machine, cafeteria, campus store). Which brand of bottled water is sold? Contact the Food and Drug Administration (see Gross's last paragraph) to find out what information the federal government has collected on that brand. Is it spring water? tap water from another location? safe to drink? What ingredients does it contain? Have any problems been associated with it? Report your findings in a letter to the campus newspaper.

2. Study the contents label of one of your favorite snacks. What are the ingredients? Consult a dictionary to "translate" those ingredients. Does your appetite diminish as a result? Describe the snack, including what you thought its ingredients were and what the ingredients really are. Conclude with a recommendation for other consumers.

3. Gross suggests that perhaps the public has been fooled by the bottled-water industry. What other products do people buy without really needing them? Find an ad for one such product and describe how it works—how it creates a need where there is none. Attach the ad to your description.

---

7. leaching: dissolving, draining away
8. endocrine: hormonal
9. carboy: oversized bottle
10. *caveat emptor*: a warning in Latin meaning "buyer beware"
11. petrochemicals: compounds derived from petroleum or natural gas

Four Directions

AMY TAN

Have you ever possessed a certain skill or strength, and then, as you grew, lost it? Amy Tan, a Chinese-American novelist who lives in San Francisco, writes about a young chess player who seemed unbeatable—at age ten.

I was ten years old. Even though I was young, I knew my ability to play chess was a gift. It was effortless, so easy. I could see things on the chessboard that other people could not. I could create barriers to protect myself that were invisible to my opponents. And this gift gave me supreme confidence. I knew at exactly what point their faces would fall when my seemingly simple and childlike strategy would reveal itself as a devastating and irrevocable[1] course. I loved to win.

And my mother loved to show me off, like one of my many trophies she polished. She used to discuss my games as if she had devised the strategies.

"I told my daughter, 'Use your horses to run over the enemy,'" she informed one shopkeeper. "She won very quickly this way." And of course, she had said this before the game—that and a hundred other useless things that had nothing to do with my winning.

To our family friends who visited she would confide, "You don't have to be so smart to win chess. It is just tricks. You blow from the North, South, East, and West. The other person becomes confused. They don't know which way to run."

I hated the way she tried to take all the credit. And one day I told her so, shouting at her on Stockton Street, in the middle of a crowd of people. I told her she didn't know anything, so she shouldn't show off. She should shut up. Words to that effect.

That evening and the next day she wouldn't speak to me. She would say stiff words to my father and brothers, as if I had become invisible and she was talking about a rotten fish she had thrown away but which had left behind its bad smell.

I knew this strategy, the sneaky way to get someone to pounce back in anger and fall into a trap. So I ignored her. I refused to speak and waited for her to come to me.

After many days had gone by in silence, I sat in my room, staring at the sixty-four squares of my chessboard, trying to think of another way. And that's when I decided to quit playing chess.

Of course I didn't mean to quit forever. At most, just for a few days. And I made a show of it. Instead of practicing in my room every night, as I always did, I marched into the living room and sat down in front of the television with my brothers, who stared at me, an unwelcome intruder. I used my brothers to further my plan; I cracked my knuckles to annoy them.

"Ma!" they shouted. "Make her stop. Make her go away."

But my mother did not say anything.

Still I was not worried. But I could see I would have to make a stronger move. I decided to sacrifice a tournament that was coming up in one week. I would refuse to play in it. And my mother would certainly have to speak to me about this. Because the sponsors and the benevolent associations[2] would start calling her, asking, shouting, pleading to make me play again.

And then the tournament came and went. And she did not come to me, crying, "Why are you not playing chess?" But I was crying inside, because I learned that a boy whom I had easily defeated on two other occasions had won.

"It was as though I had lost my magic armor."

1

2

3

4

5

6

7

8

9

10

11

12

13

---

1. irrevocable: impossible to cancel or halt
2. benevolent associations: charities

I realized my mother knew more tricks than I had thought. But now I was tired 14
of her game. I wanted to start practicing for the next tournament. So I decided to
pretend to let her win. I would be the one to speak first.

"I am ready to play chess again," I announced to her. I had imagined she 15
would smile and then ask me what special thing I wanted to eat.

But instead, she gathered her face into a frown and stared into my eyes, as if 16
she could force some kind of truth out of me.

"Why do you tell me this?" she finally said in sharp tones. "You think it is so 17
easy. One day quit, next day play. Everything for you is this way. So smart, so
easy, so fast."

"I said I'll play," I whined. 18

"No!" she shouted, and I almost jumped out of my scalp. "It is not so easy any- 19
more."

I was quivering, stunned by what she said, in not knowing what she meant. 20
And then I went back to my room. I stared at my chessboard, its sixty-four
squares, to figure out how to undo this terrible mess. And after staring like this for
many hours, I actually believed that I had made the white squares black and the
black squares white, and everything would be all right.

And sure enough, I won her back. That night I developed a high fever, and she 21
sat next to my bed, scolding me for going to school without my sweater. In the
morning she was there as well, feeding me rice porridge flavored with chicken
broth she had strained herself. She said she was feeding me this because I had
the chicken pox and one chicken knew how to fight another. And in the afternoon, she sat in a chair in my room, knitting me a pink sweater while telling me
about a sweater that Auntie Suyuan had knit for her daughter June, and how it
was most unattractive and of the worst yarn. I was so happy that she had become
her usual self.

But after I got well, I discovered that, really, my mother had changed. She no 22
longer hovered over[3] me as I practiced different chess games. She did not polish
my trophies every day. She did not cut out the small newspaper item that mentioned my name. It was as if she had erected[4] an invisible wall and I was secretly
groping each day to see how high and how wide it was.

At my next tournament, while I had done well overall, in the end the points 23
were not enough. I lost. And what was worse, my mother said nothing. She
seemed to walk around with this satisfied look, as if it had happened because she
had devised this strategy.

I was horrified. I spent many hours every day going over in my mind what I 24
had lost. I knew it was not just the last tournament. I examined every move, every
piece, every square. And I could no longer see the secret weapons of each piece,
the magic within the intersection of each square. I could see only my mistakes, my
weaknesses. It was as though I had lost my magic armor. And everybody could
see this, where it was easy to attack me.

Over the next few weeks and later months and years, I continued to play, but 25
never with that same feeling of supreme confidence. I fought hard, with fear and
desperation. When I won, I was grateful, relieved. And when I lost, I was filled
with growing dread, and then terror that I was no longer a prodigy,[5] that I had
lost the gift and had turned into someone quite ordinary.

When I lost twice to the boy whom I had defeated so easily a few years before, 26
I stopped playing chess altogether. And nobody protested. I was fourteen.

---

3. hovered over: paid close attention to
4. erected: built
5. prodigy: a person with enormous talents in a particular area

Discussion and Writing Questions

1. Why did the child and her mother fight? Do you think the mother really wanted "all the credit" for herself (paragraph 5)? Why did she refuse to speak to the child after their argument?

2. The mother and daughter almost seem locked in a chess match of their own after their argument. What do you think is happening between them? Does the daughter's age—adolescence—have anything to do with it?

3. Why do you suppose the narrator says she had lost more than the last tournament, she had lost her "magic armor" (paragraph 24)?

4. The narrator says that "nobody protested" when she gave up chess permanently at age fourteen (paragraph 26). Do you think people might have protested if she were a boy? Why or why not?

Writing Assignments

1. Did you possess a talent or strength as a young person that you later lost? What happened? What caused you to change?

2. Adolescence is for most people a time of enormous change, and change often produces great anxiety. Was there an incident in your adolescence that caused you such anxiety—because you or your surroundings were somehow changing? Describe this incident.

3. Research suggests that once they reach adolescence, many girls give up asserting themselves—in sports, in class, and in student government, for example—because they feel pressure to be "feminine." Do you think this is true? Discuss why or why not, using yourself or a young woman you know as an example.

Emotional Intelligence

Daniel Goleman

How important to a person's success is IQ—that is, his or her score on an intelligence test? According to a widely read recent book, other personality traits and skills are even more important than IQ. The author, Daniel Goleman, calls these traits and skills *emotional intelligence*. How would you rate your emotional IQ?

It was a steamy afternoon in New York City, the kind of day that makes people sullen[1] with discomfort. I was heading to my hotel, and as I stepped onto a bus, I was greeted by the driver, a middle-aged man with an enthusiastic smile.   1

"Hi! How're you doing?" he said. He greeted each rider in the same way.   2

As the bus crawled uptown through gridlocked traffic, the driver gave a lively commentary: there was a terrific sale at that store . . . a wonderful exhibit at this museum . . . had we heard about the movie that just opened down the block? By the time people got off, they had shaken off their sullen shells. When the driver called out, "So long, have a great day!" each of us gave a smiling response.   3

That memory has stayed with me for close to twenty years. I consider the bus driver a man who was truly successful at what he did.   4

Contrast him with Jason, a straight-A student at a Florida high school who was fixated[2] on getting into Harvard Medical School. When a physics teacher gave   5

---

1. sullen: gloomy
2. fixated: rigidly focused

Jason an 80 on a quiz, the boy believed his dream was in jeopardy.[3] He took a butcher knife to school, and in a struggle the teacher was stabbed in the collarbone.

How could someone of obvious intelligence do something so irrational? The answer is that high IQ does not necessarily predict who will succeed in life. Psychologists agree that IQ contributes only about 20 percent of the factors that determine success. A full 80 percent comes from other factors, including what I call *emotional intelligence.*

Following are some of the major qualities that make up emotional intelligence, and how they can be developed:

1. Self-awareness. The ability to recognize a feeling as it happens is the keystone of emotional intelligence. People with greater certainty about their emotions are better pilots of their lives.

Developing self-awareness requires tuning in to . . . gut feelings. Gut feelings can occur without a person being consciously aware of them. For example, when people who fear snakes are shown a picture of a snake, sensors on their skin will detect sweat, a sign of anxiety, even though the people say they do not feel fear. The sweat shows up even when a picture is presented so rapidly that the subject has no conscious awareness of seeing it.

Through deliberate effort we can become more aware of our gut feelings. Take someone who is annoyed by a rude encounter for hours after it occurred. He may be oblivious[4] to his irritability and surprised when someone calls attention to it. But if he evaluates his feelings, he can change them.

Emotional self-awareness is the building block of the next fundamental of emotional intelligence: being able to shake off a bad mood.

2. Mood Management. Bad as well as good moods spice life and build character. The key is balance.

We often have little control over *when* we are swept by emotion. But we can have some say in *how long* that emotion will last. Psychologist Dianne Tice of Case Western Reserve University asked more than 400 men and women about their strategies for escaping foul moods. Her research, along with that of other psychologists, provides valuable information on how to change a bad mood.

Of all the moods that people want to escape, rage seems to be the hardest to deal with. When someone in another car cuts you off on the highway, your reflexive[5] thought may be, *That jerk! He could have hit me! I can't let him get away with that!* The more you stew, the angrier you get. Such is the stuff of hypertension and reckless driving.

What should you do to relieve rage? One myth is that ventilating[6] will make you feel better. In fact, researchers have found that's one of the worst strategies. Outbursts of rage pump up the brain's arousal system, leaving you more angry, not less.

A more effective technique is "reframing," which means consciously reinterpreting a situation in a more positive light. In the case of the driver who cuts you off, you might tell yourself: *Maybe he had some emergency.* This is one of the most potent ways, Tice found, to put anger to rest.

Going off alone to cool down is also an effective way to defuse anger, especially if you can't think clearly. Tice found that a large proportion of men cool down by going for a drive—a finding that inspired her to drive more defensively. A safer alternative is exercise, such as taking a long walk. Whatever you do, don't waste the time pursuing your train of angry thoughts. Your aim should be to distract yourself.

> "How could someone of obvious intelligence do something so irrational?"

---

3. jeopardy: danger
4. oblivious: totally unaware
5. reflexive: automatic
6. ventilating: "letting off steam," raving

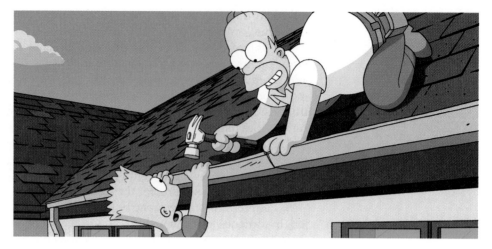

Bart and Homer Simpson attempt a roof repair. If you are familiar with the Simpsons, choose one of them and rate him or her in the five categories of emotional intelligence.

The Everett Collection.

The techniques of reframing and distraction can alleviate[7] depression and anxiety as well as anger. Add to them such relaxation techniques as deep breathing and meditation and you have an arsenal of weapons against bad moods. "Praying," Dianne Tice also says, "works for all moods." | 18

3. Self-motivation. Positive motivation—the marshaling[8] of feelings of enthusiasm, zeal, and confidence—is paramount for achievement. Studies of Olympic athletes, world-class musicians, and chess grandmasters[9] show that their common trait is the ability to motivate themselves to pursue relentless training routines. | 19

To motivate yourself for any achievement requires clear goals and an optimistic, can-do attitude. Psychologist Martin Seligman of the University of Pennsylvania advised the MetLife insurance company to hire a special group of job applicants who tested high on optimism, although they had failed the normal aptitude test. Compared with salesmen who passed the aptitude test but scored high in pessimism, this group made 21 percent more sales in their first year and 57 percent more in their second. | 20

A pessimist is likely to interpret rejection as meaning *I'm a failure; I'll never make a sale.* Optimists tell themselves, *I'm using the wrong approach,* or *That customer was in a bad mood.* By blaming failure on the situation, not themselves, optimists are motivated to make that next call. | 21

Your . . . positive or negative outlook may be inborn, but with effort and practice, pessimists can learn to think more hopefully. Psychologists have documented that if you can catch negative, self-defeating thoughts as they occur, you can reframe the situation in less catastrophic terms. | 22

4. Impulse Control. The essence of emotional self-regulation is the ability to delay impulse in the service of a goal. The importance of this trait to success was shown in an experiment begun in the 1960s by psychologist Walter Mischel at a preschool on the Stanford University campus. | 23

Children were told that they could have a single treat, such as a marshmallow, right now. However, if they would wait while the experimenter ran an errand, they could have two marshmallows. Some preschoolers grabbed the marshmallow immediately, but others were able to wait what, for them, must have seemed an endless twenty minutes. To sustain themselves in their struggle, they covered their eyes so they wouldn't see the temptation, rested their heads on their arms, | 24

---

7. alleviate: reduce, make better
8. marshaling: gathering together, using
9. chess grandmasters: experts at the game of chess

talked to themselves, sang, even tried to sleep. These plucky kids got the two-marshmallow reward.

The interesting part of this experiment came in the follow-up. The children who as four-year-olds had been able to wait for the two marshmallows were, as adolescents, still able to delay gratification in pursuing their goals. They were more socially competent and self-assertive, and better able to cope with life's frustrations. In contrast, the kids who grabbed the one marshmallow were, as adolescents, more likely to be stubborn, indecisive, and stressed.   25

The ability to resist impulse can be developed through practice. When you're faced with an immediate temptation, remind yourself of your long-term goals—whether they be losing weight or getting a medical degree. You'll find it easier, then, to keep from settling for the single marshmallow.   26

5. People Skills. The capacity to know how another feels is important on the job, in romance and friendships, and in the family. We transmit and catch moods from each other on a subtle, almost imperceptible level. The way someone says thank you, for instance, can leave us feeling dismissed, patronized, or genuinely appreciated. The more adroit[10] we are at discerning the feelings behind other people's signals, the better we control the signals we send.   27

The importance of good interpersonal skills was demonstrated by psychologists Robert Kelley of Carnegie-Mellon University and Janet Caplan in a study at Bell Labs in Naperville, Ill. The labs are staffed by engineers and scientists who are all at the apex[11] of academic IQ tests. But some still emerged as stars while others languished.[12]   28

What accounted for the difference? The standout performers had a network with a wide range of people. When a non-star encountered a technical problem, Kelley observed, "he called various technical gurus and then waited, wasting time while his calls went unreturned. Star performers rarely faced such situations because they built reliable networks *before* they needed them. So when the stars called someone, they almost always got a faster answer."   29

No matter what their IQ, once again it was emotional intelligence that separated the stars from the average performers.   30

Discussion and Writing Questions

1. Goleman names five qualities that contribute to emotional intelligence. What are they?

2. Describe someone you observed recently who showed a high level of emotional intelligence in a particular situation. Then describe someone who showed a low level of emotional intelligence in a particular situation. Which of the five qualities did each person display or lack?

3. Did it surprise you to read that "ventilating" is one of the worst ways to handle rage? Instead, experts suggest several techniques. Suppose you are in the following situation, and your first reaction is anger: *You ask a salesperson for help in choosing a CD player. As she walks right past you, she tells you that the boxes and labels will give you all the information you need.* What might you do to calm yourself down?

4. In paragraphs 24 and 25, Goleman discusses a now-famous study of children and marshmallows. What was the point of this study? Why does Goleman say that the most interesting part of the study came later, when the children reached adolescence?

———
10. adroit: skilled
11. apex: top, topmost point
12. languished: stayed in one place

Writing Assignments

1. Write a detailed portrait of a person whom you consider an "emotional genius." Develop your paper with specific examples of his or her skills.

2. Daniel Goleman claims that weak emotional qualities can be strengthened with practice. Choose one of the five qualities (self-awareness, people skills, and so forth) and recommend specific ways a person could improve in that area. Your audience is people who wish to improve their emotional intelligence; your purpose is to help them do so.

3. Review or read "The Gift" on page 403, and evaluate the emotional intelligence of Jermaine Washington. Washington saved a friend's life by giving her one of his kidneys after her two brothers and her boyfriend refused to be donors. Most people in their town still think Washington was "crazy" to make this decision. What do you think? Does he have a high level of emotional intelligence? a low level? Why?

Quotation Bank

This collection of wise and humorous statements has been assembled for you to read, enjoy, and use in a variety of ways as you write. You might choose some quotations that you particularly agree or disagree with and use them as the basis of journal entries and writing assignments. When you write a paragraph or an essay, you may find it useful to include a quotation to support a point you are making. You may simply want to read through these quotations for ideas and for fun. As you come across other intriguing statements by writers, add them to the list— or write some of your own.

Learning

Teachers open the door, but you must enter by yourself.
  —CHINESE PROVERB

Only the educated are free.
  —EPICTETUS

The mind is a mansion, but most of the time we are content to live in the lobby.
  —DR. WILLIAM MICHAELS

Pay attention to what they tell you to forget.
  —MURIEL RUKEYSER

Prejudices, it is well known, are most difficult to eradicate from the heart whose soil has never been loosened or fertilized by education; they grow there, firm as weeds among stones.
  —CHARLOTTE BRONTË

The day someone quits school he is condemning himself to a future of poverty.
  —JAIME ESCALANTE

The purpose of a liberal arts education is to liberate the human being to exercise his or her potential to the fullest.
  —BARBARA M. WHITE

Love

We can only learn to love by loving.
  —IRIS MURDOCH

So often when we say "I love you," we say it with a huge "I" and a small "you."
  —ARCHBISHOP ANTHONY

Choose your life's mate carefully. From this one decision will come 90 percent of all your happiness or misery.
  —H. JACKSON BROWNE, JR.

A divorce is like an amputation; you survive, but there's less of you.
  —MARGARET ATWOOD

Gold and love affairs are difficult to hide.
  —SPANISH PROVERB

Marriage is our last best chance to grow up.
—Joseph Barth

No partner in a love relationship should feel that she has to give up an essential part of herself to make it viable.
—May Sarton

Power without love is reckless and abusive, and love without power is sentimental and anemic.
—Martin Luther King, Jr.

Love doesn't just sit there, like a stone, it has to be made, like bread, remade all the time, made new.
—Ursula K. Le Guin

To be loved, be lovable.
—Ovid

Work and Success

The best career advice to give the young is, find out what you like doing best and get someone to pay you for doing it.
—Katherine Whilehaen

If there is any one secret of success, it lies in the ability to get the other person's point of view and see things from that person's angle as well as from your own.
—Henry Ford

If you have built castles in the air, your work need not be lost; that is where they should be. Now put foundations under them.
—Henry David Thoreau

I think most of us are looking for a calling, not a job. Most of us, like the assembly line worker, have had jobs that are too small for our spirit.
—Nora Watson

A celebrity is a person who works hard all his [or her] life to become well known, then wears dark glasses to avoid being recognized.
—Fred Allen

If at first you don't succeed, skydiving is not for you.
—Francis Roberts

You've got to believe. Never be afraid to dream.
—Gloria Estefan

If you aren't fired with enthusiasm, you will be fired with enthusiasm.
—Vince Lombardi

A good reputation is more valuable than money.
—Publius

Money is like manure. If you spread it around, it does a lot of good, but if you pile it up in one place, it stinks like hell.
—Clint W. Murchison

Measure a thousand times and cut once.
—TURKISH PROVERB

It is never too late to be what you might have been.
—GEORGE ELIOT

Family and Friendship

Making the decision to have a child—it's momentous. It is to decide forever to have your heart go walking around outside your body.
—ELIZABETH STONE

Govern a family as you would fry small fish—gently.
—CHINESE PROVERB

Nobody who has not been in the interior of a family can say what the difficulties of any individual in that family may be.
—JANE AUSTEN

Everything that irritates us about others can lead us to understanding of ourselves.
—MORTON HUNT

A true friend is someone who thinks that you are a good egg even though he knows that you are slightly cracked.
—BERNARD MELTZER

The only way to have a friend is to be one.
—RALPH WALDO EMERSON

Wisdom for Living

It is not easy to find happiness in ourselves, and it is not possible to find it elsewhere.
—AGNES REPPELIER

Regret is an appalling waste of energy; you can't build on it; it is good only for wallowing in.
—KATHERINE MANSFIELD

Smooth seas do not make a skillful sailor.
—AFRICAN PROVERB

Don't be afraid your life will end; be afraid that it will never begin.
—GRACE HANSEN

Flowers grow out of dark moments.
—KORITA KENT

Pick battles big enough to matter, small enough to win.
—JONATHAN KOZOL

A fanatic is one who can't change his [or her] mind and won't change the subject.
—WINSTON CHURCHILL

Take your life into your own hands and what happens? A terrible thing: no one to blame.
　　—Erica Jong

My life, my *real* life, was in danger, and not from anything other people might do but from the hatred I carried in my own heart.
　　—James Baldwin

No one can make you feel inferior without your consent.
　　—Eleanor Roosevelt

When you come to a fork in the road, take it.
　　—Yogi Berra

Writing

Writing, like life itself, is a voyage of discovery.
　　—Henry Miller

I am a Dominican, hyphen, American. As a writer, I find that the most exciting things happen in the realm of that hyphen—the place where two worlds collide or blend together.
　　—Julia Alvarez

I think best with a pencil in my hand.
　　—Anne Morrow Lindbergh

Writing is the hardest work in the world not involving heavy lifting.
　　—Pete Hamill

I never travel without my diary. One should always have something sensational to read on the train.
　　—Oscar Wilde

A professional writer is an amateur who didn't quit.
　　—Richard Bach

APPENDIX
1

Parts of Speech Review

A knowledge of basic grammar terms will make your study of English easier. Throughout this book, these key terms are explained as needed and are accompanied by ample practice. For your convenience and reference, the following is a short review of the eight parts of speech.

Nouns

Nouns are the names of persons, places, things, animals, activities, and ideas.*

Persons:	Ms. Caulfield, Dwayne, accountants
Places:	Puerto Rico, Vermont, gas station
Things:	sandwich, Sears, eyelash
Animals:	whale, ants, Dumbo
Activities:	running, discussion, tennis
Ideas:	freedom, intelligence, humor

Pronouns

Pronouns replace or refer to nouns or other pronouns. The word that a pronoun replaces is called its *antecedent*.**

My partner succeeded; *she* built a better mousetrap!

These computers are amazing; *they* alphabetize and index.

Everyone should do *his* or *her* best.

All students should do *their* best.

Pronouns take different forms, depending on how they are used in a sentence. They can be the subjects of sentences (*I, you, he, she, it, we, they*) or the objects of verbs and prepositions (*me, you, him, her, it, us, them*). They also can show possession (*my, mine, your, yours, his, her, hers, its, our, ours, their, theirs*).

---

*For more work on nouns, see Chapter 19.
**For more work on pronouns, see Chapter 20.

Subject:	*You* had better finish on time.
	Did *someone* leave a laptop on the chair?
Object of verb:	Bruno saw *her* on Thursday.
Object of preposition:	That CD is for *her*.
Possessive:	Did Adam leave *his* sweater on the dresser?

Verbs

Verbs can be either action verbs or linking verbs. Verbs can be single words or groups of words.*

Action verbs show what action the subject of the sentence performs.

> Leila *bought* a French dictionary.
>
> Ang *has opened* the envelope.

Linking verbs link the subject of a sentence with a descriptive word or words. Common linking verbs are *be, act, appear, become, feel, get, look, remain, seem, smell, sound,* and *taste.*

> This report *seems* well organized and complete.
>
> You *have been* quiet this morning.

The **present participle** of a verb is its *-ing* form. The present participle can be combined with some form of the verb *to be* to create the progressive tenses, or it can be used as an adjective or a noun.

Geraldo *was waiting* for the report.	*(past progressive tense)*
The *waiting* taxis lined up at the curb.	*(adjective)*
Waiting for trains bores me.	*(noun)*

The **past participle** of a verb can be combined with helping verbs to create different tenses, it can be combined with forms of *to be* to create the passive voice, or it can be used as an adjective. Past participles regularly end in *-d* or *-ed,* but irregular verbs take other forms (*seen, known, taken*).

He *has edited* many articles for us.	*(present perfect tense)*
This report *was edited* by the committee.	*(passive voice)*
The *edited* report reads well.	*(adjective)*

---

*For more work on verbs, see Unit 3.

Every verb can be written as an *infinitive: to* plus the *simple form* of the verb.

> She was surprised *to meet* him at the bus stop.

Adjectives

Adjectives describe or modify nouns or pronouns. Adjectives can precede or follow the words they describe.*

> *Several green* chairs arrived today.
>
> Collins Lake is *dangerous* and *deep*.

Adverbs

Adverbs describe or modify verbs, adjectives, or other adverbs.**

> Brandy reads *carefully*.   (*adverb describes verb*)
>
> She is *extremely* tired.   (*adverb describes adjective*)
>
> He wants a promotion *very* badly.   (*adverb describes adverb*)

Prepositions

A **preposition** begins a *prepositional phrase.* A **prepositional phrase** contains a preposition (a word such as *at, in, of,* or *with*), its object (a noun or pronoun), and any adjectives modifying the object.†

Preposition	Object
after	*work*
on	the blue *table*
under	the broken *stairs*

---

*For more work on adjectives, see Chapter 21.
**For more work on adverbs, see Chapter 21.
†For more work on prepositions, see Chapter 22.

Conjunctions

Conjunctions are connector words.

Coordinating conjunctions (*and, but, for, nor, or, so, yet*) join two equal words or groups of words.*

> Shanara is soft-spoken *but* sharp.
>
> Ms. Chin *and* Mr. Warburton attended the technology conference.
>
> He printed out the spreadsheet, *and* Ms. Helfman faxed it immediately.
>
> She will go to Norfolk Community College, *but* she will also continue working at the shoe store.

Subordinating conjunctions (*after, because, if, since, unless,* and so on) join an independent idea with a dependent idea.

> *Whenever* Alexi comes to visit, he takes the family out to dinner.
>
> I haven't been sleeping well *because* I've been drinking too much coffee.

Interjections

Interjections are words such as *ouch* and *hooray* that express strong feeling. They are rarely used in formal writing.

If the interjection is the entire sentence, it is followed by an exclamation point. If the interjection is attached to a sentence, it is followed by a comma.

> *Hey!* You left your wallet in the phone booth.
>
> *Oh,* she forgot to send in her tax return.

A Reminder

REMEMBER: The same word may be used as a different part of speech.

> Terrance *thought* about the problem. (*verb*)
>
> Your *thought* is a good one. (*noun*)

---

*For more work on conjunctions, see Chapters 13 and 14.

Some Guidelines for Students of English as a Second Language

Count and Noncount Nouns

Count nouns refer to people, places, or things that are separate units. You can often point to them, and you can always count them.

Count Noun	Sample Sentence
computer	The writing lab has four *computers*.
dime	There are two *dimes* under your chair.
professor	All of my *professors* are at a conference today.
notebook	I carry a *notebook* in my backpack.
child	Why is your *child* jumping on the table?

Noncount nouns refer to things that are wholes. You cannot count them separately. Noncount nouns may refer to ideas, feelings, and other things that you cannot see or touch. Noncount nouns may refer to food or beverages.

Noncount Noun	Sample Sentence
courage	It takes *courage* to study a new language.
equipment	The company sells office *equipment*.
happiness	We wish the bride and groom much *happiness*.
bread	Who will slice this loaf of *bread*?
meat	Do you eat *meat*, or are you a vegetarian?
coffee	The *coffee* turned cold as we talked.

For a more complete list of noncount nouns, visit <http://grammar.ccc.commnet.edu/grammar/noncount.htm>.

Plurals of Count and Noncount Nouns

Most count nouns form the plural by adding -s or -es. Some count nouns have irregular plurals.*

---

*For work on singular and plural nouns, see Chapter 19.

Plurals of Count Nouns

ship/ships	video game/video games
flower/flowers	nurse/nurses
library/libraries	knife/knives
child/children	woman/women

Noncount nouns usually do not form the plural at all. It is incorrect to say *homeworks, equipments,* or *happinesses.*

PRACTICE 1

Write the plural for every count noun. If the noun is a noncount noun, write *no plural.*

1. mountain _____
2. wealth _____
3. forgiveness _____
4. student _____
5. generosity _____

6. man _____
7. assignment _____
8. homework _____
9. knowledge _____
10. bravery _____

Some nouns have both a count meaning and a noncount meaning. Usually, the count meaning is concrete and specific. Usually, the noncount meaning is abstract and general.

Count meaning: All the *lights* in the classroom went out.
Noncount meaning: What is the speed of *light*?

Count meaning: Odd *sounds* came from the basement.
Noncount meaning: The speed of *sound* is slower than the speed of light.

Food and beverages, which are usually noncount nouns, may also have a count meaning.

Count meaning: This store sells *fruits, pies,* and *teas* from different countries.
Noncount meaning: Would you like some more *fruit, pie,* or *tea*?

Articles with Count and Noncount Nouns

Indefinite Articles

The words *a* and *an* are **indefinite articles.** They refer to one *nonspecific* (indefinite) thing. For example, "a man" refers to *any* man, not to a specific, particular man. **The article *a* or *an* is used before a singular count noun.***

Singular Count Noun	With Indefinite Article
question	a question
textbook	a textbook
elephant	an elephant
umbrella	an umbrella

———
*For when to use *an* instead of *a,* see Chapter 32.

The indefinite article *a* or *an* is never used before a noncount noun.

Noncount Noun	Sample Sentence
music	*Incorrect:* I enjoy a music.
	Correct: I enjoy music.
health	*Incorrect:* Her father is in a poor health.
	Correct: Her father is in poor health.
patience	*Incorrect:* Good teachers have a patience.
	Correct: Good teachers have patience.
freedom	*Incorrect:* We have a freedom to choose our courses.
	Correct: We have freedom to choose our courses.

PRACTICE 2

The indefinite article *a* or *an* is italicized in each sentence. Cross out *a* or *an* if it is used incorrectly. If the sentence is correct, write *correct* on the line provided.

1. My friends give me *a* help when I need it.   _____

2. The counselor gives her *an* advice about   _____
   which courses to take.

3. *An* honesty is the best policy.   _____

4. We have *an* answer to your question.   _____

5. They have *an* information for us.   _____

Definite Articles

The word *the* is a **definite article.** It refers to one (or more) *specific* (definite) things. For example, "the man" refers not to *any* man but to a specific, particular man. "The men" (plural) refers to specific, particular men. The article *the* also is used after the first reference to a thing (or things). For instance, "I got a new cell phone. The phone has a built-in MP3 player." **The article *the* is used before singular and plural count nouns.**

Definite (*The*) and Indefinite Articles (*A/An*) with Count Nouns

I saw *the* film. (singular; refers to a specific film)

I saw *the* films. (plural; refers to more than one specific film)

I saw *a* film. (refers to any film; nonspecific)

I enjoy seeing *a* good film. (refers to any good film; nonspecific)

I like *a* film that has an important message. (refers to any film that has an important message; nonspecific)

I saw *a* good film. *The* film was about the life of a Cuban singer. (refers to a specific film)

The definite article *the* is used before a noncount noun only if the noun is specifically identified.

Noncount Noun	Sample Sentence
fitness	*Incorrect:* He has *the* fitness. (not identified)
	Correct: He has *the* fitness of a person half his age. (identified)
	Incorrect: The fitness is a goal for many people. (not identified)
	Correct: Fitness is a goal for many people. (not identified, so no *the*)
art	*Incorrect:* I do not understand *the* art. (not identified)
	Correct: I do not understand *the* art in this show. (identified)
	Incorrect: The art touches our hearts and minds. (not identified)
	Correct: Art touches our hearts and minds. (not identified, so no *the*)

PRACTICE 3

The definite article *the* is italicized whenever it appears below. Cross it out if it is used incorrectly. If the sentence is correct, write *correct* on the line provided.

1. She dresses with *the* style.   _____

2. *The* beauty of this building surprises me.   _____

3. This building has *the* beauty of a work of art. _____

4. *The* courage is an important quality.   _____

5. Alex has *the* wealth but not *the* happiness.   _____

Verb + Gerund

A **gerund** is a noun that is made up of a verb plus *-ing*. The italicized words below are gerunds.

> *Playing* solitaire on the computer helps some students relax.
>
> I enjoy *hiking* in high mountains.

In the first sentence, the gerund *playing* is the simple subject of the sentence.* In the second sentence, the gerund *hiking* is the object of the verb enjoy.** Some common verbs are often followed by gerunds.

---

*For more on simple subjects, see Chapter 6, Part A.
**For more on objects of verbs, see Chapter 20, Part F, "Pronouns as Objects."

Some Common Verbs That Can Be Followed by a Gerund

Verb	Sample Sentence with Gerund
consider	Would you *consider taking* a course in psychology?
discuss	Let's *discuss buying* a scanner.
enjoy	I *enjoy jogging* in the morning before work.
finish	Sue *finished studying* for her nursing exam.
keep	*Keep trying* and you will succeed.
postpone	The Brookses *postponed visiting* their grandchildren.
quit	Three of my friends *quit smoking* this year.

The verbs listed above are *never* followed by an infinitive (*to* + the simple form of the verb).*

Incorrect: Would you consider *to take* a course in psychology?

Incorrect: Let's discuss *to buy* a scanner.

Incorrect: I enjoy *to jog* in the morning before work.

PRACTICE 4

Write a gerund after each verb in the blank space provided.

1. Dave enjoys _____ television in the evening.

2. Have you finished _____ for tomorrow's exam?

3. T.J. is considering _____ to Mexico next month.

4. I have postponed _____ until I receive the results of the test.

5. We are discussing _____ a car.

Preposition + Gerund

A preposition** may be followed by a gerund.

> I forgive you *for stepping* on my toe.
>
> Elena believes *in pushing* herself to her limits.
>
> We made the flight *by running* from one terminal to another.

A preposition is *never* followed by an infinitive (*to* + the simple form of the verb).

Incorrect: I forgive you *for **to step*** on my toe.

Incorrect: Elena believes *in **to push*** herself to her limits.

Incorrect: We made the flight *by **to run*** from one terminal to another.

_____

*For more on infinitives, see Chapter 12, Part E.
**For more on prepositions, see Chapter 22.

PRACTICE 5

Write a gerund after the preposition in each blank space provided.

1. We have succeeded in _____ the DVD you wanted.

2. You can get there by _____ left at the next corner.

3. Thank you for _____ those striped socks for me.

4. I enjoy sports like _____ and _____ .

5. Between _____ to school and _____ , I have little time for _____ .

Verb + Infinitive

Many verbs are followed by the **infinitive** (*to* + the simple form of the verb).

Some Common Verbs That Can Be Followed by an Infinitive

Verb	Sample Sentence
afford	Carla can *afford* ***to buy*** a new outfit whenever she wants.
agree	I *agree* ***to marry*** you a year from today.
appear	He *appears* ***to be*** inspired by his new job.
decide	Will they *decide* ***to drive*** across the country?
expect	Jamal *expects* ***to graduate*** next year.
forget	Please do not *forget* ***to cash*** the check.
hope	My nephews *hope* ***to visit*** Santa Fe this year.
intend	I *intend* ***to study*** harder this semester than I did last semester.
mean	Did Frank *mean* ***to leave*** his lunch on the kitchen table?
need	Do you *need* ***to stop*** for a break now?
plan	Justin *plans* ***to go*** into advertising.
promise	Sharon has *promised* ***to paint*** this wall green.
offer	Did they really *offer* ***to babysit*** for a month?
refuse	Sean *refuses* ***to walk*** another step.
try	Let's *try* ***to set*** up this tent before dark.
wait	On the other hand, we could *wait* ***to camp*** out until tomorrow.

PRACTICE 6

Write an infinitive after the verb in each blank space provided.

1. The plumber promised _____ the sink today.

2. My son plans _____ a course in electrical engineering.

3. We do not want _____ late for the meeting again.

4. They refused _____ before everyone was ready.

5. I expect _____ Jorge next week.

Verb + Either Gerund or Infinitive

Some verbs can be followed by *either* a gerund *or* an infinitive.

Some Common Verbs That Can Be Followed by a Gerund or an Infinitive

Verb	Sample Sentence
begin	They *began* **to laugh.** (infinitive)
	They *began* **laughing.** (gerund)
continue	Fran *continued* **to speak.** (infinitive)
	Fran *continued* **speaking.** (gerund)
hate	Juan *hates* **to drive** in the snow. (infinitive)
	Juan *hates* **driving** in the snow. (gerund)
like	My daughter *likes* **to surf** the Net. (infinitive)
	My daughter *likes* **surfing** the Net. (gerund)
love	Phil *loves* **to watch** soccer games. (infinitive)
	Phil *loves* **watching** soccer games. (gerund)
start	Will you *start* **to write** the paper tomorrow? (infinitive)
	Will you *start* **writing** the paper tomorrow? (gerund)

PRACTICE 7

For each pair of sentences, first write an infinitive in the space provided. Then write a gerund.

1. a. (infinitive) Laurel hates _____ in long lines.

   b. (gerund) Laurel hates _____ in long lines.

2. a. (infinitive) When will we begin _____ dinner?

   b. (gerund) When will we begin _____ dinner?

3. a. (infinitive) Carmen loves _____ in the rain.

   b. (gerund) Carmen loves _____ in the rain.

4. a. (infinitive) The motor continued _____ noisily.

   b. (gerund) The motor continued _____ noisily.

5. a. (infinitive) Suddenly, the people started _____.

   b. (gerund) Suddenly, the people started _____.

Acknowledgments

Page 386: Excerpt from Diane Sawyer, "Daring to Dream Big," *Guideposts*, March 1986 and March 2005, p. 27. Reprinted with permission from *Guideposts* magazine. Copyright © 1986 by *Guideposts*, Carmel, New York, 10512. All rights reserved.

Pages 387–388: Excerpt, "A Homemade Education," from *The Autobiography of Malcolm X* by Malcolm X and Alex Haley, 1964. Copyright © 1964 by Alex Haley and Malcolm X. Copyright © 1965 by Alex Haley and Betty Shabazz, from *The Autobiography of Malcolm X* by Malcolm X and Alex Haley. Used by permission of Random House, Inc.

Pages 388–390: Ellen Goodman, "Don't Share Your Life with Me," *Boston Globe* (as reprinted in *Miami Herald*, June 14, 2004). *Miami Herald* by Ellen Goodman. Copyright 2004 by *Miami Herald*. Reproduced with permission of *Miami Herald* in the format Textbook via Copyright Clearance Center.

Pages 390–393: Excerpt, "Mrs. Flowers," from *I Know Why the Caged Bird Sings* by Maya Angelou, copyright © 1969 and renewed 1997 by Maya Angelou. Used by permission of Random House, Inc.

Pages 394–395: As attached, Leonard Pitts Jr., "Beauty Is Not Just Smaller Than Life," *Miami Herald*, January 31, 2003, Metro Section B. *Miami Herald* by Leonard Pitts Jr. Copyright © 2003 by *Miami Herald*. Reproduced with permission of *Miami Herald* in the format Textbook via Copyright Clearance Center.

Pages 396–398: "Hot Dogs and Wild Geese," from *Funny in Farsi* by Firoozah Dumas, copyright © 2003 by Firoozah Dumas. Used by permission of Villard Books, a division of Random House, Inc.

Pages 400–402: Julia Alvarez, "My English," copyright © 1998 by Julia Alvarez, from *Something to Declare*, published by Plume, an imprint of Penguin Group (USA), in 1999 and originally in hardcover of Algonquin Books of Chapel Hill. Reprinted by permission of Susan Bergholz Literary Services, New York. All rights reserved.

Pages 403–404: "The Gift," from Courtland Milloy, "Giving Up a Kidney for a Friend," *The Washington Post*, 12/23/92, p. D1. © 1992, The Washington Post Writers Group. Reprinted with permission.

Pages 405–406: "Montgomery, Alabama, 1955" from *Rosa Parks: My Story* by Rosa Parks with Jim Haskins, copyright © 1992 by Rosa Parks. Used by permission of Dial Books for Young Readers, a Division of Penguin Young Readers Group, a Member of Penguin Group (USA) Inc., 345 Hudson Street, New York, NY 10014. All rights reserved.

Pages 406–408: Michaela angela Davis, "Quitting Hip-Hop," *Essence*, October 2004, volume 35, issue 6, p. 155. Reprinted by permission of the author.

Pages 408–409: Ana Veciana-Suarez, "You Can Take This Job and . . . Well, It Might Surprise You," *Miami Herald*, July 13, 2003, p. 2K. Copyright 2003 by *Miami Herald*. Reproduced with permission of *Miami Herald* in the format Textbook via Copyright Clearance Center.

Pages 410–412: "Papa, the Teacher" from *Papa, My Father* by Leo Buscaglia. Copyright © 1989 Leo F. Buscaglia. Reprinted by permission.

Pages 413–415: "Another Road Hog with Too Much Oink," copyright © 2000 by Dave Barry, from *Dave Barry Is Not Taking This Sitting Down* by Dave Barry. Used by permission of Crown Publishers, a division of Random House, Inc.

Pages 415–416: "Stuff" by Richard Rodriguez. Copyright © 1998 by Richard Rodriguez. Originally aired on the *NewsHour with Jim Lehrer* (PBS) on April 27, 1998. Reprinted by permission of Georges Borchardt, Inc., on behalf of the author.

Pages 418–420: "In This Arranged Marriage, Love Came Later" by Shoba Narayan. Reprinted by permission of The Elizabeth Kaplan Literary Agency.

Pages 421–422: Jack Riemer, "Playing a Violin with Three Strings," *Houston Chronicle*, February 10, 2001. Reprinted by permission of Rabbi Jack Riemer.

Pages 423–424: "One Man's Kids" from Daniel Meier, "About Men: One Man's Kids," *New York Times*, November 1, 1987. Copyright © 1987, Daniel Meier. Reprinted by permission.

Pages 425–426: "The Hidden Life of Bottled Water," by Liza Gross, as appeared in *Sierra*, May/June 1999, pp. 66–67. Reprinted by permission of *Sierra*.

Pages 427–428: "Four Directions," from *The Joy Luck Club* by Amy Tan, copyright © 1989 by Amy Tan. Used by permission of G. P. Putnam's Sons, a division of Penguin Group (USA) Inc.

Pages 429–432: From "Emotional Intelligence" by Daniel Goleman, copyright © 1995 by Daniel Goleman. Used by permission of Bantam Books, a division of Random House, Inc.

Index

a/an, 443, 444
a/an/and, 362
accept/except, 363
Action verbs, 71–72, 439
Active voice, 142–145
Addresses (location), 315–316
Adjectives
comparative, 258–259, 262, 264
  demonstrative, 263, 264
  explanation of, 254, 264
  good or *well*, 257–258, 264
  past participles as, 145–147, 439
  review of, 440
  superlative, 260–262, 264
Adverbs
  comparative, 258–259, 262, 264
  conjunctive, 200–205
  explanation of, 254–255, 264
  good or *well*, 257–258, 264
  review of, 440
  superlative, 260–262, 264
Agreement
  in past tense, 124
  in present tense, 96–98
  pronoun-antecedent, 236
  subject-verb, 102–111, 115
and, 247
Antecedents. *See also* Pronouns
  explanation of, 235, 252, 438
  use of, 235, 236
anybody, 237
anyone, 237
Apostrophes
  for contractions, 321–322, 327
  to show possession, 323–327
Appositives
  commas to set off, 313–314
  explanation of, 313
Articles
  with count and noncount nouns, 443–444
  definite, 444–445
  indefinite, 443–444
as, 249, 252, 269
as if, 269
Audience, 5–6
awful/awfully, 255

bad/badly, 255
badly/worse/worst, 262, 264
bad/worse/worst, 262
been/being, 363
Body of essays
  explanation of, 53
  generating ideas for, 56
  selecting and arranging ideas in, 57
Body of paragraphs
  examples of, 24–25
  explanation of, 16
  generating ideas for, 23–24
Brainstorming
  examples of, 11, 23, 25
  explanation of, 11
  to narrow topics, 18
  for paragraph development, 24
  for topic sentences, 25
bright/brightly, 264
buy/by, 364
by the way, 314

can/could, 160–161
Capitalization
  of quotations, 329, 330, 332
  rules for, 304–307
  semicolons and, 198, 205

Clustering
  example of, 12
  to narrow topics, 18
  for paragraph development, 24
Coherence
  arranging by order of importance for, 43–45
  space order for, 41–42
  time order for, 39–41
Collective nouns, 239–240
Commas
  with addresses, 315–316
  with coordinating conjunctions, 176, 180, 190, 316–317
  with dates, 315
  with direct address, 312–313
  general rules for, 318
  with *-ing* modifiers, 213
  with introductory phrases, 311–312
  with items in series, 310–311
  with nonrestrictive clauses, 210, 211
  with parenthetical expressions, 314
  with quotations, 329
  to set off appositives, 313–314
  with subordinating conjunctions, 183–184, 188, 316–317
Comma splices
  correction of, 190
  explanation of, 190, 194
Comparatives
  explanation of, 258–259
  list of troublesome, 262
Comparisons, 249–250, 252
Complete sentences, 21, 82–85
Complete subjects, 67
Computer spell checks, 350, 351
Concise language, 46–48
Conclusion, of essays, 53
Conjunctions
  coordinating, 176–179, 190, 441
  review of, 441
  subordinating, 181–188, 190, 441
Conjunctive adverbs. *See also* Transitional expressions
  explanation of, 200–201, 205
  list of common, 201
  punctuation of, 202–205
Consistency
  in person, 287–288
  in tense, 282–284
Consonants
  doubling final, 352–355, 360
  explanation of, 352
  suffix beginning with, 355, 356
Contractions
  apostrophes for, 321–322, 327
  explanation of, 321
  negative, 164, 165
Controlling ideas, 20
Coordinating conjunctions
  commas with, 176, 180, 190, 316–317
  to correct comma splice, 190
  explanation of, 176, 180, 218
  list of, 176
  review of, 441
  semicolons with, 198
Count nouns
  articles with, 443–444
  explanation of, 442
  plural of, 442–443

Dates, 315
-d/-ed verb endings
  for past participles, 130, 134, 148, 439

for past tense, 118, 121, 126
Definite articles, 444–445
Demonstrative adjectives, 263, 264
Dictionaries
  to check spelling, 350, 360
  noun plurals in, 227
Diener, Ed, 225
Direct address, 312–313
Direct quotations
  ending, 330–331
  explanation of, 328, 332
  punctuation for, 329–330, 332
  split, 329–330
Double negatives, 164–166
Drafts
  final, 31–32
  first, 26–27, 57

-e, 355–356, 360
each, 237, 241
each/each one/every one, 110
each of, 231, 240, 241
-ed, 352, 353
-ed/-d verb endings
  for past participles, 130, 134, 148, 439
  for past tense, 118, 121, 126
ei/ie, 358, 360
either/neither, 110, 115
either of, 240
either one of, 240
-er, 259, 352
-es/-s
  for plural nouns, 226, 227, 233
  for third person singular, 97, 108, 115
Essays
  body of, 53, 56, 57
  checklist for writing, 58
  conclusion of, 53
  example of, 53
  explanation of, 52–53
  Internet strategies for writing, 58
  narrowing subject for, 55
  paragraphs in, 53
  selecting and arranging ideas for, 57
  structure of, 54
  thesis statement for, 55–56
  writing and revising, 57
-est, 261, 352
everybody, 237
everyone, 237, 238
every one of, 240
Exact language, 45–46
Examples
  adding support by using, 36–39
  transitional expressions to introduce, 37
except/accept, 363

-f/-fe, 226–227
fine/find, 364
First drafts
  of essays, 57
  of paragraphs, 26–27
  revisions to, 31–32
First person, 287
Fixed-form helping verbs
  can/could as, 160–161
  examples of, 158
  explanation of, 158, 166
  use of, 159–160
  will/would as, 161–163
Focused freewriting. *See also* Freewriting
  example of, 10
  explanation of, 9–10
Fragments. *See* Sentence fragments

Index of Rhetorical Modes

This index classifies the practices, paragraphs, and essays in this text according to the type of writing pattern, or rhetorical mode, they employ. Writing that contains errors, as many practice exercises do, is usually not included; however, exceptions are four Writers' Workshops and two other passages—marked *with errors*—in which otherwise excellent writing warrants inclusion here.

Index to the Readings

Rhetorical Index to the Readings

Notes

Notes

Notes

Notes

Notes

Notes